SEMANTICS – ADVANCES IN THEORIES AND MATHEMATICAL MODELS

Edited by **Muhammad Tanvir Afzal**

Semantics – Advances in Theories and Mathematical Models
Edited by Muhammad Tanvir Afzal

Published by InTech
Janeza Trdine 9, 51000 Rijeka, Croatia

Publishing Process Manager Vedran Greblo

Technical Editor Teodora Smiljanic

Cover Designer InTech Design Team

Additional hard copies can be obtained from orders@intechopen.com

Semantics – Advances in Theories and Mathematical Models,
Edited by Muhammad Tanvir Afzal
p. cm.
ISBN 978-953-51-0535-0

For EU product safety concerns:
IN TECH d.o.o., Prolaz Marije Krucifikse Kozulić 3, 51000 Rijeka, Croatia,
info@intechopen.com or visit our website at intechopen.com.

Meet the editor

Muhammad Tanvir Afzal, PhD., is an Assistant Professor in the department of Computer Science at Mohammad Ali Jinnah University, Islamabad, Pakistan, adjunct professor at Graz University of Technology, Graz, Austria, editor-in-chief of a reputed journal such as: Journal of Universal Computer Science, and group leader of an active research group: Centre for Distributed and Semantic Computing. He earned his PhD with distinction from Graz University of Technology, Austria and secured Gold Medal in his Masters from Quaid-i-Azam University, Islamabad, Pakistan. He has published over 50 research articles in reputed journals and conferences. His research activities encompass the area of Semantic Web, Social Web, Sentiment Analysis, Digital Libraries, eLearning, and Information Integration. He is editor/reviewer/session chair of many journals and conferences. He is supervising/co-supervising number of PhD students in Austria, Pakistan, and Malaysia, and is involved in number of international research projects.

Contents

Preface

Semantics is the research area touching the diversified domains such as: Philosophy, Information Science, Linguistics, Formal Semantics, Philosophy of Language and its constructs, Query Processing, Semantic Web, Pragmatics, Computational Semantics, Programming Languages, and Semantic Memory etc. The current book is a nice blend of number of great ideas, theories, mathematical models, and practical systems in diversified domains.

The book has been divided into two volumes. The current one is the first volume which highlights the advances in theories and mathematical models in the domain of Semantics. This volume has been divided into four sections and ten chapters. The sections include: 1) Background, 2) Queries, Predicates, and Semantic Cache, 3) Algorithms and Logic Programming, and 4) Semantic Web and Interfaces.

Section 1 presents the background and motivations for the term "Semantics". This section has two chapters. First chapter debates about the meaning of the Semantics from different perspectives whereas the second chapter presents insights about Knowledge reasoning and beliefs, subsequently, probabilistic belief logic such as: PBL_w has been proposed and discussed.

Section 2 focuses on queries, predicates and semantic cache. This section has been divided into two chapters. The first chapter debates on the structure of the query, the structure of the answers, and predicate-argument relationships. Second chapter is in the domain of semantic cache. The authors present a survey of semantic cache query processing and semantic reasoners.

Section 3 presents two chapters from the domain of Algorithms and Logic Programming. The first chapter presents an extended version of Schellekens technique to provide the asymptotic upper and lower bounds of running time of a recursive algorithm, Furthermore, the relationship between denotational semantics and asymptotic complexity led to form a mathematical approach that model the running time and the meaning of recursive algorithms. Second chapter presents a semantic framework for declarative debugging of wrong and missing computed answers in Constraint Functional-Logic Programming.

Section 4 elaborates the work in the areas of Semantic Web and Interfaces. This section includes four chapters. First chapter discusses Spatialization of the Semantic Web to manage spatial data using Semantic Web framework. The framework, ArchaeoKM, briefly conceptualizes the 4Ks such as: Knowledge Acquisition, Knowledge Management, Knowledge Visualization and Knowledge Analysis. A case study of industrial archaeology has been discussed in details. Second chapter presents a representation system based on Ontology for quality indicators. Third chapter presents a system for semantic modeling and the numerical processing to define strategies based on domain knowledge and 3D processing knowledge. The chapter, on one hand presents a brief introduction of semantic technologies such as: RDF, OWL, SWRL, DL, while one the other hand, a system has been proposed, designed, and implemented for integrating 3D processing and spatial topological components within its framework. The last chapter presents 'Command – Causalities – Consequences Wisdom' C^3W semantics temporal entanglement modelling for human – machine interfaces.

I would like to thank authors who participated to conclude such a nice worth-reading book. I am also thankful to In-Tech Open access Initiative for making accessible all of the chapters online free of cost to the scientific community.

Dr. Muhammad Tanvir Afzal
Department of Computer Science
Mohammad Ali Jinnah University, Islamabad,
Pakistan

Section 1

Background

1

Let Us First Agree on what the Term "Semantics" Means: An Unorthodox Approach to an Age-Old Debate

Emanuel Diamant
VIDIA-mant,
Israel

1. Introduction

Semantics, as a facet of human language, has always attracted the attention of notable philosophers and thinkers. Wikipedia relates the first insights into semantic theory to Plato, the great Greek philosopher of the ancient times, somewhere about the end of the 4th century BC (Wikipedia, 2011). Nevertheless, despite the long history of investigations, the notion of semantics remains elusive and enigmatic. Only in the second half of the passed century (and partially on the verge of the current one) some sort of a consensual definition had emerged.

Alfred Tarski defined semantics as "a discipline which, speaking loosely, deals with certain relations between expressions of a language and the objects… 'referred to' by those expressions" (Tarski, 1944).

Jerry Fodor defines semantics as "a part of a grammar of (a) language. In particular, the part of a grammar that is concerned with the relations between symbols in the language and the things in the world that they refer to or are true of" (Fodor, 2007).

In the latest issue of "The Handbook of Computational Linguistics", David Beaver and Joey Frazee give another, slight different, definition of semantics: "Semantics is concerned with meaning: what meanings are, how meanings are assigned to words, phrases and sentences of natural and formal languages, and how meanings can be combined and used for inference and reasoning" (Beaver & Frazee, 2011).

The list of such citations can be extended endlessly. Nevertheless, an important and an interesting point must be mentioned here - the bulk of citations presuppose a tight link between semantics and the language that it is intended to work for. And that is not surprising - language was always seen as an evolutionary feature that has made us human, that is, a thing that has facilitated our ability to interact and cooperate with other conspecies. It is commonly agreed that the spoken language was the first and the ultimate tool that has endowed us (humans) with the ability to communicate, thus enormously improving our chances of survival.

But speaking about the spoken language and its role in human communication, we cannot avoid the inevitable, and somewhat provocative, question: "What actually is being communicated?" The first answer which comes to mind is - language. But we have just agreed that language is only a tool that has emerged to reify our ability to communicate.

I will not bother you with rhetorical questions. My answer is simple, fair and square: Semantics - that is what we communicate to our conspecies using the language as a tool for communication.

It is perfectly right to stress that spoken language was the most ancient enabling technology evolutionary evolved for communication purposes. However, in the course of human development other means of communication have gradually emerged - cave paintings, written languages, book-printing and, in more modern times, various electrical (telegraph, telephony) and electronic (radio, television, internet) forms of communication. What were they all intended to communicate?

You will possibly reject my speculations, but I will insist - Semantics that is what we are all communicating! And it does not matter if in our modern age you prefer to call it not "Semantics" but "Information". (I hope my readers would easily agree that 13,900,000 results for a Google inquiry about "information communication" (and 2,720,000 results for "communicating information") are enough convincing to justify the claim that information is the major subject that's being communicated nowadays).

You will possibly remind me that the first attempt to integrate the terms "Semantics" and "Information" was made about 60 years ago by Yehoshua Bar-Hillel and Rudolf Carnap (Bar-Hillel & Carnap, 1952). As to my knowledge, they were the first who coined the term "Semantic Information". They have sincerely believed that such a merging can be possible: "Prevailing theory of communication (or transmission of information) deliberately neglects the semantic aspects of communication, i. e., the meaning of the messages… Instead of dealing with the information carried by letters, sound waves, and the like, we may talk about the information carried by the sentence, 'The sequence of letters (or sound waves, etc.). .. has been transmitted' " (Bar-Hillel & Carnap, 1952).

However, they were not successful in their try to unite the mathematical theory of information and semantics. The mainstream thinking of that time was determined by the famous saying of The Mathematical Theory of Communication fathers (Claude E. Shannon and Warren Weaver): "These semantic aspects of communication are irrelevant to the engineering problem… It is important to emphasize, at the start, that we are not concerned with the meaning or the truth of messages; semantics lies outside the scope of mathematical information theory", (Shannon & Weaver, 1949).

I hope my readers are aware that denying any relations between semantics and information was not the most inspiring idea of that time. On the contrary, for many years it has hampered and derailed the process of understanding the elusive nature of them both, semantics and information alike (Two concepts that in course of human history have become the most important features of human's life).

The aim of this chapter was to avoid the historical pitfalls and not to repeat the mistakes and misconceptions so proudly preached by our predecessors. I will try to prove the existence of a firm link between semantics and information and I will make my best trying to share with you my understanding of their peculiarities, which have been unveiled in course of my research into the subject of our discourse.

2. What is information?

The question "What is information?" is as old and controversial as the question "What is semantics?" I will not bore you with re-examining what the most prominent thinkers of our time have thought and said about the notion of "Information". In the chapter's reference list I provide some examples of their viewpoints (Adams, 2003; Floridi, 2005; Sloman, 2011) with only one and a single purpose in mind - curious readers by themselves would decide how relevant and useful (for our discussion about semantics/information interrelations) these scholar opinions are.

2.1 Visual information, the first steps

My personal interaction with information/semantics issues has happened somewhere in the mid-1980s. At that time I was busy with home security and surveillance systems design and development. As known, such systems rely heavily on visual information acquisition and processing. However - What is visual information? - nobody knew then, nobody knows today. But, that has never restrained anybody from trying again and again to meet the challenge.

Deprived from a suitable understanding what visual information is, computer vision designers have always tried to find their inspirations in biological vision analogs, especially human vision analogs. Although underlying fundamentals and operational principles of human vision were obscure and vague, still the research in this field was always far more mature and advanced. Therefore the computer vision society has always considered human vision conjectures as the best choice to follow.

A theory of human visual information processing has been established about thirty years ago by the seminal works of David Marr (Marr, 1982), Anne Treisman (Treisman & Gelade, 1980), Irving Biederman (Biederman, 1987) and a large group of their followers. Since then it has become a classical theory, which dominates today all further developments both in human and the computer vision. The theory considers human visual information processing as an interplay of two inversely directed processing streams. One is an unsupervised, bottom-up directed process of initial image information pieces discovery and localization (The so-called low-level image processing). The other is a supervised, top-down directed process, which conveys the rules and the knowledge that guide the linking and binding of these disjoint information pieces into perceptually meaningful image objects (The so-called high-level or cognitive image processing).

While the idea of low-level processing from the very beginning was obvious and intuitively appealing (therefore, even today the mainstream of image processing is occupied mainly with low-level pixel-oriented computations), the essence of high-level processing was always obscure, mysterious, and undefined. The classical paradigm said nothing about the roots of high-level knowledge origination or about the way it has to be incorporated into the introductory low-level processing. Until now, however, the problem was usually bypassed by capitalizing on the expert domain knowledge, adapted to each and every application case. Therefore, it is not surprising that the whole realm of image processing had been fragmented and segmented according to high-level knowledge competence of the respected domain experts.

2.2 Visual information and Marr's edges

Actually, the idea of initial low-level image information processing had been initially avowed by Marr (Marr, 1978). (By the way, Marr was the first who originally coined the term "visual information"). According to Marr's theory, image edges are the main bearers of visual information, and therefore, image information processing has always been occupied with edge processing duties.

Affected by the mainstream pixel-based (edge-based) bottom-up image exploration philosophy, I have at first only slightly diverged from the common practice. But slowly I have begun to pave my own way. Initially I have invented the Single Pixel Information Content measure (Diamant, 2003). Then, experimenting with it, I have discovered the Information Content Specific Density Conservation principle (Diamant, 2002). (The reverse order of publication dates does not mean nothing. Papers are published not when the relevant work is finished, but when you are lucky to meet the personal views of a tough reviewer).

The Information Content Specific Density Conservation principle says that when an image scale is successively reduced, Image Specific Information Density remains unchanged. That explains why we usually launch our observation with a general, reduced scale preview of a scene and then zoom in on the relevant scene part that we are interested in. That also indicates that we perceive our objects of interest as dimensionless items. Taking into account these observations, Information Content Specific Density Conservation phenomenon actually leads us to a conclusion that information itself is a qualitative (not a quantitative) notion with a clear smack of a narrative.

It is worth to be mentioned that similar investigations have been performed at a later time by MIT researchers (Torralba, 2009), and similar results have been attained considering the use of a reduced scale (32x32 pixels) images. However, that was done only in qualitative experiments conducted on human participants (but not as a quantitative work).

It is not surprising therefore that The Information Content Specific Density Conservation principle has inevitably led me to a conclusion that image information processing has to be done in a top-down fashion (and not bottom-up as it is usually considered). Further advances on this path supported by insights borrowed from Solomonoff's theory of Inference (Solomonoff, 1964), Kolmogorov's Complexity theory (Kolmogorov, 1965), and Chaitin's Algorithmic Information theory (Chaitin, 1966) have promptly led me to a full-blown theory of Image Information Content discovery and elucidation (Diamant, 2005).

2.3 Visual information, a first definition

In the mentioned above theory of Image Information Content discovery and elucidation I have proposed for the first time a preliminary definition of "What is information". In the year 2005 it had sounded as follows:

First of all, information is a description, a certain language-based description, which Kolmogorov's Complexity theory regards as a program that, being executed, trustworthy reproduces the original object. In an image, such objects are visible data structures from which an image is comprised of. So, a set of reproducible descriptions of image data structures is the information contained in an image.

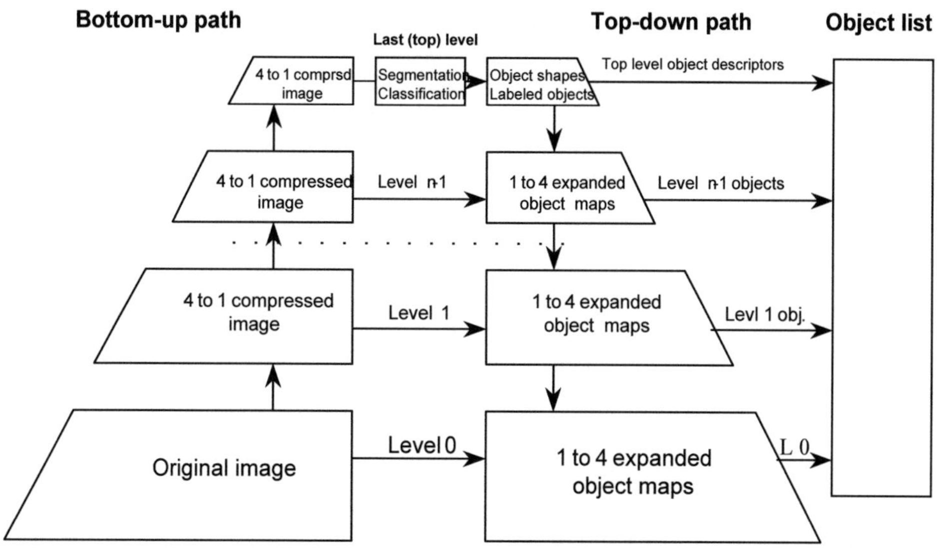

Fig. 1. The block-diagram of image contained information elucidation.

The Kolmogorov's theory prescribes the way in which such descriptions must be created: At first, the most simplified and generalized structure must be described. (Recall the Occam's Razor principle: Among all hypotheses consistent with the observation choose the simplest one that is coherent with the data). Then, as the level of generalization is gradually decreased, more and more fine-grained image details (structures) become revealed and depicted. This is the second important point, which follows from the theory's pure mathematical considerations: Image information is a hierarchy of decreasing level descriptions of information details, which unfolds in a coarse-to-fine top-down manner. (Attention, please! Any bottom-up processing is not mentioned here! There is no low-level feature gathering and no feature binding!!! The only proper way for image information elicitation is a top-down coarse-to-fine way of image processing!)

The third prominent point, which immediately pops-up from the two just mentioned above, is that the top-down manner of image information elicitation does not require incorporation of any high-level knowledge for its successful accomplishment. It is totally free from any high-level guiding rules and inspirations.

Following the given above principles, a practical algorithm for image information content discovery has been proposed and put in work. Its block-schema is provided in Fig. 1.

As it can be seen at Fig. 1, the proposed block-diagram is comprised of three main processing paths: the bottom-up processing path, the top-down processing path and a stack where the discovered information content (the generated descriptions of it) is actually accumulated.

As it follows from the schema, the input image is initially squeezed to a small size of approximately 100 pixels. The rules of this shrinking operation are very simple and fast: four non-overlapping neighbor pixels in an image at level L are averaged and the result is assigned to a pixel in a higher (L+1)-level image. Then, at the top of the shrinking pyramid, the image is segmented, and each segmented region is labeled. Since the image size at the top is significantly reduced and since in the course of the bottom-up image squeezing a severe data averaging is attained, the image segmentation/labeling procedure does not demand special computational resources. Any well-known segmentation methodology will suffice. We use our own proprietary technique that is based on a low-level (single pixel) information content evaluation (Diamant, 2003), but this is not obligatory.

From this point on, the top-down processing path is commenced. At each level, the two previously defined maps (average region intensity map and the associated label map) are expanded to the size of an image at the nearest lower level. Since the regions at different hierarchical levels do not exhibit significant changes in their characteristic intensity, the majority of newly assigned pixels are determined in a sufficiently correct manner. Only pixels at region borders and seeds of newly emerging regions may significantly deviate from the assigned values. Taking the corresponding current-level image as a reference (the left-side unsegmented image), these pixels can be easily detected and subjected to a refinement cycle. In such a manner, the process is subsequently repeated at all descending levels until the segmentation/classification of the original input image is successfully accomplished.

At every processing level, every image object-region (just recovered or an inherited one) is registered in the objects' appearance list, which is the third constituting part of the proposed scheme. The registered object parameters are the available simplified object's attributes, such as size, center-of-mass position, average object intensity and hierarchical and topological relationship within and between the objects ("sub-part of…", "at the left of…", etc.). They are sparse, general, and yet specific enough to capture the object's characteristic features in a variety of descriptive forms.

In such a way, a set of pixel clusters (segments, structures formed by nearby pixels with similar properties) is elucidated and depicted providing an explicit representation of the information contained in a given image. That means, taking the relevant segment description we can reconstruct it trustworthy and rigorously, because (by definition) every such a description contains all the information needed for the item's (or the whole set of items, that is an entire image) successful reconstruction.

2.4 Visual information = Physical information

One interesting thing has already been mentioned above – the top-down coarse-to-fine image information elucidation does not require any high-level knowledge incorporation for its successful accomplishment. It is totally free from any high-level guiding rules and inspirations (Which is in a striking contrast with the classic image information processing theories). It deals only with natural (physical) structures usually discernible in an image, which originate from natural aggregations of similar nearby data elements (e.g., pixels in the case of an image). That was the reason why I have decided to call it "Physical Information".

To summarize all what we have learned until now we can say:

- **Physical Information is a description of data structures** usually discernable in a data set (e.g., pixel clusters or segments in an image).
- **Physical Information is a language-based description,** according to which a reliable reconstruction of original objects (e.g., image segments) can be attained while the description is carried out (like an execution of a computer program).
- **Physical Information is a descending hierarchy** of descriptions standing for various complexity levels, a top-down coarse-to-fine evolving structure that represents different levels of information details.
- **Physical Information is** the only information that can be extracted from a raw data set (e.g., an image). Later it can be submitted to further suitable image processing, but at this stage it is the only information available.

To my own great surprise, solving the problem of physical (visual) information elucidation did not promote me even in the smallest way to my primary goal of image recognition, understanding and interpretation - they have remained elusive and unattainable as ever.

3. What is semantics?

3.1 Semantics – the physical information's twin

It is clear that physical information does not exhaust the whole visual information that we usually expect to reveal in an image. But on the other hand, it is perfectly clear that relying on our approach the only information that could be extracted from an image is the physical information, and nothing else. What immediately follows from this is that the other part of visual information, the high-level knowledge that makes grouping of disjoint image segments meaningful, is not an integral part of image information content (as it is traditionally assumed). It cannot be seen more as a natural property of an image. And it has to be seen as a property of a human observer that watches and scrutinizes an image.

This way I came to the conclusion that the notion of visual information must be disintegrated to two composite parts - physical information and semantic information.

The first is contained in an image while the other is contained in the observer's head. The first can be extracted from an image while the second - and that is an eternal problem - cannot be studied by opening the human's head in order to verify its existence or to explore its peculiarities. But, if we are right in our guess that semantics is information, then we have some general principals, some insights, which can be drawn from physical information studies and applied to our semantics investigations.

In such a case, all previously defined aspects of the notion of information must also hold in the case of semantic information. That is, we can say - Semantics is a language-based description of the structures that are observable in a given image. While physical

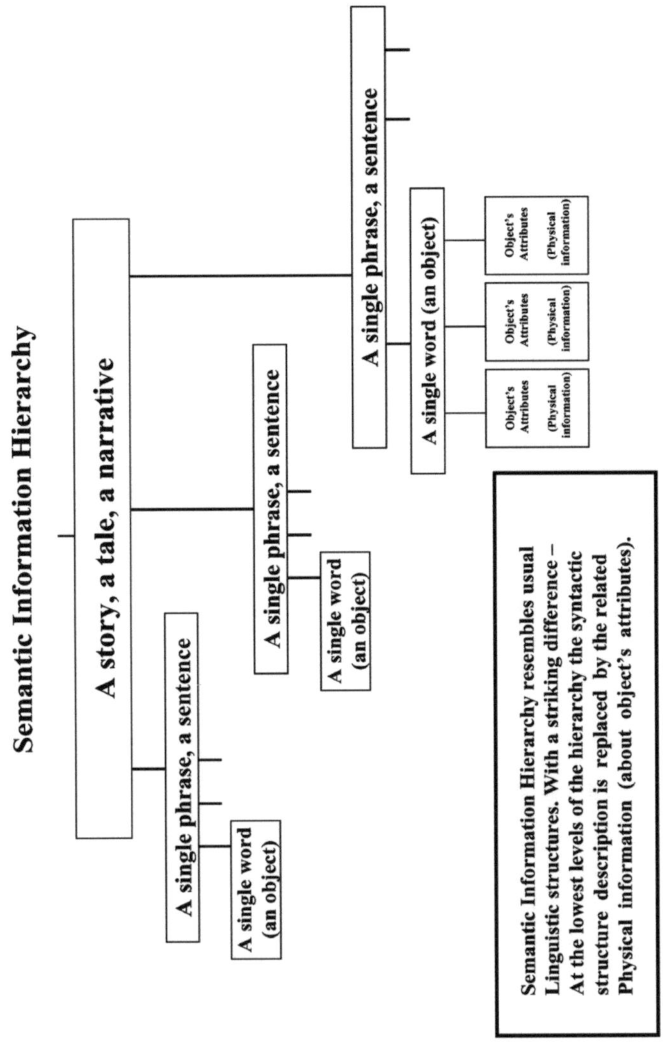

Fig. 2. Semantic Information hierarchical arrangement.

information describes structures formed by agglomeration of physical data elements (e.g., image pixels), semantic information describes structures formed by interrelations among data clusters (or segments) produced by preliminary pixel arrangements.

Bearing in mind this difference between semantic and physical information, we will proceed with what must be common to all information descriptions. That is, as all other information descriptions, semantics has to be a hierarchical structure which evolves in a top-down coarse-to-fine manner. Unlike physical information, which can be based on a variety of languages (be reminded - mathematics is also a sort of a language), semantic information is commonly based on the human natural language descriptions. This is the reason why historically semantics was always strongly tied with human language.

In this regard, I hope that a hypothetical semantic information hierarchical arrangement depicted in Fig. 2 can be seen as a trustworthy representation of the inner semantic information architecture. It must also be mentioned that this architecture resembles the structure of a written document, a piece of literary artwork, a tale, a paper, a narrative. As usual, it begins with a title, which is immediately followed by an abstract. From the abstract it descends to the paragraphs of the text body, and then it descends to phrases, which, in turn, are further decomposed into single separate words that build up a phrase.

3.2 Semantics – physical information's interpretation

At this stage, the standard linguistic semantic decomposition goes down to the syntactic components of a word. And this is not accidental - what traditional linguistics calls syntax in our case (information framework) should be called physical information (attributes), or more precisely - the underlying physical information contained in a single semantic word. That is shown in Fig. 2 as the lowest level of semantics hierarchy.

What must be specially emphasized is that these attributes (united, generalized by a higher level semantic word) could be: 1) multiple representations of different word's physical information components, which belong to the same modality; and 2) representations of different word's physical information components, which belong to different modalities. That is - the word's attributes could be represented as visual information (e.g., our case), acoustical information (as in the case of a spoken language), or any other type of physical information, including letters of a certain alphabet (as in a classical linguistic case, when a written language is used as an information bearer). It can also be a mixture of different modalities, where all physical information components are pointing (leading) to the same semantic word.

Now we can switch to the most important part of our discussion: From where semantics hierarchy does initially emerge? How it comes into existence? Somewhere in above I have mentioned that physical information is a description of structures formed by grouping of nearby data elements (I prefer to call them primary data structures) and semantic information is a description of structures formed by grouping of these nearby primary structures (I prefer to call them secondary data structures). While primary data structures are formed by grouping of nearby data elements tied by similarity in some physical property (e.g., pixel's color or brightness in an image), secondary data structures are formed without any grouping rules compliance. That means that secondary structures production (and their further naming/description) is a subjective arbitrary process, guided by mutual agreements and conventions among a specific group of observers which are involved in this (semantic) convention establishment.

This is a very important point, because what follows from it is that a new member of this specific company can not gain the established semantic conventions independently and autonomously. The conventions have to be given (transferred) to his disposal in a complete form from the outside (from the other community members) and then must be incorporated into his semantic information hierarchy. That is, fused and memorized in this hierarchy.

Publications dealing with some similar and related issues of internet documents understanding refer to this process as "a priory knowledge" acquisition and sharing. What is meant by "knowledge" is usually undefined and not considered. I think that my

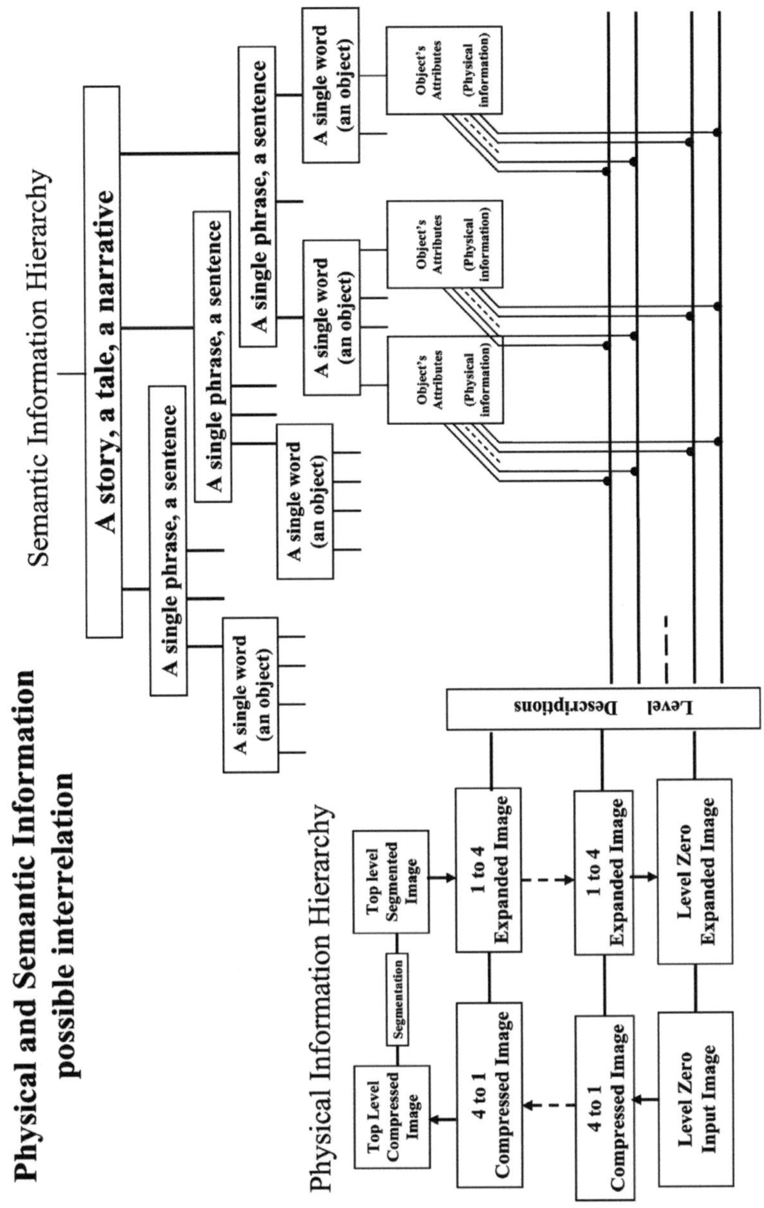

Fig. 3. Physical and Semantic Information interaction block-schema.

definition of semantic information makes it crystal clear – "Knowledge" is "Semantic information" brought from the outside and memorized into the information processing system.

And yet, the time is ripe to verify what does it means "semantic information processing"? My answer is depicted in Fig. 3 where I show how physical and semantic information are interrelated in a general information processing system.

The examination of the Fig. 3 must be prefaced with a commonplace statement that human sensory system (as well as all other so-called artificial intelligence systems) provides us only with raw sensor data and nothing else beside the data. Then, at the system's input, this sensor data is processed and physical information is being extracted from it. This physical information is fed in into the semantic information processing part, where it is matched or is being associated with the physical information stored (memorized) at the lowest level of the semantic hierarchy. If a match of physical information details in the input and in the stored information is attained and the details grouping conventions are satisfied, then a semantic label (an object's name) is "fired" on the first semantic level of the hierarchy. The names of adjacent objects are verified in the same manner (the so-called word's context is affirmed) and the named object finds its place in a suitable phrase or expression.

Thus the meaning of object's label (the semantics of natural language object's name) is revealed by the whole phrase in which the object (the object's name, the noun) was placed in as a suitable and a legitimate part. The semantics of a label (of a word) is defined now not only by its nearest linguistic neighbors, but by the whole phrase and the entire story text in which it is being submerged.

4. Generalization

Approaching the end of the chapter, I would like to generalize the partial clarifications that were just given above. My research motivation was inspired by home security visual scene analysis and understanding goals. Therefore, my main concern was with visual information processing. However, I think it would be wise to broaden the scope of my findings.

I can faithfully state now that every information gathering starts with sensor data acquisition and accumulation. The body of data is not a random collection of data elements, but exhibits undeniable structures discernible in the data. These structures emerge as a result of data elements agglomeration shaped by similarity in their physical properties. Therefore, such structures could be called primary or physical data structures.

In the eyes of an external observer these primary data structures are normally grouped and tied together into more larger and complex aggregations, which could be called secondary data structures. These secondary structures reflect human observer's view on the arrangement of primary data structures, and therefore they could be called meaningful or semantic data structures. While formation of primary data structures is guided by objective (natural, physical) properties of data elements, ensuing formation of secondary structures is a subjective process guided by human habits and customs, mutual agreements and conventions.

Description of structures observable in a data set has to be called "Information". Following the given above explanation about the structures discernible in every data set, two types of information must be declared therefore - Physical Information and Semantic Information. They are both language-based descriptions; however, physical information can be described with a variety of languages, while semantic information can be described only with natural human language used.

Every information description is a top-down evolving coarse-to-fine hierarchy of descriptions representing various levels of description complexity (various levels of description details). Physical information hierarchy is located at the lowest level of the semantic hierarchy. The process of data interpretation is reified as a process of physical information extraction from the input data, followed by a process of input physical information association with physical information stored at the lowest level of a semantic hierarchy. In this way, input physical information becomes named with an appropriate linguistic label and framed into a suitable linguistic phrase (and further – in a story, a tale, a narrative), which provides the desired meaning for the input physical information.

5. Conclusions

In this chapter I have proposed a new definition of information (as a description, a linguistic text, a piece of a story or a tale) and a clear segregation between two different types of information – physical and semantic information. I hope, I have clearly explained the (usually obscured and mysterious) interrelations between data and physical information as well as the relations between physical information and semantic information. Consequently, usually indefinable notions of "knowledge", "memory" and "learning" have also received their suitable illumination and explanation.

Traditionally, semantics is seen as a feature of human language communication praxis. However, the explosive growth of communication technologies (different from the original language-based communication) has led to an enormous diversification of matters which are being communicated today – audio and visual content, scientific and commercial, military and medical health care information. All of them certainly bear their own non-linguistic semantics (Pratikakis et al, 2011). Therefore, attempts to explain and to clarify these new forms of semantics are permanently undertaken, aimed to develop tools and services which would enable to handle this communication traffic in a reasonable and meaningful manner. In the reference list I provide some examples of such undertakings: "The Semantics of Semantics" (Petrie, 2009), "Semantics of the Semantic Web" (Sheth et al, 2005), "Geospatial Semantics" (Di Donato, 2010), "Semantics in the Semantic Web" (Almeida et al, 2011).

What is common to all those attempts is that notions of data, information, knowledge and semantics are interchanged and swapped generously, without any second thought about what implications might follow from that. In this regard, even a special notion of Data Semantics was introduced (Sheth, 1995) and European Commission and DARPA are pushing research programs aimed on extracting meaning and purpose from bursts of sensor data (Examples of such research roadmaps could be found in my last presentation at The 3-rd Israeli Conference on Robotics, November 2010, available at my website http://www.vidia-mant.info). However, as my present definition claims – data and information are not interchangeable, physical information is not a substitute for semantic information, and data is semantics devoid (semantics is a property of a human observer, not a property of the data).

Contrary to the widespread praxis (Zins, 2007), I have defined semantics as a special kind of information. Revitalizing the ideas of Bar-Hillel and Carnap (Bar-Hillel & Carnap, 1952) I have recreated and re-established (on totally new grounds) the notion of semantics as the notion of Semantic Information.

Considering the crucial role that information usage, search for, exchange and exploration have gained in our society, I dare to think that clarifying the notion of semantic information will illuminate many shady paths which Semantic Web designers and promoters are forced to take today, deprived from a proper understanding of semantic information peculiarities. As a result, information processing principles are substituted by data processing tenets

(Chignell & Kealey, 2010); the objective nature of physical information is confused with the subjective nature of semantic information. For that reason, Semantic Web search engines are continue to be built relying on statistics of linguistic features. I hope my chapter will let to avoid such lapses.

6. References

Adams, F. (2003). The Informational Turn in Philosophy, Minds and Machines 13: 471-501, 2003. Available from http://www.arquitetura.eesc.usp.br/laboratorios/lei/sap5865/2007/leituras/Mind_and_machines.pdf

Almeida, M.; Souza, R. & Fonseca, F. (2011). Semantics in the semantic web: a critical evaluation, *Knowledge Organization Journal*. Vol. 38, n.3 p. 187-203. 2011. Available from: http://mba.eci.ufmg.br/downloads/spec_subm_KO_last.pdf

Bar-Hillel, Y. & Carnap, R. (1952). An outline of a theory of semantic information, *Technical report No. 247, October 27, 1952*, Available from http://www.survivor99.com/lcg/information/CARNAP-HILLEL.pdf

Beaver, D. & Frazee, J. (2011). Semantics, In: *The Handbook of Computational Linguistics*, Ruslan Mitkov (ed.), Available from http://semanticsarchive.net/Archive/DAzYmYzO/semantics_oup.pdf

Biederman, I.(1987). Recognition-by-Components: A Theory of Human Image Understanding, *Psychological Review*, vol. 94, no. 2, pp. 115-147, 1987.

Chaitin, G. (1966). On the length of programs for computing finite binary sequences. *Journal of the ACM*, Vol. 13, pp. 547-569, 1966.

Chignell, M. & Kealey, R. (2010). Supplementing Semantics with Statistics in the Personal Web, Available from: http://research.cs.queensu.ca/home/cordy/SPW/Proceedings/ChignellKealeyPWSPaperV2.pdf

Diamant, E. (2002). Image Segmentation Scheme Ruled by Information Density Optimization, Submitted to *British Machine Vision Conference (BMVC-2002)* and decisively rejected there. Available from: http://www.vidia-mant.info.

Diamant, E. (2003). Single Pixel Information Content, *Proceedings SPIE*, Vol. 5014, pp. 460-465, IST/SPIE 15th Annual Symposium on Electronic Imaging, Santa Clara, CA, January 2003. Available from: http://www.vidia-mant.info.

Diamant, E. (2004). Top-Down Unsupervised Image Segmentation (it sounds like an oxymoron, but actually it isn't), *Proceedings of the 3rd Pattern Recognition in Remote Sensing Workshop (PRRS'04)*, Kingston University, UK, August 2004. Available from: http://www.vidia-mant.info.

Diamant, E. (2005). Searching for image information content, its discovery, extraction, and representation, *Journal of Electronic Imaging*, Vol. 14, Issue 1, January-March 2005. Available from: http://www.vidia-mant.info.

Di Donato, P. (2010). Geospatial Semantics: A Critical Review, In: ICCSA 2010, Part I, LNCS 6016, pp. 528–544, Available from http://www.labsita.org/wp-content/uploads/2010/05/didonato-geospatial-semantics.pdf

Floridi, L. (2005). Semantic Conceptions of Information, *First published Wed Oct 5, 2005; substantive revision Fri Jan 28, 2011*, Available from

http://www.illc.uva.nl/~seop/entries/information-semantic/
Fodor, J. (2007). Semantics: an interview with Jerry Fodor. *ReVEL.* Vol. 5, No. 8, 2007. Available from http://www.revel.inf.br/site2007/_pdf/8/entrevistas/revel_8_interview_jerry_fodor.pdf
Harrub, B.; Thompson, B. & Miller, D. (2003). The Origin of Language and Communication, Available from http://www.trueorigin.org/language01.asp
Kolmogorov, A. (1965). Three approaches to the quantitative definition of information, *Problems of Information and Transmission,* Vol. 1, No. 1, pp. 1-7, 1965.
Marr, D. (1978). Representing visual information: A computational approach, *Lectures on Mathematics in the Life Science,* Vol. 10, pp. 61-80, 1978.
Marr, D. (1982). Vision: A Computational Investigation into the Human Representation and Processing of Visual Information, Freeman, San Francisco, 1982.
Petrie, C. (2009). The Semantics of "Semantics", IEEE Internet Computing, September/October 2009 Available from: http://www-cdr.stanford.edu/~petrie/online/peer2peer/semantics.pdf
Pratikakis, I.; Bolovinou, A.; Gatos, B. & Perantonis, S. (2011). Semantics extraction from images, In: *Knowledge-Driven Multimedia Information Extraction and Ontology Evolution* , Lecture Notes in Computer Science, Volume 6050/2011, Available from: http://dl.acm.org/citation.cfm?id=2001072
Schyns, P. & Oliva, A. (1994). From blobs to boundary edges: Evidence for time and spatial scale dependent scene recognition, *Psychological Science,* v. 5, pp. 195 - 200, 1994.
Shannon, C. E. (1948). The mathematical theory of communication, *Bell System Technical Journal,* Vol. 27, pp. 379-423 and 623-656, July and October 1948. Available from: http://cm.bell-labs.com/cm/ms/what/shannonday/paper.html
Shannon, C. & Weaver, W. (1949). The Mathematical Theory of Communication, University of Illinois Press, 1949.
Sheth, A. (1995). Data Semantics: what, where and how?. In: *Proceedings of DS-6'1995.* pp.601~610, Available from: http://knoesis.wright.edu/library/download/S96-Data-Semantics.pdf
Sheth, A., Ramakrishnan, C., & Thomas, C. (2005), Semantics for the Semantic Web: The implicit, the formal and the powerful, *International Journal on Semantic Web & Information Systems,* vol. 1, no. 1, pp. 1–18, Jan - March 2005. Available from: http://knoesis.cs.wright.edu/library/download/SRT05-IJ-SW-IS.pdf
Sloman, A. (2011). What's information, for an organism or intelligent machine? How can a machine or organism mean? Available from http://www.cs.bham.ac.uk/~axs
Solomonoff, R. J. (1964). A formal theory of inductive inference. *Information and Control,* Part 1: Vol. 7, No. 1, pp. 1-22, March 1964; Part 2: Vol. 7, No. 2, pp. 224-254, June 1964.
Torralba, A. (2009). How many pixels make an image? *Visual Neuroscience,* Vol. 26, Issue 1, pp. 123-131, 2009. Available from: http://web.mit.edu/torralba/www/.
Treisman, A. & Gelade, G. (1980). A feature-integration theory of attention, *Cognitive Psychology,* vol. 12, pp. 97-136, Jan. 1980.
Wikipedia. (2011a). Language, Available from http://en.wikipedia.org/wiki/Language
Wikipedia. (2011b). Semantics, Available from http://en.wikipedia.org/wiki/Semantics
Zins, C. (2007). Conceptual Approaches for Defining Data, Information, and Knowledge, *Journal of the American society for information science and technology,* 58(4):479–493, 2007, Available from http://www.success.co.il/is/zins_definitions_dik.pdf

2

Probabilistic Belief Logics for Uncertain Agents

Zining Cao[1,2]
[1]*Department of Computer Science and Technology, Nanjing Universityof Aero. & Astro., Nanjing*
[2]*Provincial Key Laboratory for Computer Information Processing Technology, Soochow University, Suzhou*
P. R. China

1. Introduction

The study of knowledge and belief has a long tradition in philosophy. An early treatment of a formal logical analysis of reasoning about knowledge and belief came from Hintikka's work [15]. More recently, researchers in such diverse fields as economics, linguistics, artificial intelligence and theoretical computer science have become increasingly interested in reasoning about knowledge and belief [1–5, 10–13, 18, 20, 24]. In wide areas of application of reasoning about knowledge and belief, it is necessary to reason about uncertain information. Therefore the representation and reasoning of probabilistic information in belief is important.

There has been a lot of works in the literatures related to the representation and reasoning of probabilistic information, such as evidence theory [25], probabilistic logic [4], probabilistic dynamic logic [7], probabilistic nonmonotonic logic [21], probabilistic knowledge logic [3] and etc. A distinguished work is done by Fagin and Halpern [3], in which a probabilistic knowledge logic is proposed. It expanded the language of knowledge logic by adding formulas like "$w_i(\varphi) \geq 2w_i(\psi)$" and "$w_i(\varphi) < 1/3$", where φ and ψ are arbitrary formulas. These formulas mean "φ is at least twice probable as ψ" and "φ has probability less than $1/3$". The typical formulas of their logic are "$a_1w_i(\varphi_1) + ... + a_kw_i(\varphi_k) \geq b$", "$K_i(\varphi)$" and "$K_i^b(\varphi)$", the latter formula is an abbreviation of "$K_i(w_i(\varphi) \geq b)$". Here formulas may contain nested occurrences of the modal operators w_i and K_i, and the formulas in [4] do not contain nested occurrences of the modal operators w_i. On the basis of knowledge logic, they added axioms of reasoning about linear inequalities and probabilities. To provide semantics for such logic, Fagin and Halpern introduced a probability space on Kripke models of knowledge logic, and gave some conditions about probability space, such as OBJ, SDP and $UNIF$. At last, Fagin and Halpern concluded by proving the soundness and completeness of their probabilistic knowledge logic.

Fagin and Halpern's work on probabilistic epistemic logic is well-known and original. However, there are several aspects worth further investigation: First, the completeness proof of Fagin and Halpern can only deal with the finite set of formulas for that their method reduces the completeness to the existence of a solution of a set of finitely many linear inequalities. In the case of an infinite set of formulas, their method reduces the problem to the existence of a solution of infinitely many linear inequalities with infinitely many variables, which does not seem to be captured by the axioms in [3] for their language only contains finite-length formulas. Second, their inference system includes axioms about linear inequalities and probabilities, which makes the system complicated. Third, the semantics in [3] was given by adding a probability space on Kripke structure, correspondingly there are restrictions on probability spaces and accessible relations, but in fact a simpler model is possible for the semantics of probabilistic epistemic logic.

Kooi's work [18] combines the probabilistic epistemic logic with the dynamic epistemic logic yielding a new logic, $PDEL$, that deals with changing probabilities and takes higher-order information into account. The syntax of $PDEL$ is an expansion of Fagin and Halpern's logic by introducing formula "$[\varphi_1]\varphi_2$", which can be read as "φ_2 is the case, after everyone simultaneously and commonly learns that φ_1 is the case". The semantics of $PDEL$ is essentially same as Fagin and Halpern's semantics, which is based on a combination of Kripke structure and probability functions. Kooi proved the soundness and weak completeness of $PDEL$, but like Fagin and Halpern's paper, completeness of $PDEL$ was not given.

In [22], the authors also propose a probabilistic belief logic, called PEL, which is essentially a restricted version of the logic proposed by Fagin and Halpern. But in this chapter, the inference system was not given and the corresponding properties such as soundness and completeness of PEL were not studied.

In [16], Hoek investigated a probabilistic logic $P_F D$. This logic is enriched with operators $P_r^>, (r \in [0,1])$ where the intended meaning of $P_r^> \varphi$ is "the probability of φ is strictly greater than r". The author gave a completeness proof of $P_F D$ by the construction of a canonical model for $P_F D$ considerably. Furthermore, the author also proved finite model property of the logic by giving a filtration-technique for the intended models. Finally, the author prove the decidability of the logic. In [16], the logic $P_F D$ is based on a set F, where F is a finite set and $\{0,1\} \subseteq F \subseteq [0,1]$. The completeness of $P_F D$ was not proved in [16] for the case that F is infinite. Hoek presented this problem as an open question and considered it as a difficult task. He think this problem may be tackled by introducing infinitary rules.

In this chapter, we propose some probabilistic belief logics. There is no axiom and rule about linear inequalities and probabilities in the inference system of probabilistic belief logics. Hence the inference system looks simpler and uniform than Fagin and Halpern's logic. We also propose a simpler semantics for probabilistic belief logics, where is no accessible relation and can be generalized to description semantics of other probabilistic modal logics. Moreover, we present the new completeness proofs for our probabilistic belief logics, which can deal with infinite sets of formulas.

The remainder of the chapter is organized as follows: In Section 2, we propose a probabilistic belief logic, called PBL_ω. We provide the probabilistic semantics of PBL_ω, and prove the soundness and completeness of PBL_ω with respect to the semantics. We are unable to prove or disprove the finite model property of PBL_ω in this chapter even though we conjecture it holds. We turn to look at a variant of PBL_ω, which has the finite model property. In Section 3, we present a weaker variant of PBL_ω, called PBL_f, which is the same as PBL_ω but without *Axiom* 6 and *Rule* 6. We give the semantics of PBL_f and prove the soundness and finite model property of PBL_f. As a consequence, the weak completeness of PBL_f is given, i.e., for any finite set of formulas Γ, $\Gamma \models_{PBL_f} \varphi \Rightarrow \Gamma \vdash_{PBL_f} \varphi$. But there is an infinite inference rule, namely *Rule* 5, in PBL_f, which is inconvenient for application. Therefore we consider another variant PBL_r in Section 4. The axioms and rules of PBL_r are same as PBL_f except for *Rule* 5. PBL_r has a syntax restriction that the probability a in the scope of $B_i(a, \varphi)$ must be a rational number. The soundness and finite model property of PBL_r are proved. From the finite model property, we obtain the weak completeness of PBL_r. Note that a logic system has the compactness property if and only if the weak completeness is equivalent to the completeness in that logic. The compactness property does not hold in PBL_r, for example, $\{B_i(1/2,\varphi), B_i(2/3,\varphi), ..., B_i(n/n+1,\varphi),...\} \cup \{\neg B_i(1,\varphi)\}$ is not satisfied in any PBL_r-model, but any finite subset of it has a model. Therefore the weak completeness of PBL_r is not equivalent to the completeness. PBL_r is proved to be weak complete. Furthermore, the decidability of PBL_r is shown. In Section 5, we mainly compare our logics with the logic in [3] in terms of their syntax, inference system, semantics and proof technique. The chapter is concluded in Section 6.

2. PBL_ω and its probabilistic semantics

In this section, we first review the standard belief logic system and the standard Kripke semantics. Some examples are given to illustrate why it is necessary to extend belief to probabilistic belief. Then we introduce a probabilistic belief logic PBL_ω.

In belief logic, the formula $B_i\varphi$ says that agent i believes φ. Consider a system with n agents, say $1,...,n$, and we have a nonempty set Φ of primitive propositions about which we wish to reason. We construct formulas by closing off Φ under conjunction, negation and modal operators B_i, for $i = 1,...,n$ (where $B_i\varphi$ is read as "agent i believes φ").

The semantics to these formulas is given by means of Kripke structure [19]. A Kripke structure for belief (for n agents) is a tuple $(S,\pi,R_1,...,R_n)$, where S is a set of states, $\pi(s)$ is a truth assignment to the primitive propositions of Φ for each state $s \in S$, and R_i is an accessible relation on S, which satisfies the following conditions: Euclideanness $(\forall s\forall s'\forall s''(sR_is' \wedge sR_is'' \rightarrow s'R_is''))$, transitivity $(\forall s\forall s'\forall s''(sR_is' \wedge s'R_is'' \rightarrow sR_is''))$ and definality $(\forall s\exists s'(sR_is'))$.

We now assign truth values to formulas at each state in the structure. We write $(M,s)\models \varphi$ if the formula φ is true at state s in Kripke structure M.

$(M,s) \models p$ (for $p \in \Phi$) iff $\pi(s)(p) = true$

$(M,s) \models \neg\varphi$ iff $(M,s) \not\models \varphi$

$(M,s) \models \varphi \wedge \psi$ iff $(M,s) \models \varphi$ and $(M,s) \models \psi$

$(M,s)\models B_i\varphi$ iff $(M,t) \models \varphi$ for all $t \in R_i(s)$ with $R_i(s) = \{s'|(s,s') \in R_i\}$

The last clause in this definition captures the intuition that agent i believes φ in world (M,s) exactly if φ is true in all worlds that i considers possible.

It is well known that the following set of axioms and inference rules provides a sound and complete axiomatization for the logic of belief with respect to the class of Kripke structures for belief:

All instances of propositional tautologies and rules.

$(B_i\varphi \wedge B_i(\varphi \rightarrow \psi)) \rightarrow B_i\psi$

$B_i\varphi \rightarrow \neg B_i\neg\varphi$

$B_i\varphi \rightarrow B_iB_i\varphi$

$\neg B_i\varphi \rightarrow B_i\neg B_i\varphi$

$\vdash \varphi \Rightarrow \vdash B_i\varphi$

There are examples of probabilistic belief in daily life. For example, one may believe that the probability of "it will rain tomorrow" is less than 0.4; in a football game, one may believe that the probability of "team A will win" is no less than 0.7 and so on. In distribute systems, there may be the cases that "agent i believes that the probability of 'agent j believes that the probability of φ is at least a' is no less than b". Suppose there are two persons communicating by email, agent A sends an email to agent B. Since the email may be lost in network, A does not know whether B has received the email. Therefore A may believe that the probability of "B has received my email" is less than 0.99, or may believe that the probability of "B has received my email" is at least 0.8, and so on. On the other hand, B may believe that the probability of "A believes that the probability of 'B has received my email' is at least 0.9" is less than 0.8. In order to reply to A, B sends an acknowledgement email to A, A receives the email, and sends another acknowledgement email to B, now B believes that the probability of "A believes that the probability of 'B has received my first email' is equal to 1" is equal to 1. In order to represent and reason with probabilistic belief, it is necessary to extend belief logic to probabilistic belief logic. In following, we propose a probabilistic belief logic PBL_ω, the basic formula in PBL_ω is $B_i(a,\varphi)$, which says agent i believes that the probability of φ is no less than a.

2.1 Language of PBL_ω

Throughout this chapter, we let L^{PBL_ω} be a language which is just the set of formulas of interest to us.

Definition 2.1 The set of formulas in PBL_ω, called L^{PBL_ω}, is given by the following rules:

(1) If $\varphi \in$Atomic formulas set $Prop$, then $\varphi \in L^{PBL_\omega}$;

(2) If $\varphi \in L^{PBL_\omega}$, then $\neg\varphi \in L^{PBL_\omega}$;

(3) If φ_1,$\varphi_2 \in L^{PBL_\omega}$, then $\varphi_1 \wedge \varphi_2 \in L^{PBL_\omega}$;

(4) If $\varphi \in L^{PBL_\omega}$ and $a \in$[0,1], then $B_i(a,\varphi) \in L^{PBL_\omega}$, where i belongs to the set of agents $\{1,...,n\}$. Intuitively, $B_i(a,\varphi)$ means that agent i believes the probability of φ is no less than a.

2.2 Semantics of PBL_ω

We will describe the semantics of PBL_ω, i.e., a formal model that we can use to determine whether a given formula is true or false. We call the formal model probabilistic model, roughly speaking, at each state, each agent has a probability on a certain set of states.

Definition 2.2 A probabilistic model PM of PBL_ω is a tuple $(S,\pi,P_1,...,P_n)$, where

(1) S is a nonempty set, whose elements are called possible worlds or states;

(2) π is a map: $S \times Prop \rightarrow \{true, false\}$, where $Prop$ is a set of atomic formulas;

(3) P_i is a map, it maps every possible world s to a PBL_ω-probability space $P_i(s) = (S, X_{i,s}, \mu_{i,s})$.

Where $X_{i,s} \in \wp(S)$, which satisfies the following conditions:

(a) If p is an atomic formula, then $ev_{PM}(p) = \{s'|\pi(s', p) = true\} \in X_{i,s}$;

(b) If $A \in X_{i,s}$, then $S - A \in X_{i,s}$;

(c) If $A_1, A_2 \in X_{i,s}$, then $A_1 \cap A_2 \in X_{i,s}$;

(d) If $A \in X_{i,s}$ and $a \in [0,1]$, then $\{s'|\mu_{i,s'}(A) \geq a\} \in X_{i,s}$.

$\mu_{i,s}$ is a PBL_ω- finite additivity probability measure assigned to the set $X_{i,s}$, i.e., $\mu_{i,s}$ satisfies the following conditions:

(a) $\mu_{i,s}(A) \geq 0$ for all $A \in X_{i,s}$;

(b) $\mu_{i,s}(S) = 1$;

(c) (finite additivity) $\mu_{i,s}(A_1 \cup A_2) = \mu_{i,s}(A_1) + \mu_{i,s}(A_2)$, where A_1 and A_2 are disjoint members of $X_{i,s}$;

(d) If $A \in X_{i,s}$ and $\mu_{i,s}(A) \geq a$, then $\mu_{i,s}(\{s'|\mu_{i,s'}(A) \geq a\}) = 1$; if $A \in X_{i,s}$ and $\mu_{i,s}(A) < b$, then $\mu_{i,s}(\{s'|\mu_{i,s'}(A) < b\}) = 1$.

Notice that from the definition of $X_{i,s}$, we have $\{s'|\mu_{i,s'}(A) \geq a\} \in X_{i,s}$ and $\{s'|\mu_{i,s'}(A) < b\} = S - \{s'|\mu_{i,s'}(A) \geq b\} \in X_{i,s}$. Intuitively, the probability space $P_i(s)$ describes agent i's probabilities on events, given that the state is s. W is the sample space, which is the set of states that agent i considers possible. $X_{i,s}$ is the set of measurable sets. The measure $\mu_{i,s}$ does not assign a probability to all subsets of S but only to the measurable sets.

As an example, we consider a PBL_ω-model such that $PM = (S, \pi, P_1)$. Here $S = \{s_1, s_2, s_3\}$; $\pi(s_1, p) = false$, $\pi(s_2, p) = false$, $\pi(s_3, p) = true$, $\pi(s_1, q) = true$, $\pi(s_2, q) = true$, $\pi(s_3, q) = true$; P_1 is defined as follows: for every $s \in S$, $P_1(s) = (S, X_{1,s}, \mu_{1,s})$, where $X_{1,s_1} = X_{1,s_2} = \wp(S)$, $X_{1,s_3} = \{\emptyset, \{s_1, s_2\}, \{s_3\}, S\}$, $\mu_{1,s_1}(\emptyset) = \mu_{1,s_2}(\emptyset) = \mu_{1,s_3}(\emptyset) = 0$, $\mu_{1,s_1}(\{s_1\}) = \mu_{1,s_2}(\{s_1\}) = 1/2$, $\mu_{1,s_1}(\{s_2\}) = \mu_{1,s_2}(\{s_2\}) = 1/2$, $\mu_{1,s_1}(\{s_3\}) = \mu_{1,s_2}(\{s_3\}) = 0$, $\mu_{1,s_3}(\{s_3\}) = 1$, $\mu_{1,s_1}(\{s_1, s_2\}) = \mu_{1,s_2}(\{s_1, s_2\}) = 1$, $\mu_{1,s_3}(\{s_1, s_2\}) = 0$, $\mu_{1,s_1}(\{s_1, s_3\}) = \mu_{1,s_2}(\{s_1, s_3\}) = 1/2$, $\mu_{1,s_1}(\{s_2, s_3\}) = \mu_{1,s_2}(\{s_2, s_3\}) = 1/2$, $\mu_{1,s_1}(S) = \mu_{1,s_2}(S) = \mu_{1,s_3}(S) = 1$. It is easy to check that the above model satisfies the conditions in Definition 2.2. In this model, it is clear that the set of measurable sets $X_{1,s}$ and probability measure $\mu_{1,s}$ varies with s, and consequently the probability space also varies with s, hence we index probability space by s.

We now define what it means for a formula to be true at a given world s in a probabilistic model PM.

Definition 2.3 Probabilistic semantics of PBL_ω

$(PM, s) \models p$ iff $\pi(s, p) = true$, where p is an atomic formula;

$(PM, s) \models \neg\varphi$ iff $(PM, s) \not\models \varphi$;

$(PM, s) \models \varphi \wedge \psi$ iff $(PM, s) \models \varphi$ and $(PM, s) \models \psi$;

$(PM, s) \models B_i(a, \varphi)$ iff $\mu_{i,s}(ev_{PM}(\varphi)) \geq a$, where $ev_{PM}(\varphi) = \{s'|(PM, s') \models \varphi\}$.

The intuitive meaning of the semantics of $B_i(a, \varphi)$ is that agent i believes that the probability of φ is at least a in world (PM, s) if the measure of possible worlds satisfying φ is at least a.

In the above example, according to Definition 2.3, we have $(PM, s_1) \models B_1(1/2, q)$, $(PM, s_2) \models B_1(0, p \wedge q)$, $(PM, s_3) \models B_1(1, p \wedge q)$, etc.

In order to characterize the properties of probabilistic belief, we will characterize the formulas that are always true. More formally, given a probabilistic model PM, we say that φ is valid in PM, and write $PM \models \varphi$, if $(PM, s) \models \varphi$ for every state s in S, and we say that φ is satisfiable in PM if $(PM, s) \models \varphi$ for some s in S. We say that φ is valid, and write $\models \varphi$, if φ is valid in all probabilistic models, and that φ is satisfiable if it is satisfiable in some probabilistic model. We write $\Gamma \models \varphi$, if φ is valid in all probabilistic models in which Γ is satisfiable.

2.3 Inference system of PBL_ω

Now we list a number of valid properties of probabilistic belief, which form the inference system of PBL_ω.

Axioms and inference rules of proposition logic

Axiom 1. $B_i(0, \varphi)$ (For any proposition φ, agent i believes that the probability of φ is no less than 0.)

Axiom 2. $B_i(a, \varphi) \wedge B_i(b, \psi) \rightarrow B_i(max(a+b-1, 0), \varphi \wedge \psi)$ (For any φ and ψ, if agent i believes that the probability of φ is no less than a, and believes that the probability of ψ is no less than b, then agent i believes that the probability of $\varphi \wedge \psi$ is no less than $max(a+b-1, 0)$.)

Axiom 3. $B_i(a, \varphi) \rightarrow B_i(1, B_i(a, \varphi))$ (If agent i believes that the probability of φ is no less than a, then agent i believes that the probability of his belief being true is no less than 1.)

Axiom 4. $\neg B_i(a, \varphi) \rightarrow B_i(1, \neg B_i(a, \varphi))$ (If agent i believes that the probability of φ is less than a, then agent i believes that the probability of his belief being true is no less than 1.)

Axiom 5. $B_i(a, \varphi) \rightarrow B_i(b, \varphi)$, where $1 \geq a \geq b \geq 0$. (If agent i believes that the probability of φ is no less than a, and $1 \geq a \geq b \geq 0$, then agent i believes that the probability of φ is no less than b.)

Axiom 6. $B_i(a+b, \varphi \vee \psi) \rightarrow (B_i(a, \varphi) \vee B_i(b, \psi))$, where $1 \geq a+b \geq 0$. (If agent i believes that the probability of $\varphi \vee \psi$ is no less than $a+b$, then agent i believes that the probability of φ is no less than a or believes that the probability of ψ is no less than b.)

Rule 1. $\vdash \varphi \Rightarrow \vdash B_i(1, \varphi)$ (If φ is a tautology proposition, then agent i believes that the probability of φ is no less than 1.)

Rule 2. $\vdash \varphi \rightarrow \psi \Rightarrow \vdash B_i(a, \varphi) \rightarrow B_i(a, \psi)$ (If $\varphi \rightarrow \psi$ is a tautology proposition, and agent i believes that the probability of φ is no less than a, then agent i believes that the probability of ψ is no less than a.)

Rule 3. $\vdash \neg(\varphi \wedge \psi) \Rightarrow \vdash \neg(B_i(a, \varphi) \wedge B_i(b, \psi))$ for any $a, b \in [0, 1]$ such that $a+b > 1$. (If φ and ψ are incompatible propositions, then it is impossible that agent i believes that the probability of φ is no less than a, and believes that the probability of ψ is no less than b, where $a+b > 1$.)

Rule 4. $\vdash \neg(\varphi \wedge \psi) \Rightarrow \vdash B_i(a, \varphi) \wedge B_i(b, \psi) \rightarrow B_i(a+b, \varphi \vee \psi)$, where $a+b \leq 1$. (If φ and ψ are incompatible propositions, agent i believes that the probability of φ is no less than a, and believes that the probability of ψ is no less than b, where $a+b \leq 1$, then agent i believes that the probability of $\varphi \vee \psi$ is no less than $a+b$.)

Rule 5. $\Gamma \vdash B_i(a_n, \varphi)$ for all $n \in M \Rightarrow \Gamma \vdash B_i(a, \varphi)$, where $a = sup_{n \in M}(\{a_n\})$. (If agent i believes that the probability of φ is no less than a_n, where n is any element in the index set M, then agent i believes that the probability of φ is no less than a, where $a = sup_{n \in M}(\{a_n\})$.)

Rule 6. Given a set of formulas Σ, $\Gamma \cup (\cup_{\varphi \in \Sigma}(\{B_i(a, \varphi) | 0 \leq a \leq a_{i,\varphi}\} \cup \{\neg B_i(b, \varphi) | 1 \geq b > a_{i,\varphi}\})) \vdash \psi$ for any $a_{i,\varphi} \in [0,1] \Rightarrow \Gamma \vdash \psi$. (If ψ can be proved from Γ with any possible probabilistic belief of agent i for Σ, then ψ can be merely proved from Γ.)

Remark: In *Rule* 5, the index set M may be an infinite set, therefore we call *Rule* 5 an infinite inference rule. For example, let $\Gamma = \{B_i(1/2, \varphi), B_i(2/3, \varphi), ..., B_i(n/n+1, \varphi), ...\}$, we have $\Gamma \vdash B_i(n/n+1, \varphi)$ for all $n \in M = \{1, 2, ..., k, ...\}$, by *Rule* 5, we get $\Gamma \vdash B_i(1, \varphi)$ since $1 = sup_{n \in M}(\{n/n+1\})$.

In *Rule* 6, $\{B_i(a, \varphi) | 0 \leq a \leq a_{i,\varphi}\} \cup \{\neg B_i(b, \varphi) | 1 \geq b > a_{i,\varphi}\}$ means that agent i believes the probability of φ is exactly $a_{i,\varphi}$. Therefore $\Gamma \cup \{B_i(a, \varphi) | 0 \leq a \leq a_{i,\varphi}\} \cup \{\neg B_i(b, \varphi) | 1 \geq b > a_{i,\varphi}\} \vdash \psi$ for any $a_{i,\varphi} \in [0,1]$ means that under any possible probabilistic belief of agent i for φ, ψ can be proved from Γ. Intuitively, in this case, the correctness of ψ is independent of the exact probability of φ that agent i believes, so we can get ψ from Γ. In *Rule* 6, formula φ here is generalized to arbitrary set Σ of formulas. Since the premises of *Rule* 6 are infinite, it is also an infinite inference rule.

We will show that in a precise sense these properties completely characterize the formulas of PBL_ω that are valid with respect to probabilistic model. To do so, we have to consider the notion of provability. Inference system PBL_ω consists of a collection of axioms and inference rules. We are actually interested in (substitution) instances of axioms and inference rules (so we in fact think of axioms and inference rules as schemes). For example, the formula $B_i(0.7, \varphi) \wedge B_i(0.8, \psi) \rightarrow B_i(0.5, \varphi \wedge \psi)$ is an instances of the propositional tautology $B_i(a, \varphi) \wedge B_i(b, \psi) \rightarrow B_i(max(a+b-1, 0), \varphi \wedge \psi)$, obtained by substituting $B_i(0.7, \varphi)$, $B_i(0.8, \psi)$ and $B_i(0.5, \varphi \wedge \psi)$ for $B_i(a, \varphi)$, $B_i(b, \psi)$ and $B_i(max(a+b-1, 0), \varphi \wedge \psi)$ respectively. A proof in PBL_ω consists of a sequence of formulas, each of which is either an instance of an axiom in PBL_ω or follows from an application of an inference rule. (If "$\varphi_1, ..., \varphi_n$ infer ψ" is an instance of an inference rule, and if the formulas $\varphi_1, ..., \varphi_n$ have appeared earlier in the proof, then we say that ψ follows from an application of an inference rule.) A proof is said to be from Γ to φ if the premise is Γ and the last formula is φ in the proof. We say φ is provable from Γ in PBL_ω, and write $\Gamma \vdash_{PBL_\omega} \varphi$, if there is a proof from Γ to φ in PBL_ω.

2.4 Soundness of PBL_ω

We will prove that PBL_ω characterizes the set of formulas that are valid with respect to probabilistic model. Inference system of PBL_ω is said to be sound with respect to probabilistic models if every formula provable in PBL_ω is valid with respect to probabilistic models. The system PBL_ω is complete with respect to probabilistic models if every formula valid with respect to probabilistic models is provable in PBL_ω. We think of PBL_ω as characterizing probabilistic models if it provides a sound and complete axiomatization of that class; notationally, this amounts to saying that for all formulas set Γ and all formula φ, we have $\Gamma \vdash_{PBL_\omega} \varphi$ if and only if $\Gamma \models_{PBL_\omega} \varphi$. The following soundness and completeness provide a tight connection between the syntactic notion of provability and the semantic notion of validity.

Firstly, we need the following obvious lemmas.

Lemma 2.1 $\mu_{i,s}(A_1 \cup A_2) = \mu_{i,s}(A_1) + \mu_{i,s}(A_2)$, here A_1 and A_2 are any disjoint members of $X_{i,s} \Rightarrow$ for any members A_1 and A_2 of $X_{i,s}$, $\mu_{i,s}(A_1 \cup A_2) + \mu_{i,s}(A_1 \cap A_2) = \mu_{i,s}(A_1) + \mu_{i,s}(A_2)$.

Proof. $\mu_{i,s}(A_1 \cup A_2) + \mu_{i,s}(A_1 \cap A_2) = \mu_{i,s}(A_1 \cup (A_2 - A_1)) + \mu_{i,s}(A_1 \cap A_2) = \mu_{i,s}(A_1) + \mu_{i,s}(A_1 \cap A_2) + \mu_{i,s}(A_2 - A_1) = \mu_{i,s}(A_1) + \mu_{i,s}((A_1 \cap A_2) \cup (A_2 - A_1)) = \mu_{i,s}(A_1) + \mu_{i,s}(A_2)$.

Lemma 2.2 $\mu_{i,s}(A_1 \cap A_2) \geq \mu_{i,s}(A_1) + \mu_{i,s}(A_2) - 1$.

Proof. It follows from Lemma 2.1 immediately.

Lemma 2.3 $\mu_{i,s}(A_1) + \mu_{i,s}(A_2) \geq \mu_{i,s}(A_1 \cup A_2)$. If $A_1 \cap A_2 = \emptyset$, then $\mu_{i,s}(A_1) + \mu_{i,s}(A_2) = \mu_{i,s}(A_1 \cup A_2)$.

Proof. It follows from Lemma 2.1.

Now, we can prove the following proposition:

Proposition 2.1 (Soundness of PBL_ω) If $\Gamma \vdash_{PBL_\omega} \varphi$, then $\Gamma \models_{PBL_\omega} \varphi$.

Proof. We show each axiom and each rule of PBL_ω is sound, respectively.

Axiom 1: By the definition of PBL_ω-probability measure, for any s, if $A \in X_{i,s}$ then $\mu_{i,s}(A) \geq 0$. Since by the definition of $X_{i,s}$, for any φ, $ev_{PM}(\varphi) = \{s' | (PM, s') \models \varphi\} \in X_{i,s}$, we have $\mu_{i,s}(ev_{PM}(\varphi)) \geq 0$, therefore $B_i(0, \varphi)$ holds.

Axiom 2: Suppose $(PM, s) \models B_i(a, \varphi) \wedge B_i(b, \psi)$, so $\mu_{i,s}(ev_{PM}(\varphi)) \geq a$ and $\mu_{i,s}(ev_{PM}(\psi)) \geq b$. For $\mu_{i,s}$ is PBL_ω - probability measure, by Lemma 2.2, we get $\mu_{i,s}(ev_{PM}(\varphi \wedge \psi)) = \mu_{i,s}(ev_{PM}(\varphi) \cap ev_{PM}(\psi)) \geq \mu_{i,s}(ev_{PM}(\varphi)) + \mu_{i,s}(ev_{PM}(\psi)) - 1 \geq a + b - 1$, which implies $(PM, s) \models B_i(max(a + b - 1, 0), \varphi \wedge \psi)$.

Axiom 3: Suppose $(PM, s) \models B_i(a, \varphi)$, so $\mu_{i,s}(ev_{PM}(\varphi)) \geq a$. Let $\Lambda_i^a(\varphi) = \{s' | \mu_{i,s'}(ev_{PM}(\varphi)) \geq a\}$, by the definition of $\mu_{i,s}$, we get $\mu_{i,s}(\Lambda_i^a(\varphi)) = 1$. Assume $s' \in \Lambda_i^a(\varphi)$, then $s' \in ev_{PM}(B_i(a, \varphi))$, hence $\Lambda_i^a(\varphi) \subseteq ev_{PM}(B_i(a, \varphi))$, so $\mu_{i,s}(ev_{PM}(B_i(a, \varphi))) = 1$, which implies $(PM, s) \models B_i(1, B_i(a, \varphi))$.

Axiom 4: Suppose $(PM, s) \models \neg B_i(a, \varphi)$, so $\mu_{i,s}(ev_{PM}(\varphi)) < a$. Let $\Theta_i^a(\varphi) = \{s' | \mu_{i,s'}(ev_{PM}(\varphi)) < a\}$, by the definition of $\mu_{i,s}$, we get $\mu_{i,s}(\Theta_i^a(\varphi)) = 1$. Assume $s' \in \Theta_i^a(\varphi)$, then $s' \in ev_{PM}(\neg B_i(a, \varphi))$, hence $\mu_{i,s}(ev_{PM}(\neg B_i(a, \varphi))) = 1$, which implies $(PM, s) \models B_i(1, \neg B_i(a, \varphi))$.

Axiom 5: Suppose $(PM, s) \models B_i(a, \varphi)$, so $\mu_{i,s}(ev_{PM}(\varphi)) \geq a$. If $1 \geq a \geq b \geq 0$, then $\mu_{i,s}(ev_{PM}(\varphi)) \geq b$, so $(PM, s) \models B_i(b, \varphi)$, therefore $B_i(a, \varphi) \rightarrow B_i(b, \varphi)$ holds.

Axiom 6: Suppose $(PM, s) \models B_i(a + b, \varphi \vee \psi)$, then $\mu_{i,s}(ev_{PM}(\varphi \vee \psi)) \geq a + b$. Since $\mu_{i,s}(ev_{PM}(\varphi)) + \mu_{i,s}(ev_{PM}(\psi)) \geq \mu_{i,s}(ev_{PM}(\varphi) \cup ev_{PM}(\psi)) \geq a + b$, we have $\mu_{i,s}(ev_{PM}(\varphi)) \geq a$ or $\mu_{i,s}(ev_{PM}(\psi)) \geq b$. Hence $(PM, s) \models B_i(a, \varphi) \vee B_i(b, \psi)$.

Rule 1: Since $\models \varphi$, so for any possible world s, $\mu_{i,s}(ev_{PM}(\varphi)) \geq 1$, therefore $\models B_i(1, \varphi)$ holds.

Rule 2: Since $\models \varphi \rightarrow \psi$, so $ev_{PM}(\varphi) \subseteq ev_{PM}(\psi)$. Suppose $(PM, s) \models B_i(a, \varphi)$, therefore $\mu_{i,s}(ev_{PM}(\varphi)) \geq a$, by the property of PBL_ω-probability space, we get $\mu_{i,s}(ev_{PM}(\varphi)) \leq \mu_{i,s}(ev_{PM}(\psi))$. So $\mu_{i,s}(ev_{PM}(\psi)) \geq a$. Therefore $(PM, s)| = B_i(a, \psi)$, and *Rule* 2 of PBL_ω holds.

Rule 3: Suppose $\models \neg(\varphi \wedge \psi)$, so $ev_{PM}(\varphi) \cap ev_{PM}(\psi) = \emptyset$. By the property of PBL_ω-probability space and Lemma 2.3, for any possible world s, we get $\mu_{i,s}(ev_{PM}(\varphi) \cup$

$ev_{PM}(\psi)) = \mu_{i,s}(ev_{PM}(\varphi)) + \mu_{i,s}(ev_{PM}(\psi))$ and $\mu_{i,s}(ev_{PM}(\varphi) \cup ev_{PM}(\psi)) \leq 1$, therefore $\mu_{i,s}(ev_{PM}(\varphi)) + \mu_{i,s}(ev_{PM}(\psi)) \leq 1$. Assume $(PM,s) \models (B_i(a,\varphi) \wedge B_i(b,\psi))$ where $a+b>1$, then $\mu_{i,s}(ev_{PM}(\varphi)) \geq a$, $\mu_{i,s}(ev_{PM}(\psi)) \geq b$, but $a+b>1$, it is a contradiction.

Rule 4: Suppose $\models \neg(\varphi \wedge \psi)$ and for possible world s, $(PM,s) \models B_i(a,\varphi) \wedge B_i(b,\psi)$, so $ev_{PM}(\varphi) \cap ev_{PM}(\psi) = \emptyset$, $\mu_{i,s}(ev_{PM}(\varphi)) \geq a$, and $\mu_{i,s}(ev_{PM}(\psi)) \geq b$. By the property of PBL_ω-probability space and Lemma 2.3, for any possible world s, we get $\mu_{i,s}(ev_{PM}(\varphi) \cup ev_{PM}(\psi)) = \mu_{i,s}(ev_{PM}(\varphi)) + \mu_{i,s}(ev_{PM}(\psi))$. Hence, $\mu_{i,s}(ev_{PM}(\varphi)) + \mu_{i,s}(ev_{PM}(\psi)) \geq a+b$ and $\mu_{i,s}(ev_{PM}(\varphi) \cup ev_{PM}(\psi)) \geq a+b$, which means $(PM,s) \models B_i(a+b,\varphi \vee \psi)$.

Rule 5: Suppose $\Gamma \models B_i(a_n,\varphi)$ for all $n \in M$, therefore for every s, if $(PM,s) \models \Gamma$, then $(PM,s) \models B_i(a_n,\varphi)$ for all $n \in M$, so $\mu_{i,s}(ev_{PM}(\varphi)) \geq a_n$ for all $n \in M$. We get $\mu_{i,s}(ev_{PM}(\varphi)) \geq sup_{n \in M}(\{a_n\})$. Therefore, $(PM,s) \models B_i(a,\varphi)$ and $a = sup_{n\in M}(\{a_n\})$, we get $\Gamma \models B_i(a,\varphi)$ and $a = sup_{n\in M}(\{a_n\})$ as desired.

Rule 6: Suppose $\Gamma \cup (\cup_{\varphi\in\Sigma}(\{B_i(a,\varphi)|0 \leq a \leq a_{i,\varphi}\} \cup \{\neg B_i(b,\varphi)|1 \geq b > a_{i,\varphi}\})) \models \psi$ for any $a_{i,\varphi} \in [0,1]$, let $(PM,s) \models \Gamma$ and $c_{i,\varphi} = \mu_{i,s}(ev_{PM}(\varphi))$, it is clear that $c_{i,\varphi} \in [0,1]$ and $(PM,s) \models \Gamma \cup (\cup_{\varphi\in\Sigma}(\{B_i(a,\varphi)|0 \leq a \leq c_{i,\varphi}\} \cup \{\neg B_i(b,\varphi)|1 \geq b > c_{i,\varphi}))$. Since $\Gamma \cup (\cup_{\varphi\in\Sigma}(\{B_i(a,\varphi)|0 \leq a \leq a_{i,\varphi}\} \cup \{\neg B_i(b,\varphi)|1 \geq b > a_{i,\varphi}\})) \models \psi$ for any $a_{i,\varphi} \in [0,1]$, we have $(PM,s) \models \psi$, therefore $\Gamma \models \psi$.

2.5 Completeness of PBL_ω

We shall show that the inference system of PBL_ω provides a complete axiomatization for probabilistic belief with respect to a probabilistic model. To achieve this aim, it suffices to prove that every PBL_ω-consistent set is satisfiable with respect to a probabilistic model. We prove this by using a general technique that works for a wide variety of probabilistic modal logic. We construct a special structure PM called a canonical structure for PBL_ω. PM has a state s_V corresponding to every maximal PBL_ω-consistent set V and the following property holds: $(PM,s_V) \models \varphi$ iff $\varphi \in V$.

We need some definitions before giving the proof of the completeness. Given an inference system of PBL_ω, we say a set of formulas Γ is a consistent set with respect to L^{PBL_ω} exactly if false is not provable from Γ. A set of formulas Γ is a maximal consistent set with respect to L^{PBL_ω} if (1) it is PBL_ω-consistent, and (2) for all φ in L^{PBL_ω} but not in Γ, the set $\Gamma \cup \{\varphi\}$ is not PBL_ω-consistent.

Definition 2.7 The probabilistic model PM with respect to PBL_ω is $(S,P_1,...,P_n,\pi)$.

(1) $S = \{\Gamma|\Gamma$ is a maximal consistent set with respect to $PBL_\omega\}$;

(2) P_i maps every element of S to a probability space: $P_i(\Gamma) = (S,X_{i,\Gamma},\mu_{i,\Gamma})$, where $X_{i,\Gamma} = \{X(\varphi)|\varphi$ is a formula of $PBL_\omega\}$, here $X(\varphi) = \{\Gamma'|\varphi \in \Gamma'\}$; $\mu_{i,\Gamma}$ is a probability assignment: $X_{i,\Gamma} \to [0,1]$, and $\mu_{i,\Gamma}(X(\varphi)) = sup(\{a|B_i(a,\varphi) \in \Gamma\})$;

(3) π is a truth assignment as follows: for any atomic formula p, $\pi(p,\Gamma) = true \Leftrightarrow p \in \Gamma$.

Lemma 2.4 S is a nonempty set.

Proof. Since the rules and axioms of PBL_ω are consistent, S is nonempty.

Lemma 2.5 $X_{i,\Gamma}$ satisfies the conditions of Definition 2.2.

Proof. We only prove the following claim: if $A \in X_{i,\Gamma}$, then $\{\Gamma'|\mu_{i,\Gamma'}(A) \geq a\} \in X_{i,\Gamma}$. Other cases can be proved similarly. Since $A \in X_{i,\Gamma}$, so there is φ with $A = X(\varphi)$. It is clear that $X(B_i(a,\varphi)) \in X_{i,\Gamma}$, so $\{\Gamma'|\mu_{i,\Gamma'}(A) \geq a\} = \{\Gamma'|\mu_{i,\Gamma'}(X(\varphi)) \geq a\} = X(B_i(a,\varphi)) \in X_{i,\Gamma}$.

In classical logic, it is easy to see that every consistent set of formulas can be extended to a maximal consistent set, but with the infinitary rules in PBL_ω it cannot simply be proved in a naive fashion because the union of an increasing sequence of consistent sets need no longer be consistent. Therefore we give a detailed proof for this claim in the following lemma.

Lemma 2.6 For any PBL_ω-consistent set of formulas Δ, there is a maximal PBL_ω-consistent set Γ such that $\Delta \subseteq \Gamma$.

Proof. To show that Δ can be extended to a maximal PBL_ω-consistent set, we construct a sequence Γ_0, Γ_1, ... of PBL_ω-consistent sets as follows. Let ψ_1, ψ_2, ... be a sequence of the formulas in L^{PBL_ω}. This sequence is not an enumeration sequence since the cardinal number of the set of real number is not enumerable, however, we can get a well-ordered sequence of the formulas by the choice axiom of set theory.

At first, we construct Γ_0 which satisfies the following conditions:

(1) $\Delta \subseteq \Gamma_0$;

(2) Γ_0 is consistent;

(3) For any agent $i \in \{1,...,n\}$ and every $\varphi \in L^{PBL_\omega}$, there is some $c_{i,\varphi} \in [0,1]$ such that $\{B_i(a,\varphi)|0 \leq a \leq c_{i,\varphi}\} \cup \{\neg B_i(b,\varphi)|1 \geq b > c_{i,\varphi}\} \subseteq \Gamma_0$.

Let $\Sigma_0 = \Delta$, then for agent 1 and every $\varphi \in L^{PBL_\omega}$, there is some $c_{1,\varphi} \in [0,1]$ such that $\Sigma_0 \cup (\cup_{\varphi \in L^{PBL_\omega}}(\{B_1(a,\varphi)|0 \leq a \leq c_{1,\varphi}\} \cup \{\neg B_1(b,\varphi)|1 \geq b > c_{1,\varphi}\}))$ is consistent, otherwise, for all $a_{1,\varphi} \in [0,1]$, $\Sigma_0 \cup (\cup_{\varphi \in L^{PBL_\omega}}(\{B_1(a,\varphi)|0 \leq a \leq a_{1,\varphi}\} \cup \{\neg B_1(b,\varphi)|1 \geq b > a_{1,\varphi}\})) \vdash$ *false*. By *Rule* 6, we have $\Sigma_0 \vdash$ *false*, and since $\Sigma_0 = \Delta$ is consistent, it is a contradiction. Let $\Sigma_1 = \Sigma_0 \cup (\cup_{\varphi \in L^{PBL_\omega}}(\{B_1(a,\varphi)|0 \leq a \leq c_{1,\varphi}\} \cup \{\neg B_1(b,\varphi)|1 \geq b > c_{1,\varphi}\}))$, similarly, for agent i and for each $\varphi \in L^{PBL_\omega}$ there is $c_{i,\varphi} \in [0,1]$ such that $\Sigma_{i-1} \cup (\cup_{\varphi \in L^{PBL_\omega}}(\{B_i(a,\varphi)|0 \leq a \leq c_{i,\varphi}\} \cup \{\neg B_i(b,\varphi)|1 \geq b > c_{i,\varphi}\}))$ is consistent. Let $\Sigma_i = \Sigma_{i-1} \cup (\cup_{\varphi \in L^{PBL_\omega}}(\{B_i(a,\varphi)|0 \leq a \leq c_{i,\varphi}\} \cup \{\neg B_i(b,\varphi)|1 \geq b > c_{i,\varphi}\}))$ for $i \in \{1,...,n\}$ and $\Gamma_0 = \cup_{i \in \{1,...,n\}}\Sigma_i = \Sigma_n$, here $\{1,...,n\}$ is the set of agent. Since Σ_n is consistent, Γ_0 is also consistent.

Now we inductively construct the rest of the sequence according to ψ_k: (a) in the case of $k = n+1$, take $\Gamma_{n+1} = \Gamma_n \cup \{\psi_{n+1}\}$ if the set is PBL_ω-consistent and otherwise take $\Gamma_{n+1} = \Gamma_n$. (b) in the case that k is a limit ordinal, take $\Gamma_k = \cup_{n<k}\Gamma_n \cup \{\psi_k\}$ if the set is PBL_ω-consistent and otherwise take $\Gamma_k = \cup_{n<k}\Gamma_n$. Let $\Gamma = \cup\Gamma_k$. We will prove that Γ is a maximal PBL_ω-consistent set and $\Delta \subseteq \Gamma$.

Firstly, we prove that Γ_k is consistent by induction. We have already known that Γ_0 is consistent. Now we prove the claim when $k > 0$. In the case of (a), it is clear. In the case of (b), we only need to prove that $\cup_{n<k}\Gamma_n$ is consistent. Suppose $\cup_{n<k}\Gamma_n$ is not consistent, then there is a proof C of falsity from $\cup_{n<k}\Gamma_n$. If this proof does not apply *Rule* 5 and *Rule* 6, then one of Γ_n contains the formulas in the proof, since Γ_n is consistent, then there is a contradiction. If this proof does apply *Rule* 5, since our construction of Γ_0 ensures: for some $c_{i,\varphi} \in [0,1]$, $\{B_i(a,\varphi)|0 \leq a \leq c_{i,\varphi}\} \cup \{\neg B_i(b,\varphi)|1 \geq b > c_{i,\varphi}\} \subseteq \Gamma_0$, hence if $\{B_i(a_1,\varphi), B_i(a_2,\varphi), ...\}$ can be deduced from $\cup_{n<k}\Gamma_n$, then $\{B_i(a_1,\varphi), B_i(a_2,\varphi), ...\} \cup \{B_i(c,\varphi)\} \subseteq \Gamma_0$, here $c =$

$sup(\{a_m | B_i(a_m, \varphi)\})$, hence $\Gamma_0 \vdash B_i(c, \varphi)$. This proof can be transferred to a new proof D of falsity from $\cup_{n<k}\Gamma_n$ which does not apply *Rule* 5, this reduces to the case that the proof does not apply *Rule* 5. If this proof does apply *Rule* 6, since our construction of Γ_0 ensures: for any $\varphi \in \Sigma$ there is some $c_{i,\varphi} \in [0,1]$, $\cup_{\varphi\in\Sigma}(\{B_i(a,\varphi)|0 \leq a \leq c_{i,\varphi}\} \cup \{\neg B_i(b,\varphi)|1 \geq b > c_{i,\varphi}\}) \subseteq \Gamma_0$, hence if $(\cup_{n<k}\Gamma_n) \cup (\cup_{\varphi\in\Sigma}(\{B_i(a,\varphi)|0 \leq a \leq a_{i,\varphi}\} \cup \{\neg B_i(b,\varphi)|1 \geq b > a_{i,\varphi}\})) \vdash \psi$ for any $a_{i,\varphi} \in [0,1]$ then $(\cup_{n<k}\Gamma_n) = (\cup_{n<k}\Gamma_n) \cup \Gamma_0 \vdash (\cup_{n<k}\Gamma_n) \cup (\cup_{\varphi\in\Sigma}(\{B_i(a,\varphi)|0 \leq a \leq c_{i,\varphi}\} \cup \{\neg B_i(b,\varphi)|1 \geq b > c_{i,\varphi}\})) \vdash \psi$. This proof can be transferred to a new proof E of falsity from $\cup_{n<k}\Gamma_n$ which does not apply *Rule* 6, this reduces to the case that the proof does not apply *Rule* 6. Therefore a proof of falsity from $\cup_{n<k}\Gamma_n$ can be transferred to a proof without applying *Rule* 5 and *Rule* 6. This case has been discussed above.

The proof of that Γ is consistent is similar to the above proof of that $\cup_{n<k}\Gamma_n$ is consistent.

We claim that Γ is maximal, for suppose $\psi \in L^{PBL_\omega}$ and $\psi \notin \Gamma$, since ψ must appear in our sequence, say as ψ_k, here we assume k is a successor ordinal, the case of limit ordinal k can be proved similarly. If $\Gamma_k \cup \{\psi_k\}$ were PBL_ω-consistent, then our construction would guarantee that $\psi_k \in \Gamma_{k+1}$. Hence $\psi_k \in \Gamma$. Because $\psi_k = \psi \notin \Gamma$, it follows that $\Gamma_k \cup \{\psi\}$ is not PBL_ω-consistent. Hence Γ is maximal.

By the above discussion, we have a maximal PBL_ω-consistent set Γ such that $\Delta \subseteq \Gamma$.

Lemma 2.7 For any Γ, $P_i(\Gamma)$ is well defined, i.e., for any $S \in X_{i,\Gamma}$, the value of $\mu_{i,\Gamma}(S)$ is unique.

Proof. It suffices to prove the following claim: if S_1, $S_2 \in X_{i,\Gamma}$ and $S_1 = S_2$, then $\mu_{i,\Gamma}(S_1) = \mu_{i,\Gamma}(S_2)$. Since $S_1, S_2 \in X_{i,\Gamma}$, by the construction of $X_{i,\Gamma}$, there are φ and ψ such that $S_1 = X(\varphi)$ and $S_2 = X(\psi)$. Assume $S_1 = S_2$, then $X(\varphi) = X(\psi)$. It is clear that $\vdash \varphi \leftrightarrow \psi$, suppose not, w.l.o.g, assume $\vdash \varphi \rightarrow \psi$ does not hold, then by Lemma 2.6, $\{\varphi, \neg\psi\}$ is consistent and there is a maximal consistent set Γ' such that $\{\varphi, \neg\psi\} \subseteq \Gamma'$, this contradicts $X(\varphi) = X(\psi)$. Furthermore, by rule: $\vdash \varphi \rightarrow \psi \Rightarrow\vdash B_i(a,\varphi) \rightarrow B_i(a,\psi)$, we have $\vdash B_i(a,\varphi) \leftrightarrow B_i(a,\psi)$, so $\mu_{i,\Gamma}(X(\varphi)) = \mu_{i,\Gamma}(X(\psi))$.

Lemma 2.8 Let $Pro_{i,\Gamma}(\varphi) = \{a | B_i(a,\varphi) \text{ is in } \Gamma\}$, then $sup(Pro_{i,\Gamma}(\varphi)) \in Pro_{i,\Gamma}(\varphi)$.

Proof. Suppose $Pro_{i,\Gamma}(\varphi) = \{a | B_i(a,\varphi) \text{ is in } \Gamma\}$, therefore $\Gamma \vdash B_i(a_n, \varphi)$ for all $a_n \in Pro_{i,\Gamma}(\varphi)$, by *Rule* 5 of PBL_ω, $\Gamma \vdash B_i(a,\varphi)$, where $a = sup_{n\in M}(\{a_n\}) = sup(Pro_{i,\Gamma}(\varphi))$, so we get $sup(Pro_{i,\Gamma}(\varphi)) \in Pro_{i,\Gamma}(\varphi)$ as desired.

Lemma 2.9 If $A \in X_{i,\Gamma}$, then $0 \leq \mu_{i,\Gamma}(A) \leq 1$. Furthermore, $\mu_{i,\Gamma}(\emptyset) = 0$, $\mu_{i,\Gamma}(S) = 1$.

Proof. By the construction of model, it is obvious that if $A \in X_{i,\Gamma}$ then $0 \leq \mu_{i,\Gamma}(A) \leq 1$.

By rule: $\vdash \varphi \Rightarrow\vdash B_i(1,\varphi)$, therefore we have $\mu_{i,\Gamma}(S) = \mu_{i,\Gamma}(X(true)) = 1$ as desired. By axiom: $B_i(0,\varphi)$, we get $B_i(0, false)$, so $\mu_{i,\Gamma}(\emptyset) = \mu_{i,\Gamma}(X(false)) \geq 0$. By rule: $\vdash \neg(\varphi \wedge \psi) \Rightarrow\vdash B_i(a,\varphi) \wedge B_i(b,\psi) \rightarrow B_i(a+b, \varphi \vee \psi)$, where $a+b \leq 1$, we have $\mu_{i,\Gamma}(S) = \mu_{i,\Gamma}(X(true \vee false)) \geq \mu_{i,\Gamma}(X(true)) + \mu_{i,\Gamma}(X(false)) = \mu_{i,\Gamma}(S) + \mu_{i,\Gamma}(\emptyset)$, since $\mu_{i,\Gamma}(S) = 1$, $1 \geq 1 + \mu_{i,\Gamma}(\emptyset)$ holds, therefore $\mu_{i,\Gamma}(\emptyset) = 0$.

Lemma 2.10 If A_1 and A_2 are disjoint members of $X_{i,\Gamma}$, then $\mu_{i,\Gamma}(A_1 \cup A_2) = \mu_{i,\Gamma}(A_1) + \mu_{i,\Gamma}(A_2)$.

Proof. Suppose $A_i = X(\varphi_i)$, and $\vdash \neg(\varphi_1 \wedge \varphi_2)$. By *Rule* 4, $\vdash B_i(a_1,\varphi_1) \wedge B_i(a_2,\varphi_2) \rightarrow B_i(a_1+a_2, \varphi_1 \vee \varphi_2))$, therefore $\mu_{i,\Gamma}(X(\varphi_1 \vee \varphi_2)) \geq \mu_{i,\Gamma}(X(\varphi_1)) + \mu_{i,\Gamma}(X(\varphi_2))$. Since $X(\varphi_1 \vee$

$\varphi_2) = A_1 \cup A_2$, we have $\mu_{i,\Gamma}(A_1 \cup A_2) = \mu_{i,\Gamma}(X(\varphi_1 \vee \varphi_2)) \geq \mu_{i,\Gamma}(X(\varphi_1)) + \mu_{i,\Gamma}(X(\varphi_2)) = \mu_{i,\Gamma}(A_1) + \mu_{i,\Gamma}(A_2)$.

Now, we prove $\mu_{i,\Gamma}(A_1) + \mu_{i,\Gamma}(A_2) \geq \mu_{i,\Gamma}(A_1 \cup A_2)$. Suppose $\mu_{i,\Gamma}(A_1 \cup A_2) > \mu_{i,\Gamma}(A_1) + \mu_{i,\Gamma}(A_2)$. Let $\mu_{i,\Gamma}(A_1) = a_1$, $\mu_{i,\Gamma}(A_2) = a_2$, $\mu_{i,\Gamma}(A_1 \cup A_2) > a_1 + a_2$. Choose $e > 0$ such that $2e + a_1 + a_2 = \mu_{i,\Gamma}(A_1 \cup A_2)$, then $\mu_{i,\Gamma}(A_1) < a_1 + e$, $\mu_{i,\Gamma}(A_2) < a_2 + e$.

Therefore we have $\Gamma \models B_i(a_1 + a_2 + 2e, \varphi_1 \vee \varphi_2) \wedge \neg B_i(a_1 + e, \varphi_1) \wedge \neg B_i(a_2 + e, \varphi_2)$. Since Γ is a maximal consistent set, so $\Gamma \vdash B_i(a_1 + a_2 + 2e, \varphi_1 \vee \varphi_2) \wedge \neg B_i(a_1 + e, \varphi_1) \wedge \neg B_i(a_2 + e, \varphi_2)$, which contradicts *Axiom* 6 of PBL_ω.

Lemma 2.11 For any φ, let $\Delta_i^a(\varphi) = \{\Gamma' | \mu_{i,\Gamma'}(X(\varphi)) \geq a\}$. If $\mu_{i,\Gamma}(X(\varphi)) \geq a$, then $\mu_{i,\Gamma}(\Delta_i^a(\varphi)) = 1$.

Proof. It is clear that $B_i(a,\varphi) \in \Gamma \Rightarrow \Gamma \in \Delta_i^a(\varphi)$, therefore $X(B_i(a,\varphi)) \subseteq \Delta_i^a(\varphi)$. Since $B_i(a,\varphi) \rightarrow B_i(1, B_i(a,\varphi))$, so $B_i(1, B_i(a,\varphi)) \in \Gamma$, thereby $\mu_{i,\Gamma}(X(B_i(a,\varphi))) = sup(\{b | B_i(b, B_i(a,\varphi)) \in \Gamma\}) = 1$. For $X(B_i(a,\varphi)) \subseteq \Delta_i^a(\varphi)$, we have $\mu_{i,\Gamma}(\Delta_i^a(\varphi)) = 1$ as desired.

Lemma 2.12 For any φ, let $\Theta_i^a(\varphi) = \{\Gamma' | \mu_{i,\Gamma'}(X(\varphi)) < a\}$. If $\mu_{i,\Gamma}(X(\varphi)) < a$, then $\mu_{i,\Gamma}(\Theta_i^a(\varphi)) = 1$.

Proof. By the construction of the canonical model and Lemma 2.8, $\neg B_i(a,\varphi) \in \Gamma \Rightarrow \Gamma \in \Theta_i^a(\varphi)$, so $X(\neg B_i(a,\varphi)) \subseteq \Theta_i^a(\varphi)$. Since $\neg B_i(a,\varphi) \rightarrow B_i(1, \neg B_i(a,\varphi))$, so $\neg B_i(a,\varphi) \in \Gamma \Rightarrow B_i(1, \neg B_i(a,\varphi)) \in \Gamma$, thereby $\mu_{i,\Gamma}(X(\neg B_i(a,\varphi))) = sup(\{b | B_i(b, \neg B_i(a,\varphi)) \in \Gamma\}) = 1$. For $X(\neg B_i(a,\varphi)) \subseteq \Theta_i^a(\varphi)$, we have $\mu_{i,\Gamma}(\Theta_i^a(\varphi)) = 1$ as desired.

Lemma 2.13 For any Γ, $P_i(\Gamma)$ is a PBL_ω-probability space.

Proof. By Lemma 2.4-2.12, it is obvious.

Lemma 2.14 The model *PM* is a PBL_ω-probabilistic model.

Proof. It follows from Lemma 2.4 and Lemma 2.13.

The above lemmas state that the probability space $P_i(\Gamma) = (S, X_{i,\Gamma}, \mu_{i,\Gamma})$ of the model satisfies all conditions in Definition 2.2, then as a consequence, the model *PM* is a PBL_ω-probabilistic model. In order to get the completeness, we further prove the following lemma, which states that *PM* is "canonical".

Lemma 2.15 In the model *PM*, for any Γ and any φ, $(PM, \Gamma) \models \varphi \Leftrightarrow \varphi \in \Gamma$.

Proof. We argue by the cases on the structure of φ, here we only give the proof in the case of $\varphi \equiv B_i(a, \psi)$.

It suffices to prove that: $(PM, \Gamma) \models B_i(a,\psi) \Leftrightarrow B_i(a,\psi) \in \Gamma$.

If $B_i(a,\psi) \in \Gamma$, by the definition of *PM*, $\mu_{i,\Gamma}(X(\psi)) = b \geq a$, therefore $(PM, \Gamma) \models B_i(a,\psi)$.

If $B_i(a,\psi) \notin \Gamma$, by Lemma 2.8, there exists $b = sup(\{c | B_i(c,\psi) \in \Gamma\})$ such that $B_i(b,\psi) \in \Gamma$ and $a > b$. By the definition of *PM*, $\mu_{i,\Gamma}(X(\psi)) = b$, therefore $(PM, \Gamma) \not\models B_i(a,\psi)$.

Now it is ready to get the completeness of PBL_ω:

Proposition 2.2 (Completeness of PBL_ω) If $\Gamma \models_{PBL_\omega} \varphi$, then $\Gamma \vdash_{PBL_\omega} \varphi$.

Proof. Suppose not, then there is a PBL_ω - consistent formulas set $\Phi = \Gamma \cup \{\neg\varphi\}$, and there is no model PM such that Φ is satisfied in PM. For there is a PBL_ω - maximal consistent formula set Σ such that $\Phi \subseteq \Sigma$, by Lemma 2.15, Φ is satisfied in possible world Σ of PM. It is a contradiction.

Our proof of the above completeness is different from the proof in [3]. The main idea of our proof is to give a canonical model, which can be regarded as a generalization of canonical model method in Kripke semantics. In [3], Fagin and Halpern adopt another technique to get the completeness. Let φ be consistent with AX_{MEAS}, they show firstly that an i-probability formula $\psi \in Sub^+(\varphi)$ is provably equivalent to a formula of the form $\Sigma_{s\in S} c_s \mu_i(\varphi_s) \geq b$, for some appropriate coefficients c_s, where S consists of all maximal consistent subsets of $Sub^+(\varphi)$. Then for a fixed agent i and a fixed state s, they describe a set of linear equalities and inequalities corresponding to i and s, over variables of the form $x_{iss'}$, for $s' \in S$. We can think of $x_{iss'}$ as representing $\mu_{i,s}(s')$, i.e., the probability of state s' under agent i's probability distribution at state s. Assume that ψ is equivalent to $\Sigma_{s\in S} c_s \mu_i(\varphi_s) \geq b$. Observe that exactly one of ψ and $\neg\psi$ is in s. If $\psi \in s$, then the corresponding inequality is $\Sigma_{s'\in S} c_{s'} x_{iss'} \geq b$. If $\neg\psi \in s$, then the corresponding inequality is $\Sigma_{s'\in S} c_{s'} x_{iss'} < b$. Finally, we have the equality $\Sigma_{s'\in S} x_{iss'} = 1$. As shown in Theorem 2.2 in Fagin et al. [4], sinceφ_s is consistent, this set of linear equalities and inequalities has a solution $x^*_{iss'}$, $s' \in S$. From their idea, it is clear that their proof depends tightly on the axioms of linear equalities and inequalities, whereas there are no such axioms in our inference system. On the other hand, their proof cannot deal with the case of infinite set of formulas, because in this case, we will get an infinite set of linear equalities and inequalities, which contains infinite variables. But their axioms seem insufficient to describe the existence of solutions of an infinite set of linear equalities and inequalities.

Proposition 2.1 and Proposition 2.2 show that the axioms and inference rules of PBL_ω give us a sound and complete axiomatization for probabilistic belief. Moreover, we can prove the finite model property and decidability of the provability problem for some variants of PBL_ω in the following sections.

It is not difficult to see that *Axioms* 1-6 and *Rules* 1-4 are not complete for our model. Because otherwise, the compactness property of PBL_ω holds, but we can give the following example to show that the compactness property fails in PBL_ω: any finite sub set of $\{B_i(1/2,\varphi), B_i(2/3,\varphi),$ $..., B_i(n/n+1,\varphi),...\} \cup \{\neg B_i(1,\varphi)\}$ has model, whereas the whole set does not. But we do not know whether *Axioms* 1-6 and *Rules* 1-5 are complete for our model, i.e., whether *Rule* 6 is redundant in the inference system. Although we believe that *Rule* 6 is not redundant, we have no proof up to now.

3. PBL$_f$ and its inner probabilistic semantics

As is often the case in modal logics, the ideas in our completeness proof can be extended to get a finite model property. Therefore the question arises whether finite model property holds for PBL_ω, i.e., for every consistent formula φ, whether there is a finite sates model satisfies φ. Unfortunately, we cannot give a positive or negative answer here. Therefore, we seek for some weak variant of PBL_ω whose finite model property can be proved. We call the variant PBL_f, its reasoning system is the result of deleting *Axiom* 6 and *Rule* 6 from PBL_ω. In the semantics of PBL_f, we assign an inner probability space to every possible world in the model, here "inner" means the measure does not obey the additivity condition, but obeys some weak additivity conditions satisfied by inner probability measure.

The well formed formulas set L^{PBL_f} of PBL_f is the same as L^{PBL_ω}.

3.1 Semantics of PBL_f

Definition 3.1 An inner probabilistic model PM of PBL_f is a tuple $(S, \pi, P_1, ..., P_n)$, where

(1) S is a nonempty finite set whose elements are called possible worlds or states;

(2) π is a map: $S \times Prop \to \{true, false\}$, where $Prop$ is an atomic formulas set;

(3) P_i is a map, it maps every possible world s to a PBL_f-probability space $P_i(s) = (S, X, \mu_{i,s})$. Here $X = \wp(S)$.

$\mu_{i,s}$ is a PBL_f-inner probability measure assigned to the set X, which means $\mu_{i,s}$ satisfies the following conditions:

(a) $0 \le \mu_{i,s}(A) \le 1$ for all $A \in X$.

(b) $\mu_{i,s}(\emptyset) = 0$ and $\mu_{i,s}(S) = 1$.

(c) If $A_1, A_2 \in X$ and $A_1 \subseteq A_2$, then $\mu_{i,s}(A_1) \le \mu_{i,s}(A_2)$;

(d) If $A_1, A_2 \in X$ and $A_1 \cap A_2 = \emptyset$, then $\mu_{i,s}(A_1 \cup A_2) \ge \mu_{i,s}(A_1) + \mu_{i,s}(A_2)$;

(e) If $A_1, A_2 \in X$, then $\mu_{i,s}(A_1 \cap A_2) \ge \mu_{i,s}(A_1) + \mu_{i,s}(A_2) - 1$;

(f) Let $\Lambda_{i,s} = \{s' | P_i(s) = P_i(s')\}$, then $\mu_{i,s}(\Lambda_{i,s}) = 1$.

Remark: Since $X = \wp(S)$, therefore X is a constant set, and we omit the subscript of $X_{i,s}$ as was used in Definition 2.2.

It is easy to see that the conditions (d) and (e) in Definition 3.1 are weaker than the finite additivity condition in Definition 2.2. One can check that if μ is a probability measure, then inner measure μ^* induced by μ obeys the conditions (d) and (e) in Definition 3.1, i.e., the reason we call $\mu_{i,s}$ inner probability measure.

The notation $\Lambda_{i,s}$ in the condition (f) represents the set of states whose probability space is same as the probability space of state s. Therefore the condition (f) means that for any state s, the probability space of almost all states is same as the probability space of s.

Definition 3.2 Inner probabilistic semantics of PBL_f

$(PM, s) \models p$ iff $\pi(s, p) = true$, where p is an atomic formula;

$(PM, s) \models \neg\varphi$ iff $(PM, s) \not\models \varphi$;

$(PM, s) \models \varphi_1 \wedge \varphi_2$ iff $(PM, s) \models \varphi_1$ and $(PM, s) \models \varphi_2$;

$(PM, s) \models B_i(a, \varphi)$ iff $\mu_{i,s}(ev_{PM}(\varphi)) \ge a$, where $ev_{PM}(\varphi) = \{s' | (PM, s') \models \varphi\}$.

3.2 Inference system of PBL_f

The inference system of PBL_f is the same as PBL_ω except without *Axiom* 6 and *Rule* 6. *Axiom* 6 corresponds to the finite additivity property of probability. Since the inner probabilistic measure in the model of PBL_f does not obey the finite additivity property, therefore *Axiom* 6 fails with respect to the semantics of PBL_f.

3.3 Soundness of PBL_f

The proof of soundness of PBL_f is similar to the proof in Proposition 2.1, but because there are some differences between PBL_ω-probabilistic model and PBL_f-probabilistic model, there are a few differences. For example, in the following proof, we can use the property $\mu_{i,s}(A_1 \cap A_2) \geq \mu_{i,s}(A_1) + \mu_{i,s}(A_2) - 1$ directly, rather than as a corollary of finite additivity property; we apply the property $\mu_{i,s}(\Lambda_{i,s}) = 1$ (where $\Lambda_{i,s} = \{s'|P_i(s) = P_i(s')\}$) in the proof, which also differs from the last property of PBL_ω-probabilistic model (If $A \in X_{i,s}$ and $\mu_{i,s}(A) \geq a$, then $\mu_{i,s}(\{s'|\mu_{i,s'}(A) \geq a\}) = 1$; if $A \in X_{i,s}$ and $\mu_{i,s}(A) < b$, then $\mu_{i,s}(\{s'|\mu_{i,s'}(A) < b\}) = 1$.).

Proposition 3.1 (Soundness of PBL_f) If $\Gamma \vdash_{PBL_f} \varphi$, then $\Gamma \models_{PBL_f} \varphi$.

Proof. We only discuss *Axiom* 2, *Axiom* 3 and *Axiom* 4 of PBL_f, other cases can be proved similarly as in Proposition 2.1.

Axiom 2: Suppose $(PM, s) \models B_i(a, \varphi) \wedge B_i(b, \psi)$, so $\mu_{i,s}(ev_{PM}(\varphi)) \geq a$ and $\mu_{i,s}(ev_{PM}(\psi)) \geq b$. For $\mu_{i,s}$ is PBL_f-probability measure, we get $\mu_{i,s}(ev_{PM}(\varphi \wedge \psi)) = \mu_{i,s}(ev_{PM}(\varphi) \cap ev_{PM}(\psi)) \geq \mu_{i,s}(ev_{PM}(\varphi)) + \mu_{i,s}(ev_{PM}(\psi)) - 1 \geq a + b - 1$, which implies $(PM, s) \models B_i(max(a + b - 1, 0), \varphi \wedge \psi)$.

Axiom 3: Suppose $(PM, s) \models B_i(a, \varphi)$, therefore $\mu_{i,s}(ev_{PM}(\varphi)) \geq a$. Let $\Lambda_{i,s} = \{s'|P_i(s) = P_i(s')\}$, then $\Lambda_{i,s} \in X$ and $\mu_{i,s}(\Lambda_{i,s}) = 1$. Let $\Xi = \{s'|\mu_{i,s'}(ev_{PM}(\varphi)) \geq a\}$. Since $s' \in \Lambda_{i,s}$ implies $s' \in \Xi$, it is clear $\Lambda_{i,s} \subseteq \Xi$, since $\mu_{i,s}(\Lambda_{i,s}) = 1$, so $\mu_{i,s}(\Xi) = 1$. If $s' \in \Xi$, then $s' \in ev_{PM}(B_i(a, \varphi))$, therefore $\mu_{i,s}(ev_{PM}(B_i(a, \varphi))) = 1$, we get $(PM, s) \models B_i(1, B_i(a, \varphi))$ as desired.

Axiom 4: Suppose $(PM, s) \models \neg B_i(a, \varphi)$, so $\mu_{i,s}(ev_{PM}(\varphi)) < a$. Let $\Lambda_{i,s} = \{s'|P_i(s) = P_i(s')\}$, then $\Lambda_{i,s} \in X$ and $\mu_{i,s}(\Lambda_{i,s}) = 1$. Let $\Xi = \{s'|\mu_{i,s'}(ev_{PM}(\varphi)) < a\}$, for $s' \in \Lambda_{i,s}$ implies $s' \in \Xi$, it is clear $\Lambda_{i,s} \subseteq \Xi$, since $\mu_{i,s}(\Lambda_{i,s}) = 1$, so $\mu_{i,s}(\Xi) = 1$. If $s' \in \Xi$, then $s' \in ev_{PM}(B_i(a, \varphi))$, therefore $\mu_{i,s}(ev_{PM}(\neg B_i(a, \varphi))) = 1$, we get $(PM, s) \models B_i(1, \neg B_i(a, \varphi))$ as desired.

3.4 Finite model property of PBL_f

We now turn our attention to the finite model property of PBL_f. It needs to show that if a formula is PBL_f-consistent, then it is satisfiable in a finite structure. The idea is that rather than considering maximal consistent formulas set when trying to construct a structure satisfying a formula φ, we restrict our attention to sets of subformulas of φ.

Definition 3.3 Suppose ζ is a consistent formula with respect to PBL_f, $Sub^*(\zeta)$ is a set of formulas defined as follows: let $\zeta \in L^{PBL_f}$, $Sub(\zeta)$ is the set of subformulas of ζ, then $Sub^*(\zeta) = Sub(\zeta) \cup \{\neg\psi|\psi \in Sub(\zeta)\}$. It is clear that $Sub^*(\zeta)$ is finite.

Definition 3.4 The inner probabilistic model PM_ζ with respect to formula ζ is $(S_\zeta, P_{1,\zeta}, ..., P_{n,\zeta}, \pi_\zeta)$.

(1) Here $S_\zeta = \{\Gamma|\Gamma$ is a maximal consistent formulas set with respect to PBL_f and $\Gamma \subseteq Sub^*(\zeta)\}$.

(2) For any $\Gamma \in S_\zeta$, $P_{i,\zeta}(\Gamma) = (S_\zeta, X_\zeta, \mu_{\zeta,i,\Gamma})$, where $X_\zeta = \{X(\varphi)|\ X(\varphi) = \{\Gamma'|\ \varphi$ is a Boolean combination of formulas in $Sub^*(\zeta)$ and $\Gamma \vdash_{PBL_f} \varphi\}\}$; $\mu_{\zeta,i,\Gamma}$ is an inner probability assignment: $X_\zeta \rightarrow [0,1]$, and $\mu_{\zeta,i,\Gamma}(X(\varphi)) = sup(\{a|B_i(a, \varphi)$ is provable from Γ in $PBL_f\})$.

(3) π_ζ is a truth assignment as follows: For any atomic formula p, $\pi_\zeta(p, \Gamma) = true \Leftrightarrow p \in \Gamma$.

Similar to the proof of completeness of PBL_ω, we mainly need to show that the above canonical model PM_ζ is a PBL_f-inner probabilistic model. The following lemmas from Lemma 3.1 to Lemma 3.13 contribute to this purpose. Furthermore, Lemma 3.14 states that PM_ζ is "canonical", i.e., for any consistent formula $\varphi \in Sub^*(\zeta)$, there is a state s, such that $(PM_\zeta, s) \models \varphi$. Since we can prove that PM_ζ is a finite model, these lemmas imply the finite model property of PBL_f.

Lemma 3.1 S_ζ is a nonempty finite set.

Proof. Since the rules and axioms of PBL_f are consistent, S_ζ is nonempty. For $Sub^*(\zeta)$ is a finite set, by the definition of S_ζ, the cardinality of S_ζ is no more than the cardinality of $\wp(Sub^*(\zeta))$.

Lemma 3.2 X_ζ is the power set of S_ζ.

Proof. Firstly, since $Sub^*(\zeta)$ is finite, so if $\Gamma \in S_\zeta$ then Γ is finite. We can let φ_Γ be the conjunction of the formulas in Γ. Secondly, if $A \subseteq S_\zeta$, then $A = X(\vee_{\Gamma \in A} \varphi_\Gamma)$. By the above argument, we have that X_ζ is the power set of S_ζ.

Lemma 3.3 If φ is consistent (here φ is a Boolean combination of formulas in $Sub^*(\zeta)$), then there exists Γ such that φ can be proved from Γ, here Γ is a maximal consistent set with respect to PBL_f and $\Gamma \subseteq Sub^*(\zeta)$.

Proof. For φ is a Boolean combination of formulas in $Sub^*(\zeta)$, therefore by regarding the formulas in $Sub^*(\zeta)$ as atomic formulas, φ can be represented as disjunctive normal form. Since φ is consistent, so there is a consistent disjunctive term in disjunctive normal form expression of φ, let such term be $\psi_1 \wedge ... \wedge \psi_n$, then φ can be derived from the maximal consistent set Γ which contains $\{\psi_1, ..., \psi_n\}$.

Lemma 3.4 For any $\Gamma \in S_\zeta$, $P_{i,\zeta}(\Gamma)$ is well defined.

Proof. It suffices to prove the following claim: if $X(\varphi) = X(\psi)$, then $\mu_{\zeta,i,\Gamma}(X(\varphi)) = \mu_{\zeta,i,\Gamma}(X(\psi))$. If $X(\varphi) = X(\psi)$, it is clear that $\vdash \varphi \leftrightarrow \psi$. For suppose not, then $\varphi \wedge \neg\psi$ is consistent, by Lemma 3.3, there is Γ' such that $\varphi \wedge \neg\psi$ can be proved from Γ', therefore $\Gamma' \in X(\varphi)$ and $\Gamma' \notin X(\psi)$, it is a contradiction. Thus $\vdash \varphi \leftrightarrow \psi$. By rule: $\vdash \varphi \rightarrow \psi \Rightarrow \vdash B_i(a, \varphi) \rightarrow B_i(a, \psi)$, we get $\vdash B_i(a, \varphi) \leftrightarrow B_i(a, \psi)$, which means $\mu_{\zeta,i,\Gamma}(X(\varphi)) = \mu_{\zeta,i,\Gamma}(X(\psi))$.

Lemma 3.5 Let $Pro_{\zeta,i,\Gamma}(\varphi) = \{a | B_i(a, \varphi)$ can be proved from Γ in $PBL_f\}$, then $sup(Pro_{\zeta,i,\Gamma}(\varphi)) \in Pro_{\zeta,i,\Gamma}(\varphi)$.

Proof. Suppose $Pro_{\zeta,i,\Gamma}(\varphi) = \{a | B_i(a, \varphi)$ can be proved from Γ in $PBL_f\}$, therefore $\Gamma \vdash B_i(a_n, \varphi)$ for all $a_n \in Pro_{\zeta,i,\Gamma}(\varphi)$, by *Rule* 5 of PBL_f, $\Gamma \vdash B_i(a, \varphi)$, where $a = sup_{n \in M}(\{a_n\}) = sup(Pro_{\zeta,i,\Gamma}(\varphi))$, so we get $sup(Pro_{\zeta,i,\Gamma}(\varphi)) \in Pro_{\zeta,i,\Gamma}(\varphi)$ as desired.

Lemma 3.6 If $A \in X_\zeta$, then $0 \leq \mu_{\zeta,i,\Gamma}(A) \leq 1$. Furthermore, $\mu_{\zeta,i,\Gamma}(\emptyset) = 0$, $\mu_{\zeta,i,\Gamma}(S_\zeta) = 1$.

Proof. By the definition, if $B_i(a, \varphi)$ is a well formed formula, then $0 \leq a \leq 1$; furthermore, check the axioms and rules of PBL_f, any formula derived from well formed formulas is also a well formed formula, so $0 \leq \mu_{\zeta,i,\Gamma}(X(\varphi)) \leq 1$. Therefore, if $A \in X_\zeta$, then $0 \leq \mu_{\zeta,i,\Gamma}(A) \leq 1$.

By rule: $\vdash \varphi \Rightarrow \vdash B_i(1, \varphi)$, therefore we have $\mu_{\zeta,i,\Gamma}(S_\zeta) = 1$ as desired. By axiom: $B_i(0, \varphi)$, we get $B_i(0, false)$, so $\mu_{\zeta,i,\Gamma}(\emptyset) \geq 0$. By rule: $\vdash \neg(\varphi \wedge \psi) \Rightarrow \vdash B_i(a, \varphi) \wedge B_i(b, \psi) \rightarrow B_i(a + b, \varphi \vee \psi)$, where $a + b \leq 1$, we have $\vdash B_i(a, false) \wedge B_i(b, true) \rightarrow B_i(a + b, false \vee true)$, hence $\mu_{\zeta,i,\Gamma}(S_\zeta) \geq \mu_{\zeta,i,\Gamma}(S_\zeta) + \mu_{\zeta,i,\Gamma}(\emptyset)$. Since $\mu_{\zeta,i,\Gamma}(S_\zeta) = 1$, so $1 \geq 1 + \mu_{\zeta,i,\Gamma}(\emptyset)$, therefore $\mu_{\zeta,i,\Gamma}(\emptyset) = 0$ as desired.

Lemma 3.7 If $A_1, A_2 \in X_\zeta$ and $A_1 \subseteq A_2$, then $\mu_{\zeta,i,\Gamma}(A_1) \leq \mu_{\zeta,i,\Gamma}(A_2)$.

Proof. Since $A_1, A_2 \in X_\zeta$, assume $A_1 = X(\varphi)$, $A_2 = X(\psi)$. If $X(\varphi) \subseteq X(\psi)$, by rule: $\vdash \varphi \to \psi \Rightarrow \vdash B_i(a,\varphi) \to B_i(a,\psi)$, we have $\mu_{\zeta,i,\Gamma}(X(\varphi)) \leq \mu_{\zeta,i,\Gamma}(X(\psi))$. Therefore if $A_1, A_2 \in X_\zeta$ and $A_1 \subseteq A_2$, then $\mu_{\zeta,i,\Gamma}(A_1) \leq \mu_{\zeta,i,\Gamma}(A_2)$.

Lemma 3.8 If $A_1, A_2 \in X_\zeta$ and $A_1 \cap A_2 = \emptyset$, then $\mu_{\zeta,i,\Gamma}(A_1 \cup A_2) \geq \mu_{\zeta,i,\Gamma}(A_1) + \mu_{\zeta,i,\Gamma}(A_2)$.

Proof. Since $A_1, A_2 \in X_\zeta$, assume $A_1 = X(\varphi)$, $A_2 = X(\psi)$, by rule: $\vdash \neg(\varphi \wedge \psi) \Rightarrow \vdash B_i(a,\varphi) \wedge B_i(b,\psi) \to B_i(a+b, \varphi \vee \psi)$, where $a_1 + a_2 \leq 1$, we have $\mu_{\zeta,i,\Gamma}(X(\varphi) \cup X(\psi)) \geq \mu_{\zeta,i,\Gamma}(X(\varphi)) + \mu_{\zeta,i,\Gamma}(X(\psi))$. Therefore if $A_1, A_2 \in X_\zeta$ and $A_1 \cap A_2 = \emptyset$, then $\mu_{\zeta,i,\Gamma}(A_1 \cup A_2) \geq \mu_{\zeta,i,\Gamma}(A_1) + \mu_{\zeta,i,\Gamma}(A_2)$.

Lemma 3.9 For any $C, D \in X_\zeta$, $\mu_{\zeta,i,\Gamma}(C \cap D) \geq \mu_{\zeta,i,\Gamma}(C) + \mu_{\zeta,i,\Gamma}(D) - 1$.

Proof. Since $C, D \in X_\zeta$, assume $C = X(\varphi)$, $D = X(\psi)$, by axiom: $B_i(a,\varphi) \wedge B_i(b,\psi) \to B_i(max(a+b-1,0), \varphi \wedge \psi)$, we get $\mu_{\zeta,i,\Gamma}(X(\varphi) \cap X(\psi)) \geq \mu_{\zeta,i,\Gamma}(X(\varphi)) + \mu_{\zeta,i,\Gamma}(X(\psi)) - 1$.

Lemma 3.10 Let $B_i^-(\Gamma) = \{\Gamma' | \{\varphi : B_i(1,\varphi) \in \Gamma\} \subseteq \Gamma'\}$, then $\mu_{\zeta,i,\Gamma}(B_i^-(\Gamma)) = 1$.

Proof. For Γ is a finite formulas set, therefore $B_i^-(\Gamma) = X(\wedge_{B_i(1,\varphi_n) \in \Gamma} \varphi_n)$, by axiom: $B_i(a,\varphi) \wedge B_i(b,\psi) \to B_i(max(a+b-1,0), \varphi \wedge \psi)$, we have that $\wedge B_i(1,\varphi_n) \to B_i(1, \wedge \varphi_n)$, so $B_i(1, \wedge_{B_i(1,\varphi_n) \in \Gamma} \varphi_n)$ can be proved from Γ in PBL_f, so $\mu_{\zeta,i,\Gamma}(B_i^-(\Gamma)) = 1$.

Lemma 3.11 Let $\Lambda_{i,\Gamma} = \{\Gamma' | P_{i,\zeta}(\Gamma) = P_{i,\zeta}(\Gamma')\}$, then $\mu_{\zeta,i,\Gamma}(\Lambda_{i,\Gamma}) = 1$.

Proof. Suppose $\Gamma' \in B_i^-(\Gamma)$. If $B_i(a,\varphi) \in \Gamma$, by rule: $B_i(a,\varphi) \to B_i(1, B_i(a,\varphi))$, we get $B_i(1, B_i(a,\varphi)) \in \Gamma$, for $\Gamma' \in B_i^-(\Gamma)$, hence $B_i(a,\varphi) \in \Gamma'$. If $\neg B_i(a,\varphi) \in \Gamma$, by rule: $\neg B_i(a,\varphi) \to B_i(1, \neg B_i(a,\varphi))$, we get $B_i(1, \neg B_i(a,\varphi)) \in \Gamma$, for $\Gamma' \in B_i^-(\Gamma)$, hence $\neg B_i(a,\varphi) \in \Gamma'$. Therefore $B_i(a,\varphi) \in \Gamma$ iff $B_i(a,\varphi) \in \Gamma'$, which means for any $A \in X_\zeta$, $\mu_{\zeta,i,\Gamma}(A) = \mu_{\zeta,i,\Gamma'}(A)$, so $\Gamma' \in \Lambda_{i,\Gamma}$, and furthermore $B_i^-(\Gamma) \subseteq \Lambda_{i,\Gamma}$. By Lemma 3.10, $\mu_{\zeta,i,\Gamma}(B_i^-(\Gamma)) = 1$, we get $\mu_{\zeta,i,\Gamma}(\Lambda_{i,\Gamma}) = 1$ as desired.

Lemma 3.12 For any $\Gamma \in S_\zeta$, $P_{i,\zeta}(\Gamma)$ is a PBL_f-inner probability space.

Proof. By Lemma 3.6 to Lemma 3.11, we can get the claim immediately.

Lemma 3.13 The inner probabilistic model PM_ζ is a finite model.

Proof. By the definition of S_ζ, the cardinality of S_ζ is no more than the cardinality of $\wp(Sub^*(\zeta))$, which means $|S_\zeta| \leq 2^{|Sub^*(\zeta)|}$.

Similar to the proof of completeness of PBL_ω, the above lemmas show that PM_ζ is a finite PBL_f-model and the following lemma states that PM_ζ is canonical.

Lemma 3.14 For the finite canonical model PM_ζ, for any $\Gamma \in S_\zeta$ and any $\varphi \in Sub^*(\zeta)$, $(PM_\zeta, \Gamma) \models \varphi \Leftrightarrow \varphi \in \Gamma$.

Proof. We argue by cases on the structure of φ, here we only give the proof in the case of $\varphi \equiv B_i(a,\psi)$:

It suffices to prove: $(PM_\zeta, \Gamma) \models B_i(a,\psi) \Leftrightarrow B_i(a,\psi) \in \Gamma$.

If $B_i(a,\psi) \in \Gamma$, by the definition of PM_ζ, $\mu_{\zeta,i,\Gamma}(X(\psi)) = b \geq a$, therefore $(PM_\zeta, \Gamma) \models B_i(a,\psi)$.

If $B_i(a,\psi) \notin \Gamma$, by Lemma 3.5, there exists $b = sup(\{c|B_i(c,\psi) \in \Gamma\})$ such that $B_i(b,\psi) \in \Gamma$ and $a > b$. By the definition of PM_ζ, $\mu_{\zeta,i,\Gamma}(X(\psi)) = b$, therefore $(PM_\zeta, \Gamma) \not\models B_i(a,\psi)$.

From the above lemmas, we know that PM_ζ is a finite PBL_f-model that is canonical. Now it is no difficult to get the following proposition.

Proposition 3.2 (Finite model property of PBL_f) If Γ is a finite set of consistent formulas, then there is a finite PBL_f-model PM such that $PM \models_{PBL_f} \Gamma$.

Proof. By Lemma 3.14, there exists a finite PBL_f-model $PM_{\wedge\Gamma}$ such that Γ is satisfied in $PM_{\wedge\Gamma}$.

Proposition 3.3 (Weak completeness of PBL_f) If Γ is a finite set of formulas, φ is a formula, and $\Gamma \models_{PBL_f} \varphi$, then $\Gamma \vdash_{PBL_f} \varphi$.

Proof. Suppose not, then $(\wedge\Gamma) \wedge \neg\varphi$ is consistent with respect to PBL_f, by Proposition 3.2, there exists an inner probabilistic model $PM_{(\wedge\Gamma)\wedge\neg\varphi}$ such that $(\wedge\Gamma) \wedge \neg\varphi$ is satisfied in $PM_{(\wedge\Gamma)\wedge\neg\varphi}$, but this contradicts our assumption that $\Gamma \models_{PBL_f} \varphi$, thus the proposition holds.

As to PBL_ω case, the construction of canonical model like Definition 3.4 fails to get the finite model property. The main problem lies in how to define measure assignment $\mu_{\zeta,i,\Gamma}$, in Definition 3.4, $\mu_{\zeta,i,\Gamma}(X(\varphi)) = sup(\{a|B_i(a,\varphi)$ is provable from Γ in $PBL_f\})$, but *Rule* 6 fails under this definition. Thus there is an unsolved problem about how to construct a finite model with respect to a PBL_ω-consistent formula.

Usually, in the case of modal logics, one can get decidability of the provability problem from finite model property. At first, one can simply construct every model with finite (for example, say $2^{|Sub^*(\varphi)|}$) states. One then check if φ is true at some state of one of these models (note that the number of models that have $2^{|Sub^*(\varphi)|}$ states is finite). By finite model property, if a formula φ is consistent, then φ is satisfiable with respect to some models. Conversely, if φ is satisfiable with respect to some models, then φ is consistent.

But it becomes different for PBL_f. Because there may be infinitely many PBL_f-inner probability measure assigned to the set X (since real number in [0,1] is infinite), there are infinitely many probabilistic models associated to a given number of states (for example, say $2^{|Sub^*(\varphi)|}$). Therefore the above argument fails. On the contrary, in the next section, we will present another variant-PBL_r, and prove that the decidability of the provable problem holds for PBL_r.

4. PBL_r and its inner probabilistic semantics

The inference systems of PBL_ω and PBL_f both have the infinite inference rules, but in application, an infinite inference rule is inconvenient. Whether we can get the weak completeness for a variant of PBL_ω or PBL_f without *Rule* 5? In this section, we propose another probabilistic belief logic-PBL_r. The inference system of PBL_r is that of PBL_f without *Rule* 5. Another notable difference between PBL_r and PBL_f is that the probability a in the scope of $B_i(a,\varphi)$ must be a rational number. Similar to the semantics of PBL_f, we assign an inner probability space to every possible world in the model.

We prove the soundness and finite model property of PBL_r. At last, as a consequence of the finite model property, we obtain weak completeness and decidability of the provability problem of PBL_f. Roughly speaking, let Γ be a finite set of formulas, weak completeness means $\Gamma \models \varphi \Rightarrow \Gamma \vdash \varphi$, and decidability of the provability problem of PBL_f means there is an algorithm that, given as input a formula φ, will decide whether φ is provable in PBL_f.

Definition 4.1 The set of well formed formulas set of PBL_r, called L^{PBL_r}, is given by the following grammar:

(1) If φ $\in$Atomic formulas set, then $\varphi \in L^{PBL_r}$;

(2) If $\varphi \in L^{PBL_r}$, then $\neg\varphi \in L^{PBL_r}$;

(3) If φ_1,$\varphi_2 \in L^{PBL_r}$, then $\varphi_1 \wedge \varphi_2 \in L^{PBL_r}$;

(4) If $\varphi \in L^{PBL_r}$ and a is a rational number in [0,1], then $B_i(a, \varphi) \in L^{PBL_r}$.

Remark: A significant difference between PBL_r and PBL_ω (PBL_f) is that in the definition of syntax, the probability in the scope of $B_i(a, \varphi)$ in the former is a rational number.

The inner probabilistic model of PBL_r is the same as the inner probabilistic model of PBL_f, except that the value of PBL_r-inner probability measure is a rational number.

The inference system of PBL_r consists of axioms and inference rules of proposition logic and the *Axioms* 1-5 and *Rules* 1-4 of PBL_ω. But it is necessary to note that by the definition of well formed formulas of PBL_r, all the probabilities in the axioms and inference rules of PBL_r should be modified to be rational numbers. For example, *Axiom* 5 of PBL_ω: "$B_i(a, \varphi) \rightarrow B_i(b, \varphi)$, where $1 \geq a \geq b \geq 0$" should be modified as "$B_i(a, \varphi) \rightarrow B_i(b, \varphi)$, where $1 \geq a \geq b \geq 0$ and a, b are rational numbers" in PBL_r. Since the probabilities a and b in the formulas $B_i(a, \varphi)$ and $B_i(b, \psi)$ are rational numbers, so the probability $max(a + b - 1, 0)$ in the scope of $B_i(max(a+b-1, 0), \varphi \wedge \psi)$ in *Axiom* 2 and the probability $a + b$ in the scope of $B_i(a + b, \varphi \vee \psi)$ in *Rule* 4 are also rational numbers.

The proof of the soundness of PBL_r is similar to the soundness of PBL_f, and we do not give the details.

Proposition 4.1 (Soundness of PBL_r) If $\Gamma \vdash_{PBL_r} \varphi$ then $\Gamma \models_{PBL_r} \varphi$.

4.1 Finite model property and decidability of PBL_r

In order to prove the weak completeness of PBL_r, we first present a probabilistic belief logic - $PBL_r(N)$, where N is a given natural number. The finite model property of $PBL_r(N)$ is then proved. From this property, we get the weak completeness and the decidability of PBL_r.

The syntax of $PBL_r(N)$ is the same as the syntax of PBL_r except that the probabilities in formulas should be rational numbers like k/N. For example, every probability in formulas of $PBL_r(3)$ should be one of $0/3$, $1/3$, $2/3$ or $3/3$. Therefore, $B_i(1/3, \varphi)$ and $B_i(2/3, B_j(1/3, \varphi))$ are well formed formulas in $PBL_r(3)$, but $B_i(1/2, \varphi)$ is not a well formed formula in $PBL_r(3)$.

The inner probabilistic model of $PBL_r(N)$ is also the same as PBL_r except that the measure assigned to every possible world should be the form of k/N respectively. Therefore, in an inner probabilistic model of $PBL_r(3)$, the measure in a possible world may be $1/3$, $2/3$ and etc, but can not be $1/2$ or $1/4$.

The inference system of $PBL_r(N)$ is also similar to PBL_r but all the probabilities in the axioms and inference rules should be the form of k/N respectively. For example, *Axiom* 5 of PBL_ω:

"$B_i(a,\varphi) \to B_i(b,\varphi)$, where $1 \geq a \geq b \geq 0$" should be modified to "$B_i(a,\varphi) \to B_i(b,\varphi)$, where $1 \geq a \geq b \geq 0$ and a, b are the from of k_1/N, k_2/N" in *Axiom* 5 of the inference system of $PBL_r(N)$. Since the probabilities a and b in the formulas $B_i(a,\varphi)$ and $B_i(b,\varphi)$ are in the form of $k_1/N, k_2/N$, so the probability $max(a+b-1,0)$ in the scope of $B_i(max(a+b-1,0),\varphi \wedge \psi)$ in *Axiom* 2 and the probability $a+b$ in the scope of $B_i(a+b,\varphi \vee \psi)$ in *Rule* 4 are also in the form of k/N.

It is easy to see that the soundness of $PBL_r(N)$ holds. We omit the detail proof here.

Proposition 4.2 (Soundness of $PBL_r(N)$) If $\Gamma \vdash_{PBL_r(N)} \varphi$ then $\Gamma \models_{PBL_r(N)} \varphi$.

In the following, we prove the finite model property of $PBL_r(N)$. By this proposition, we can obtain the weak completeness of PBL_r immediately.

Definition 4.2 Suppose ζ is a consistent formula with respect to $PBL_r(N)$. $Sub^*(\zeta)$ is a set of formulas defined as follows: let $\zeta \in L^{PBL_r(N)}$, $Sub(\zeta)$ is the set of subformulas of ζ, then $Sub^*(\zeta) = Sub(\zeta) \cup \{\neg\psi | \psi \in Sub(\zeta)\}$. It is clear that $Sub^*(\zeta)$ is finite.

Definition 4.3 The inner probabilistic model PM_ζ with respect to formula ζ is $(S_\zeta, P_{1,\zeta}, ..., P_{n,\zeta}, \pi_\zeta)$.

(1) Here $S_\zeta = \{\Gamma | \Gamma$ is a maximal consistent formulas set with respect to $PBL_r(N)$ and $\Gamma \subseteq Sub^*(\zeta)\}$.

(2) For any $\Gamma \in S_\zeta$, $P_{i,\zeta}(\Gamma) = (S_\zeta, X_\zeta, \mu_{\zeta,i,\Gamma})$, where $X_\zeta = \{X(\varphi) | X(\varphi) = \{\Gamma' | \varphi$ is a Boolean combination of formulas in $Sub^*(\zeta)$ and $\Gamma' \vdash_{PBL_r(N)} \varphi\}\}$; $\mu_{\zeta,i,\Gamma}$ is an inner probability assignment: $X_\zeta \to [0,1]$, and $\mu_{\zeta,i,\Gamma}(X(\varphi)) = sup(\{a | B_i(a,\varphi)$ is provable from Γ in $PBL_r(N)\})$.

(3) π_ζ is a truth assignment as follows: for any atomic formula p, $\pi_\zeta(p,\Gamma) = true \Leftrightarrow p \in \Gamma$.

The following lemmas show that the above model PM_ζ is an inner probabilistic model of $PBL_r(N)$, and it is canonical: for any $\Gamma \in S_\zeta$ and any $\varphi \in Sub^*(\zeta)$, $\varphi \in \Gamma \Leftrightarrow (PM_\zeta, \Gamma) \models \varphi$. This implies the finite model property of $PBL_r(N)$.

Lemma 4.1 S_ζ is a nonempty finite set.

Proof. Since the rules and axioms of $PBL_r(N)$ are consistent, S_ζ is nonempty. For $Sub^*(\zeta)$ is a finite set, by the definition of S_ζ, the cardinality of S_ζ is no more than the cardinality of $\wp(Sub^*(\zeta))$.

Lemma 4.2 X_ζ is the power set of S_ζ.

Proof. Firstly, since $Sub^*(\zeta)$ is finite, so if $\Gamma \in S_\zeta$ then Γ is finite. We can let φ_Γ be the conjunction of the formulas in Γ. Secondly, if $A \subseteq S_\zeta$, then $A = X(\vee_{\Gamma \in A} \varphi_\Gamma)$. By the above argument, we have that X_ζ is the power set of S_ζ.

Lemma 4.3 If φ is consistent (here φ is a Boolean combination of formulas in $Sub^*(\zeta)$), then there exists Γ such that φ can be proved from Γ, here Γ is a maximal consistent set with respect to $PBL_r(N)$ and $\Gamma \subseteq Sub^*(\zeta)$.

Proof. For φ is obtainable from the Boolean connective composition of formulas in $Sub^*(\zeta)$, therefore by regarding the formulas in $Sub^*(\zeta)$ as atomic formulas, φ can be represented in disjunctive normal form. Since φ is consistent, there is a consistent disjunctive term in disjunctive normal form expression of φ, let such term be $\psi_1 \wedge ... \wedge \psi_n$, then φ can be derived from the maximal consistent set Γ that contains $\{\psi_1, ..., \psi_n\}$.

Lemma 4.4 For any $\Gamma \in S_\zeta$, $P_\zeta(\Gamma)$ is well defined.

Proof. It suffices to prove the following claim: if $X(\varphi) = X(\psi)$, then $\mu_{\zeta,i,\Gamma}(X(\varphi)) = \mu_{\zeta,i,\Gamma}(X(\psi))$. If $X(\varphi) = X(\psi)$, it is clear that $\vdash \varphi \leftrightarrow \psi$. For suppose not, $\varphi \wedge \neg\psi$ is consistent. By Lemma 4.3, there is Γ' such that $\varphi \wedge \neg\psi$ can be proved from Γ', therefore $\Gamma' \in X(\varphi)$ and $\Gamma' \notin X(\psi)$, it is a contradiction. Thus $\vdash \varphi \leftrightarrow \psi$. By rule: $\vdash \varphi \rightarrow \psi \Rightarrow \vdash B_i(a,\varphi) \rightarrow B_i(a,\psi)$, we get $\vdash B_i(a,\varphi) \leftrightarrow B_i(a,\psi)$, which means $\mu_{\zeta,i,\Gamma}(X(\varphi)) = \mu_{\zeta,i,\Gamma}(X(\psi))$.

Lemma 4.5 Let $Pro_{\zeta,i,\Gamma}(\varphi) = \{a|B_i(a,\varphi) \in \Gamma\}$, then $sup(Pro_{\zeta,i,\Gamma}(\varphi)) \in Pro_{\zeta,i,\Gamma}(\varphi)$.

Proof. By the construction of model, $Pro_{\zeta,i,\Gamma}(\varphi)$ is one of the numbers $0/N$, $1/N$,...,N/N. Since the set $0/N, 1/N, ..., N/N$ is finite, therefore $sup(Pro_{\zeta,i,\Gamma}(\varphi)) \in Pro_{\zeta,i,\Gamma}(\varphi)$.

Lemma 4.6 If $A \in X_\zeta$, then $0 \leq \mu_{\zeta,i,\Gamma}(A) \leq 1$. Furthermore, $\mu_{\zeta,i,\Gamma}(\emptyset) = 0$ and $\mu_{\zeta,i,\Gamma}(S_\zeta) = 1$.

Proof. By the construction of model, it is clear that $\mu_{\zeta,i,\Gamma}$ has the following property: if $A \in X_\zeta$, then $0 \leq \mu_{\zeta,i,\Gamma}(A) \leq 1$.

By rule: $\vdash \varphi \Rightarrow \vdash B_i(1,\varphi)$, it is clear $\mu_{\zeta,i,\Gamma}(S_\zeta) = 1$. By axiom: $B_i(0,\varphi)$, we get $B_i(0, false)$, so $\mu_{\zeta,i,\Gamma}(\emptyset) \geq 0$. By *Rule* 4 of PBL_r, we get $\mu_{\zeta,i,\Gamma}(S_\zeta) \geq \mu_{\zeta,i,\Gamma}(S_\zeta) + \mu_{\zeta,i,\Gamma}(\emptyset)$, so $1 \geq 1 + \mu_{\zeta,i,\Gamma}(\emptyset)$, which implies $\mu_{\zeta,i,\Gamma}(\emptyset) = 0$.

Lemma 4.7 If $A_1, A_2 \in X_\zeta$ and $A_1 \subseteq A_2$, then $\mu_{\zeta,i,\Gamma}(A_1) \leq \mu_{\zeta,i,\Gamma}(A_2)$.

Proof. Since $A_1, A_2 \in X_\zeta$ assume $A_1 = X(\varphi)$, $A_2 = X(\psi)$. If $X(\varphi) \subseteq X(\psi)$, by rule: $\vdash \varphi \rightarrow \psi \Rightarrow \vdash B_i(a,\varphi) \rightarrow B_i(a,\psi)$, we have $\mu_{\zeta,i,\Gamma}(A_1) \leq \mu_{\zeta,i,\Gamma}(A_2)$. Therefore if $A_1, A_2 \in X_\zeta$ and $A_1 \subseteq A_2$, then $\mu_{\zeta,i,\Gamma}(A_1) \leq \mu_{\zeta,i,\Gamma}(A_2)$.

Lemma 4.8 If $A_1, A_2 \in X_\zeta$ and $A_1 \cap A_2 = \emptyset$, then $\mu_{\zeta,i,\Gamma}(A_1 \cup A_2) \geq \mu_{\zeta,i,\Gamma}(A_1) + \mu_{\zeta,i,\Gamma}(A_2)$.

Proof. Since $A_1, A_2 \in X_\zeta$, assume $A_1 = X(\varphi)$, $A_2 = X(\psi)$. By rule: $\vdash \neg(\varphi \wedge \psi) \Rightarrow \vdash B_i(a_1,\varphi) \wedge B_i(a_2,\psi) \rightarrow B_i(a_1 + a_2, \varphi \vee \psi)$, where $a_1 + a_2 \leq 1$, we have $\mu_{\zeta,i,\Gamma}(X(\varphi) \cup X(\psi)) \geq \mu_{\zeta,i,\Gamma}(X(\varphi)) + \mu_{\zeta,i,\Gamma}(X(\psi))$. Therefore if $A_1, A_2 \in X_\zeta$ and $A_1 \cap A_2 = \emptyset$, then $\mu_{\zeta,i,\Gamma}(A_1 \cup A_2) \geq \mu_{\zeta,i,\Gamma}(A_1) + \mu_{\zeta,i,\Gamma}(A_2)$.

Lemma 4.9 For any $C, D \in X_\zeta$, $\mu_{\zeta,i,\Gamma}(C \cap D) \geq \mu_{\zeta,i,\Gamma}C) + \mu_{\zeta,i,\Gamma}(D) - 1$.

Proof. Since $C, D \in X_\zeta$, assume $C = X(\varphi)$, $D = X(\psi)$, by axiom: $B_i(a,\varphi) \wedge B_i(b,\psi) \rightarrow B_i(max(a+b-1,0), \varphi \wedge \psi)$, we get $\mu_{\zeta,i,\Gamma}(X(\varphi) \cap X(\psi)) \geq \mu_{\zeta,i,\Gamma}(X(\varphi)) + \mu_{\zeta,i,\Gamma}(X(\psi)) - 1$.

Lemma 4.10 Let $B_i^-(\Gamma) = \{\Gamma'|\{\varphi|B_i(1,\varphi) \in \Gamma\} \subseteq \Gamma'\}$, then $\mu_{\zeta,i,\Gamma}(B_i^-(\Gamma)) = 1$.

Proof. For Γ is a finite formulas set, therefore $B_i^-(\Gamma) = X(\wedge_{B_i(1,\varphi_n) \in \Gamma}\varphi_n)$, by axiom: $B_i(a,\varphi) \wedge B_i(b,\psi) \rightarrow B_i(max(a+b-1,0), \varphi \wedge \psi)$, we have that $\wedge B_i(1,\varphi_n) \rightarrow B_i(1, \wedge\varphi_n)$, so $B_i(1, \wedge_{B_i(1,\varphi_n)\in\Gamma}\varphi_n)$ can be proved from Γ in $PBL_r(N)$, so $\mu_{\zeta,i,\Gamma}(B_i^-(\Gamma)) = 1$.

Lemma 4.11 Let $\Lambda_{i,\Gamma} = \{\Gamma'|P_{i,\zeta}(\Gamma) = P_{i,\zeta}(\Gamma')\}$, then $\mu_{\zeta,i,\Gamma}(\Lambda_{i,\Gamma}) = 1$.

Proof. Suppose $\Gamma' \in B_i^-(\Gamma)$. If $B_i(a,\varphi) \in \Gamma$, by rule: $B_i(a,\varphi) \rightarrow B_i(1, B_i(a,\varphi))$, we get $B_i(1, B_i(a,\varphi)) \in \Gamma$, for $\Gamma' \in B_i^-(\Gamma)$, hence $B_i(a,\varphi) \in \Gamma'$. If $\neg B_i(a,\varphi) \in \Gamma$, by rule: $\neg B_i(a,\varphi) \rightarrow B_i(1, \neg B_i(a,\varphi))$, we get $B_i(1, \neg B_i(a,\varphi)) \in \Gamma$, for $\Gamma' \in B_i^-(\Gamma)$, hence $\neg B_i(a,\varphi) \in \Gamma'$. Therefore $B_i(a,\varphi) \in \Gamma$ iff $B_i(a,\varphi) \in \Gamma'$, which means for any $A \in X_\zeta$, $\mu_{\zeta,i,\Gamma}(A) = \mu_{\zeta,i,\Gamma'}(A)$, so $\Gamma' \in \Lambda_{i,\Gamma}$, and furthermore $B_i^-(\Gamma) \subseteq \Lambda_{i,\Gamma}$. For $\mu_{\zeta,i,\Gamma}(B_i^-(\Gamma)) = 1$, we get $\mu_{\zeta,i,\Gamma}(\Lambda_{i,\Gamma}) = 1$ as desired.

Lemma 4.12 For any $\Gamma \in S_\zeta$, $P_{i,\zeta}(\Gamma)$ is a $PBL_r(N)$-inner probability space.

Proof. By Lemma 4.2 to Lemma 4.11, we can get the claim immediately.

Lemma 4.13 The inner probabilistic model PM_ζ is a finite model.

Proof. By the definition of S_ζ, the cardinality of S_ζ is no more than the cardinality of $\wp(Sub^*(\zeta))$, which means $|S_\zeta| \leq 2^{|Sub^*(\zeta)|}$.

Lemma 4.14 In the canonical $PBL_r(N)$-model PM_ζ, for any $\Gamma \in S_\zeta$ and any $\varphi \in Sub^*(\zeta)$, $\varphi \in \Gamma \Leftrightarrow (PM_\zeta, \Gamma) \models \varphi$.

Proof. We prove the lemma by induction on the structure of φ. In the following, we only prove that $B_i(a, \psi) \in \Gamma \Leftrightarrow (PM_\zeta, \Gamma) \models B_i(a, \psi)$.

If $B_i(a, \psi) \in \Gamma$, by the construction of PM_ζ, $\mu_{\zeta,i,\Gamma}(X(\psi)) = b \geq a$, we get $(PM_\zeta, \Gamma) \models B_i(a, \psi)$.

If $B_i(a, \psi) \notin \Gamma$, then $\neg B_i(a, \psi) \in \Gamma$, by the construction of PM_ζ and Lemma 4.5, since $sup(Pro_{\zeta,i,\Gamma}(\psi)) \in Pro_{\zeta,i,\Gamma}(\psi)$, so we have $sup(Pro_{\zeta,i,\Gamma}(\psi)) = b < a$, and $\mu_{\zeta,i,\Gamma}(X(\psi)) = b$, which implies $(PM_\zeta, \Gamma) \models \neg B_i(a, \psi)$, therefore $(PM_\zeta, \Gamma) \not\models B_i(a, \psi)$.

Proposition 4.3 (Finite model property of $PBL_r(N)$) If Γ is a finite set of consistent formulas, then there is a finite model PM such that $PM \models_{PBL_r(N)} \Gamma$.

Proof. By Lemma 4.14, there exists a finite $PBL_r(N)$-model $PM_{\wedge\Gamma}$ such that Γ is satisfied in $PM_{\wedge\Gamma}$.

Since any inner probabilistic model of $PBL_r(N)$ is also an inner probabilistic model of PBL_r, and any formula of PBL_r can be regarded as a formula of $PBL_r(N)$, given a consistent PBL_r-formula ζ, we can construct a $PBL_r(N)$-inner probabilistic model PM_ζ that satisfies formula ζ by the above lemmas. Since PM_ζ is also PBL_r-inner probabilistic model, so we can construct a PBL_r- inner probabilistic model PM_ζ that satisfies the given consistent PBL_r-formula ζ, this implies the finite model property of PBL_r.

Proposition 4.4 (Finite model property of PBL_r) If Γ is a finite set of consistent formulas, then there is a finite model PM such that $PM \models_{PBL_r} \Gamma$.

Proof. Let $a_1, a_2, ..., a_n$ be all rational numbers occur in the formulas in Γ. There are natural numbers $k_1, k_2, ..., k_n, N$ such that $a_i = k_i/N$. Firstly, since the axioms and rules of $PBL_r(N)$ is also the axioms and rules of PBL_r, therefore it is clear that if a finite set of formulas Γ is consistent with PBL_r, then it is also consistent with $PBL_r(N)$. By Proposition 4.3, there is a finite model of $PBL_r(N)$, PM, satisfying Γ. Since the model of $PBL_r(N)$ is also a model of PBL_r, so we get the proposition.

Proposition 4.5 (Weak completeness of PBL_r) If Γ is a finite set of formulas, φ is a formula, and $\Gamma \models_{PBL_r} \varphi$, then $\Gamma \vdash_{PBL_r} \varphi$.

Proof. Suppose not, then $(\wedge\Gamma) \wedge \neg\varphi$ is consistent with respect to PBL_r, by Proposition 4.4, there exists an inner probabilistic model $PM_{(\wedge\Gamma)\wedge\neg\varphi}$ such that $(\wedge\Gamma) \wedge \neg\varphi$ is satisfied in $PM_{(\wedge\Gamma)\wedge\neg\varphi}$, but this contradicts our assumption that $\Gamma \models_{PBL_r} \varphi$, thus the proposition holds.

From Proposition 4.4, we can get a procedure for checking if a formula φ is PBL_r-consistent. We simply construct every probabilistic model with $2^{|Sub^*(\varphi)|}$ states (Remember that in the construction of the finite model of φ, the values of inner probability measure are in the form of k/N, where N is a constant natural number. Since there are finite numbers having the form of k/N, where $0 \leq k \leq N$, therefore the number of inner probability measures assigned to the measurable sets is also finite, and consequently, the number of models with $2^{|Sub^*(\varphi)|}$ states is finite). We then check if φ is true at some state of one of these models. By Proposition 4.4, if a formula φ is PBL_r -consistent, then φ is satisfiable with respect to some models. Conversely, if φ is satisfiable with respect to some models, then φ is PBL_r-consistent.

As a consequence, we can now show that the provability problem for PBL_r is decidable.

Proposition 4.6 (Decidability of PBL_r) The provability problem for PBL_r is decidable.

Proof. Since φ is provable in PBL_r iff $\neg\varphi$ is not PBL_r-consistent, we can simply check if $\neg\varphi$ is PBL_r-consistent. By the above discussion, there is a checking procedure. Hence the provability problem for PBL_r is decidable.

5. Comparison of Fagin and Halpern's logic with our work

The probabilistic knowledge logic proposed by Fagin and Halpern in [3] is a famous epistemic logic with probabilistic character. In this section, we mainly compare the logic in [3] with our logics in terms of their syntax, inference system, semantics and proof technique.

1. Syntax. The basic formulas of logic in [3] can be classified into two categories: the standard knowledge logic formula such as $K_i\varphi$, and the probability formula such as $a_1w_i(\varphi_1) + ... + a_kw_i(\varphi_k) \geq b$. The formula $K_i^b(\varphi)$ is an abbreviation for $K_i(w_i(\varphi) \geq b)$, intuitively, this says that "agent i knows that the probability of φ is greater than or equal to b". Except the difference of knowledge and belief operators, the formula $K_i^b(\varphi)$ is similar to the formula $B_i(b,\varphi)$ of this chapter. But in this chapter, $B_i(b,\varphi)$ is a basic formula, and there is no formula such as $a_1w_i(\varphi_1) + ... + a_kw_i(\varphi_k) \geq b$, because $a_1w_i(\varphi_1) + ... + a_kw_i(\varphi_k) \geq b$ contains non-logical symbols such as "$\times$", "$+$" and "$\geq$", and accordingly, the language and reasoning system have to deal with linear inequalities and probabilities. We get a tradeoff between expressive power and complexity, and the only basic formula of this chapter is $B_i(b,\varphi)$, which makes the syntax and axioms of our logic system simpler.

2. Inference system. The inference system in [3] consists of four components: the first component includes axioms and rules for propositional reasoning; the second component includes the standard knowledge logic; the third component allows us to reason about inequalities (so it contains axioms that allow us to deduce, for example, that $2x \geq 2y$ follows from $x \geq y$); while the fourth is the only one that has axioms and inference rules for reasoning about probability. It is worthy to note that $W3$ ($w_i(\varphi \wedge \psi) + w_i(\varphi \wedge \neg\psi) = w_i(\varphi)$) in [3] corresponds to finite additivity, not countable infinite additivity, i.e., $\mu(A_1 \cup A_2 \cup ... \cup A_n...) = \mu(A_1) + \mu(A_2) + ... + \mu(A_n) + ...$, if $A_1, ..., A_n, ...$ is a countable collection of disjoint measurable sets. As Fagin and Halpern indicated, they think it is enough to introduce an axiom corresponding to finite additivity for most applications. They could not express countable infinite additivity in their language.

In this chapter, there are two components in our inference systems: the first component includes axioms and rules for propositional reasoning; the second component includes axioms and rules for probabilistic belief reasoning. In our system, when one perform reasoning, one need not to consider different kinds of axioms and rules that may involve linear inequalities or probabilities. In order to express the properties of probability (such as finite additivity, monotonicity or continuity) by probabilistic modal operator directly instead of by inequalities and probabilities, we introduce some new axioms and rules. While in Fagin and Halpern's paper, these properties are expressed by the axioms for linear inequalities or probabilities. Similar to Fagin and Halpern's logic system, we only express finite additivity, but not countable infinite additivity, because we cannot express such property in our language, in fact, we believe that this property cannot be expressed by finite length formula in reasoning system. On the other hand, we think the finite additivity property is enough for the most of meaningful reasoning about probabilistic belief.

3. Semantics. In [3], a Kripke structure for knowledge and probability (for n agents) is a tuple $(S, \pi, K_1, ..., K_n, P)$, where P is a probability assignment, which assigns to each agent $i \in \{1, ..., n\}$ and state $s \in S$ a probability space $P(i,s) = (S_{i,s}, X_{i,s}, \mu_{i,s})$, where $S_{i,s} \subseteq S$.

To give semantics to formula such as $w_i(\varphi) \geq b$, the obvious way is $(M,s) \models w_i(\varphi) \geq b$ iff $\mu_{i,s}(S_{i,s}(\varphi)) \geq b$, here $S_{i,s}(\varphi) = \{s' \in S_{i,s} | (M,s') \models \varphi\}$. The only problem with this definition is that the set $S_{i,s}(\varphi)$ might not be measurable (i.e., not in $X_{i,s}$), so that $\mu_{i,s}(S_{i,s}(\varphi))$ might not be well defined. They considered two models. One model satisfies $MEAS$ condition (for every formula φ, the set $S_{i,s}(\varphi) \in X_{i,s}$) to guarantee that this set is measurable, and the corresponding inference system AX_{MEAS} has finite additivity condition $W3$. The other model does not obey $MEAS$ condition, and the corresponding inference system AX has no finite additivity condition $W3$. To deal with the problem in this case, they adopted the inner measures $(\mu_{i,s})^*$ rather than $\mu_{i,s}$, here $(\mu_{i,s})^*(A) = sup(\{\mu_{i,s}(B) | B \subseteq A \text{ and } B \in X\})$, here $sup(A)$ is the least upper bound of A. Thus, $(M,s) \models w_i(\varphi) \geq b$ iff $(\mu_{i,s})^*(S_{i,s}(\varphi)) \geq b$.

Similar to the model of AX_{MEAS} in [3], in the model of PBL_ω, $X_{i,s}$ satisfies the following conditions: (a) If p is an atomic formula, then $ev_{PM}(p) = \{s' | \pi(s', p) = true\} \in X_{i,s}$; (b) If $A \in X_{i,s}$, then $S_{i,s} - A \in X_{i,s}$; (c) If $A_1, A_2 \in X_{i,s}$, then $A_1 \cap A_2 \in X_{i,s}$; (d) If $A \in X_{i,s}$ and $a \in [0,1]$, then $\{s' | \mu_{i,s'}(A) \geq a\} \in X_{i,s}$. From these conditions, we can prove by structural induction that for every formula φ, the set $ev_{PM}(\varphi) \in X_{i,s}$. Therefore, the model of PBL_ω also satisfies the condition $MEAS$. Moreover, similar to the model of AX_{MEAS}, probability measure in the model of PBL_ω satisfies finite additivity property.

In contrast with PBL_ω, the models of PBL_f and PBL_r are similar to the model of AX in [3]. There is an inner probability measure rather than probability measure in the models of PBL_f and PBL_r. In the model of AX, the semantics of formula is given by inner probability measure induced by probability measure. Meanwhile, in the models of PBL_f and PBL_r, we introduce inner probability measure directly, which satisfies some weaker additivity properties.

Since there is no accessible relation in our model, we need not to consider the conditions about accessible relations. The only conditions we have to consider are probability space at different states, which simplifies the description and construction of model.

4. Proof technique of completeness. In [3], they prove the completeness by reducing the problem to the existence of solution of a finite set of linear inequalities. But this method does not provide the value of measure assigned to every possible world, and just assures the existence of measure. Moreover, this method cannot provide completeness property in the case of infinite set of formulas, which needs some linear inequalities axioms to characterize the existence of solutions of infinitely many linear inequalities that contain infinitely many variables. This seems impossible when we have only finite-length formulas in the language. In this chapter, the proof for completeness is significant different from the proof in [3]. There are no auxiliary axioms such as the probability axioms and linear inequality axioms, which are necessary in the proof of [3]. We prove the completeness by constructing the model that satisfies the given consistent formulas set, our proof can also be used to deal with the case of infinite set of formulas. Furthermore, our proof can be generalized to get the completeness of other probabilistic logic systems because it depends very lightly on the concrete axioms and rules.

6. Conclusions

In this chapter, we proposed probabilistic belief logics PBL_ω, PBL_f and PBL_r, and gave the respective probabilistic semantics of these logics. Furthermore we proved the soundness and completeness of PBL_ω, the finite model property of PBL_f and the decidability of PBL_r. The above probabilistic belief logics allow the reasoning of uncertain information of agent in artificial intelligent systems.

The probabilistic semantics of probabilistic belief logic can also be applied to describe other probabilistic modal logic by adding the respective restricted conditions on probability space. Just as different assumptions about the relationship between worlds, can be captured with different axioms in modal logics, different assumptions about the interrelationships between probability assignment spaces at different states, can also be captured axiomatically. Furthermore, the completeness proof in this chapter can be applied to prove the completeness of other probabilistic modal logics.

It seems to us that some further research directions lie in the following several problems: whether the finite model property for PBL_ω holds, whether the decidability for the provability problem of PBL_ω or PBL_f holds, moreover, if the decidability holds, what is the complexity of the corresponding provability problem. These problems seem to be much more difficult and remain open. The techniques used in classical modal logics are not suit to solve such problems, and some new techniques may be necessary.

7. Acknowledgment

This work was supported by the National Natural Science Foundation of China under Grants No. 60873025, and the Foundation of Provincial Key Laboratory for Computer Information Processing Technology of Soochow University under Grant No. KJS0920.

8. References

[1] R. J. Aumann. Agreeing to disagree. The Annals of Statistics, 1976, 4(6): 1236-1239.

[2] F. Bacchus. Representing and reasoning with probabilistic knowledge: a logical approach to probabilities. Cambridge, Mass. : MIT Press, 1990.

[3] R. Fagin and J. Y. Halpern. Reasoning about knowledge and probability. J ACM, 1994, 41(2): 340-367.

[4] R. Fagin, J. Y. Halpern and N. Megiddo. A logic for reasoning about probabilities, Information and Computation. 1990, 87(1/2): 78-128.

[5] R. Fagin, J. Y. Halpern, Y. Moses and M. Y.Vardi. Reasoning about knowledge. Cambridge, Massachusetts: The MIT Press, 1995. /2): 78-128.

[6] M. Fattorosi-Barnaba and G. Amati. Modal Operators with Probabilistic Interpretations i. Studia Logica, 1987, XLVI(4):383-393.

[7] Y. Feldman. A decidable prepositional probabilistic dynamic logic with explicit probabilities. Information and Control, 1984, 63: 11-38.
[8] D. Fudenberg and J. Tirole. Game theory. Cambridge, Massachusetts: The MIT Press, 1991.
[9] D. Gillies. Philosophical Theories of Probability, Philosophical issues in science, London and New York: Routledge, 2000.
[10] J. Y. Halpern. The relationship between knowledge, belief, and certainty. Annals of Mathematics and Artificial Intelligence 1991, 4: 301-322.
[11] J. Y. Halpern. Lexicographic probability, conditional probability, and nonstandard probability. In Proceedings of the Eighth Conference on Theoretical Aspects of Rationality and Knowledge, 2001, 17-30.
[12] J. Y. Halpern and Y. Moses. Knowledge and common knowledge in a distributed environment. J ACM, 1990, 37(3): 549-587.
[13] J. Y. Halpern and M. R. Tuttle. Knowledge, probability, and adversaries,. J.ACM, 1993, 40(4): 917-962.
[14] S. Hart and M. Sharir. Probabilistic temporal logics for finite and bounded models. In Proceedings of the 16th ACM Symposium on Theory of Computing, 1984, ACM, New York, 1-13.
[15] J. Hintikka. Knowledge and belief. Ithaca, NY: Cornell University Press, 1962.
[16] W. van der Hoek. Some considerations on the logic PFD: A logic combining modality and probability. J. Applied Non-Classical Logics, 7(3):287-307, 1997.
[17] H. J. Keisler. Probability quantifiers, in J. Barwise and S. Feferman, Eds. Model-theoretical logics, 509-556, Springer-Verlag, New York/Berlin, 1985.
[18] B. P. Kooi. Probabilistic Dynamic Epistemic Logic. Journal of Logic, Language and Information 2003, 12: 381-408.
[19] S. Kripke. A semantics analysis of modal logic, I: Normal modal propositional calculi. Z. Math. Logik Grundl. Math, 1963, 9: 67-96.
[20] A. Laux and H. Wansing. (eds) Knowledge and belief in philosophy and artificial intelligence, Akademie Verlag GmbH, Berlin, 1995.
[21] T. Lukasiewicz. Weak nonmonotonic probabilistic logics, KR2004, Whistler, Canada, 2004.
[22] B. Milch and D. Koller. Probabilistic Models for Agent's Beliefs and Decisions. Proc. 16th Conference on Uncertainty in Artificial Intelligence 2000: 389-396.
[23] J. Pearl. Probabilistic reasoning in intelligent systems: Networks of plausible inference. Morgan Kaufmann, San Mateo, CA, USA, 1988.
[24] A. S. Rao and M. P. Georgeff. Modeling rational agents within a BDI-architecture. Proceeding of KR-91, 1991, San Mateo, CA, USA, 473-484.
[25] G. Shafer. A mathematical theory of evidence. Princeton University Press, Princeton, N.J, 1976.

Section 2

Queries, Predicates, and Semantic Cache

3

Queries and Predicate – Argument Relationship

Savina Raynaud
Università Cattolica del Sacro Cuore – Milan
Italy

1. Introduction

Queries are essential for retrieving information. For those who surf the net they can play a crucial role. But the relationship between questions and answers involves many classical topics, not only in the language sciences, especially in pragmatics, but also in philosophy. It would be surprising if the results of such an old, even ancient, inquiry did not inspire interesting solutions to present-day research.

In fact, semantics was born at the beginning of philosophical enquiry, for its own sake. Philosophy, conceived as a demand of wisdom and truth requesting the exercise of thought (and good will), has the *logos* as its specific resource. Given that *logos* is both uttered thought and thoughtful word, the mood of reflecting upon speeches and their role in finding and telling the truth, asking questions and giving answers, has been present since the beginning. As is often the case, an important motivation to meditate and speculate upon logos came out of a crisis, with its attacks and instrumental claims about language and human discourse. We could identify the Sophist movement, during the development of democracy in the Greek *poleis*, in the fifth century B.C., as such a factor.

Plato and Aristotle are the obvious significant responses to the Sophists' extraordinary argumentation skills, resting upon relativistic claims. Dialogue between master and disciple as well as an inspection of *organon* structures emerged as conditions which granted a positive and safe attitude towards truth, knowledge, virtue… in short, a good life.

What was Aristotelic Organon about? The name, meaning instrument, designated, according to Andronicus of Rhodes (40 B.C.), Aristotle's works on logic, philosophy of language and of sciences, valid arguments and fallacies. These treatises were so specifically designed as *praeambula* to assuring a self-conscious and self-controlled intellectual activity, that they constituted a basic *corpus* providing safe methodological - deontological premises to those who wanted to cultivate philosophy, or simply true knowledge, concerning good and happiness in personal and socio-political life, moral virtues or human skills such as art, persuasion, the creation of laws and cathartic tragedies. Even more fundamentally, however, they concerned being in the physical world and beyond it: through living beings (animals and humans) and celestial bodies, up to their first causes to their final end.

How could this huge scenario disclose its secrets and reveal its hidden structure without a self-confident appeal to human powers, and above all to the capacities of human knowledge? How was it possible to observe the human way of proceeding from thought to truth without observing those "observable forms of thought" which were human discourse, arguments, propositions and their constituents? Was it even conceivable to grasp the inner organisation of thoughts without articulating them into nouns and verbs, premises and conclusions, while inquiring into their mutual relations? After Plato's evaluation of dialogue as the genuine path to remembering apparently unknown truths and to conquering uncontroversial knowledge, it was Aristotle's enterprise to direct attention to that object-making of our thinking activity which, during his day, was particularly evidenced by the wide diffusion of writing. Written words meant linguistically shaped thoughts.

To follow a human way of thinking meant following a human way of speech. This is why semantics entered the heart of human inquiry about human pretention of truth. The same pretention which motivates queries expecting answers. A kind of tension towards avoiding mistaken and misleading steps which caused another great philosophical movement, that of the Stoics, who cultivated logic in order to argue about ethics. Many of us are unaware that most of the grammatical tools through which we still analyse language today come from the Stoics: the names of cases (nominative, genitive ...), of verbal diatheses (active, passive, reflexive) etc.

This speculative attitude towards language did not only occur in the philosophical schools of the classical world.

For the same reasons - the unavoidable relations between the adventures of thought, especially the most audacious and universal on one side and its linguistic expression and importance for communication and dialectic argumentation on the other - semantics was also considered highly important in the Medieval universities. This took the form of *gramaticae speculativae* and grammars *de modis significandi,* and the relationships between *modi essendi, intelligendi* and *significandi* were explored.

Another crisis marked a new historical turn, from the Middle Ages to the modern era. The multiplication of national languages, the progressive neglect of Latin as a common language, the scientific revolution together with political conflicts led to another crisis. It was a semiotic crisis together with a new semantic demand. From Locke to Leibniz, from Port-Royal to the *Encyclopédie,* many new questions arose: about the affordability of ideas linking words and world, or - from a reduced horizon - about connections between words and thoughts and their invariant structures in spite of the diversity of idioms, or otherwise about the possibility of building artificial languages to provide good demonstrations, to allow the construction of *machines à penser.*

It would be sufficient to look at the categories of ancient grammars to see how heavily they were charged with semantic functions: nouns called substantives, adjectives characterised as qualifiers, possessives, demonstratives, conjunctions labelled as final, causal, concessive etc.

One of the permanent aims animating linguistics as a science over the last two centuries remains the distinction, if not a separation between form and function, between the description (or generation, or historical reconstruction) of formal linguistic devices (often conceived as a sufficient task) and the ascription of prototypical, but not unexceptionable functions.

Over the last two centuries, in fact, language has been a focus of attention for a multitude of disciplines: linguistics, semiotics, philosophy of language, psycholinguistics and cognitive sciences were born and developed while sharing the same basic area but seen from quite different perspectives.

What characterises philosophical semantics above all is the triangular relation among signs, thoughts, things (states of affaires, events, situations): whereas linguistic semantics has mainly dealt with, and still deals with, intra-linguistic relations. Referential semantics has thus become central to the philosophy of language, going from existential judgements (does what is spoken about exist?) to the role of determinants (definite vs. indefinite descriptions, indexicality, singular vs. plural reference), up to the different ways of referring (proper names vs. common nouns), or to the scope of operators such as quantifiers or negation etc.

Cognitive semantics is devoted rather to the skills and performances involved in processing semantic information.

Very often, in semantic inquiries, the order of magnitude has gone from the minimum of single words (searched as terms of synonymic or antonymic relations, for instance) to the maximum of propositional units evaluable as true or false. Only gradually and rather recently have intermediate structures such as noun- and verb phrases with their determinants, syntactic relations, nominal or pronominal substitutions, up to single speech acts or conversational turns become objects of inquiry.

In the following paragraphs we shall see how and why.

2. The structure of a query

2.1 Questions … about queries, questions and /or queries

Let us begin by stating whether a question and a query are the same.

A question is a sort of speech act, with its particular illocutionary force and standard structure.

In ordinary language, it is marked either by a typical intonation (in oral communication) or by a dedicated interpunction, a question mark (in written communication), often together with further markers, such as introductory interrogative lexical items (pronouns, adjectives, adverbs, such as the 5 *wh*), a typical word order (e.g. VSO vs. SVO etc.), some special devices (auxiliary verbs, correlated adverbial or adjectival forms, such as, in English, 'to do', 'ever' vs. 'never', 'any' vs. 'some' etc.).

'Query' is the term used to define what users enter into a web search engine, in order to retrieve information. Its normal form is that of an item being identified as a query by being placed in a special field designed to be filled in with some subject, key-word or quotation in the context of a search-engine interface. Such a context helps the authors of queries to save time and energy in the self-activation of their queries as such. Formats for queries already serve as devices to make the subject of a query recognisable as such.

In computing, a query language is a language in which queries are passed to and information retrieved from a database or information system.

2.2 The problem of ranking and the struggle for escaping carelessness

Usually, grammars introduce interrogative structures after the affirmative ones.

Such an expository and explanatory order seems to suggest the idea of a sort of precedence in ranking of so-called declarative or assertive sentences vs. interrogative and also negative ones.

Is this ranking the right one?

a. On the linguistic/grammatical side, it seems more a matter of didactical priorities than of intrinsic communicative dynamics. In fact, answers follow questions. Furthermore, both in interrogative and in declarative moods negation comes as a meta-operation, something which intervenes upon an already imposed structure, a super-imposed structure.
b. Another trend in favour of such ranking has been the long-held attitude in philosophy of considering only statements as sentences *par excellence*. Their excellence is due to their relationship to truth. They were known as *orationes perfectae*, both in the sense of accomplished, (and therefore complete), utterances, and in the sense of being able to reach the top, the truth. Austin calls such an overestimation of declarative sentences compared to all other kinds of sentences a 'descriptive fallacy': "To overlook these possibilities in the way once common is called the 'descriptive' fallacy". Which possibilities? "It was for too long the assumption of philosophers - Austin claims - that the business of a 'statement' can only be to 'describe' some states of affairs, or to 'state some fact', which it must do either truly or falsely. ... But now, in recent years, many things which would once have been accepted without question as 'statements' by both philosophers and grammarians have been scrutinized with new care. ... First came the view ... that a statement (of fact) ought to be 'verifiable', and this led to the view that many 'statements' are only what may be called pseudo-statements. First and most obviously, many 'statements' were shown to be ... strictly nonsense... so that it was natural to go on to ask, as a second stage, whether many apparent pseudo-statements really set out to be 'statements' at all. ... for example, 'ethical propositions' are perhaps intended, solely or partly, to evince emotion or to prescribe conduct or to influence it in special ways. ... It has come to be seen that many special perplexing words embedded in apparently descriptive statements do not serve to indicate some specially odd additional feature in the reality reported, but to indicate (not to report) the circumstances in which the statement is made or reservations to which it is subject or the way in which it is to be taken and the like."(Austin, 1962). We shall return to this fallacy shortly.

2.3 Different kinds of questions: yes-no questions vs. completive questions, closed vs. open questions

In any case, what traditionally has contributed to establishing such a questionable ranking, or the idea that interrogative structures are modifications, transformations[1] of declarative

[1] Cf. (Chomsky, 1957) and beyond, minimalism included (Chomsky, 1995), for his transformational grammar.
Indeed, "Under generativist approaches, non-subject questions - like passives – are formed by movement. However, whereas passives are formed by NP-movement, questions are formed by movement of the auxiliary from I to C (**subject-auxiliary inversion**) and - for *wh*-questions – by movement of the *wh*-word from within VP to SPEC CP (***wh*-movement**) [...]. Interestingly – observe Ben Ambridge and Elena V.M. Lieven – a preferential-looking study [...] has shown that children aged

ones, is, in my opinion, an unconscious preference shown towards one kind of questions only, the so-called "oriented" ones.

In a case such as:

1. Peter won the game →
2. Did Peter win the game? the proper order seems to be the proposed one. But if we consider
3. Who won the game? or
4. What did Peter win?

(3) and (4) clearly show that to ask is something which comes first - has a certain priority - in the development of our knowledge, and pushes forward the development of knowledge itself[2].

According to the usual classification, interrogative sentences are of two kinds: partial and general, completive (wh-questions) or oriented (yes-no questions)[3].

The purpose of completive questions is to inquire about the identity of a missing element in the information available to the speaker. The questioned identity may be that of a person

---

as young as 1;8 are able to respond appropriately (i.e. differentially) to subject and object *wh*-questions (*What hit the book?* Vs. *What did the book hit?*), suggesting early knowledge of (from a generativist perspective) inversion.
The challenge for generativist account is therefore to explain why, given that knowledge of subject-auxiliary inversion is acquired early (or, indeed, is innate), errors are relatively common among learners of English. […] Most common are **non-inversion** (or **uninversion**) **errors** (e.g. **What she can eat?* […] where the auxiliary appears in post-subject position. Various types of **auxiliary-doubling errors** are also observed, particularly for negative questions (e.g. **What does she doesn't like*?) […]
Under constructivist approaches, questions are not formed by movement. Rather, questions are independent constructions and undergo the same acquisition process as any other: children begin with rote-learned holophrases (e.g. *What is he doing?; What is he eating?*) and gradually schematize across these to form low-level lexically specific slot-and-frame-patterns (e.g. *What is [THING] [PROCESS]?*). Finally, children analogize across these schemas (or instances of these schemas in the form of actual utterances) to yield fully abstract constructions (e.g. *Wh-word AUX SUBJECT VERB?*).
The prediction of this account is that children will show effects of lexical-specificity: they will show good performance with question that can be formed using a well-learned schema, but poor performance for questions where a ready-made schema is unavailable and a more creative strategy is acquired. […] Rowland and Pine (2000: 164) argue that 'the child lexically specific knowledge is likely to centre round wh-word + auxiliary combinations, rather than auxiliary + subject combinations' [apparently, completive rather than oriented questions]. This is because the range of *wh*-words and auxiliaries is relatively narrow (perhaps especially in speech to young children), whereas the range of subjects is potentially infinite." (Ambridge, Lieven, 2011).
Concluding their paragraphs about the acquisition of questions, Ambridge and Lieven propose some solutions for both the generativist approach and the constructivist one, such as "to posit some role for lexical learning" in the first case, or to specify "the precise nature of the early schemas themselves", "to explain precisely how children move from lexically-specific construction schemas to a fully abstract *wh*-question construction".
Evidently, such an interesting "theoretical contrasting" should be developed not only about English as an object-language, but also about highly typologically differentiated languages.

[2] The skill of asking questions seems typical of humans and cannot be learned by primates, not even by those who were trained to learn human languages: see Jordania (2006).

[3] See, among others, Gobber, 1999, Weber 1993.

('who'), a thing ('what'), a time ('when'), a place ('where'), or a reason ('why'), according to the typical pronominal or adverbial heads of interrogative phrases.

The purpose of oriented questions is to ascertain the truth or falsity of a statement, or at least to make explicit the assent or dissent given by the addressee to the state of affairs under question.

Both completive and oriented questions belong to the so-called "closed" questions, because the task given to the answerer is a rather quick and delimited one. Alternatively, "open" questions are those which cannot be answered in a way correspondent to the structure of the question, i.e. just confirming or disconfirming the set-up orientation, or by just completing the missing constituent. Open questions are those which require an active and long-lasting cooperation by the addressee: the task of answering has to be articulated step by step, and it is not excluded that the goal of a definite answer cannot be achieved. Some well-known or lesser known questions remain open for a long time, even for centuries[4].

2.4 A larger scale: questions vs. requests

Beyond these two classes of questions another kind of speech acts needs to be recalled: that of requests. Latin distinguished these two acts at a lexical level: while *petere* means "to ask" for knowledge, *quaerere* means "to ask" in order to obtain something. 'Queries' may just be questions asked in order to obtain/retrieve information.

The distinction between questions and requests always deserves to be taken into consideration, in order to avoid that "intellectualistic" or theoreticist attitude, according to which we just speak for the sake of knowledge. As Austin claimed, with words we do things. Nevertheless we have to bear in mind that sometimes we ask questions instead of requiring something, accomplishing a so-called indirect speech act: e.g., when we ask "are you getting down at the next stop?", when we need to get past to get off the bus.

This whole family of speech acts (asking questions, making requests etc.) was already included by Wittgenstein in his *Philosophical Investigations*[5] among the (almost innumerable) language games which he claimed needed to be taken into consideration without restricting one's attention to declarative sentences.

It was quite probably "the first" Wittgenstein, i.e. the author of the *Tractatus Logico-Philosophicus*, that Austin had especially (but not exclusively) in mind when he reminded philosophers of the descriptive fallacy. "Grammarians, indeed", - Austin admitted – "have regularly pointed out that not all 'sentences' are [used in making] statements: there are, traditionally, besides (grammarians') statements, also questions and exclamations, and sentences expressing commands or wishes or concessions " (Austin, 1962). In any case, the difficult balance between assertiveness and its counterparts deserves to be put in evidence much earlier, in the roots of Western philosophical tradition. After Plato's sympathetic witnessing of Socrates' midwifing ability, with its connected erotetic method (the art of asking questions), a whole tradition came down to us, according to which apophantic speech only (the term is Aristotelic: declaratory) had to be considered in logic. Questions,

[4] http://www.openquestions.com/
[5] §§ 21-23.

being neither true nor false, disappeared from the philosophical investigations for a long time.

This happened in spite of the role assigned by Aristoteles himself to wonder: "For it is owing to their wonder that men both now begin and at first began to philosophize; they wondered originally at the obvious difficulties, then advanced little by little and stated difficulties about the greater matters, e.g. about the phenomena of the moon and those of the sun and of the stars, and about the genesis of the universe" (*Metaphysics*, Book I).

A pioneer's exception in introducing questions in logic was Richard Whately's *Elements of Logic* (1826), which included erotetic logic (see now Brozek, 2011), i.e. the logic of questioning. "Every Argument" - he writes - "consists of two parts; that which is *proved;* and that *by means of which* it is proved: the former is called, *before* it is proved, the *question; when proved,* the *conclusion* (or *inference*)" (Whately, 1826). Thus questions move inferential activity. Furthermore, Whately devotes two chapters of his work to introducing proper distinctions, the ignorance of which produces "*undetected* Verbal Questions and fruitless Logomachy".

Such distinctions - warns Whately - allow us to avoid confusion between Verbal and Real Questions. "For to trace any error to its source, will often throw more light on the subject in hand than can be obtained if we rest satisfied with merely detecting and refuting it."(*ibid.*). Such was his reply to George Cambell's *Philosophy of Rhetoric* (1776), where he had "maintained, or rather assumed, that Logic is applicable to Verbal controversy alone". Evidently Whately intended to sweep away those controversies which are merely verbal, in order to deal just with those which are genuine, real ones.

He states: "*Every* Question that can arise, is in fact a Question whether a certain Predicate is or is not applicable to a certain subject, or *what* Predicate is applicable [...]. But sometimes the Question turns on the meaning and extent of the *terms* employed; sometimes on the *things* signified by them. If it be made to appear, therefore, that the opposite sides of a certain Question may be held by persons not differing in their *opinion of the matter* in hand, then that Question may be pronounced Verbal; as depending on the different senses in which they respectively employ the *terms*. If, on the contrary, it appears that they employ the terms in the same sense, but still differ as to the application of one of them to the other, then it may be pronounced that the Question is Real, that they differ as to the opinions they hold of the *things* in Question. [...] It is by no means to be supposed that all Verbal Questions are trifling and frivolous; it is often of the highest importance to settle correctly the meaning of a word, either according to ordinary use, or according to the meaning of any particular writer, or class of men; but when Verbal Questions are *mistaken* for Real, much confusion of thought and unprofitable wrangling will be generally the result. [...] It is evidently of much importance to keep in mind the above distinctions, in order to avoid, on the one hand, stigmatizing as Verbal controversies, what in reality are not such, merely because the Question turns on the applicability of a certain Predicate to a certain subject; or, on the other hand, falling into the opposite error of mistaking words for things, and judging of men's agreement or disagreement in opinion in every case, merely from their agreement or disagreement in the terms employed." (Whately, 1826).

2.5 Performing questions / queries and formalising them

This connection between judgement and agreement should lead to overcoming the threshold that divides the theoretical and practical sides involved in our subject, questions and queries.

Indeed, Austin plays an important role in opening[6] new paths to pragmatics, identifying the character of questions, promises and the like.

"To perform a locutionary act is in general, we may say, also and *eo ipso* to perform an *illocutionary* act, as I propose to call it. To determine what illocutionary act is so performed we must determine in what way we are using the locution: asking or answering a question [...] When we perform a locutionary act, we use speech: but in what way precisely are we using it on this occasion? [...] These issues penetrate a little but not without confusion into grammar [...], but we constantly do debate them, in such terms as whether certain words (a certain locution) *had the force of* a question, or *ought to have been taken as* an estimate and so on. [...] I shall refer to [...] the doctrine of 'illocutionary forces'" (Austin, 1962).

It was few years later, in 1969, that John Searle published *Speech Acts*. In the very first pages it was stated: "The unit of linguistic communication is not, as has generally been supposed, the symbol, word or sentence, or even the token of the symbol, word or sentence, but rather the production or issuance of the symbol, word or sentence in the performance of the speech act." (Searle, 1969). " The general form of (many kinds of) illocutionary acts is

$$F\ (p)$$

where the variable "F" takes illocutionary force indicating devices as values and "*p*" takes expressions for propositions. We can symbolize different kinds of illocutionary acts in the form, e.g.,

$\vdash (p)$ for assertions
$!\ (p)$ for requests
$Pr\ (p)$ for promises
$W\ (p)$ for warnings
$?\ (p)$ for yes - no questions

and so on. Except for yes-no questions the symbolism for questions must represent propositional functions and not complete proposition, because except in yes -no questions the speaker asking a question does not express a complete proposition. Thus, "How many people were at the party?" is represented as

? (*X* number of people were at the party)

"Why did he do it?" is represented as

---

[6] For truth's sake, the evaluation about who opens what is the result of a historical judgement. To be well informed and impartial, the historians of culture and ideas should open their views towards the global scene: what happens, on the contrary, is too often that different kinds of barriers (linguistic, ideological, due to mutually ignored traditions and so on) forbid such a world-wide view. On our specific subject, a widespread mistake or simply a naiveté is to take the deep and well-known unity of pragmatics belonging to the English-speaking world of analytic philosophy as the very first trend in metalinguistic thought overcoming the gap between theoretic and pragmatic approach, viewing the speaking activity as related not only to the domain of knowledge, but also to that of action. Just confining ourselves to the Western/Central European situation, we shouldn't ignore the old and large stream of German-speaking scholars, who however do not belong to/create an actual common school, such as Bernard Bolzano, Gottlob Frege, Alexius Meinong. They all well understood that questions do not only reveal a lack of something, but also compel their addressees to fill such a gap. See Gobber, 2011.

? (He did it because ...)

But "Did you do it?", a yes –no question, is represented as

? (You did it)

In so far as we confine our discussion to simple subject predicate propositions, with a singular definite referring term as subject, we can represent the distinctions in the form

F (RP)

"*R*" for the referring expression and the capital *P* for the predicating expression." (Searle, 1969, as the following table).

		Request	*Question*
	Propositional Content	Future act *A* of *H*	Any proposition or propositional function
	Preparatory	1. *H* is able to do *A*. *S* believes *H* is able to do *A*. 2. It is not obvious to both *S* and *H* that *H* will do *A* in the normal course of events of his own accord.	1. *S* does not know "the answer", i.e., does not know if the proposition is true, or, in the case of the propositional function, does not know the information needed to complete the proposition truly (but see comment below). 2. It is not obvious to both *S* and *H* that *H* will provide the information at that time without being asked.[7]
Types of rules	Sincerity	*S* wants *H* to do *A*.	*S* wants this information.
	Essential	Counts as an attempt to get *H* to do *A*.	Counts as an attempt to elicit this information from *H*.
	Comment	*Order* and *command* have the additional preparatory rule that *S* must be in a position of authority over *H*. *Command* probably does not have the 'pragmatic' condition requiring non-obviousness. Furthermore in both, the authority relationship infects the essential condition because the utterance counts as an attempt to get *H* to do *A in virtue of the authority of S over H.*	There are two kind of questions (*a*) real questions, (*b*) exam questions. In real questions *S* wants to know (find out) the answer; in exam questions, *S* wants to know if *H* knows.

Table 1. Types of illocutionary act.

[7] A further preparatory rule should be: "S believes that H knows 'the answer', i.e. if the proposition is true or, in case of propositional function, the element needed to complete the proposition truly". I owe the suggestion of this addition to Aldo Frigerio.

In 1985 Searle and Vanderveken publish *Foundations of Illocutionary Logic*. Questions are, once more, mentioned among speech acts considered as illocutionary acts. Therefore questions too consist of an illocutionary force F and a propositional content P. Illocutionary logic aims to formalize the logical properties of illocutionary forces. In the case of questions, the authors consider requests and asks within the class of English directives.

According to the meanings attributed to the occurring symbols[8], definitions of 'request' and 'ask' are as follows:

"*request* (!)

A request is a directive illocution that allows for the possibility of refusal. A request can be granted or refused by the hearer. Thus ‖request‖ differs from ‖direct ‖only by the fact that mode (‖request‖) (i, P) = I iff $i \hat{\prod}_{!} P$ and the speaker in i allows the hearer the possibility of refusing to carry out the future course of action represented by P. "Request" is the paradigmatic directive verb, but since it is special in having a rather polite mode of achievement of its illocutionary point, it cannot be taken as the primitive directive.

ask.

"Ask" has two quite distinct uses. One is in the notion of asking a question and the second is in the notion of asking someone to do something. Questions are always directives, for they are attempts to get the hearer to perform a speech act. In the simple directive sense, "ask" names the same illocutionary force as "request". In the sense of "ask a question" it means request that the hearer perform a speech act to the speaker, the form of which is already determined by the propositional content of the question. Thus if the question is a yes-no question requesting an assertive, the speaker expresses the propositional content of the answer in asking the question; and all that the hearer is asked to do is affirm or deny that propositional content. For example, to ask someone whether it is raining is to request him to perform a true assertion with the propositional content that it is or that it is not raining.

The illocutionary force of the illocutionary act that is requested to be performed in case of asking a question is not necessarily assertive. When the minister in the wedding chapel asks "Do you take this woman to be your lawful wedded wife?", he is asking for a response

---

[8] ‖ ‖ is the function that assigns to each illocutionary verb the force or type of speech act that it names;
i is a variable for possible contexts of utterance;
P is a variable for propositions;
$\hat{\prod}$ names a relation between contexts of utterance and propositions that determines the condition of commitment to illocutionary point $\prod$;
I names the integer one or the truth value: truth, or the success value : success;
$\in$ is the sign of membership;
Prop names the set of all propositions;
A is a variable for illocutionary acts;
b_i is a variable for hearers;
a_i is a variable for speakers; it names the speaker of context of utterance i;
t is a variable for moments of time;
l is a variable for places of utterance;
w is a variable for possible words
Prop $_{\|ask\|}$ (i) is the set of all propositions which respect the conditions imposed by the illocutionary force ‖ask‖ on the propositional content P in a context i.

("Yes I do", or "No I do not") that is a declaration and not an assertion. Thus ‖ask‖ (in the simple directive sense) = ‖request‖ and ‖ask?‖ in the sense of yes-no question differs from ‖direct‖ only by the fact that $P \in \text{Prop}_{\|ask\|}(i)$ iff, for some illocution A, $P(w) = 1$ iff for some $t > t_i$, A is performed in $< b_i, a_i, t, l, w >$.

In wh-questions the form of the question contains a propositional function, and the hearer is requested to fill in a value of the free variable in the propositional function in such a way as to produce a true complete proposition. Thus, for example, the question "How many people went to the party?" is of the form "I request you, you tell me the correct value of x in 'x number of people went to the party'." A full characterization of the logical form of wh-questions cannot be made in this study, because it would require the definition of the notions of a property, a relation and an elementary proposition, all of which are part of first order illocutionary logic." (Searle, Vanderveken, 1985).

2.6 Triggers

Sometimes old mythology helps to show simply and synthetically the deep roots - the foundations - of what technical treatments of ever-green topics just foreshadow.

If we read Plato's Symposion, we find the story told by Diotima to Socrates about the birth of Eros (love) from Poros (Πόρος, "resource" or "plenty") and Penia (Πενία, poverty).[9] According to Plato, love "is also a philosopher: or lover of wisdom, and being a lover of wisdom is in a mean between the wise and the ignorant."

This tale can serve as a helpful hint to understand the formal affinity between indefinite and interrogative adjectives/pronouns: constantly related throughout typologically different languages[10].

What does this structural similarity mean? It underlines the strong relationship between lack of determinacy (poverty) and the need to overcome it (in order to attain plentifulness). If somebody is not able to determine, to define something, s/he is in a position of having to ask somebody else to fill this gap. To be in this position does not necessarily imply acting upon it, adopting those decisions, using those devices where triggers such as *wh*-words are at work for retrieving missing information, for extracting knowledge, mining data or for receiving the cooperation requested.

---

[9] "What then is Love?" I asked; "Is he mortal?" "No." "What then?" "As in the former instance, he is neither mortal nor immortal, but in a mean between the two." "What is he, Diotima?" "He is a great spirit (daimon), and like all spirits he is intermediate between the divine and the mortal." "And what," I said, "is his power?" "He interprets," she replied, "between gods and men, conveying and taking across to the gods the prayers and sacrifices of men, and to men the commands and replies of the gods; he is the mediator who spans the chasm which divides them, and therefore in him all is bound together, and through him the arts of the prophet and the priest, their sacrifices and mysteries and charms, and all, prophecy and incantation, find their way. For God mingles not with man; but through Love all the intercourse, and converse of god with man, whether awake or asleep, is carried on. The wisdom which understands this is spiritual; all other wisdom, such as that of arts and handicrafts, is mean and vulgar. Now these spirits or intermediate powers are many and diverse, and one of them is Love. "And who," I said, "was his father, and who his mother?" "The tale," she said, "will take time; nevertheless I will tell you…" The tale can be read in The Internet Classics Archive:
http://classics.mit.edu//Plato/symposium.html.

[10] http://wals.info/chapter/46

We are all familiar with the expression "to break the ice". To ask proper questions at the right moment may be a good way to break the ice. But sometimes it is so difficult to detect the extension and the boundaries of what we ignore that no questions arise, whereas at some other times correct, precise, punctual questions addressed to the right addressee at the right moment can pave the way to quite important self-disclosures, intelligent and far-seeing insights, real turning points. The quality of interviews and interrogatories depends on the skills of their authors and on the cooperation they are able to gain.

There are crucial structures which are capable of building answers, as well as questions and requests. These structures are the strategic means to order words syntactically and semantically, in a way which is suitable for "filling" the gaps (of knowledge/action) identified by questions/requests; strategic insofar as they themselves are non-saturated tools, unaccomplished structures, and yet still able to activate accomplishments, and form a bridge to the expected items.

Predication is such a structure, propositional functions are its developments on the way towards complete propositions.

3. The structure of an answer

3.1 From interrogative/indefinite items to definite references

Basically, an answer looks like an assertion (affirmative or negative) or a consent / refusal, perhaps accompanied by the requested action or even converted into it, without words. It depends on the trigger, whether a question or a request[11].

According to Paul Grice, in order for our wording to be effective, our interaction with one another has to follow the "cooperative principle": "make your contribution such as it is required, at the stage at which it occurs, by the accepted purpose or direction of the talk exchange in which you are engaged."

To complement a question or a request means, therefore, to replace indefiniteness with definiteness, thanks to the force appointed to an item to be fulfilled or to the confirmation/disconfirmation of the suspended orientation included.

Too often these alternative possibilities have been replaced in the metalinguistic representation by an oversimplification, i.e. by the reduction of answers to judgements, because of the importance of truth values.

Our choice here, however, is whatever the reply is, to consider its core, or rather the condition of the possibility not only of answers but of queries too; that is to say predication and the structure it involves.

Generally speaking, predicates are conceived as terms of a relation, the output of the act of saying something about something else, of attributing (or applying) something to something

---

[11] Nevertheless, we have to consider this distinction not as a clear-cut one: indeed with the notion of indirect speech act Searle recalls that "for example, a speaker may utter the sentence *Can you reach the salt?* and mean it not merely as a question but as a request to pass the salt [...], cases in which one illocutionary act is performed indirectly by way of performing another." (Searle, 1975)

else, as expressions of properties or relations belonging to one or more objects, or the result of making concepts fall into one another.

Actually, in logical-grammatical training, we meet predicates first. Predication as such remains in the background. On the contrary, it is consistent with a pragmatic framework to put the act first and its result afterwards.

Our claim is that without predication we cannot ensure neither the right assessment of the interrogative items in questions (where *wh*-placeholders need to be substituted and their empty place filled), nor the nuclear structure upon which the illocutionary force of the answers can be exerted.

Moreover, we think that while underlining predication as a main device, at the same time we show answers as works in progress, towards the identification of definite references or events, or towards the definition of a yes- or no-answer. In fact, if we consider that, according to a certain semantic paradigm (the Fregean and the Neo-fregean one), truth values are the referents of assertions, we can say that predication allows answers to gain reference both locally and globally (at the level of single constituents and at the level of whole sentences, if assertive, as such).

Once the primacy of the act of predication upon predicates and consequently upon predication as a result is stated (words like predic-*ation* always work both as a *nomen actionis* and as a *nomen rei actae*), we can proceed as follows:

- first we will treat predication as the basic syntagmatic act,
- then we will see its correlates and
- eventually we will consider the whole structure it builds, from the point of view of the two main paradigms according to which such a structure has been conceived, the Aristotelian and the Fregean one.

3.2 The basic syntagmatic act is predication

Let us consider the etymology of 'predicate', in English a noun with exactly the same form as the verb (but in the infinitive, not participle mood). Why is this so? According to the reconstruction offered by the Oxford English Dictionary 'predicate' comes from "Middle French *predicat* (French *prédicat*) that which is said of a subject (1370), quality (1466) and its etymon post-classical Latin *praedicatum*[12] that which is said of a subject (6th cent. in Boethius; earlier in senses doctrine, precept (4th cent.), prediction (late 2nd or early 3rd cent. in Tertullian), use as noun of neuter past participle of classical Latin *praedicāre.* ".

Therefore, if somebody predicates something of something else or of somebody else, then we obtain predicates. We can sum up the whole scene as a predication. Why do I underline such an obvious remark? Because sometimes this "ontogenetic", dynamic reconstruction has been forgotten, leaving as a result the static relation between predicates and their correlates as ready-made.

---

[12] Gr. *kategoroúmenon*, from *kategoréo*, a typical expression recalling the *agorà* in the *polis*, and its role of attracting citizens called to select (*katà*, in front of everybody, publicly) candidates submitted to public evaluation for the future governance of the *polis* itself.

Beyond this, what was the result of an operation of junction and construction has been considered to be something already given, to be analysed, resolved into its parts. This is why traditionally we became acquainted with the practise of grammatical *analysis* centred upon the parts of speech (the whole, i.e. the speech, remaining almost completely out of systematic consideration), and with the practice of logical *analysis* centred upon logical terms (literally, ends of the proposition: see predicate calculus), rather than upon the unity of proposition itself and of propositions with each other (propositional calculus).

Moreover, the two analyses tended towards reciprocal emancipation: instead of a systematic correlation among forms and functions, a frequent matter was that of the "liberation" or "emancipation" of grammar from the yoke of logic and of logic from the yoke of grammar[13].

This caused some confusions and worry throughout long history of Western logic and philosophy.

It would be useful, to begin with, to recall that some technical terms on the matter could work, as *predication*, both as *nomina actionis* and as *nomina rei actae*, such as *articulation, proposition* and *function*. Similarly, not only *predicate*, but also *subject* come from Latin *praedicatum* and *subjectum*, in their turn translations of the past *and* passive Greek participles *kategoroumenon* and *hypokeimenon*: the first one a real passive form, the latter an interesting deponent.

But what could be seen "on the run" was, and still is, rather considered as an achieved goal.

Two independent developments in the 20th century helped to change this point of view, in linguistics as well as in philosophy, the first, functionalism in classical structuralism and the second, pragmatics in analytical philosophy.

"*The basic syntagmatic act,* and at the same time the intrinsic sentence-forming act, is *the predication*", states the second of the 1929 theses of the Prague Linguistic Circle (Vachek 1983). Behind the collective authorship of that text, there was one particular author, Vilém Mathesius, the founder of the Circle, with his syntactical investigations[14]. In 1926 he wrote:

[13] See (Sériot, Samain, 2008), with a precious extension of the *status quaestionis* to Eastern European and Russian studies.

[14] Although being a detail in the huge panorama here sketchily outlined, it is worth mentioning the particular approach developed by Mathesius himself and by a Swedish Anglicist he quotes as well, K.F. Sundén, in the previous decades (Sundén 1904, 1916) : they both ended up researching "sentencehood" through predic*ation*, and elliptical predication especially, i.e. through effective, though reduced structures, deviating from the canonical bi-member sentences, yet recognisable and understandable as true sentences only via a cooperative inference of the addressee, who had to capture specific semantic intentions orienting each act of predication. Sundén (1916) begins his essay *The Predicational Categories in English* thus: "It is a matter of general observation that the connexion between subject and predicate may from a semological point of view be of different kinds. We are not then alluding to the particular and accidental relation brought about by the different tenses, moods or tense-aspects of the predicate, but to the general qualification of the subject conditioned by the material import of the predicate itself. In other words, we are referring to the different manners in which the predicate qualifies the subject. It

"A full analysis of the basic grammatical function - e.g. the function of the subject and predic*ation*, [...] the real nature of sentence form*ation* - can be achieved only with the help of the static [not genetically comparative] method by which linguistic phenomena are not unduly separated from the *action of speaking*. [...] In the field of *syntax* the general shift of interest from the external aspect of *language* to its *inner life* is exemplified by the emphasizing of the stylistic principle and by the substitution of the functional conception for the traditional formal point of view. Finer methods of linguistic analysis have brought *to light the importance of what I should call the* double-faced character of linguistic phenomena. It consists [of] a *continuous fluctuation between the general and the individual*. [...] Linguistic research can either concentrate on what has already become a common possession of all members of the linguistic community or it can study the individual efforts of linguistic creation. The traditional school of linguistics has so exclusively limited itself to the study of commonly accepted means of expression that the individual speaker has disappeared from its ken. As a reaction against this too objective conception of language, a school of an extreme linguistic subjectivism chiefly represented by Professor K. Vossler has appeared, which following the ideas of Wilhelm von Humboldt and Benedetto Croce regards the act of linguistic expression as something [as] individual as artistic creation. [...] The proposition maintained by Professor Spitzer '*Nihil est in syntaxi quod non fuerit in stylo*' very clearly shows how the greatest stress is laid by him and his friends on the individual share in linguistic expression. Linguistics as a whole can derive from stylistic syntax and stylistic semasiology a double benefit. [But, Mathesius replies,] It is good that the rule, often neglected, has been emphasized again [...] In the study of language, of course, individual utterances are analysed as specimens of the linguistic possibilities of the whole community... . The time has really come for general linguistic problems to be systematically studied. [...] The basic functions of linguistic expression should be analysed and the means of linguistic expression catalogued. This means *showing how in all kinds of languages the subject and the predicate are expressed*, which are *the possible forms of* the active, passive, perceptive, qualificative, possessive, etc. *predication*, how the attributive qualification is expressed, *which aspects* of activity or of status *can be expressed in the predication*, etc. It is self-evident that such problems cannot be solved but by the functional and static [i.e. synchronic, as opposed to diachronic] method of research." (Mathesius, 1926; italics mine).

---

is this difference that should be the leading principle for a classification of the predicative connexions [...] or for short 'predication'. [...] Thus 'connexion' is meant to denote one of the two principal categories of combination of morphemes that occur in language ['connexion', term employed by Noreen, on the whole corresponding to Wundt's '*geschlossene Wortgruppe*', as implies that a principal and an accessory element are being combined, in this case equivalent to a subject and a predicate, in contradistinction to 'adjunctive (adjundct) connexion' (Wundt's '*offene Wortverbindung*', that implies a combination already made between a principal and an accessory member, in this case a determinatum and a determinandum: *the laughing child* vs. *the child is laughing*], the other [combination] being called 'adhexion', in which the members combined are independent of each other, e.g. 'You *and* I'; 'he is reading, *but* she is writing'.
A distinction of the different kinds of predicative connexion as met with in Indo-European languages, has not yet been instituted by current grammar. This neglect renders it difficult, may impossible to deal properly with the predicational changes of verbs [...] It is indispensable to make this classification if we want to view the verbal changes of meaning we are going to deal with [the phenomenon of transitive verbs used in English as predicate-verbs in the active form with a passive sense: close (of a flower), conjoin (of roots), divide (of a shell)], in the light of their predicational functions."

In a nutshell, syntagmatic acts precede syntax as composition precedes its metalinguistic analysis[15].

With a strong similarity, in his *Speech Acts* John Searle identifies predication and reference within the level of expressions, before inquiring into their meaning and their being speech acts. He states: "… in the utterance […] a speaker is characteristically performing at least three distinct kinds of acts: (*a*) the uttering of words (morphemes, sentences); (*b*) referring and predicating; *c*) stating, questioning, commanding, promising etc.

Let us assign names to these under the general heading of speech acts:

a. uttering words (morphemes, sentences) = performing *utterance acts.*
b. referring and predicating = performing *propositional acts.*
c. stating, questioning, commanding, promising etc. = performing *illocutionary acts.*

[…] The distinction between reference and predication holds, and the correct description is to say that the predicate expression is used to ascribe a property. I do not claim that this description has any *explanatory* power at all. Nobody who does not already have a prior understanding of what it is to use a predicate expression can understand this remark […] At this stage I only claim that it is literally true […] (Searle 1969).

Essentially, summing up cause and effect, act and result has to be done not only for the sake of completeness, but also on the assumption that linguistic structures and their semantics largely underdetermine their meanings and the meaning of their relations, which are often defined by the context in which they occur[16]. In other words: predicates are not prefab, they are just semi-processed products. They need to be determined within the sentences they belong to, and further assigned to the utterances they are constituents of.

Now that this primacy of predication upon predicates (so to speak) has been grasped, let us move on to the two main models about predicates, that of Aristotle and that of Frege[17].

Before sketching an essential outline of their doctrines, it is worth noting the wide influence of models, especially the Aristotelian one, with which not only philosophers became (and still become) acquainted, but also ordinary people, usually young pupils during their first years of school.

3.3 Predicates and their correlates, or the sentence as a unit

Predication is the act of predicating (saying) something about something else. So we have, *in nuce*, the legitimate expectancy of a second term of relation, of the predicative relation: what is predicated about.

---

[15] On this very point, of the border between generality and individuality, ten years later Mathesius stated: "The sentence is not entirely the product of a transitory moment, is not entirely determined by the individual situation, and, consequently, does not entirely belong to the sphere of speech, but depends in its general form on the grammatical system of the language in which it is uttered. […] In language we have the word in its conceptual meaning and the sentence as abstract pattern, whereas in speech we have the word as referring to concrete reality and the sentence as concrete utterance." (Mathesius 1936). See (Raynaud, 2008).

[16] See (Frigerio, 2010 a), (Frigerio, 2010 b).

[17] The eminency of Aristotle's and Frege's contributions throughout the whole history of logic are widely recognised: see (Dummett, 1973).

Nearly everybody would label this second term of relation 'subject', due to a more than bi-millenarian tradition: a really successful transmission of high culture (Aristotelian logic) to basic education, passed down from the school-teaching of ancient languages to that of modern ones, without so much as a blink.

This so well-known schema has induced and still induces another apparently obvious expectancy: that predication involves a two-element structure, be it a question or an answer, or whatever.

Rather than a relation, this should grant a correlation: if P, then C (= Correlate to P). Immediately after, or even simultaneously, a further if-then (→) prevision: if P, then S (= Subject).

But even the briefest glance at real conversations, texts, or messages of any sort would contradict such a prevision, a prevision to be contradicted in many ways, upwards and downwards. Sometimes only one element is enough, sometimes even five or six constituents take place. What has to be corrected? The idea of a correlation to be expected? Its structure as a regular two-element structure? Its epistemological status as a regulative ideal instead of a statistical regularity?

Let us proceed step by step.

Firstly:

The expectancy of a correlation is a legitimate one; on one condition however, that of recognising it as a regulative ideal only. This means that we cannot take for granted that in each sentence we will find such an evident correlation. We have elliptical sentences, condensed utterances, such as *'Why?', 'What?', 'Fire!', 'Come!' 'Yes.', 'No'*. Sometimes the predicate is absent /cut off because it is the same as in the previous sentence, sometimes it is present but includes the person it refers to, sometimes just an adverb of affirmation or negation is sufficient to substitute the whole predicative correlation. In any case the correlation seems, though not always , to be active.

But is the predicative relation always a relation to one element (typically the subject), i.e. a monadic relation?

The short (though not careless) answer should be: what is necessary is the unity of the sentence (query or answer), whether the unity be simple or complex.

If we look for a classical image suggesting the idea of one thing being able to look like (and also function as) two, we should recall the image of an elbow or of a knee: being part of an arm or leg does not prevent them articulating the movement of their own limbs. As demonstrated, this basic biological image supports the concept of *articulation,* an ancient and evergreen metalinguistic tool (Laspia, 1997).

Such a deep feeling of the original and fundamental unit of any sentence (in this case, specifically, and especially, queries and answers), and, at the same time, of the dynamic role of predication in the sentence, is well attested to by nearly all of the major authors , those who represent real milestones along the path of metalinguistic thought, such as Aristotle, Humboldt, Frege, Peirce, Bühler and Tesnière, to mention some of the most eminent.

Nevertheless, the tone with which this eminent choir has sung throughout the centuries deserves our careful attention.

Let us begin with Aristotle's insistence upon the "equivalence" between a noun and a definition (Laspia, 2005), expressed through a judgement of identity:

"Since definition [*horismòs*] means 'an account [*lógos*] of what a thing is', obviously one kind of definition will be an explanation [*lógos*] of the meaning of the name, or of an equivalent denomination [*e logos héteros onomatódes*]" (*Analytica posteriora* B 10, 93 b 29-31).

"The starting-point is from definition; and definition results from the necessity of [...] meaning something; because the formula, which [...] term implies, will be a definition." (*Metaphysica* Γ 7, 1012 a 23-4).

A reading of the whole dialogue "The Sophist" would be helpful in revealing the reasons why nouns and verbs came on to the philosophical scene: they actually fulfill the requirements of those who seek to discern truth from falsity, or rather of those who contrast the thesis of the indiscernibility of truth and falsity. From this point of view Plato and Aristotle are much closer to each other than usually thought. "Discourse is never composed of nouns alone spoken in succession, nor of verbs spoken without nouns. [...] For instance, 'walks', 'runs', 'sleeps' and the other verbs which denote actions, even if you utter all there are of them in succession, do not make discourse for all that. No, - replies Theaethetus to the Stranger - of course not. And again, when 'lion', 'stag', 'horse', and all other names of those who perform these actions are uttered, such a succession of words does not yet make discourse; for in neither case do the words uttered indicate action or inaction or existence of anything that exists or does not exist, until the verbs are mingled with the nouns; then the words fit, and their first combination [*symploké*] is a sentence, about the first and shortest form of discourse.[...] When one says 'a man learns' [...] he does not merely gives names, but he reaches a conclusion by combining (*symplékon*) verbs with nouns. [...] So, then, just as of things some fit each other and some do not, so too some vocal signs do not fit, but some of them do fit and form discourse (*lógos*)." (Plato *Sophista* 261 d - 262 e)

"Verbs by themselves, then, are nouns, and they stand for or signify something, for the speaker stops his process of thinking and the mind of the hearer acquiesces. However, they do not as yet express positive or negative judgements. [...] A sentence is significant speech, of which this or that part may have meaning - as something, that is, that is uttered but not as expressing a judgement of a positive or negative character. [...] But while every sentence has meaning, [...] not all can be called propositions." (*De interpretatione* 3, 16 b 22-5; 4, 16 b 27-29; 4, 17 a 1-4).

Although not all sentences prove to be units as in the case of a definition, Aristotle nevertheless explains what, in each case, keeps the noun and the verb together, the subject and the predicate: it is the verb 'to be', which paraphrases the relating function of the verb: "The two propositions, 'man walks', 'man is walking' mean just the same thing. "(*De interpretatione* 12, 21 b 9-10)

The term 'copula', although first introduced only in the XIIth century, by Abelard, and therefore not originally Aristotelian, with its huge diffusion, testifies to the "popularity" of the Aristotelian model.

We have already mentioned the objection of descriptive fallacy (§ 2.2) which can be recalled as important due to the reductionism of the proposed formalisation: S is P[18] .

Less attracted by the referential and defining purport of speech and more focused on its building dynamics is Humboldt's view.

Perhaps it would be worth mentioning the subjectivist turn (not yet about sentences, but rather concerning nouns and verbs) taken in the modern era and testified to by Arnauld and Lancelot's *Grammaire générale et raisonnée,*: "The subject of our thoughts, are either things, such as the earth, the sun, water, wood, what we normally call substance. Or the way things are; like being round, being red, being hard, being wise etc. what we call accidents. [...] Because those [the words] which refer to substance, are called "substantive nouns or names"; and those which refer to attributes, signalling the subject to which these attributes pertain, adjectival nouns.

And that is the origin of substantive and adjectival nouns. But we didn't stop there: and it so happens that we didn't so much stop at meaning [*signification*], but rather at the manner of meaning [*manière de signifier*]. Because the substance is what exists in its own right, we have given the name substantive nouns to all those which exist by themselves in the discourse, without needing any other name, even if they signify accidents. [...] The verb itself should have no other use than to signify the link that we make in our minds between the two terms of the proposition. But there is only the verb "to be" which we call substantive which has this simplicity, we can even say that it only has this simplicity in the third person of the present tense, "is" and in certain contexts."(Arnauld-Lancelot, 1660; italics, beyond examples and technical terms, are mine).

The reflexion on language takes its leave of an insurmountable correspondence between linguistic and world structures. The shape of speech -as is now accepted - depends largely on the activity of speakers. Wilhelm von Humboldt, after a life-long and world-wide empirical research on languages, sums up his theoretical views with great efficacy:

"*Framing the sentence.* The grammatically formed *word* [...] in the composition of its elements, and in its unity as a whole, is destined to enter, again as an element, into the *sentence.* So language must here form, higher unity - higher, not merely because it is of greater extent, but also because it depends more exclusively on the ordering inner form of the sense of language, in that sound can only operate on it an auxiliary fashion. [...] If *we start from the sentence, as is originally more correct, since every utterance, however incomplete, does really constitute a closed thought in the speaker's mind,* then languages which employ this method [as the Mexican] by no means shatter the unity of the sentence, but try, rather, to knit its construction even more tightly together. But they manifestly derange the boundaries of verbal unity by carrying them over into the domain of sentential unity. [...] The Mexican method of incorporation testifies in this to a correct sense of sentence-formation, that it attaches the designation of its relations precisely to the verb, and thus to the point at which the sentence ties itself together into unity. [...]

---

[18] While attending corpus linguistics studies, I was prompted to reconsider the role of predication in the vast field of illocutionary forces and in relation to a variety of objects. It was a rather shocking experience, similar to that of going out in the open air rather than contemplating a panorama from a single window.

Sound forms and grammatical requirements. Grammatical formation arises from the *laws of thinking* in language, and rests on the *congruence of sound-forms* with the latter. [...] But deficiency on the one point always reacts back at once upon the other. The perfecting of language demands that every word be stamped as a specific *part of speech*, and carry within it those properties that a philosophical analysis perceives therein. It thus itself presupposes inflection. So the question now is as to how the simplest part of completed language formation, the minting of a word by *inflection* into a part of speech, can be supposed to proceed within the mind of a people? Reflective *consciousness* of the language cannot be presumed in connection with its origin, and would also harbour no creative power for the forming of sounds. Every advantage that a language possesses in this truly vital portion of its organism proceeds originally from the living *sensory world-outlook.* [...] An intuition proceeding from the liveliest and most harmonious exertion of powers exhausts everything presented in the intuited, and does not confound the particular, but separates it out in clarity. Now from recognition of this dual relation of objects, from the feeling of their right relationship and the vividness of the impression evoked by each one of them, inflection[19] arises, as if automatically, as the verbal expression of what is intuited and felt.

At the same time, however, it is remarkable to see in what various ways the mental outlook arrives here at *sentence-formation.* It does not set out from a prototype, does not laboriously put the sentence together, but achieves this without any forethought, in that it merely confers shape in sound upon the sharp and fully-registered impression of the object. In that this happens correctly each time, and according to the same feeling, the thought becomes coordinated out of the words so formed. [...]

Spontaneous positing in languages. There are points in the grammatical structure of languages at which this synthesis, and the power that produces it, come nakedly and directly in view, as it were, and with which all the rest of the language-structure is then also necessarily most intimately connected. Since *the synthesis* we are speaking of *is not a state [Beschaffenheit], nor even properly a deed [Handlung], but itself a real action,* always passing with the moment, there can be no special *sign* for it in the words, and the endeavour to find such a sign would already in itself bear witness to a lack of true strength in the act, in that its nature was misunderstood. The real presence of the synthesis must reveal itself *immaterially,* as it were, in the language. [...] We may call this act in general - as I have done here in this particular case [if, in a language, a root is marked out by a suffix as a substantive] - the act of *spontaneous positing* by bringing-together (synthesis). It recurs everywhere in language. [...]

The *verb* (to speak first of this by itself) *differs in a sharply determinate way from the noun,* and from the other parts of speech that might possibly occur in a simple sentence, in that to it alone is assigned the act of *synthetic positing* as a grammatical function. Like the declined noun, it arose through such an act, in the fusion of its elements, with the stem, but it has also received this form in order to have the office and capacity of itself again performing this act with regard to the sentence. Between it and the other words of the simple sentence, there is therefore a difference which forbids us to count it along with them in the same category. *All the other words of the sentence are like dead matter lying there for combination; the verb alone is the*

[19] Regarding Leibniz's idea of reducing relations to properties, and therefore the possibility of conceiving, for instance, a declinable root of a verb, with the entities around it as a basis of property with its modifications, see (Orilia, 2000).

centre, containing and disseminating life. Through one and the same synthetic act, it conjoins, by *being*, the *predicate* with the *subject*, yet in such a way that the being which passes, with an energetic predicate, into an action, becomes attributed to the subject itself, so that what is *thought* as merely capable of conjunction becomes, in *reality*, a state or process. [...] *The thought, if one may put it so concretely, departs through the verb, from its inner abode, and steps across into reality.*" (Humboldt, 1999; italics added).

We note with surprise both the profound consonance and the logical and semantic refinement which are apparent between these last lines and the following, written some decades later (1835-1892), always in Germany, by Gottlob Frege:

"[...] In every judgement, [a judgement, for me, is not the mere comprehension of a thought, but the admission of its truth] no matter how trivial, the step from the level of thoughts to the level of reference (the objective), has already been taken.

One might be tempted to regard the relation of the thought to the True not as that of sense to reference, but rather as that of subject to predicate. [...] The truth claim arises [...] from the form of the declarative sentence [...] It follows that the relation of the thought to the True may not be compared with that of subject to predicate. Subject and predicate (understood in the logical sense) are indeed elements of thought; they stand on the same level for knowledge. By combining subject and predicate, one reaches only a thought, never passes from sense to reference, never from a thought to its truth value. One moves at the same level but never advances from one level to the next. A truth value cannot be a part of a thought, any more than, say, the Sun can, for it is not a sense but an object. (Frege, 1952) [...]

Judgements can be regarded as advances from a thought to a truth value. Naturally this cannot be a definition. Judgement is something quite peculiar and incomparable. One might also say that judgements are distinctions of parts within truth values. Such distinction occurs by a return to the thought." (Frege, 1952)

One year earlier (1891) Frege had stated a parallelism between equations and statements. "The linguistic form of equations is a statement.... " (Frege, 1952)[20]

"I am concerned to show that the argument does not belong with the function, but goes together with the *function to make up a complete whole*; for the function by itself must be called incomplete, in need of supplementation or 'unsaturated'. And in this respect functions differ fundamentally from numbers. Since such is the essence of the function, we can explain why, on the one hand, we recognize the same function in '$2{\cdot}1^3 + 1$' and '$2{\cdot}2^3 + 2$', even though these expressions stand for different numbers, whereas, on the other hand, we do not find one and the same function in '$2{\cdot}1^3 + 1$' and '$4 - 1$' in spite of their equal numerical values. Moreover, we now see how people easily led to regard the form of the expression as what is essential to the function. We recognize the *function* in the expression by imagining the latter *as split up*, and *the possibility of thus splitting it up is suggested by its structure.*

The two parts into which the mathematical expression is thus split up, the sign of the argument and the expression of the function, are *dissimilar*; for the argument is a number, a whole complete in itself, as the function is not. (We may compare this with the division of a line by a point. One is inclined in that case to count the dividing-point along with both

[20] Cf. (Raynaud, 2002).

segments; but if we want to make a clean division, i.e. so as not to count anything twice over or leave anything out, then we may only count the dividing-point along with one segment. This segment thus becomes fully complete in itself, and may be compared to the argument; whereas the other is lacking in something - vid. the dividing-point, which one may call its endpoint, does not belong to it. Only by completing it with this endpoint, or with a line that has two endpoints, do we get from it something entire." (Frege, 1952 [24-25]).

The "entirety" of the whole starts to become the *Leitmotiv* of so many and so various contributions. Frege emphasises the idea by using two different images: incompleteness means in need of supplementation, while unsaturatedness (chemical suggestion[21]) is a segment without an endpoint.

Another author, a great logician and semiotician well-endowed with chemical competences[22], Charles Sanders Peirce, more or less in the same period (1892-1906), was developing a model which would be accepted and spread from the 20th century onwards.

"A Predicate", Peirce wrote in 1906, "is either non-relative, or a *monad*, that is, is explicitly indefinite in one extensive respect, as is 'black'; or it is a dyadic relative, or dyad, such as 'kills', or it is a polyadic relative, such as 'gives'. These things must be diagrammatized in our system." (Peirce 4.543)

In 1892, the same year in which Frege published his *On Sense and Reference*, Peirce stated: "A rhema is somewhat closely analogous to a chemical atom or radical with unsaturated bonds. A non-relative rhema is like a univalent radicle; it has but one unsaturated bond. A relative rhema is like a multivalent radical. The blanks of a rhema can only be filled by terms, or, what is the same thing, by 'something which' (or the like) followed by a rhema; or, two can be filled together by means of 'itself' or the like. So, in chemistry, unsaturated bonds can only be saturated by joining two of them, which will usually, though not necessarily, belong to different radicles. If two univalent radicles are united, the result is a saturated compound. So, two non-relative rhemas being joined give a complete proposition. [...] And we may say that all rhemata are either singular, dual, or plural," (Peirce, 3.421).

But even more important than this multiplication of terms around the predicate is Peirce's thesis of the difference between verbs and proper nouns (or pronouns).

"The proposition, or sentence, signifies that an eternal fitness, or truth, attaches certain hecceities to certain parts of an idea" (Peirce 3.461). "It is - in fact - the connection of an indicative word [of an index] to a symbolic word which makes an assertion (Peirce 4.56)[23].

Such a 'dissimilarity' (Frege), or 'asymmetry' (Mathesius), is the condition of that 'fitness' Peirce writes about. Without it, instead of an 'attachment' (Peirce) or of the unity of a line where segments meet (Frege), of an intertwining (Plato), or of a 'synthesis' or a '*syntheke*'[24] (Aristotle), a couple (Abelard), we would have just a co-presence[25], a juxtaposition, a mere addition.

---

[21] See Picardi, 1994.

[22] Peirce completed an M.A in chemistry in 1862, and a Bachelor of Science in 1863 at Harvard University.

[23] Cf. (Fumagalli, 1995). The last two quoted passages are dated 1896 and 1893 respectively.

[24] See Lo Piparo, 2003.

[25] Against the "two-term theory," see (Geach, 1972). About a medieval semantics of verb not "reabsorbed" by the semantics of noun see (Marmo, 2004).

In order to arrive at conclusions which oppose mere cumulativity, Bühler writes some memorable pages, at the opening of the fourth part of his *Theory of Language*, on "The Make-up of Human Speech: Elements and Compositions", contrasting the *incipit* of Leibniz's *Monadology* about composites as accumulation or *aggregatum* of simples with the Aristotelian concept of *synthesis*, later encountered in Kant, Hegel, Cassirer, Wundt. He then states: "the old disjunctive question has found a new home in our contemporaries' minds, but with various new names; psychologists who profess the 'idea of *Gestalt*' or some 'holistic view' normally draw boundaries and erect barriers in its name against the *'amas ou aggregatum'* because hardly anyone wants to be counted among the 'atomists' or elementarians. [...] On the one hand anyone can mention the so-called summative wholes as an example of an aggregate in the strict sense; and on the other hand the sentence is a handy illustration as a last resort to make even the blind see that Leibniz's analysis cannot be generally applied: it is said that the sentence is obviously more than and different from an aggregate of words. [...] We rather will remain on the ground of sematology and try to find out whether *both* claims can be understood and maintained in one breath with respect to significative structures, namely the claim that they are aggregates in one respect and synthemata in another. That is precisely what they are; we shall only be able to gain a correct view of the relationship of the words to the sentence unit by changing the aspect under which we regard the issue, by shifting the approach; we must make this shift of attitude [...]. The nature of this shift can be stated without a trace of mystery or of mysticism or paradox. If there are two different sort of thing in the sentence, namely symbols and a field, then two separate counts can without contradiction reach the result **n** in the former case and the result **1** in the latter case. Leibniz, the productive mathematician, will be quite right if he determines the result n as a sum of units; but the one field unit will not be a merely symbolic sum." (Bühler, 2011).

We could continue quoting *ad infinitum*, but the purpose here is merely to underline the fact that two different directions need be followed in a complementary way while respectively producing (encoding) and understanding (decoding) a message (a text), at least a sentence to begin with: top-down in the first case - from the whole communicative intention to its segmentation in predication -, bottom-up in the second - from lexemes and morphemes to phrases and their structure. Compositionality (the value of totality is a function of the value of its parts) is then plausible; this, though, is secondary to the primacy of the thesis that the totality is more than the sum of its parts, a thesis according to which we are able to explain sentences as units at their sources.

Ultimately we would like to reflect a convergent approach shared by the fathers of the two main contemporary grammatical models: dependency grammar and constituency grammar.

Lucien Tesnière, to whom the so-called dependency grammars are ascribed, opens his *Esquisse d'une syntaxe structural* (1953) as follows:

"*CONNECTION.* In the sentence *Alfred sings*, how many elements are there?

Two, we would normally answer: *Alfred* and *sings*.
Only one, would be the guess of those who feel the unity of the sentence.
Three, we say, taking into account the two previous answers:

1. = Alfred
2. = sings

3. = finally and **above all**, the link which unites unit *Alfred* and *sings*, and without which we would only have two independent **ideas**, with no relationship between them, and no organised thought.

We will give to this link, without which there is no possible sentence, the name **connection.**

The connection is the soul of the sentence, its vital and organising principle. It ensures **structural function**. [...]

STEMMA. The structure of the sentence depends upon the architecture of its connections. **Structural syntax** is the science which studies this architecture.

The **stemma** is the graphical representation of the architecture of the connections. [...] The stemma may be **linear** or **forked**. The forked stemma may have a **bifurcation**, a **trifurcation** or an even more complex ramification:

LINEAR STEMMA	FORKED STEMMA	
	Bifurcation	Trifurcation
Alfred sings	*Alfred hits Bernard*	*Alfred gives the book to Charles*
sings | *Alfred*	*hits* /\ *Alfred* *Bernard*	*gives* / | \ *Alfred* *the book* *to Charles*

[...]

STEMMATIC ANALYSIS. The structural syntax method consists essentially of reconstituting the stemma of a given utterance, that is to recognise the internal architecture. The establishment of the stemma constitutes **stemmatic analysis**, which includes both grammatical analysis and logical analysis and which it replaces in a positive and advantageous manner. [...]

VERB. The verb is the **node of nodes.** It is the verb which, directly or indirectly, controls the whole sentence. As such, it appears at the top of the stemma. This is why, when we establish a stemma, a good way is to start with the verb. [...]

The immediate subordinates of the verb are the **agents** and the **circonstants.**

AGENTS. We give the name agents to the subordinates of the verb which participate in any way in the action. [...]

CIRCONSTANTS. We give the name circonstants to the subordinates of the verb which indicate the circumstances of the action: time, place, manner, etc. The number of the circonstants is unlimited. " (Tesnière, 1953).

In order to remind ourselves that predication is the basic structure of both queries and answers, we refer to Tesnière's proposal about '*interrogation*':

"In the sentence : *Alfred sings*, three questions may arise (which confirms that there are three elements) :

- *Who sings?*

- *What does Alfred do?*
- *Does Alfred sing?*

NUCLEAR INTERROGATION. In the sentence: *Who sings?* the question concerns the subordinate **nucleus**, which is emptied of the meaning *Alfred*, and where only the interrogative word *Who? exists.* We would say that there is a **nuclear interrogation.**

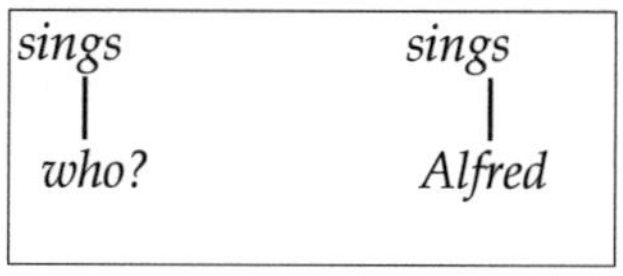

When the nuclear interrogation is made with an empty nucleus, the corresponding response is made with a full nucleus: *Who sings? Alfred sings.* It is even enough to fill the nucleus without repeating the rest of the sentence: *Who sings? Alfred.*

The sentence: *What does Alfred do?* is also a nuclear interrogation. *What does Alfred do? Alfred sings* or simply: *He sings.* The only difference is that this time the question is on the controlling nucleus.

To summarise, the sentence: *Alfred sings,* having two nuclei, can give rise to two nuclear interrogations. We can see from this that a phrase can give rise to **as many nuclear interrogations as it has nuclei**.

Nuclear interrogations are made via **question words,** of which the main ones are:

For agents: *who? – what?*
For circonstants: *where? – when? – how?- why?*
For epithet: *which?*
For example: *Which book is Alfred looking at? Alfred is looking at the red book* or simply: *The red one.*

CONNECTIONAL INTERROGATION. In the sentence: *Does Alfred sing?* the two nuclei *Alfred* and *sings* are full. The question is therefore not nuclear. Effectively, *Alfred* and the action of *singing* are given. What we don't know is whether the two notions should be joined together, that is, if there is a **connection** between them. The questions is thus about the connection. We would say there is a **connectional interrogation.** [...]

If the connectional interrogation is made with a full nucleus, the corresponding response is made with an empty one. This is why a single word is enough: *yes* or *no*:

Does Alfred sing? - Yes.

Yes means : *There is a connection.*

No means : *There is not a connection.*

To summarise, the phrase *Alfred sings* can give rise to three questions, two nuclear and one connectional." (Tesnière, 1953).

As far as Chomsky is concerned, here we shall only recall that in generative, or more precisely in phrase-structure grammar, the start variable (or start symbol) S represents the whole sentence.

So far we have reached the 1950s.

For the 1960s I wish to mention two independent semantic turns within two different traditions: František Daneš' *Three-level Approach to Syntax* (1964) and following articles and Charles Fillmore's *The Case for Case* (1968) with its further developments.

Without being able to dwell upon each of these contributions, I think both of them deserve to be appreciated for their awareness of the importance of a sharp distinction and at the same time a strict correlation between the formal and the functional level (as typical of the Prague School) or, in other words, between the syntactic and the semantic levels of linguistic analysis (as was gradually being evidenced within the generative trend).

Distinction does not mean separation. On the contrary, distinction allows better outlined relations, those which let the new generation of Czech linguists identify semantic patterns (something like the predicational categories already investigated by Sundén) such as: *process; agent–action–the object of action; the bearer of state–state; individual–predication of a feature to it; individual–placing it into a class; etc.* (Daneš, 1964).

"The framework of Functional Generative Description [FGD]", states Petr Sgall, "has been designed so as to handle sentence structure in its anthropocentric aspects, i.e. based on syntactic dependency (the core of which, at least in most European languages, is the pattern of actor and action) and comprising the topic-focus articulation, i.e. specifying sentences not just as abstract objects, but as anchored in interactive context; this opens a way to understand them as operations on the hearer's states of mind.

FGD offers a basis for a relatively economic description, since the sentence representation having the shape of a dependency tree (with the verb at its root) contains only nodes corresponding to lexical items proper, rather than to nonterminals and function morphemes." (Sgall, 2006); paper originally published in 1997).

In the report of Charles Fillmore's *The Case for Case*, his work is introduced in these terms: "The grammatical notion 'case' deserves a place in the base component of the grammar of every language. It is argued that past research has not led to valid insights on case relationships and that what is needed is a conception of base structure in which case relationships are primitive terms of the theory and in which such concepts as 'subject' and 'direct object' are missing." (Fillmore, 1967).

More than forty years later, we can conclude that the cognitive turn in linguistics has become stronger. The notion of case has evolved into that of frame. The latter, together with the notion of script, had, in the meantime, gained ground[26].

It would be fruitful to compare the finite set, the list of cases with the results of other similar enterprises: tectogrammatical roles in Prague Dependency Treebank[27], Chomsky's thematic roles/Theta Roles[28].

[26] (Minsky, 1974); (Schank, Abelson,1977).

[27] http://ufal.mff.cuni.cz/pdt2.0/doc/manuals/en/t-layer/html/ch11s05s01.html

[28] In generative grammar, a theta role or θ-role is the formal device for representing syntactic argument structure (number and type of noun phrases) required by a particular verb. Thematic roles or relations are their semantic correspondents. Theta comes from thematic.

What we eventually want to do is to make explicit some conclusions which can be arrived at from the wide perspective so far explored:

1. Factual oversimplifications are not admitted: verbs usually cannot be alone, but sometimes they can (I'm not speaking about ellipses), given that zerovalent verbs exist (as atmospheric verbs in many languages) (Malchukov, Sievierska, 2011).
2. Metalinguistic oversimplifications are not admitted either: neither the correlation subject-property (suggested by Aristotle) nor that of agent-action (suggested by Tesnière's terminology) always stand, and not everywhere: they are merely *pars pro toto* representations[29].
3. However, what can be seen as an interesting, though covert, convergence between two main models of predication is something underlying the conviction about sentence unit: that is to say that both the Aristotelian paraphrase 'man is walking' for 'man walks' and the Fregean symbolic transcription W (m) = 1, or W (m) = 0[30] attest to the feeling of a relationship, of a reference from the foreground to the background, from the present being to the whole one, from the determined knowledge to the totality of what can be judged, as Frege calls it (*das Beurteilbare*, the judgeable), from the objects the sentence is about, to the world (actual or possible) it has been assigned to.

To better understand this fundamental belonging of the "case in question" to what it is included within, without being reducible to it, is a worthwhile goal: the result will be to understand that difficult but stimulating balance which is provided by relating something determined to something abstract, a dream - as Peirce would say - to an index[31], thoughts to worlds and worlds to thoughts.

3.4 Predication without or before judgement. Propositions vs. propositional functions

Just a couple of further statements before leaving the subject of predication.

As widely considered, we need predication before judging[32]. We need it to ask questions, to make requests, to give orders, to plea, to pray, to express wonder and so on. Predication deserves attention as an act of thinking, as a logical and psychological matter, as a semiotic, linguistic ability, as a communicative deed. Before judgements we utter questions, doubts, hypotheses, shaping our thoughts while still suspending our evaluations.

Formalising this distinction means distinguishing between propositional functions and propositions, between unsaturated connections and saturated ones. Saturated through what device? Completed by what?, if ever …

3.5 Affirming or denying

In a sentence deprived of its context no linguistic evidence (in the etymological sense of the word, i.e. seeable verbal constituents) can be displayed as the marker of an accomplished

---

[29] Regarding the importance of an ontology of events, for predicates referring to events, see (Davidson, 1980).

[30] The formula means that the predicate 'walk' being saturated by its argument identifies the truth value: either 1 (true) or 0 (false).

[31] "A verb by itself signifies a mere dream, an imagination unattached to any particular occasion. It calls up in the mind an *icon*" (Peirce 3.459).

[32] See (Davidson, 2005).

saturation (or, rather, as the mark of an ended task). No morpheme, no lexeme proper; intonation, rather, an unsuspended one; word order, possibly. But most of all, the plain intonation of an assertion contrasted with, for example, the rising intonation of a question.

What does this mean? Different authors in different contexts have underlined the presence of a covert constituent in judging: the personal assent or dissent which determines the affirmative or negative structure of predication itself in assertions, and constitutes its illocutionary force.

After having quoted Frege's expressions on this point (3.3), let us recall Brentano's statements about the role of assenting (or dissenting) while judging: once an object is given in presentation, with our judgements we express its acceptance or rejection (Brentano, 1995).

This way of considering the further commitment involved through an act of judgement helps us gain a unified perspective on the two different kinds of questions mentioned in § 2.3. Any assertion - this is the suggestion - qualifies itself as a yes or no answer, even if apparently no question at all has generated it; completive questions just pave the way for oriented questions. Answers will then confirm or deny the orientation proposed, thus underlining the strict relationship between predicate as sentence-centre and predication as basic syntagmatic act, whatever illocutionary act may follow, be it an assertion or not.

4. Tools and resources: from WordNet to FrameNet *et alia*

After having reconstructed some basic steps of the more than bi-millennial thread of philosophic-linguistic thought, the next move must be that one of a recognition of data, in order to check the validity of theoretical contributions. From this point of view we are now in a privileged position, that of scholars favoured by the creation of a specific area of studies, computational linguistics and related resources, which support and provide inspiration to the theorists.

From the works of ancient grammarians to those of present-day linguists, the interplay between data and theory has always been of vital importance in developing sound, deep competences.

The work is hard, but well worth the effort and avoids restricting ourselves to armchair philosophy (Austin 1956/57) or armchair linguistics (Fillmore 1992).

"**Armchair linguistics** - writes Fillmore - does not have a good name in some linguistics circles. A caricature of the armchair linguist is something like this. He sits in a deep soft comfortable armchair, with his eyes closed and his hands clasped behind his head. Once in a while he opens his eyes, sits up abruptly shouting, "Wow, what a neat fact!", grabs his pencil, and writes something down. Then he paces around for a few hours in the excitement of having come still closer to knowing what language is really like.

(There isn't anybody exactly like this, but there are some approximations).

Corpus linguistics does not have a good name in some linguistics circles. A caricature of the corpus linguist is something like this. He has all of the primary facts that he needs, in the form of a corpus of approximately one zillion running words, and he sees his job as that of deriving secondary facts from his primary facts. At the moment he is busy determining the relative frequencies of the eleven parts of speech as the first word of a sentence versus as the second word of a sentence.

(There isn't anybody exactly like this, but there are some approximations).

These two don't speak to each other very often, but when they do, the corpus linguist says to the armchair linguist, 'Why should I think that what you tell me is true?', and the armchair linguist says to the corpus linguist, 'Why should I think that what you tell me is interesting?'" (Fillmore, 1992).

By 'linguistic resources' we mean "Collections of data which primarily document communicative acts of humans by some form of recording and/or descriptions, both directly as in corpora, or at higher levels of abstraction in lexicons and ontologies. The primary data can be text, video recording and/or audio tracks."[33]

In 2010 a new initiative was launched by LREC (Language Resources and Evaluation Conference) in its 7th edition, the

Compilation of a *Map of Language Resources, Technologies and Evaluation,* "a collective enterprise of the LREC community, as a first step towards the creation of a very broad, community-built, Open Resource Infrastructure; [...] The map was intended to monitor the use and creation of language resources (datasets, tools, etc.)"[34].

We will now mention some of the main resources available, which can enable data collection *and* annotation at different levels about them, in a bottom-up direction.

4.1 WordNet and MultiWordNet

Firstly we shall start with lexical units, just words: WordNet "is a large lexical database of English. Nouns, verbs, adjectives and adverbs are grouped into sets of cognitive synonyms (synsets), each expressing a distinct concept. Synsets are interlinked by means of conceptual-semantic and lexical relations"[35]. From the point of view of our subject, predication and predicate-argument relationship, of particular note is that "The majority of the WordNet's relations connect words from the same part of speech (POS). Thus, WordNet really consists of four sub-nets, one each for nouns, verbs, adjectives and adverbs, with few cross-POS pointers. Cross-POS relations include the "morphosemantic" links that hold among semantically similar words sharing a stem with the same meaning: observe (verb), observant (adjective) observation, observatory (nouns). In many of the noun-verb pairs the semantic role of the noun with respect to the verb has been specified: {sleeper, sleeping_car} is the LOCATION for {sleep} and {painter}is the AGENT of {paint}, while {painting, picture} is its RESULT."

MultiWordNet is a multilingual lexical database, aligned with Princeton WordNet[36].

http://multiwordnet.fbk.eu/english/home.php

---

[33] From the Glossary of INTERA project:: http://www.mpi.nl/INTERA/

[34] http://www.informatik.uni-trier.de/~ley/db/conf/lrec/lrec2010.html: see especially section 0.33, Question Answering.

[35] http://wordnet.princeton.edu/

[36] http://multiwordnet.fbk.eu/english/home.php

4.2 Treebanks and annotated corpora

The creation of annotated corpora at different levels (layers) constitutes a further development and a sound premise for a good selection of metadata. Here, we refer only to the creation of annotated corpora in a great deal of different languages at the syntactic level, treebanks, and to the systematically planned discussion about the relationship between annotation as such, and the adoption of apparatus according to which annotation needs to be done (not only manually, but also automatically, of course): the Treebanks and Linguistic Theories (TLT) conference series[37].

4.3 PropBank *et relata*

From lexicon (and lexicography) through syntax: the step towards propositions has been taken and the results can be viewed in the realised and on-going project of PropBank, which adds predicate-argument relations to the syntactic trees of Penn-Treebank (concerning English language), thus achieving a corpus of text annotated with information about basic semantic propositions. In connection with this project, a continuation aims at creating Parallel PropBanks (the English-Chinese Treebank/PropBank)[38].

Based upon PropBank, once again top-down observation and analysis has been carried out, generating a verb index[39] (a system which merges links and web pages from four different natural language processing projects) and an index of nouns[40], the goal of which is to mark the sets of arguments that cooccur with nouns in PropBank. They are the Unified Verb Index and Nombank.

4.4 FrameNet and Semlink. Towards increasing semantic annotation and resource combination

In order to expand the annotation from the syntactic to the semantic level and to achieve frames passing through verbs and valences, other resources have been produced and are still under construction, their development being possible in relation to different corpora and languages: VerbNet[41] (the largest on-line verb lexicon currently available for English) and valence lexica[42] according to the PDT-ValencyLexicon[43] model.

The most refined annotation on the semantic level of predicate-argument relationship is still provided by FrameNet[44], Fillmore's Project, is consistent with his life-long research into

---

[37] The list of the first seven conferences is published at http://tlt8.unicatt.it/Links.htm ; the addresses of the last three edition are the following: http://tlt8.unicatt.it/ ; http://math.ut.ee/tlt9/index.html ; http://tlt10.cl.uni-heidelberg.de/ See also, for a case study regarding a particular predicative structure, (Bamman, Passarotti, Crane, 2008).

[38] http://verbs.colorado.edu/~mpalmer/projects/ace.html

[39] http://verbs.colorado.edu/verb-index/

[40] http://nlp.cs.nyu.edu/meyers/NomBank.html

[41] http://verbs.colorado.edu/~mpalmer/projects/verbnet.html

[42] Cf. http://jochenleidner.posterous.com/english-valency-lexicon-online

[43] See (Hajič, J., Panevová, J., Urešová, Z., Bémová, A., Kolářová, V., Pajas, P., 2003) and http://ufal.mff.cuni.cz/PDT-Vallex/ PDT-Vallex contains at the time of writing (January 2012) over 11000 valency frames for more than 7000 verbs. It has been built in close connection with the Prague Czech-English Dependency Treebank project.

[44] https://framenet.icsi.berkeley.edu/fndrupal/

cases, first, and then frames. "The FrameNet project is building a lexical database of English that is both human- and machine-readable, based on annotating examples of how words are used in actual texts. From the student's point of view, it is a dictionary of more than 10,000 word senses, most of them with annotated examples that show the meaning and usage. For the researcher in Natural Language Processing, the more than 170,000 manually annotated sentences provide a unique training dataset for semantic role labeling, used in applications such as information extraction, machine translation, event recognition, sentiment analysis, etc. For students and teacher of linguistics it serves as a valence dictionary, with uniquely detailed evidence for the combinatorial properties of a core set of the English vocabulary."

As it is already evident both from a strategic, epistemological point of view and from a practical one, resource compatibility and unification are highly appreciable and not only as a goal to be pursued in the future. SemLink, for instance, is "the effort to map between complementary lexical resources: WordNet, FrameNet , VerbNet and PropBank. The goal is to develop a broad-coverage, unified English resource that has a fine granularity and rich semantics of Word-Net and Frame-Net, that is a platform for syntactically based generalizations based on VerbNet, and that provides PropBank style effective training data for supervised Machine Learning techniques." (Palmer, 2009)

We would like to conclude our quick survey by quoting Martha Palmer's words at the conclusion of the same paper: "Efforts to link the PropBank/VerbNet and FrameNet resources to one another and to WordNet, and to define semantics for the roles used by each resource, are a likely avenue for future improvements in semantic role labeling systems, and will benefit Question-Answering, Information Extraction and other NLP applications." Let's pursue such avenues.

5. Conclusion

We have considered the differences between questions and requests, and their co-presence in the structure of queries.

Because of the so-called "descriptive fallacy" in philosophy of language, it took rather a long time to give them the attention they were due. Thanks to pragmatics, this oversight has been rectified.

Asking questions testifies to the strong relationship between lack of determinacy (poverty, both in knowledge and in action) and the need to overcome it (in order to attain plentifulness). Interrogative structures are devices where triggers such as *wh*-words or suspended assent are at work to retrieve missing information, extract knowledge, or receive the cooperation requested.

Answers are therefore not only assertions, but also permissions, prohibitions, orders, suggestions, etc. The logico-linguistic structure which is always required across this variety of speech acts and which makes possible the wording of questions and requests is predication.

Even in elliptical or simply verbless sentences, predication is at work albeit implicit or implied. To be at work means that it is a necessary condition for the complete efficiency and comprehensibility of the sentence itself. To be at work, then, means that the addressee/hearer/reader has to bear in mind, or retrieve, the predication, where the absence of recognition would prevent him/her from understanding the meaning, i.e. the semantics of the sentence. In crosstalk such as "Ready?" "Not yet.", no verb appears, but predication is easily recognisable, as implicit (in the question) or implied (in the answer): Implicit, specifically as *a part of* the first turn "[Are you] ready?", and implied as *the whole* turn upon which negation operates. The role of negation is in fact that of an operator, the scope of which is the whole preceding sentence structure: [It is] not yet [true that I am ready]", i.e. the preceding sentence deprived of its interrogative mood, that is to say without the suspension of assent typical of oriented questions, and shifted to the second person (addressee) to the first one (sender).

During our reconstruction of the basic views on such an evergreen topic in logic and linguistic inquiries as predication, we have argued that some routes need to be modified:

i. Before predicates, theory must put predication as the basic syntagmatic act. This means the adoption of a pragmatic framework.
ii. Before articulating predicative relations, the sentence unit must be asserted and the reasons investigated, thus avoiding both factual and metalinguistic oversimplification. Bottom-up approaches need to be balanced by top-down approaches, which deserve a certain priority due to the causative role of the speaker and of his/her communicative intention, which gives rise to the actualisation of the speech act and to the processing of its constituents by the addressee. Compositionality is a function of (con)textuality and not vice versa.
iii. 'Dissimilarity', or 'asymmetry' of components (typically nouns and verbs) is the condition of 'fitness' which joins sentence constituents. Without it, we would merely have a co-presence, a juxtaposition, a simple addition. Beyond this, both Aristotelian and Fregean models attest to the feeling of a further (second step) relationship, a reference from the foreground to the background, from the present being (through the copula) to being as such; from single, determined objects of the spoken domain to the universe of discourse (the co-domain instituted as the truth or falsehood which the predicate-argument relationship refers to); from the objects the sentence is about, to the world (actual or possible) it has been assigned to. Moreover, this asymmetry is also active on another layer, that of communicative dynamism (topic-focus articulation, functional sentence perspective). Within the speech, participants in the conversation / communication exchange need to move from what is known to something new; they need to increase their already shared world of reference to new information / action upon it.
iv. Higher units, such as texts, may be further requested, but at least questions/requests and answers cannot be mutually isolated. Moreover, a useful insight into a textual (macro)structure can be derived from the identification of the question(s) and request(s) which may be considered, albeit implicitly, to be the source of the text itself.
v. The newest solutions proposed to capture the structure of the predicative link - which keeps queries and answers together- support the idea of a semantic unity displayed through a plurality of roles and their gradual identification or confirmation: this is what concepts such as functions, cases, stemmas, frames and scripts suggest - barring gaps at the beginning – who does what?, when does this happen? etc. – which have to be filled as an on-going task.
vi. Unproven or simply intuited theoretical endeavours deserve access to data, as rich and varied as possible, in order to test their validity. In the privileged position made possible by computational linguistic tools and resources, philosophers of language,

logicians, linguists and other scholars, aware of the multi-secular history of human thought on these topics, can now also carry out field-work. Mutual advantage is expected.

6. References

Ambridge, B., Lieven, E.V.M. (2011). *Child Language Acquisition. Contrasting Theoretical Approaches*, Cambridge University Press, Cambridge

Aristotle, (1955). *The Organon. The Categories, On Interpretation,* by H.B. Cook; *Prior Analytics,* by H. Tredennick, Harvard University Press - William Heinemann Ltd, Cambridge Mass. - London

(1956). *The Metaphysics. Books I-IX,* by H. Tredennick, Harvard University Press - William Heinemann Ltd,Cambridge Mass. - London

(1959). *Posterior Analytics,* by H. Tredennick; *Topica,* by E.S. Forster, Harvard University Press - William Heinemann Ltd, Cambridge Mass. - London

Arnauld, A., Lancelot, C. (1966 ; 1660[1] -1676[2]). *Grammaire générale et raisonnée ou La Grammaire de Port-Royal,* Edition Critique présentée par H. E. Brekle, Tome I. Nouvelle impression en facsimilé de la troisième édition de 1676, Friedrich Frommann Verlag (Günther Holzboog), Stuttgart - Bad Cannstatt

Austin, J. L. (1956/57). *A Plea for Excuses.* In *Proceedings of the Aristotelian Society,* 57, pp. 1-30; repr. in Id. (1961). *Philosophical papers,* ed. by Urmson J. O., Warnock G. J., Oxford University Press, Oxford, pp. 175-204

(1962). *How to Do Things with Words,* Clarendon Press, Oxford

Bamman D., Passarotti M., Crane G. (2008). *A Case Study in Treebank Collaboration and Comparison: Accusativus cum Infinitivo and Subordination in Latin,* «Prague Bulletin of Mathematical Linguistics», 90, pp. 109-122

Belnap Jr., N.D. (1966). *Questions, Answers, and Presuppositions,* «The Journal of Philosophy» 63 (20), pp. 609-611

Brentano, F. (1995). *Psychology from an Empirical Standpoint,* 2nd revised edition, Routledge, London

Brozek, A., (2011). *Theory of Questions. Erotetics through the Prism of its Philosophical Background and Practical Applications,* Rodopi, Amsterdam

Bühler, K. (2011). *Theory of Language. The Representational Function of Language,* John Benjamins Publishing Co., Amsterdam / Philadelphia

Chomsky, N. (1957). *Syntactic Structures,* Mouton, The Hague - Paris

(1995). *The Minimalist Program,* the MIT Press, Cambridge Mass. London

Daneš, Fr. (1964): A three-level approach to syntax. In: J. Vachek (ed.), *Travaux linguistiques de Prague 1: L'École de Prague d'aujourd'hui,* pp. 225–240, Éditions de l'Académie Tchécoslovaque des Sciences, Prague

Davidson, D. (1980). *Essays on Actions and Events.* Oxford University Press, Oxford

(2005). *Truth & Predication,* Harvard University Press, Cambridge Mass. - London

Dummett, M. (1973). *Frege: Philosophy of Language,* Duckworth, London

Fillmore Ch. J. (1968) *The Case for Case.* In Bach and Harms (Ed.): Universals in Linguistic Theory, pp. 1-88, Holt, Rinehart, and Winston, New York

(1992). *"Corpus linguistics" or "Computer-aided armchair linguistics"* in Svartvik J. (ed), *Directions in Corpus Linguistics*, Proceeding of Nobel Symposium 82, Stockholm, 4-8 August 1991, pp. 35-60, Mouton De Gruyter, Berlin,

Frege, G. (1952). *Function and Concept.* In Geach, P., Black, M. (eds), *Translations from the Philosophical Writings of Gottlob Frege*, pp. 21-41, Basil Blackwell, Oxford

Frigerio, A. (2010 a). *L'unità dell'enunciato. Indeterminismo semantico e determinazioni pragmatiche*, Mimesis, Milano-Udine

(2010 b). *L'enunciato come sistema. Il principio di composizionalità e i suoi limiti.* In L. Urbani Ulivi (a cura di), *Strutture di mondo. Il pensiero sistemico come specchio di una realtà complessa*, pp. 155-173, Il Mulino, Bologna

Fumagalli, A. (1995). *Il reale nel linguaggio. Indicalità e realismo nella semiotica di Peirce*, Vita e Pensiero, Milano

Geach, P. (1972). *Logic Matters*, Basil Blackwell, Oxford

Gobber, G. (1999). *Pragmatica delle frasi interrogative. Con applicazioni al Tedesco, al Polacco e al Russo*, Pubblicazioni dell'I.S.U. - Università Cattolica, Milano

(2011). *Sulla semantica della domanda tra Otto e Novecento: Bolzano, Frege, Meinong*, In: *Januam linguarum reserare. Saggi in onore di Bona Cambiaghi*, a cura di C. Bosisio, pp. 26-34, Le Monnier Università, Firenze

Grice, P. (1975). *Logic and Conversation*, In: *Syntax and Semantics, 3: Speech Acts*, ed. P. Cole & J. Morgan, Academic Press, New York. Repr. in *Studies in the Way of Words*, ed. H. P. Grice, pp. 22–40, Harvard University Press (1989), Cambridge, MA

Hajič, J., Panevová, J. Zdeňka Urešová, Z., Bémová, A., Kolářová, V., Pajas, P. (2003). PDT-VALLEX: Creating a Large-coverage Valency Lexicon for Treebank Annotation, In: *Proceedings of The Second Workshop on Treebanks and Linguistic Theories*, pp. 57-68, Copyright © Vaxjo University Press, Vaxjo, Sweden, ISBN 91-7636-394-5, ISSN 1651-0267

Humboldt, W. von (1999). *On Language. On the Diversity of Human Language Construction and Its Influence on the Mental Development of the Human Species*, ed. by M. Losonsky, transl. by P. Heath, Cambridge University Press, Cambridge

Jordania, J. (2006). *Who Asked the First Question? The Origins of Human Choral Singing, Intelligence, Language and Speech*, Logos, Tbilisi; full text online (pdf version): http://www.polyphony.ge/uploads/whoaskthefirst.pdf

Laspia, P. (1997). *L'articolazione linguistica. Origini biologiche di una metafora*, La Nuova Italia, Roma

(2005). *Definizione e predicazione: Aristotele e Frege a confronto*, Edizioni della Fondazione Nazionale «Vito Fazio-Allmayer»

Lo Piparo, F. (2005). *Aristotele e il linguaggio. Cosa fa di una lingua una lingua*, Laterza, Roma-Bari

Malchukov, A., Sievierska, A. (2011). *Impersonal Constructions. A Cross-Linguistic Perspective*, John Benjamins Publishing Co., Amsterdam / Philadelphia

Marmo, C. (2004). *Una semantica del verbo nella grammatica e nella teologia tra XII e XIII secolo.* In A. Maierù, L. Valente (eds), *Medieval Theories on Assertive and Non-assertive Language. Acts of the 14th European Symposium on Medieval Logic and Semantics*, Rome, June 11-15, 2002, Lessico Intellettuale Europeo, Leo S. Olschki Editore, Firenze

Mathesius, V. (1926). *New Currents and Tendencies in Linguistic Research*. In: *MNHMA: Festschrift for Josef Zubatý*, pp. 188–203 Praha; Repr. in J. Vachek (ed.) (1983). *Praguiana: Some Basic and Less Known Aspects of the Prague Linguistic School. An Anthology of Prague School Papers* , pp. 45–63, Academia, Prague

(1936). *Deset let Pražského linguistického kroužku*, «Slovo a slovesnost» 2, pp. 137–145. Engl. transl. In J. Vachek (ed.), (1966) *The Linguistic School of Prague: An Introduction to its Theory and Practice*, pp. 137–151, Indiana University Press, Bloomington

Minsky, M.A. (1974). *A framework for representing knowledge*. MIT-AI Laboratory Memo 306, June; Repr. In Wiston, P. H. (ed.), (1975)*The psychology of computer Vision*, McGraw Hill, New York

Orilia, F. (2000). *Argument Deletion, Thematic Roles, and Leibniz's Logico-grammatical Analysis of Relations*, «History and Philosophy of Logic», pp. 147-162

Palmer, M. (2009). "*Semlink: Linking PropBank, VerbNet and FrameNet."In Proceedings of the Generative Lexicon Conference*. Sept. 2009, Pisa, Italy GenLex-09

Peirce, Ch. S. (1931-35). *Collected Papers of Charles Sanders Peirce*, ed by Ch. Hartshorne, P. Weiss, voll. 1-6, Harvard University Press - The Belknap Press, Cambridge Mass.

Picardi, E. (1994). *La chimica dei concetti. Linguaggio, logica, psicologia 1879-1927*, Il Mulino, Bologna

Plato (1952). *Sophist*, with an English Translation by H. N. Fowler, William Heinemann Ltd - Harvard University Press, London -Cambridge Mass.

Prior, M., Prior, A. (1955). *Erotetic Logic* «The Philosophical Review» 64 (1), gennaio, pp. 43-59

Raynaud, S. (2002). *Equazione e giudizio. Sulla teoria della denotazione degli enunciati dichiarativi in Frege*. In S. Poggi (a cura di), *Le leggi del pensiero tra logica, ontologia e psicologia. Il dibattito austro-tedesco (1830-1930)*, pp. 117-172, Unicopli, Milano

(2008). *The Basic Syntagmatic Act is Predication*. «Slovo a Slovesnost», vol. LXVIII (4), pp. 49-66

Schank, R.C., Abelson, R. (1977). *Scripts, plans, goals and understanding*, N.J. Erlbaum, Hillsdale

Searle, J. (1969). *Speech Acts. An Essay in the Philosophy of Language*, Cambridge University Press, Cambridge

(1975). *Indirect Speech Acts*, In: *Syntax and Semantics, 3: Speech Acts*, ed. P. Cole & J. Morgan, Academic Press, New York. Repr. in Searle, J. (1979). *Expression and Meaning*, pp. 30-57, Cambridge University Press, Cambridge

Searle, J., Vanderveken, D. (1985). *Foundations of Illocutionary Logic*, Cambridge University Press, Cambridge

Sériot, P., Samain, D. (éd.) (2008). *La structure de la proposition: histoire d'un métalangage*, Cahiers de l'ILSL, n° 25, Centre de Linguistique et des Sciences du Langage de l'Université de Lausanne (Suisse), Lausanne

Sgall, P. (2006). *Language in its Multifarious Aspects*. The Carolinum Press, Prague

Sundén, K. F. (1916). *Essays I-II: I. The Predicational Categories in English. II. A Category of Predicational Change in English*, University Press Edv. Berling, Uppsala

Tesnière, L. (1953). *Esquisse d'une syntaxe structurale*, Klincksieck, Paris

Vachek, J. (1983). *Praguiana: Some Basic and Less Known Aspects of the Prague Linguistic School: An Anthology of Prague School Papers*, Academia, Prague

Weber, E.G. (1993). *Varieties of Questions in English Conversation*, Benjamins, Amsterdam Philadelphia

Whately, R. (1826). *Elements of Logic*, J. Mawman, London; repr. Facs. ed. by P. Dessì, (1988), Clueb, Bologna

4

Semantic Cache Reasoners

Muhammad Azeem Abbas, Muhammad Abdul Qadir
and Muhammad Tanvir Afzal
Centre for Distributed and Semantic Computing,
Faculty of Engineering and Applied Sciences,
Mohammad Ali Jinnah University Islamabad,
Pakistan

1. Introduction

Semantic caching (Ren, Q et al., 2003),(Dar et al., 1996) is said to be a technique for storing data and their corresponding semantic descriptions. Concept of semantic cache itself is quite simple but the reasoning required to evaluate any query over a semantic cache can be very complex (Godfrey P. and Gryz J., 1997). The reasoning over stored semantics is a determination process to know how query and cache formulas are related semantically. This reasoning is termed as semantic cache query processing (Ren, Q et al., 2003),(Dar et al., 1996). In this chapter we demonstrate several semantic cache query processing techniques for relational queries, web queries, xml queries, answering queries form materialized views and logic based subsumption analysis queries.

Mainly there are two types of semantic query processing approaches, structured-semantics and unstructured-semantics. In structured-semantics original problem or query is represented in a structure that has the ability to contain semantics along with its structure. Examples of structured-semantics are ontology, resource description framework (RDF) and extensible markup language (XML) etc. Unstructured-semantics approaches perform reasoning for semantic extraction from structures that do not posses semantics in their representations. Semantic cache query processing is an example of unstructured-semantics reasoning. Since standard query language (SQL) is structured but it do not contains semantics of data to be answered against a query and query itself.

In this chapter we demonstrate several semantic cache reasoners for unstructured-semantics. All of these semantic cache reasoning techniques represent query language to a mediate structured-semantic representation for semantic extraction.

2. Semantic cache query processing

In general research a semantic cache system can be grouped into two parts i) cache management and ii) query processing. Strategies for data management, replacing, coalescing, and indexing results of previously evaluated queries are mainly the part of semantic cache management. Query processing involves techniques that compute available and unavailable data from a semantic cache by performing some sort of reasoning over semantic descriptions. Also query processing technique handles local query execution, retrieval of unavailable data from a remote server and formulation of the end results. In this chapter we focus on semantic cache query processing.

At finer granularity semantic cache is a collection of semantic regions or semantic segments. Associated semantics for a cached query, which is a query specification (Lee et al., 1999) are stored in semantic cache along with resultant data is called a semantic region (Dar et al., 1996) or semantic segment (Ren et al., 2003).

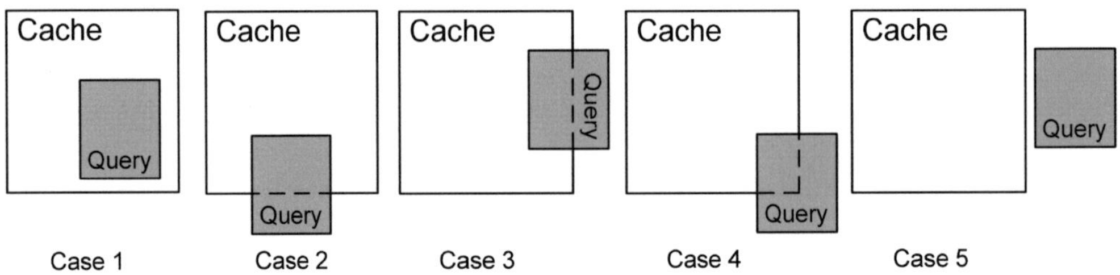

Fig. 1. Relationship between Cached Query (Q_C) and User Query (Q_U).

Formal definition of semantic segment can be seen in (Ren et al., 2003). A query processing technique can perform reasoning over semantic segments to determine whether cached data fully or partially or do not contributes to an incoming query. If the incoming query is fully answerable from a semantic cache, then no communication with the server is required. Similarly a partial answer to a query will reduce the amount of data retrieved from the server.

In case of a partial answer, the user query is trimmed into two disjoint sub queries (Keller A.M. and Basu J., 1996): the query executed locally called Probe Query (ProbQ) and the query sent to the server named Remainder Query (RemQ) (Dar et al., 1996). The previous literature (Ren, Q et al., 2003),(Dar et al., 1996),(Lee et al., 1999),(Godfrey P. and Gryz J., 1997),(Keller A.M. and Basu J., 1996) shows that this trimming is performed on the basis of relationship between the content of a semantic segment and the result required by an incoming query. Possible cases of the relationship between the incoming query and the semantics stored in the cache (as reported in the literature) is shown in Figure 1. White boxes represent previously stored query results and gray boxes shows incoming user queries. In Figure 1 rows (tuples) are represented horizontally and columns (attributes) are vertically and only select-project queries are considered. In each case a user query overlaps semantic cache region in a certain way. Case 2 depicts a horizontal partition in which some part of the incoming query tuples satisfied by cache semantics. Where in case 3, a projection of the query is available in cache and some attributes are missing, this situation is called a vertical partition. This figure represents that a partial answer is possible in case 2,3 and 4, where a user query can be fully answered from the cache in case 1. This figure is used to evaluate a semantic cache query processing scheme, too, i.e. whether a scheme incorporates all the cases or not. We argue that due to this misleading diagram, the missing implicit semantics are not being considered in the previous query processing techniques. Therefore, in this thesis we have adopted a new way of comparing the semantics of a user query and the cache semantics in the coming sections.

2.1 Semantic cache query processing criteria

Previous surveys (Bashir M. F. and Qadir M. A., 2006a), (Ahmad, M and Qadir, M.A., 2008), (Jónsson B. Þór et al., 2006), (Hao X et al., 2005), (Halevy, A.Y., 2001), (Makki K. S and Andrei S, 2009) conducted over semantic cache query processing identified two main parameters for evaluation i.e. Maximum Data Retrieval (MDR) and fast query processing. Quantification of the MDR was not given in those surveys. Here we quantify it with the test, data from server ($\mathbf{D_s}$) intersection data from cache ($\mathbf{D_c}$) should be empty set i.e. $\mathbf{D_s \cap D_c = \Phi}$. In general any technique which retrieves maximum possible or complete results from local cache in tractable time with this given quantification is said to be an efficient semantic cache query processing technique.

2.2 Query

A select-project query is a tuple < Q_{UA}, Q_{UR}, Q_{UP},Q_{UD}>, where Q_{UA} is *Select Clause* of query which contains projected attributes. Q_{UR} is the *From Clause* which contains relation of a database D, from which data is to be retrieved. Q_{UP} is *Where Clause* which contains conjunctive or disjunctive compare predicates, a compare predicate is of the form $P = a\ op\ c$, where $a \in A$ *{Attributes Set}*, $op \in \{<,\leq,>,\geq,=\}$, c is a constant in a specific domain (Ren et al., 2003), Q_{UD} is the *resultant data* of this query. A query can be represented as $\pi_{QUA}\ \sigma_{QUP}\ (Q_{UR})$ in relational algebra.

2.3 Amending query

A query that only request a key attribute of a relation from a remote server to extract known available data from cache is called an amending query. When we know that some data is available in semantic cache but could not extract it precisely. Than we request the server for a key attribute for a user query and extract cached attributes (data) against those keys from cache. Requesting only keys require less computation on database server and low bandwidth over network, in general.

Consider the following employee database information provided in example 1 below, which shall be used throughout evaluation in this chapters. The semantic cache model we follow is similar to the relational database model. The basic building blocks of the relational model are attributes (columns), rows (tuple), tables (relations) and relation schema. The schema defines the relations and the attributes with their data type in each relation. A row or a tuple is a set of attribute's instances.

2.4 Example 1

Consider an employee database with a relation name *Emp (Empid, Ename,Department, Age, Salary,Exp)*. The domain of the *Age, Salary, Department* and *Exp* attributes of *Emp* are {20,…,100},{0.1K,…,1K,…15K},{CS, EE, BI, BA},{1,..,50} respectively as shown in Figure 2. Also suppose that a cache already has following cached queries shown in Figure 3.

3. Query processing techniques

Work on query processing over semantic cache is mainly classified in query intersection (Lee et al., 1999), query trimming (Keller A.M. and Basu J., 1996),(Ren, Q et al., 2003), answering queries using views (Levy A.Y et al., 1996), (Duschka O.M. and Genesereth M.R.

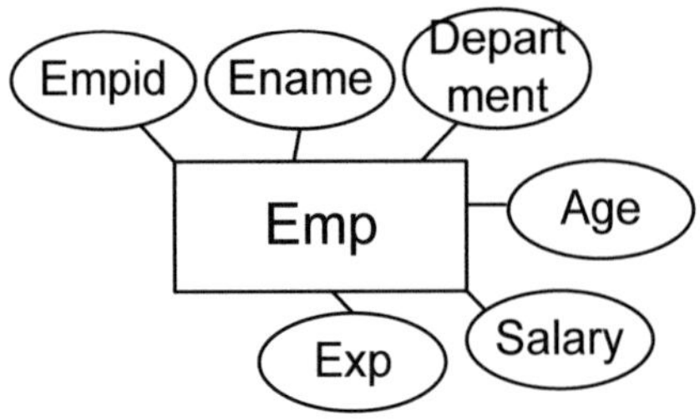

Fig. 2. Employee relation.

$$Q_{C1} \leftarrow \pi_{\,Ename,\, Department}\ \sigma_{\,Age \geq 50}\ (Emp);$$
$$Q_{C2} \leftarrow \pi_{\,Age,\, Department}\ (Emp);$$
$$Q_{C3} \leftarrow \pi_{\,Ename,\, Department}\ \sigma_{\,Salary > 10k}\ (Emp);$$
$$Q_{C4} \leftarrow \pi_{\,Age,\, Salary}\ \sigma_{\,Salary \leq 30k}\ (Emp);$$
$$Q_{C5} \leftarrow \pi_{\,Ename,\, Salary,\, Exp}\ (Emp);$$
$$Q_{C6} \leftarrow \pi_{\,Age}\ \sigma_{\,Age < 70}\ (Emp);$$
$$Q_{C7} \leftarrow \pi_{\,Age,Salary,Exp}\ \sigma_{\,Salary \geq 1K \wedge Salary <= 40K}$$

Fig. 3. Cached Queries.

1997), (Pottinger R. and Levy A. 2000), semantic cache for web queries (Chidlovskii B and Borghoff U. M., 2000), (Qiong L and Jaffrey F. N., 2001), xml based semantic cache (Mandhani B. and Suciu D., 2005), (Sanaullah, M., 2008) and description logic based subsumption analysis in semantic cache (Baader et al., 1991a) (Hollunder et al., 1990) techniques.

3.1 Query intersection

Query processing for the five scenarios similar to Figure 1 and one additional scenario which shows cache as a subset of incoming queries (reverse of case 1 of Figure 1) was presented by Lee (1999, pp.28-36). Against each scenario probe and remainder query were computed based on cache and query intersection or difference. Intersection and difference of cache semantics and a posed query were mentioned at a very abstract level.

Definition of intersection (Lee et al., 1999) between semantics of cache region Q_C and a user query Q_U on relation R is shown in statement (i) of Figure 4. This intersection consists of two parts. One is the common projected attributes while the other is combined condition of a user and cached query predicates (Shown in statement (ii) of Figure 4). A query or cache semantics are represented as a triple < π_Q, σ_Q, $operand_Q$ >. π_Q is the projected attributes, $operand_Q$ is the base relation. Where any predicate condition (σ_Q) is represented as a value domain list $\{d_{Q,1}, d_{Q,2}, ..., d_{Q,n}\}$ and a condition is satisfiable if none of the value domain is null. We elaborate this concept with an example.

Consider the database schema information provided in example 1 above. A user query Q_U over cached query Q_{C1} of Figure 3 are represented as triple < π_Q, σ_Q, $operand_Q$ > in statement (iv) and (iii) of Figure 4 respectively. The query Q_U is statisfiable (or completely answerable) from Q_{C1} because intersection of projected attributes is not empty and there is no null value domain in predicate condition. According to Lee (1999, pp.28-36) two queries are disjoint if either intersection of their projected attributes is empty or there is no combined condition between user and cached query predicates.

$$Q_U \cap Q_C = \langle Q_{UA} \cap Q_{CA}, Q_{UP} \cap Q_{CP}, R \rangle \quad \text{(i)}$$
$$\pi_{QUA \cap QCA}, \sigma_{QUP \cap QCP} \quad \text{(ii)}$$
$$Q_{C1} = \langle \{Ename, Department\}, \{-,-,-,\{50,\ldots,100\},-\}, Emp \rangle \quad \text{(iii)}$$
$$Q_U = \langle \{Ename, Department\}, \{-,-,-,\{55,\ldots,100\},-\}, Emp \rangle \quad \text{(iv)}$$

Fig. 4. Query Intersection (Lee et al., 1999).

3.2 Query trimming

The concept of query trimming was introduced by (Keller A.M. and Basu J., 1996) and formally given by Ren (2003, pp.192-210). Ren (2003, pp.192-210) gave a comprehensive algorithm for query processing. In the start of the algorithms it is checked if the user query attributes are subset of cached semantics attributes, then perform query trimming based upon the implication or satisfiability of predicates. If the user query attributes is not a subset of cached semantics attributes, then there may be some common attributes. In this case, if query predicate implies cache predicates or there are common predicates between the query and cache semantics, then form the probe and remainder query as per the logic given by the algorithm. In other words the logic is based on checking implication and satisfiability of a user and cached query predicates (based upon the already published material, as explained in the next section) and finding common part between the user and cached query attributes.

Much work has been contributed towards finding implication and satisfiablity between a user and cached query predicates (Guo S et al., 1996), (Härder T. and Bühmann A., 2008). Simplified concept of implication and satisfiability is, let us have a user query predicate Q_{UP} and semantic segment predicate Q_{CP}, then there are three scenarios:

- $Q_{UP} \rightarrow Q_{CP}$, i.e. User predicate implies segment predicates, implying that the whole answer of Q_{UP} is contained in Q_{CP}.
- ($Q_{UP} \wedge Q_{CP}$ is satisfiable), implying that part of Q_{UP} answer is contained in Q_{CP}.
- ($Q_{UP} \wedge Q_{CP}$ is unsatisfiable), implying that there is no common part between Q_{UP} and Q_{CP}.

Remainder queries were trimmed again after comparing with other semantic cache segments with the same algorithm. It continues until it is decided that the cache does not further contribute to the query answering. This approach forms an iterative behavior, which was handled by a proposed query plan tree structure. This plan tree expresses the relationship of cache items and query subparts.

Query trimming techniques have some short comings, such as time and space efficiency, and complexity of the trimming process (Makki K. S and Andrei S, 2009), (Makki K. S and Rockey M., 2010). When query is trimmed into probe ($Q_{UP} \wedge Q_{CP}$) and remainder ($Q_{UP} \neg \wedge Q_{CP}$) part, the negation of the cached query predicate in remainder part make it much more expanded term if it contains disjunctions. This expansion created by negation of a term was shown with example (Makki K. S and Andrei S, 2009).

A relational query can be visualized as a rectangle with boundaries set by query predicate values. So according to (Makki K. S and Andrei S, 2009), (Makki K. S and Rockey M., 2010) semantic cache query processing based on query trimming is problem of finding intersection between two finite rectangles. Six cases that are extended form of Figure 1.1 are given in (Makki K. S and Andrei S, 2009), (Makki K. S and Rockey M., 2010) to show relationship between rectangles of user and cached queries. These rectangular representations do not depict implicit knowledge present in the semantics of user and cached queries. An technique named Flattening Bi-dimensional Interval Constraints (FBIC) was proposed (Makki K. S and Andrei S, 2009). Based on FBIC an algorithm for handling disjunctive and conjunctive queries was given by Makki (Makki K. S and Rockey M., 2010). The algorithm works for only single disjunctive case, where conjunctive cases are same as provided by (Makki K. S and Andrei S, 2009).

Finding intersection between rectangles of user and cached queries was done by comparing Bounds (Lower or Upper) of both rectangles. But computing comparable bounds were not given (Makki K. S and Andrei S, 2009), (Makki K. S and Rockey M., 2010).

3.3 Satisfiability and implication

Finding whether there exists a satisfiable part between two formulas or whether one implies the other is central to many database problems such as query containment, query equivalence, answering queries using views and database cache. So according to Guo (Guo S et al., 1996) implication is defined as "S implies T, denoted as $S \rightarrow T$, if and only if every assignment that satisfies S also satisfies T". Similarly satisfiability is defined as "S is satisfiable if and only if there exists at least one assignment for S that satisfies T." (Guo S et al., 1996) had given algorithm to compute implication, satisfiability and equivalence for given conjunctive formulas in integer and real domain. Let us have a formula (*Salary* < *20K AND Salary* > *8K AND Department* = *'CS'*) is satisfiable, because the assignment {12K/*Salary* , CS/*Department*} satisfies the formula. Similarly a formula (*Salary* >*10K OR Salary* < *12K)* is a tautology, because every assignment under this formula is satisfiable.

Satisfiability and implication results in databases (Guo et al., 1996),(J.D. Ullman, 1989),(A.Klug, 1988),(Rosenkrantz and Hunt, 1980), (Sun et al., 1989) are relevant to the computation of probe and remainder query in semantic cache query processing for a class of queries that involve inequalities of integer and real domain. Previous work models the problem into graph structure.

Rosenkrantz and Hunt (Rosenkrantz and Hunt, 1980) provided an algorithm of complexity $O(|Q|^3)$ for solving satisfiability problem; the expression S to be tested for satisfiability is the conjunction of terms of the form $X\ op\ C$, $X\ op\ Y$, and $X\ op\ Y + C$.

Guo et al. (Guo et al., 1996) provided an algorithm (GSW) for computing satisfiability with complexity $O(|Q|^3)$ involving complete operator set and predicate type X op C, X op Y and X op Y + C. Here we demonstrate GSW algorithm (Guo et al., 1996) for finding implication and satisfiability between two queries.

The GSW algorithm starts with transforming all inequalities into normalized form through given rules. It was proved by Ullman (J.D. Ullman, 1989) that these transformations still holds equality. After these transformation remaining operator set become $\{\leq, \neq\}$.

(1) $(X \geq Y+C) \equiv (Y \leq X - C)$
(2) $(X < Y + C) \equiv (X \leq Y + C) \wedge (X \neq Y + C)$
(3) $(X > Y + C) \equiv (Y \leq X - C) \wedge (X \neq Y + C)$
(4) $(X = Y + C) \equiv (Y \leq X - C) \wedge (X \leq Y + C)$
(5) $(X < C) \equiv (X \leq C) \wedge (X \neq C)$
(6) $(X > C) \equiv (X \geq C) \wedge (X \neq C)$
(7) $(X = C) \equiv (X \leq C) \wedge (X \geq C)$

Satisfiability of a conjunctive query Q is computed by constructing a connected weighted-directed graph $G_Q=(V_Q,E_Q)$ of Q after above transformation. Where V_Q are the nodes representing predicate attributes of an inequality and E_Q represent an edge between two nodes. An inequality of the form X op Y + C has X and Y nodes and an edge between them with C weight. The inequality X op C is transformed to X op V_0 + C by introducing a dummy node V_0.

According to GSW (Guo et al., 1996) algorithm, for any query Q if a negative-weighted cycle (a cycle whose sum of edges weight is negative) found in G_Q then Q is unsatisfiable. Otherwise Q is satisfiable. Testing satisfiability among user query Q_U and cached segment Q_S require us to construct a graph ($G_{Qu \wedge Qs}$) of ($Q_U \wedge Q_S$) and check $G_{Qu \wedge Qs}$ for any negative weighted cycle. Negative weighted cycle is found through Floyd-Warshall algorithm (R.W. Floyd, 1962). Complexity of Floyd-Warshall algorithm is $O(|V|^3)$, so finding satisfiability become $O(|Q_U \wedge Q_S|^3)$.

An algorithm with $O(|S|^3 + K)$ complexity for solving the implication problem between two conjunctive inequalities S and T was presented by Ullman (J.D. Ullman, 1989) and Sun (Sun et al., 1989). Conjunctive queries of the form X op Y were studied by (A.Klug, 1988) and (Sun et al., 1989). Implication between conjunctive queries of the form X op Y +C was addressed by GSW algorithm (Guo et al., 1996) with complexity $O(|Q_U|^2 + |Q_C|)$. GSW Implication (Guo et al., 1996) requires that Q_U is satisfiable. At first the implication algorithm constructs the closure of Q_U i.e., a universal set that contains all those inequalities that are implied by Q_U. Then, $Q_U \rightarrow Q_S$ if Q_S is a subset of the Q_U closure.

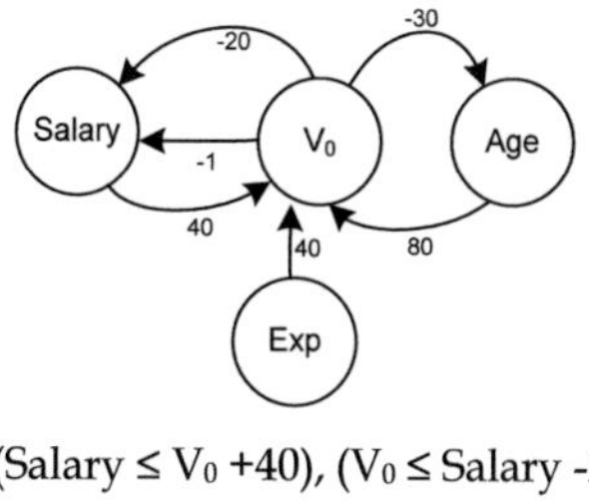

	Salary	V_0	Age	Exp
Salary	20	40	10	∞
V_0	-20	20	-30	∞
Age	60	80	50	∞
Exp	20	40	10	0

[($V_0 \leq$ Salary -1), (Salary $\leq V_0$ +40), ($V_0 \leq$ Salary -20), ($V_0 \leq$ Age -30), (Age $\leq V_0$ +80), (Exp $\leq V_0$ +40)]

Fig. 5. (a) [$Q_{U1} \wedge Q_S$] and $G_{QU1 \wedge QS}$ (b) Shortest Path Table

Example 2: Let us have a user query $Q_{U1} = \pi_{\text{Age,Salary,Exp}}\ \sigma_{\text{Salary}\geq 20K \wedge \text{Age}\geq 30 \wedge \text{Age}\leq 80 \wedge \text{Exp}\leq 40}$ over cached segment Q_{C7} of Example 1. The directed weighted graph $G_{QU1 \wedge QC7}$ of $Q_{U1} \wedge Q_{C7}$ is shown in Figure 5(a). Q_{U1} is satisfiable with respect to Q_{C7}, as there is no negative weighted cycle in $G_{QU \wedge QC7}$.

3.4 Bucket algorithm

As discussed earlier, a user of data integration system poses query in term of mediated schema, because root sources are transparent in such systems. A module of data integration system translate/reformulate a user query that refers directly to the root sources. Several reputed algorithms exist for such query reformulation/rewriting (Levy A.Y et al., 1996), (Duschka O.M. and Genesereth M.R. 1997), (Pottinger R. and Levy A. 2000). In context of semantic cache the root sources are the cache segments and the mediated schema is the cache description. The goal of the bucket algorithm (Levy A.Y et al., 1996) is to reformulate a user query that is posed on the mediated (virtual) schema into a query that refers directly to the available (local/cached) data sources. This reformulation is known as query-rewriting. Both the query and the sources are described by select-project-join queries that may include atoms of arithmetic comparison predicates. The bucket algorithm returns the maximally-contained rewriting of the query using the views. This rewriting is a maximally-contained but not an equivalent one.

We demonstrate working (in context of semantic cache query processing) of bucket algorithm with example.

$$Q_{C1} \leftarrow \pi_{Ename,\ Department}\ \sigma_{Age \geq 50}\ (Emp);$$

$$Q_{C2} \leftarrow \pi_{Age,\ Department}\ (Emp);$$

$$Q_{C3} \leftarrow \pi_{Age,\ Department}\ \sigma_{Exp < 15}\ (Emp);$$

$$Q_{U} \leftarrow \pi_{Age,\ Department}\ \sigma_{Exp > 20\ \wedge\ Age < 70}\ (Emp);$$

Fig. 6. User Query (Q_U) Over Cached Queries

Let us have Q_{C1}, Q_{C2} and Q_{C3} (shown in Figure 6) in cache, and a user query Q_U (shown in Figure 6) is posed over them. As shown in Table 1 below, according to bucket algorithm both cached queries Q_{C1} and Q_{C2} are candidate selection for its bucket. Since there is no inconsistency between user query predicate and cached queries (i.e. $Age \geq 55$ consistent with $Age < 70$) when compared in isolation (atomically). Where Q_{C3} is excluded due to predicate inconsistency (i.e. $Exp < 15$ inconsistent with $Exp > 20$). In second step of bucket algorithm, elements of buckets are combined together to form a rewriting of the user query. The rewritten query (Q') in this case is shown in Figure 7 below.

Emp(Empid,Ename,Department,Age,Salary,Exp)
Q_{C1}(Ename', Department) *Q_{C2}(Age, Department)*

Table 1. Contents of Bucket. The attribute not required by user query is shown as primed attribute.

$$Q' \leftarrow \pi_{Age,\ Department}\ \sigma_{Age < 70}\ (Q_{C1}, Q_{C2});$$

Fig. 7. Rewritten Query Q′.

3.4.1 Example

We follow the results produced by maximally-contained query rewriting algorithm named bucket algorithm (Levy A.Y et al., 1996) provided above. The predicate (*Exp* > *20*) is pruned because query cannot be executed over cached data as there is no information present against *Exp* attribute. Further more if the rewritten query (*Q′* shown in Figure 7) executed locally, it will give unnecessary/incorrect results. These results are maximally-contained or maximum data retrieval (MDR) but the results contain tuples that are not part of the actual user query (Q_U). Figure 8 (a) shows the collective dataset of cached queries Q_{C1} and Q_{C2} (Figure 6). The rewritten query (*Q′*) executed over cached data is shown in Figure 8 (b). The data items shown as strike circle (-●-) in Figure 8 (b) are the required results of user query (Q_U). Where results retrieved by the rewritten query (*Q′*) are not the precise answer for the user query (Q_U).

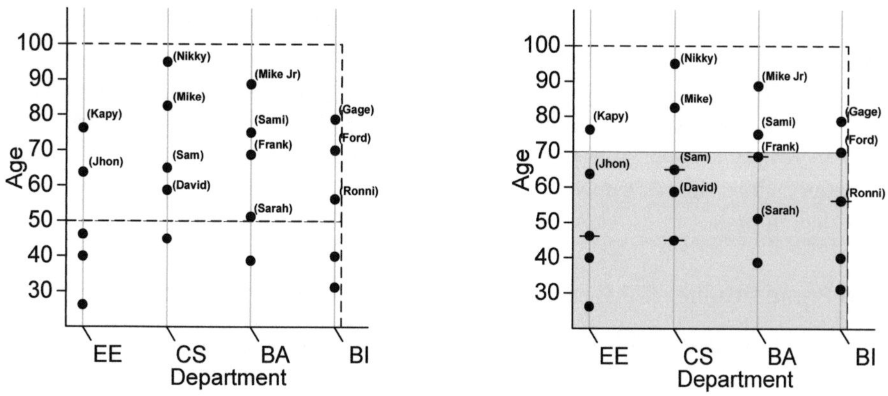

Fig. 8. (a) Collective Data of Cached Query Q_{C1} and Q_{C2}. (b) Rewritten Query Q′ Over Cached Query Q_{C1} and Q_{C2}.

Bucket algorithm does not compute probe and remainder queries separately. So there is no way to determine the available and unavailable answer from the cache.

3.5 Semantic reasoning for web queries

A web-based cache system is different from data caching. In web cache, special proxy servers store recently visited pages for later reuse. A uniform resource locater (URL) is a user query that is posed over web cache system. Any page in cache is being used whenever a user given URL matches the cache page header. This type of caching strategy is similar to page-caching, where binary results (complete answer or no-answer) are possible but partial answer cannot be determined.

However, searching performed over web resources through Boolean queries (keywords conjunction with AND & NOT operators) do not work in a plain page caching system. Because the user query in this case is not a URL, and extracting qualified tuples against an individual keyword or whole query from page headers is not possible (Chidlovskii B and Borghoff U. M., 2000), (Qiong L and Jaffrey F. N., 2001). Semantic cache was introduced as an alternative to plain page caching where cache is managed as semantic regions.

Web queries over web resources are different than queries posed over databases. As there is no attribute and predicate part in web queries, also it neither contain join operator. And the problem of answering web-queries can be reduced to *set containment problem.*

There is a lot of research work on semantic caching for web queries. Such as (Chidlovskii B and Borghoff U. M., 2000) addressed both semantic cache management and query processing of web queries for meta-searcher systems. Their technique is based on a signature file method. In which a signature is given to every semantic region for processing all cases (similar to Figure 1) of containment and intersection.

A cache model was proposed for database applications using web techniques (Anton J. et al., 2002). Cache elements were stored as web pages/sub pages called fragments and sub fragments with their header information called template. Fragments can be indexed or shared among different templates. Fragments, sub-fragments and templates were updated or expired based on their unique policy which included expiration, validation and invalidation information. In this case data retrieval is performed by matching template information with requested query and subsequent fragments or sub-fragments are returned. Partial answer retrieval is possible in this technique as sub-fragments alone can be resulted to a user query. But still this technique is closer to page cache technique, where each fragment is itself a page.

3.6 Pattern Prime Product (PPT) reasoning for XML queries

The information that is available on the web is unstructured, extensible mark-up language XML is used to provide the structure to the web information/data. As described above the querying mechanism for current web is keyword based search. Keyword based search is considered to be the non-semantic (Mandhani B. and Suciu D., 2005), (Sanaullah, M., 2008).

A novel method of checking containment is proposed by Gang Wu and Juanzi Li (Gang Wu and Juanzi Li, 2010). Each node in the query is assigned a unique prime number and then the product of these prime numbers is calculated by a specific method. This product is called Pattern's Prime producT (PPT). The query is stored in the cache along with this PPT.

On each next issued query the same procedure is followed to assign unique prime numbers to each node and if any node of the query matches with any existing stored view's node then the same prime number is assigned to new node as it was allotted to previously stored node. The PPT of the new query is calculated and then divided by the PPT of all stored views. If any of stored views completely divides the PPT of the query then that view is selected and rest are rejected. The selected view further processed to make sure whether the occurrences of the nodes in the query and view is similar, i.e $Qk = Vk$ where k is the position of kth axis node. The PPT of each infix is also checked.

3.6.1 Example

An XML document is shown in Figure 9. A user issues a query /lib/book and as a result the technique loads all the results of "lib", "book" nodes in the cache and assigns prime numbers to each node i.e. "lib"=2, "book"=3. After assigning the prime numbers a prime product is calculated as follows.

(2*3), here 6 is the Tree Pattern Prime Product of the view.

Now if the user again issues the query /lib/book/author then each node in the query is assigned the same prime number as it was previously assigned to the nodes in the view. Here 2 is assigned to "lib" and 3 is assigned to "book". "author" appeared first time so a new prime number i.e. 5 is assigned to author node. Dividing the prime product of query (90) by the prime product of view (6) will yields the result 15, means query is completely divided by the view. If the prime product of a view completely divides the prime product of a query then it further checks the following conditions. Whether the order of appearance of each axis node in the view and query is similar and if the answer is true then it means that the query is contained in the view.

3.6.2 Example

If a query contains predicates, for example A[b[b[a]]]/c/d the tree of this query is shown in figure 9. The prime product is calculated as shown below

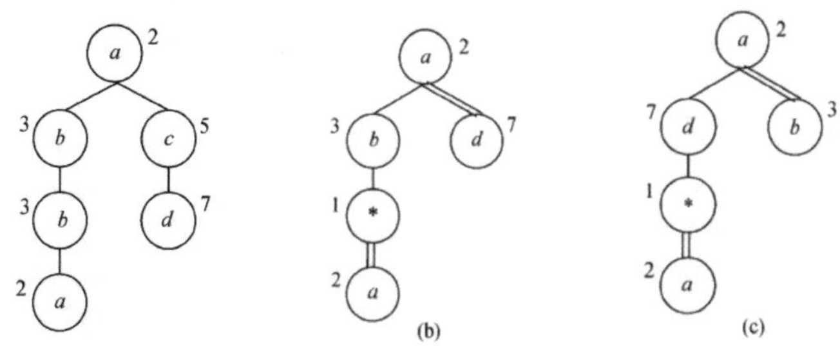

Fig. 9. Prime Product Calculation.

PPT of b=(2*3)*(3*1)*(1*2)*(2*7) = 504
PPT of c= (2*7)*(7*1)*(1*2)*(2*3) = 1176

Now only the PPT of b completely divides the PPT of the query so b is selected in the first condition of the algorithm.

This algorithm retrieves the results of all axis nodes given in the query for example if we issue following query to the document shown in figure 1 "\lib\book[price>30]". Then apart from the presence of a predicate it retrieves all the result of book node and stores it in the cache. This action requires more cache space.

3.7 Subsumption analysis reasoning

Description logics (a language of logic family) DL claims that it can express the conceptual domain model/ontology of the data source and provide evaluation techniques. Since structured query language (SQL) is a structured format, it can be classified under subsumption relationship. A well known technique named Tabulex provides structural subsumption of concepts. Description logic (DL) is assumed to be useful for semantic cache query processing and management (Ali et al. 2010). The relational queries can be modelled / translated in DL and DL inference algorithms can be used to find query containments. The translation of relational query to DL may have not the same spirit as that of querying languages for DL systems, but is sufficient for finding the query containment of relational queries (Ali et al. 2010). The subsumption reasoning (containment) of the semantics of the data to be cached is very useful in eliminating the redundant semantics and minimizing the size of semantic cache for the same amount of data.

The tableaux algorithm (Baader et al., 1991a) (Hollunder et al., 1990) is instrumental to devise a reasoning service for knowledge base represented in description logic. All the facts of knowledge base are represented in a tree of branches with intra-branch logical AND between the facts and inter-branch logical OR, organized as per the rules of tableaux algorithm (Baader et al., 2003). A clash in a branch represents an inconsistency in that branch and the model in that branch can be discarded. The proof of subsumption or unsatisfiability can be obtained if all the models (all the branches) are discarded this way (Baader et al., 2003).

The proposed solution (Ali et al. 2010) consists of two basic steps: First user query (relational) is translated into DL. The translated query is then evaluated for subsumption relationship with previously stored query in the cache by using the sound and complete subsumption algorithm given in (Baader et al., 91b) (Lutz et al., 2005).

3.7.1 Example

Considering, another scenario having predicates conditions with disjunctive operator in Figure 10. All the three branches yields to clash in checking *Q3 ⊑ Q4;* therefore, *Q4* contain *Q3*. In first branch (Line 8 in Figure 10) after applying the *Or rule, Emp* and *¬Emp* yields to clash. In second branch (Line 9 in Figure 10) *ename* and *¬ename* yields to clash, and in third *branch (Line 10* Figure 10), *≥30k(sal)* and *≤19k(sal)* yields to clash. All tree branches (Line 8, 9, 10 of Figure 10) yield to clash in opening the tableaux algorithm; therefore, *Q3 ⊑ Q4*.

1. Q3: Select ename, age from Emp where sal ≥ 30k
2. Q4: Select ename from Emp where sal ≥ 20k ⊔ age ≥20
3. *Q3 ⊑ Q4*
4. *Q3 ⊓ ¬Q4*
5. (Emp ⊓ ename ⊓ age ⊓ ≥ 30k(sal)) ⊓ ¬(Emp ⊓ ename ⊓ ≥ 20k(sal) ⊔ ≥20(age))
6. (Emp ⊓ ename ⊓ age ⊓ ≥ 30k(sal)) ⊓ (¬Emp ⊔ ¬ename ⊔ 19k(sal) ⊓ 19(age)) **Move negation inward**
7. (Emp , ename , age , ≥ 30k(sal) , ¬Emp ⊔ ¬ename ⊔ 19k(sal) , 19(age)) **AND rule**
8. Emp , ename , age , ≥ 30k(sal) , ¬Emp, , 19(age) **Clash**
9. Emp , ename , age , ≥ 30k(sal), ¬ename, 19(age) **Or Rule** **Clash**
10. Emp , ename , age , ≥ 30k(sal), 19k(sal) , 19(age)) **Clash**
11. *Q3 ⊑ Q4* ***All branches leads to Clash***

Fig. 10. Query Containment using Tableux.

4. Conclusion

In this chapter we demonstrated several reasoning techniques of query processing in semantic cache. This chapter provides overview of semantic cache application in different domains such as relational databases, web queries, answering from views, xml based queries and description logic based queries.

Semantic cache query processing techniques are unstructured-semantics approaches, in which semantics are extracted from structured representations that have no semantics within their representations.

5. Acknowledgment

We would like to acknowledge Mr. Ishtique Ahmad for providing help on XML based semantic cache, Mr. Tariq Ali for DL based subsumption analysis, and Mr. Munir Ahmed for providing useful feedbacks.

6. References

A. Klug, "On Conjunctive Queries Containing Inequalities," *ACM*, vol. 35, no. 1, pp. 146-160, Jan. 1988.

Ahmad, M and Qadir, M.A., (2008). "Query Processing Over Relational Databases with Semantic Cache: A Survey", 12th IEEE International Multitopic Conference 2008, INMIC08.

Ahmad, M and Qadir, M.A., "Query Processing and Enhanced Semantic Indexing for Relational Data Semantic Cache", Center for Distributed and Semantic Computing, Mohammad Ali Jinnah University, Islamabad, Pakistan 2007.

Ahmed M. U., Zaheer R. A., and Qadir M. A., "Intelligent Cache Management for Data Grid", Australasian Workshop on Grid Computing and e-Research (AusGrid 2005).

Ali, T., Qadir, M. A., Ahmed, M., Translation of Relational Queries into Description Logic for semantic Cache Query Processing, International Conference on Information and Emerging Technologies (ICIET) 2010.

Andrade H., Kurc T., Sussman A., Saltz J., "Active semantic caching to optimize multidimensional data analysis in parallel and distributed environments" Elsevier Journal on Parallel Computing, volume 33, pp 497-520, 2007.

Anton J., Jacobs L., Liu X., Parker J., Zeng Z. and Zhong T., "Web caching for database applications with Oracle Web Cache", Proceedings of the 2002 ACM SIGMOD international conference on Management of data, June 03-06, 2002, Madison, Wisconsin.

Baader, F., Hollunder, B., A terminological knowledge representation system with complete inference algorithm. In: Proc. Workshop on Processing Declarative Knowledge, PDK-91Lecture Notes in Artificial Intelligence, Springer, Berlin, pp. 67–86, 1991.

Baader, F., Hanschke, P. A schema for integrating concrete domains into concept languages. In Proc. of the 12th Int. Joint Conf. on Artificial Intelligence (IJCAI'91), pages452–457, 1991.

Baader, F., McGuinness, D., Nardi, D., Patel-Schneider, P., The Description Logic Handbook: Theory, Implementation and Applications. Cambridge University Press, 2003.

Bashir M F. and Qadir M. A., "Survey on Efficient Content Matching over Semantic Cache", 10th IEEE International Multitopic Conference 2006, INMIC06.

Bashir M F. and Qadir M. A., "HiSIS: 4-Level Hierarchical Semantic Indexing for Efficient Content", 10th IEEE International Multitopic Conference 2006, INMIC06.

Bashir M.F., Zaheer R.A., Shams Z.M. and Qadir M.A.. "SCAM: Semantic Caching Architecture for Efficient Content Matching over Data Grid". AWIC, Springer Heidelberg, Berlin, 2007. pp. 41-46.

Bashir, M.F and Qadir, M.A., "ProQ - Query Processing Over Semantic Cache For Data Grid", Master's Thesis, Center for Distributed and Semantic Computing, Mohammad Ali Jinnah University, Islamabad, Pakistan 2007.

Brunkhorst I. and Dhraief H., "Semantic Caching in Schema-based P2P-Networks", DBISP2P 2005/2006, LNCS 4125, pp. 179-186, 2007. Springer-Verlag Berlin Heidelberg 2007.

Chidlovskii B and Borghoff U. M., "Signature file methods for semantic query caching". In: Proc. 2nd European Conf. on Digital Libraries, September, 1998, Heraklion, Greece, Berlin Heidelberg New York: Springer, LNCS 1513, pp. 479–498

Chidlovskii B., Borghoff U. M., "Semantic caching of Web queries", The International Journal on Very Large Data Bases, v.9 n.1, p.2-17, March 2000.

Dar S, M. J. Franklin, B. T. Jonson, D. Srivastava, M. Tan, "Semantic Data Caching and Replacement", in proceedings of 22nd VLDB Conference, Mumbai, 1996.

Duschka O.M. and Genesereth M.R. "Query planning in infomaster". In: Proc.ACM Symposium on Applied Computing. pp 109–111, San Jose, Calif., USA, 1997.

Gang Wu and Juanzi Li, "Semantic Web", Intech Publisher 2010, pp 97-106.

Godfrey P. and Gryz J., "Semantic Query Caching for Heterogeneous Databases," Proc. KRDB Conf. Very Large Databases, vol. 6, pp. 1-6, 1997.

Guo S., Sun W., and Weiss M.A., "Solving Satisfiability and Implication Problems in Database Systems," ACM Trans. Database Systems, vol. 21, no. 2, pp. 270-293, 1996.

Halevy, A.Y., "Answering queries using views", VLDB J., vol. 10, pp. 270-294, 2001.

Hao X., Zhang T., and Li L., "The Inter-clause Optimization Technique in Semantic Caching Query Evaluation", Journal of Information & Computational Science volume 2, no. 1, pp 27-33, 2005.

Härder T. and Bühmann A., "Value complete, column complete, predicate complete", VLDB Journal, 2008, pp 805-826.

Hector García-Molina, Jeffrey D. Ullman and Jennifer Widom., "Database Systems: the Complete Book", GOAL Series, 2001.

Hollunder, B., Nutt, W., Subsumption algorithms for concept languages. Research Report RR-90-04, Deutsches Forschungszentrum fur Kunstliche Intelligenz GmbH (DFKI), April 1990.

J.D. Ullman, Principles of Database and Knowledge-Base Systems, vol. 11. Computer Science Press, 1989.

Jónsson B. Þór., Arinbjarnar M., Þórsson B., Franklin M. J., Srivastava D., "Performance and overhead of semantic cache management", ACM Transactions on Internet Technology (TOIT), v.6 n.3, p.302-331, August 2006.

Keller A.M. and Basu J., "A Predicate-Based Caching Scheme for Client-Server Database Architectures," VLDB J., vol. 5, no. 2, pp. 35-47, Apr. 1996.

Lee D. and Chu W. W., "Semantic Caching via Query Matching for Web Sources", CIKM, ACM, 1999.

Lee K.C.K, H.V. Leong, and A. Si, "Semantic Query Caching in a Mobile Environment," Mobile Computing and Comm. Rev., vol. 3, no. 2, pp. 28-36, Apr. 1999.

Levy A.Y., Rajaraman A., Ordille J. J., "Querying Heterogeneous Information Sources Using Source Descriptions", Proceedings of the 22th International Conference on Very Large Data Bases, p.251-262, September 03-06, 1996

Levy A.Y. "Logic-based techniques in data integration", Minker J (ed.) Logic-based artificial intelligence. Kluwer Academic, Dordrecht, 2000, pp 575–595

Lutz, C., Milicic., M. A tableau Algorithm for Description Logics with Concrete Domains and GCIs, Tableaux 2005, LNAI 3702, pp. 201-216, 2005

Makki K. S and Andrei S. "Utilizing Semantic Caching in Ubiquitous Environment", IWCMC'09, June 21-24,2009, Leipzig, Germany.

Makki K. S and Rocky M., "Query Visualization for Query Trimming in Semantic Caching", IEEE 24th International Conference on Advanced Information Networking and Applications Workshops (WAINA), 2010.

Mandhani B. , Suciu D., "Query caching and view selection for XML databases", Proceedings of the 31st international conference on Very large data bases (VLDB), 2005, Trondheim, Norway.

Nama B., Shin M., Andrade H., and Sussman A., "Multiple query scheduling for distributed semantic caches", In Proc. of Journal of Parallel and Distributed Computing, 70-(2010) pp. 598-611

Pottinger R. and Levy A. "A scalable algorithm for answering queries using views". In: Proc. of VLDB. pp 484-495, Cairo, Egypt, 2000.

Qiong L and Jeffrey F. N., "Form-Based Proxy Caching for Database-Backed Web Sites", Proceedings of the 27th International Conference on Very Large Data Bases, p.191-200, 2001.

Ren, Q., Dunham, M.H., and Kumar, V., (2003). "Semantic Caching and Query Processing". IEEE Transactions on Knowledge and Data Engineering, IEEE Computer Society, 2003, pp. 192-210.

Rosenkrantz D.J. and Hunt H.B., "Processing Conjunctive Predicates and Queries," Proc. Conf. Very Large Databases, pp. 64- 71, 1980.

R.W. Floyd, "Algorithm 97 Shortest Path" *Comm. ACM,* vol. 5, no. 6, p. 345, June 1962.

Safaeei A.A, Haghjoo M. Abdi S., "Semantic cache schema for query processing in mobile databases", 3rd IEEE International Conference on Digital Information Management, 2008. ICDIM 2008.

Sanaullah, M., Qadir, M.A., and Ahmad, M., (2008) "SCAD-XML: Semantic Cache Architecture for XML Data Files using XPath with Cases and Rules ". 12th IEEE

International Multitopic Conference, INMIC 2008, IEEE, Karachi, Pakistan, December 2008.

Sun, X., Kamell, N. N., AND NI, L.M. 1989. Processing implication on queries. *IEEE Trans. Softw. Eng.* 5, 10 (Oct.), 168–175.

The TimesTen Team Mid-tier caching: the TimesTen approach. In: SIGMOD Conference, pp. 588–593 (2002).

Section 3

Algorithms and Logic Programming

A Common Mathematical Framework for Asymptotic Complexity Analysis and Denotational Semantics for Recursive Programs Based on Complexity Spaces

Salvador Romaguera[1] and Oscar Valero[2]
[1]*Instituto Universitario de Matemática Pura y Aplicada, Universitat Politècnica de València*
[2]*Departamento de Ciencias Matemáticas e Informática, Universidad de las Islas Baleares*
Spain

1. Introduction

In Denotational Semantics one of the aims consists of giving mathematical models of programming languages so that the meaning of a recursive algorithm can be obtained as an element of the constructed model.

Most programming languages allow to construct recursive algorithms by means of a recursive definition expressing the meaning of such a definition in terms of its own meaning. In order to analyze the correctness of such recursive definitions, D.S. Scott developed a mathematical theory of computation which is based on ideas from order theory and topology (Davey & Priestley, 1990; Scott, 1970; 1972). From the Scott theory viewpoint, the meaning of such a denotational specification is obtained as the fixed point of a nonrecursive mapping, induced by the denotational specification, which is at the same time the topological limit of successive iterations of the nonrecursive mapping acting on a distinguished element of the model. Moreover, the order of Scott's model represents some notion of information so that each iteration of the nonrecursive mapping, which models each step of the program computation, is identified with an element of the mathematical model which is greater than (or equal to) the other ones associated with the preceding iterations (preceding steps of the program computation) because each iteration gives more information about the meaning than those computed before. Hence the aforesaid meaning of the recursive denotational specification is modeled as the fixed point of the nonrecursive mapping which is obtained as the limit, with respect to the so-called Scott topology, of the increasing sequence of successive iterations. Consequently, the fixed point captures the amount of information defined by the increasing sequence, i.e. the fixed point yields the total information about the meaning provided by the elements of the increasing sequence, and it does not contain more information than can be obtained from the elements of such a sequence.

A typical and illustrative example of such recursive definitions is given by those recursive algorithms that compute the factorial of a nonnegative integer number by means of the following recursive denotational specification:

$$fact(n) = \begin{cases} 1 & \text{if } n = 1 \\ nfact(n-1) & \text{if } n > 1 \end{cases}. \tag{1}$$

Of course the above denotational specification has the drawback that the meaning of the symbol *fact* is expressed in terms of itself. Hence the symbol *fact* can not be replaced by its meaning in the denotational specification (1), since the meaning, given by the right-hand side in (1), also contains the symbol. Following the original ideas of Scott, the meaning of the specification (1), i.e. the entire factorial function, is obtained as the unique total function that is a fixed point of the nonrecursive functional ϕ_{fact} defined on the set of partial functions ordered by extension (see (Davey & Priestley, 1990) for a detailed description of the set of partial functions) by

$$\phi_{fact} f(n) = \begin{cases} 1 & \text{if } n = 1 \\ nf(n-1) & \text{if } n > 1 \text{ and } n-1 \in \text{dom} f \end{cases},$$

where the successive iterations acting over the partial function f_1 ($\text{dom} f_1 = 1$ and $f_1(1) = 1$) hold that $\phi^n_{fact} f_1(m) = 1$ if $m = 1$ and $\phi^n_{fact} f_1(m) = m!$ for all $m \leq n$. Thus, the increasing with respect to the extension order sequence of iterations $(\phi^n_{fact}(f_1))_{n \in \mathbb{N}}$ models each step of the computation of the factorial of a nonnegative integer number by a recursive algorithm using the specification (1) and, in addition, the limit of the sequence with respect to the Scott topology is exactly the meaning of the symbol *fact* which provides the factorial of each nonnegative integer number. Furthermore, each iteration provides more information about the symbol *fact* (i.e. about the entire factorial function) than the preceding ones.

Since Scott's mathematical theory of computation was introduced, it has been wondered in the literature whether such a model can be applied to other fields of Computer Science which differ from Denotational Semantics. A positive answer to the posed question was provided by M.P. Schellekens in (Schellekens, 1995). In fact, Schellekens showed that the original Scott idea of getting, via fixed point techniques, the meaning of a denotational specification as the topological limit of "successive approximations" is helpful in Asymptotic Complexity Analysis. Concretely, Schellekens introduced a novel mathematical method to provide asymptotic upper bounds of the complexity of those algorithms whose running time of computing satisfies a recurrence equation of Divide and Conquer type in such a way that the original ideas of Scott, namely, the meaning is a fixed point and is the limit of a sequence of successive iterations of a functional acting on a distinguished element, are respected but now the fixed point technique is new. Furthermore, in Schellekens' method the topology, intrinsic to the Scott model, is induced by a "distance" tool which provides, in addition, a measure of the degree of approximation of the elements that form the model. This fact yields an advantage over the Scott model because in the latter one quantitative data approach is not available.

Motivated by the fact that Schellekens' method successfully applies the Scott ideas for Denotational Semantics to the asymptotic complexity analysis of algorithms and that, in addition, the aforesaid method improves the Scott one in the sense that it allows to provide quantitative information, not only qualitative, about the degree of approximation of the elements that form the model, the propose of this chapter is twofold.

On one hand, we will show that Schellekens' method, and thus the original ideas of Scott, is useful to obtain asymptotic upper bounds of complexity for a class of recursive algorithms whose running time of computing leads to recurrence equations different from the Divide and Conquer ones. Moreover, we improve the original Schellekens's method by introducing a new fixed point technique which allows to obtain lower asymptotic bounds for the running time of computing of the aforesaid algorithms. We will illustrate and validate the developed method applying our results to provide the asymptotic complexity (upper and lower bounds) of the running time of computing of a celebrated recursive algorithm that computes the Fibonacci sequence (see, for instance, (Cull et al., 1985)).

On the other hand, we will introduce a generalized mathematical method, in the spirit of Schellekens and based on the mathematical approach given in (Romaguera & Schellekens, 2000), which will be useful to formally describe the running time of computing of algorithms that perform a computation using recursive denotational specifications and the meaning, and thus the correctness, of such a denotational specification simultaneously. In order to validate the new results we will apply them to provide, at the same time, the program correctness and the asymptotic complexity class (upper and lower bounds) of the running time of a recursive program that computes the factorial function via the denotational specification (1).

The remainder of the chapter is organized as follows: In Section 2 we recall a few pertinent concepts from asymptotic complexity analysis of algorithms. Section 3 is devoted to introduce the method of Schellekens, and its relationship to the above exposed Scott ideas, which provides an upper bound of the asymptotic complexity for those algorithms whose running time of computing leads to a Divide and Conquer recurrence equation. The utility of the method is illustrated by means of the application given by Schellekens to obtain an asymptotic upper bound of the average running time of computing of Mergesort. In order to analyze the complexity of the recursive algorithm that computes the Fibonacci sequence via the Schellekens approach, in Section 4 we will introduce the new method based on successive approximations and fixed point techniques that allow us to describe the complexity class (asymptotic upper and lower bounds) for the running time of computing of recursive algorithms more general than the Divide and Conquer ones. Moreover, in Section 5 we give the generalized mathematical method which is useful to describe formally the running time of computing of algorithms that perform a computation using recursive denotational specifications as well as their program correctness . Finally, in Section 6 we summarize the aims achieved and the advantages of our new mathematical methodologies with respect to the Schellekens and Scott ones.

2. Fundamentals of Asymptotic Complexity Analysis

From now on, the letters $\mathbb{R}^+$ and $\mathbb{N}$ will denote the set of nonnegative real numbers and the set of positive integer numbers, respectively.

Our basic reference for complexity analysis of algorithms is (Brassard & Bratley, 1988).

In Computer Science the complexity analysis of an algorithm is based on determining mathematically the quantity of resources needed by the algorithm in order to solve the problem for which it has been designed.

A typical resource, playing a central role in complexity analysis, is the running time of computing. Since there are often many algorithms to solve the same problem, one objective of the complexity analysis is to assess which of them is faster when large inputs are considered. To this end, it is required to compare their running time of computing. This is usually done by means of the asymptotic analysis in which the running time of an algorithm is denoted by a function $T : \mathbb{N} \rightarrow (0, \infty]$ in such a way that $T(n)$ represents the time taken by the algorithm to solve the problem under consideration when the input of the algorithm is of size n. Of course the running time of an algorithm does not only depend on the input size n, but it depends also on the particular input of the size n (and the distribution of the data). Thus the running time of an algorithm is different when the algorithm processes certain instances of input data of the same size n. As a consequence, it is usually necessary to distinguish three possible behaviors when the running time of an algorithm is discussed. These are the so-called best case, the worst case and the average case. The best case and the worst case for an input of size n are defined by the minimum and the maximum running time of computing over all inputs of size n, respectively. The average case for an input of size n is defined by the expected value or average running time of computing over all inputs of size n.

In general, given an algorithm, to determine exactly the function which describes its running time of computing is an arduous task. However, in most situations is more useful to know the running time of computing of an algorithm in an "approximate" way than in an exact one. For this reason the Asymptotic Complexity Analysis focus its interest on obtaining the "approximate" running time of computing.

In order to recall the notions from Asymptotic Complexity Analysis which will be useful for our aim later on, let us assume that $f : \mathbb{N} \rightarrow (0, \infty]$ denotes the running time of computing of a certain algorithm under study. Moreover, consider that there exists a function $g : \mathbb{N} \rightarrow (0, \infty]$ such that there exist, simultaneously, $n_0 \in \mathbb{N}$ and $c \in \mathbb{R}^+$ satisfying $f(n) \leq cg(n)$ for all $n \in \mathbb{N}$ with $n \geq n_0$ ($\leq$ and $\geq$ stand for the usual orders on $\mathbb{R}^+$). Then, the function g provides an asymptotic upper bound of the running time of the studied algorithm. Hence, if we do not know the exact expression of the function f, then the function g gives an "approximate" information of the running time of the algorithm for each input size n, $f(n)$, in the sense that the algorithm takes a time to process the input data of size n bounded above by the value $g(n)$. Following the standard notation, when g is an upper asymptotic bound of f we will write $f \in \mathcal{O}(g)$.

In the analysis of the complexity of an algorithm, besides obtaining an upper asymptotic bound, it is useful to assess an asymptotic lower bound of the running time of computing. In this case the Ω-notation plays a central role. Indeed, the statement $f \in \Omega(g)$ means that there exist $n_0 \in \mathbb{N}$ and $c \in \mathbb{R}^+$ such that $cg(n) \leq f(n)$ for all $n \in \mathbb{N}$ with $n \geq n_0$. Of course, and similarly to the $\mathcal{O}$-notation case, when the time taken by the algorithm to process an input data of size n, $f(n)$, is unknown, the function g yields an "approximate" information of the running time of the algorithm in the sense that the algorithm takes a time to process the input data of size n bounded below by $g(n)$.

Of course, when the complexity of an algorithm is discussed, the best situation matches up with the case in which we can find a function $g : \mathbb{N} \rightarrow (0, \infty]$ in such a way that the running time f holds the condition $f \in \mathcal{O}(g) \cap \Omega(g)$, denoted by $f \in \Theta(g)$, since, in this case, we obtain a "tight "asymptotic bound of f and, thus, a total asymptotic information about the time taken by the algorithm to solve the problem under consideration (or equivalently to process the input data of size n for each $n \in \mathbb{N}$). From now on, we will say that f belongs to the asymptotic complexity class of g whenever $f \in \Theta(g)$.

In the light of the above, from an asymptotic complexity analysis viewpoint, to determine the running time of an algorithm consists of obtaining its asymptotic complexity class.

3. Quasi-metric spaces and Asymptotic Complexity Analysis: the Schellekens approach

In 1995, Schellekens introduced a new mathematical framework, now known as the Complexity Space, with the aim to contribute to the topological foundation for the Asymptotic Complexity Analysis of Algorithms via the application of the original Scott ideas for Denotational Semantics, that is via the application of fixed point and successive approximations reasoning, (Schellekens, 1995). This framework is based on the notion of a quasi-metric space.

Following (Künzi, 1993), a quasi-metric on a nonempty set X is a function $d : X \times X \to \mathbb{R}^+$ such that for all $x, y, z \in X$:

(i) $d(x,y) = d(y,x) = 0 \Leftrightarrow x = y$;
(ii) $d(x,y) \leq d(x,z) + d(z,y)$.

Of course a metric on a nonempty set X is a quasi-metric d on X satisfying, in addition, the following condition for all $x, y \in X$:

(iii) $d(x,y) = d(y,x)$.

A quasi-metric space is a pair (X, d) such that X is a nonempty set and d is a quasi-metric on X.

Each quasi-metric d on X generates a T_0-topology $\mathcal{T}(d)$ on X which has as a base the family of open d-balls $\{B_d(x,\varepsilon) : x \in X, \varepsilon > 0\}$, where $B_d(x,\varepsilon) = \{y \in X : d(x,y) < \varepsilon\}$ for all $x \in X$ and $\varepsilon > 0$.

Given a quasi-metric d on X, the function d^s defined on $X \times X$ by

$$d^s(x,y) = \max\left(d(x,y), d(y,x)\right),$$

is a metric on X.

A quasi-metric space (X, d) is called bicomplete whenever the metric space (X, d^s) is complete.

A well-known example of a bicomplete quasi-metric space is the pair $((0,\infty], u_{-1})$, where

$$u_{-1}(x,y) = \max\left(\frac{1}{y} - \frac{1}{x}, 0\right),$$

for all $x, y \in (0,\infty]$. Obviously we adopt the convention that $\frac{1}{\infty} = 0$. The quasi-metric space $((0,\infty], u_{-1})$ plays a central role in the Schellekens framework. Indeed, let us recall that the complexity space is the pair $(\mathcal{C}, d_{\mathcal{C}})$, where

$$\mathcal{C} = \{f : \mathbb{N} \to (0, \infty] : \sum_{n=1}^{\infty} 2^{-n} \frac{1}{f(n)} < \infty\},$$

and $d_{\mathcal{C}}$ is the quasi-metric (so-called complexity distance) on $\mathcal{C}$ defined by

$$d_{\mathcal{C}}(f,g) = \sum_{n=1}^{\infty} 2^{-n} u_{-1}(f(n), g(n)) = \sum_{n=1}^{\infty} 2^{-n} \max\left(\frac{1}{g(n)} - \frac{1}{f(n)}, 0\right).$$

According to (Schellekens, 1995), since every reasonable algorithm, from a computability viewpoint, must hold the "convergence condition" $\sum_{n=1}^{\infty} 2^{-n} \frac{1}{f(n)} < \infty$, it is possible to associate each algorithm with a function of $\mathcal{C}$ in such a way that such a function represents, as a function of the size of the input data, its running time of computing. Motivated by this fact, the elements of $\mathcal{C}$ are called complexity functions. Moreover, given two functions $f, g \in \mathcal{C}$, the numerical value $d_{\mathcal{C}}(f,g)$ (the complexity distance from f to g) can be interpreted as the relative progress made in lowering the complexity by replacing any algorithm P with complexity function f by any algorithm Q with complexity function g. Therefore, if $f \neq g$, the condition $d_{\mathcal{C}}(f,g) = 0$ can be read as f is "at least as efficient" as g on all inputs (note that $d_{\mathcal{C}}(f,g) = 0 \Leftrightarrow f(n) \leq g(n)$ for all $n \in \mathbb{N}$). In fact, the condition $d_{\mathcal{C}}(f,g) = 0$ provides that $f \in \mathcal{O}(g)$.

Notice that the asymmetry of the complexity distance $d_{\mathcal{C}}$ plays a central role in order to provide information about the increase of complexity whenever an algorithm is replaced by another one. A metric will be able to yield information on the increase but it, however, will not reveal which algorithm is more efficient.

The utility of the complexity space in complexity analysis of algorithms was also illustrated by Schellekens in (Schellekens, 1995). In particular, he introduced a mathematical method to provide asymptotic upper bounds of the running time of computing for Divide and Conquer algorithms. To this end, Schellekens used the below fixed point theorem which is a quasi-metric version of the celebrate Banach's fixed point theorem.

Theorem 1. *Let f be a contractive mapping from a bicomplete quasi-metric space (X,d) into itself with contractive constant s. Then f has a unique fixed point x_0 and, in addition, $\lim_{n\to\infty} f^n(x) = x_0$ for all $x \in X$.*

Let us remark that a mapping f from a quasi-metric space (X,d) into itself it is called contractive provided that there exists $s \in [0,1)$ such that for all $x, y \in X$

$$d(f(x), f(y)) \leq s d(x,y).$$

In this case, s is called a contractive constant of f.

Next we recall the aforenamed method with the aim of motivating our subsequent work, given in Sections 4 and 5.

A Divide and Conquer algorithm solves a problem of size n ($n \in \mathbb{N}$) splitting it into a subproblems of size $\frac{n}{b}$, for some constants a, b with $a, b \in \mathbb{N}$ and $a, b > 1$, and solving them separately by the same algorithm. After obtaining the solution of the subproblems, the algorithm combines all subproblem solutions to give a global solution to the original problem. The recursive structure of a Divide and Conquer algorithm leads to a recurrence equation for the running time of computing. In many cases the running time of a Divide and Conquer algorithm is the solution to a Divide and Conquer recurrence equation, that is a recurrence equation of the form

$$T(n) = \begin{cases} c & \text{if } n = 1 \\ aT(\frac{n}{b}) + h(n) & \text{if } n \in \mathbb{N}_b \end{cases}, \tag{2}$$

where $\mathbb{N}_b = \{b^k : k \in \mathbb{N}\}$, $c > 0$ denotes the complexity on the base case (i.e. the problem size is small enough and the solution takes constant time), and $h(n)$ represents the time taken by the algorithm in order to divide the original problem into a subproblems and to combine all subproblems solutions into a unique one ($h \in \mathcal{C}$ with $h(n) < \infty$ for all $n \in \mathbb{N}$).

Notice that for Divide and Conquer algorithms, it is typically sufficient to obtain the complexity on inputs of size n with n ranges over the set $\mathbb{N}_b$ (see (Brassard & Bratley, 1988) for a fuller description).

Mergesort (in all behaviors) and Quicksort (in the best case behavior) are typical and well-known examples of Divide and Conquer algorithms whose running time of computing satisfies the recurrence equation (2) (we refer the reader to (Brassard & Bratley, 1988) and (Cull et al., 1985) for a detailed discussion about the both aforasaid algorithms).

In order to provide the asymptotic behavior of the running time of computing of a Divide and Conquer algorithm satisfying the recurrence equation (2), it is necessary to show that such a recurrence equation has a unique solution and, later, to obtain the asymptotic complexity class of such a solution. The method introduced by Schellekens allows us to show that the equation (2) has a unique solution, and provides an upper asymptotic complexity bound of the solution in the following way:

Denote by $\mathcal{C}_{b,c}$ the subset of $\mathcal{C}$ given by

$$\mathcal{C}_{b,c} = \{f \in \mathcal{C} : f(1) = c \text{ and } f(n) = \infty \text{ for all } n \in \mathbb{N} \backslash \mathbb{N}_b \text{ with } n > 1\}.$$

Since the quasi-metric space $(\mathcal{C}, d_{\mathcal{C}})$ is bicomplete (see Theorem 3 and Remark in page 317 of (Romaguera & Schellekens, 1999)) and the set $\mathcal{C}_{b,c}$ is closed in $(\mathcal{C}, d^s_{\mathcal{C}})$, we have that the quasi-metric space $(\mathcal{C}_{b,c}, d_{\mathcal{C}}|_{\mathcal{C}_{b,c}})$ is bicomplete.

Next we associate a functional $\Phi_T : \mathcal{C}_{b,c} \longrightarrow \mathcal{C}_{b,c}$ with the Divide and Conquer recurrence equation (2) as follows:

$$\Phi_T(f)(n) = \begin{cases} c & \text{if } n = 1 \\ \infty & \text{if } n \in \mathbb{N} \backslash \mathbb{N}_b \text{ and } n > 1 \\ af(\frac{n}{b}) + h(n) & \text{otherwise} \end{cases}. \tag{3}$$

Of course a complexity function in $\mathcal{C}_{b,c}$ is a solution to the recurrence equation (2) if and only if it is a fixed point of the functional Φ_T. Under these conditions, Schellekens proved (Schellekens, 1995) that

$$d_{\mathcal{C}}|_{\mathcal{C}_{b,c}}(\Phi_T(f), \Phi_T(g)) \leq \frac{1}{a} d_{\mathcal{C}}|_{\mathcal{C}_{b,c}}(f, g), \tag{4}$$

for all $f, g \in \mathcal{C}_{b,c}$. So, by Theorem 1, the functional $\Phi_T : \mathcal{C}_{b,c} \longrightarrow \mathcal{C}_{b,c}$ has a unique fixed point and, thus, the recurrence equation (2) has a unique solution.

In order to obtain the asymptotic upper bound of the solution to the recurrence equation (2), Schellekens introduced a special class of functionals known as improvers.

Let $C \subseteq \mathcal{C}$. A functional $\Phi : C \longrightarrow C$ is called an improver with respect to a function $f \in C$ provided that $\Phi^n(f) \leq \Phi^{n-1}(f)$ for all $n \in \mathbb{N}$. Of course $\Phi^0(f) = f$.

Observe that an improver is a functional which corresponds to a transformation on algorithms in such a way that the iterative applications of the transformation yield, from a complexity point of view, an improved algorithm at each step of the iteration.

Taking into account the exposed facts, Schellekens stated the following result in (Schellekens, 1995).

Theorem 2. *A Divide and Conquer recurrence of the form (2) has a unique solution f_T in $\mathcal{C}_{b,c}$ suh that $\lim_{n\to\infty} \Phi_T^n(g) = f_T$ for all $g \in \mathcal{C}_{b,c}$. Moreover, if the functional Φ_T associated with (2) is an improver with respect to some function $g \in \mathcal{C}_{b,c}$, then the solution to the recurrence equation satisfies that $f_T \in \mathcal{O}(g)$.*

Of course the preceding theorem states a few relationships between the Schellekens framework and the Scott one (see Section 1). Concretely, the solution to a recurrence equation of type (2) is the fixed point $f_T \in \mathcal{C}_{b,c}$ of the nonrecursive functional Φ_T, which can be seen as the topological limit of the sequence of the successive iterations $(\Phi_T^n(g))_{n\in\mathbb{N}}$ where Φ_T is an improver with respect to $g \in \mathcal{C}_{b,c}$. Note that in this case the functional Φ_T plays the role of the nonrecursive functional ϕ_{fact} introduced in Section 1 and that the role of meaning of the factorial recursive denotational specification, i.e. the factorial function, is now played by the running time of computing f_T. Moreover, the facts that functional Φ_T is an improver and $\lim_{n\to\infty} \Phi_T^n(g) = f_T$ in $(\mathcal{C}_{b,c}, d^s|_{\mathcal{C}_{b,c}})$ yield that each iteration gives more information about the solution to the recurrence equation (the running time of computing) than the preceding ones and, in addition, one has that the information about the running time of computing of the algorithm under study is exactly that which can be obtained from the elements of such a sequence. Hence the role of the distinguished element f_1 and the successive approximations sequence $(\phi^n(f_1))_{n\in\mathbb{N}}$ of the Scott framework, is now played by the sequence of improved running time versions of the Divide and Conquer algorithm under study, $(\Phi_T^n(g))_{n\in\mathbb{N}}$, and the complexity function $g \in \mathcal{C}_{b,c}$ with respect to which the nonrecursive functional Φ_T is an improver. These analogies between the Schellekens and Scott techniques give relevance to the former one with respect to the standard and classical techniques to analyze the complexity of algorithms. Simultaneously, the framework based on the complexity space presents an advantage with respect to the Scott one. Indeed, the framework of Schellekens counts on a topology induced by a quasi-metric (the complexity distance) which allows to measure the information about the fixed point of the nonrecursive functional contained in each element of the sequence of successive approximations and the framework of Scott has not available, in general, quantitative data approach.

In order to validate Theorem 2 and to illustrate its usefulness, Schellekens obtained an upper asymptotic bound of the running time of Mergesort (in the average case behavior). In this particular case, the Mergesort running time of computing satisfies the following particular case of recurrence equation (2):

$$T(n) = \begin{cases} c & \text{if } n = 1 \\ 2T(\frac{n}{2}) + \frac{n}{2} & \text{if } n \in \mathbb{N}_2 \end{cases}. \tag{5}$$

It is clear that Theorem 2 shows that the recurrence equation (5) has a unique solution f_T^M in $\mathcal{C}_{2,c}$. In addition, it is not hard to check that the functional Φ_T induced by the recurrence equation (5), and given by (3), is an improver with respect to a complexity function $g_k \in \mathcal{C}_{2,c}$ (with $k > 0$, $g_k(1) = c$ and $g_k(n) = kn\log_2 n$ for all $n \in \mathbb{N}_2$) if and only if $k \geq \frac{1}{2}$. Note that under the assumption that the functional Φ in (3) is monotone, this is the case for the functional Φ_T induced by (5), to show that Φ_T is an improver with respect to $f \in C$ is equivalent to verify that $\Phi_T(f) \leq f$.

Therefore, by Theorem 2, we can conclude that $f_T^M \in \mathcal{O}(g_{\frac{1}{2}})$, i.e. Theorem 2 provides a new formal proof, inspired by the original Scott fixed point approach, of the well-known fact that the running time of computing f_T^M of Mergesort (in the average case behavior) belongs to $\mathcal{O}(n\log_2 n)$, i.e. that the complexity function $g_{\frac{1}{2}}$, or equivalently $\mathcal{O}(n\log_2 n)$, gives an asymptotic upper bound of f_T^M.

Furthermore, it must be stressed that in (Schellekens, 1995) it was pointed out that an asymptotic lower bound of the running time of Mergesort (in the average case behavior) belongs to $\Omega(n\log_2 n)$. However, to show this standard arguments, which are not based on the use of fixed point techniques, were followed. So Schellekens proved that Mergesort running time (in the average case behavior) belongs to the complexity class $\Theta(n\log_2 n)$, but the unique, strictly speaking, novel proof of the last fact was given when the asymptotic upper bound was obtained.

4. An extension of Schellekens' approach: the general case of recursive algorithms

Although the most natural is to think that the running time of computing of Divide and Conquer algorithms is always the solution to a Divide and Conquer recurrence equations of type (2), there are well-known examples, like Quicksort (worst case behaviour), of Divide and Conquer algorithms whose complexity analysis does not lead with a recurrence equation of the aforesaid type (Cull et al., 1985). In particular, the running time of computing (worst case behavior) for the aforenamed algorithm is the solution to the recurrence equation given by

$$T(n) = \begin{cases} c & \text{if } n = 1 \\ T(n-1) + jn & \text{if } n \geq 2 \end{cases}, \tag{6}$$

with $j > 0$ and where c is the time taken by the algorithm in the base case. Observe that in this case it is not necessary to restrict the input size of the data to a set $\mathbb{N}_b$ as defined in the preceding section.

Clearly, the recurrence equation (6) can not be retrieved as a particular case of the Divide and Conquer family of recurrence equations (2). However, the main and strong relationship between Mergesort and Quicksort is given by the fact that both are recursive algorithms. Obviously, the class of recursive algorithms is wider than the Divide and Conquer one. An illustrative example, which does not belong to the Divide and Conquer family, is provided by the recursive algorithm, which we will call Hanoi, that solves the Towers of Hanoi puzzle (Cull et al., 1985; Cull & Ecklund, 1985). In this case, under the uniform cost criterion assumption, the running time of computing is the solution to a recurrence equation given by

$$T(n) = \begin{cases} c & \text{if } n = 1 \\ 2T(n-1) + d & \text{if } n \geq 2 \end{cases}, \tag{7}$$

where $c, d > 0$ and where c represents the time taken by the algorithm to solve the base case. Of course, to distinguish three possible running time behaviors for Hanoi is meaningless, since the input data distribution is always the same for each size n.

In (Romaguera et al., 2011), the fact that the class of recursive algorithms is wider than the Divide and Conquer inspired to wonder whether one can obtain a family of recurrence equations in such a way that the complexity analysis of those algorithms whose running time of computing is a solution either to recurrence equations associated with Quicksort (in the worst case behavior) and Hanoi or to a Divide and Conquer one can be carried out from it and, in addition, whether such a complexity analysis can be done via an extension of the fixed point technique of Schellekens.

A positive answer to the preceding questions was also given in (Romaguera et al., 2011). Concretely, it was shown two things.

On one hand, it was pointed out that the recurrence equations that yield the running time of computing of the above aforesaid algorithms can be considered as particular cases of the following general one:

$$T(n) = \begin{cases} c & \text{if } n = 1 \\ aT(n-1) + h(n) & \text{if } n \geq 2 \end{cases}, \tag{8}$$

where $c > 0$, $a \geq 1$ and $h \in \mathcal{C}$ such that $h(n) < \infty$ for all $n \in \mathbb{N}$.

Of course, the discussion of the complexity of the Divide and Conquer algorithms introduced in Section 3 can be carried out from the family of recurrence equations of type (8). This is possible because the running time of computing of the aforementioned algorithms leads to recurrence equations can be seen as a particular case of our last general family of recurrence equations. Indeed, a Divide and Conquer recurrence equation

$$T(n) = \begin{cases} c & \text{if } n = 1 \\ aT(\frac{n}{b}) + h(n) & \text{if } n \in \mathbb{N}_b \end{cases}, \tag{9}$$

can be transformed into the following one

$$S(m) = \begin{cases} c & \text{if } m = 1 \\ aS(m-1) + r(m) & \text{if } m > 1 \end{cases}, \tag{10}$$

where $S(m) = T(b^{m-1})$ and $r(m) = h(b^{m-1})$ for all $m \in \mathbb{N}$. (Recall that $\mathbb{N}_b = \{b^k : k \in \mathbb{N}\}$ with $b \in \mathbb{N}$ and $b > 1$).

Observe that the analysis of the recurrence equation family (10) allows immediately to study the Divide and Conquer recurrence equations.

On the other hand, the Schellekens fixed point technique was extended and applied to discuss the complexity class (asymptotic upper and lower bounds) of those algorithms whose running time of computing is the solution to a recurrence equation of type (8). Of course, it was introduced an improvement over the original Schellekens method in order to obtain asymptotic lower bounds of the running time of computing of algorithms. This was done by means of a new kind of functionals defined on the complexity space and called worseners (see Subsection 4.2 for the definition). Furthermore, the applicability of the new results to Asymptotic Complexity Analysis was illustrated by discussing the complexity class of the running time of computing, among others, of Quicksort (in the worst case behavior) and Hanoi.

Nevertheless, a recursive algorithm whose running time does not hold a recurrence equation of type (8) can be found, for instance, in (Cull et al., 1985). The aforementioned algorithm, that we will call Fibonacci, computes the value of the Fibonacci sequence at any given index n with $n \in \mathbb{N}$. The running time of computing of Fibonacci matches up with the solution to a recurrence equation given as follows:

$$T(n) = \begin{cases} 2c & \text{if } n = 1 \\ 3c & \text{if } n = 2 \\ T(n-1) + T(n-2) + 4c & \text{if } n > 2 \end{cases}, \tag{11}$$

where c represents the time taken by the computer to perform a basic operation. Again, similarly to Hanoi, to distinguish three possible running time behaviors is meaningless.

It is clear that the recurrence equation (11) can not be retrieved as a particular case from the family of recurrence equations (8). Consequently, the latter family of recurrence equations is not be able to model the complexity of Fibonacci. However, the running time of computing of all above recursive algorithms, including Fibonacci, can be modeled as the solution to a recurrence equation of the below general family:

$$T(n) = \begin{cases} c_n & \text{if } 1 \leq n \leq k \\ \sum_{i=1}^{k} a_i T(n-i) + h(n) & \text{if } n > k \end{cases}, \tag{12}$$

where $h \in \mathcal{C}$ such that $h(n) < \infty$ for all $n \in \mathbb{N}$, $k \in \mathbb{N}$, $c_i > 0$ and $a_i \geq 1$ for all $1 \leq i \leq k$.

Inspired by the previous exposed fact our purpose in this section is to go more deeply into the Schellekens fixed point technique for the complexity analysis of algorithms and to demonstrate that such techniques can be successfully used to obtain the complexity class of those recursive algorithms whose running time is a solution to a recurrence equation of type (12). In particular we prove, by means of a new fixed point theorem, the existence and uniqueness of the solution to a recurrence equation of type (12). Moreover, we introduce, based on the fixed point theorem, a technique in the spirit of Schellekens and Scott to get the the complexity class (an asymptotic upper and lower bound) of such a solution. Concretely, our technique to obtain asymptotic upper bounds is based on, following the Schellekens original ideas, the use of improver functionals induced by the recurrence equation. Nevertheless, following (Romaguera et al., 2011), we provide asymptotic lower bounds of the solution via worseners functionals which capture, similarly to the improvers one but in a dual way, the original "successive approximations" spirit of Scott's approach.

Furthermore, we prove that in order to provide the complexity class of an algorithm whose running time satisfies a recurrence equation of type (12) is enough to search among all complexity functions for which the functional associated to the recurrence equation is an improver and a worsener simultaneously. Finally, with the aim, on one hand, to validate our new results and, on the other hand, to show the potential applicability of the developed theory to Asymptotic Complexity Analysis, we end the section discussing the complexity class of the running time of Fibonacci.

4.1 The fixed point: existence and uniqueness of solution

Fix $k \in \mathbb{N}$. Consider the subset $\mathcal{C}_{c,k}$ of $\mathcal{C}$ given by

$$\mathcal{C}_{c,k} = \{f \in \mathcal{C} : f(n) = c_n \text{ for all } 1 \leq n \leq k\}.$$

Define the functional $\Psi_T : \mathcal{C}_{c,k} \longrightarrow \mathcal{C}_{c,k}$ by

$$\Psi_T(f)(n) = \begin{cases} c_n & \text{if } 1 \leq n \leq k \\ \sum_{i=1}^{k} a_i f(n-i) + h(n) & \text{if } n > k \end{cases}, \tag{13}$$

for all $f \in \mathcal{C}_{c,k}$.

It is clear that a complexity function in $\mathcal{C}_{c,k}$ is a solution to a recurrence equation of type (12) if and only if it is a fixed point of the functional Ψ_T.

The next result is useful to supply the bicompleteness of the quasi-metric space $(\mathcal{C}_{c,k}, d_{\mathcal{C}}|_{\mathcal{C}_{c,k}})$.

Proposition 3. *The subset $\mathcal{C}_{c,k}$ is closed in $(\mathcal{C}, d_{\mathcal{C}}^s)$.*

Proof. Let $g \in \overline{\mathcal{C}_{c,k}}^{d_{\mathcal{C}}^s}$ and $(f_i)_{i \in \mathbb{N}} \subset \mathcal{C}_{c,k}$ with $\lim_{i \to \infty} d_{\mathcal{C}}^s(g, f_i) = 0$. First of all we prove that $g \in \mathcal{C}$. Indeed, given $\varepsilon > 0$, there exist $i_0, n_0 \in \mathbb{N}$ such that $d_{\mathcal{C}}^s(g, f_i) < \varepsilon$ whenever $i \geq i_0$ and $\sum_{n=n_0+1}^{\infty} 2^{-n} \frac{1}{f_{i_0}(n)} < \varepsilon$. Whence

$$\begin{aligned}
\sum_{n=n_0+1}^{\infty} 2^{-n} \frac{1}{g(n)} &= \sum_{n=n_0+1}^{\infty} 2^{-n} \left(\frac{1}{g(n)} - \frac{1}{f_{i_0}(n)} + \frac{1}{f_{i_0}(n)} \right) \\
&\leq \sum_{n=n_0+1}^{\infty} 2^{-n} \left| \frac{1}{g(n)} - \frac{1}{f_{i_0}(n)} \right| + \sum_{n=n_0+1}^{\infty} 2^{-n} \frac{1}{f_{i_0}(n)} \\
&\leq 2d_{\mathcal{C}}^s(g, f_{i_0}) + \sum_{n=n_0+1}^{\infty} 2^{-n} \frac{1}{f_{i_0}(n)} \\
&< 3\varepsilon.
\end{aligned}$$

Now suppose for the purpose of contradiction that $g \notin \mathcal{C}_{c,k}$. Then there exists $n_1 \in \mathbb{N}$ with $1 \leq n_1 \leq k$ such that $g(n_1) \neq c_{n_1}$. Put $\varepsilon = 2^{-n_1} \left| \frac{1}{g(n_1)} - \frac{1}{c_{n_1}} \right|$. Then there exists $i_0 \in \mathbb{N}$ such that $d_{\mathcal{C}}^s(g, f_i) < \frac{\varepsilon}{2}$ whenever $i \geq i_0$. Thus

$$\sum_{n=1}^{\infty} 2^{-n} \left| \frac{1}{g(n)} - \frac{1}{f_i(n)} \right| < \varepsilon,$$

whenever $i \geq i_0$. As a result we have that

$$\varepsilon = 2^{-n_1}\left|\frac{1}{g(n_1)} - \frac{1}{c_{n_1}}\right| \leq \sum_{n=1}^{\infty} 2^{-n}\left|\frac{1}{g(n)} - \frac{1}{f_{i_0}(n)}\right| < \varepsilon,$$

which is a contradiction. So $g(n) = c_n$ for all $1 \leq n \leq k$. Therefore we have shown that $\overline{\mathcal{C}_{c,k}}^{d^s_{\mathcal{C}}} = \mathcal{C}_{c,k}$ and, thus, that $\mathcal{C}_{c,k}$ is closed in $(\mathcal{C}, d^s_{\mathcal{C}})$. ■

Since the metric space $(\mathcal{C}, d^s_{\mathcal{C}})$ is complete and, by Proposition 3, the subset $\mathcal{C}_{c,k}$ is closed in $(\mathcal{C}, d^s_{\mathcal{C}})$ we immediately obtain the following consequence.

Corollary 4. *The quasi-metric space $(\mathcal{C}_{c,k}, d_{\mathcal{C}}|_{\mathcal{C}_{c,k}})$ is bicomplete.*

The next result provides the existence and uniqueness of solution to a recurrence equation of type (12).

Theorem 5. *The functional Ψ_T is contractive from $(\mathcal{C}_{c,k}, d_{\mathcal{C}}|_{\mathcal{C}_{c,k}})$ into itself with contractive constant*

$$\left(\max_{1\leq i\leq k} \frac{1}{a_i}\right)\left(\frac{2^k-1}{2^k}\right).$$

Proof. Let $f, g \in \mathcal{C}_{c,k}$. Then we prove that

$$d_{\mathcal{C}}|_{\mathcal{C}_{c,k}}(\Psi_T(f), \Psi_T(g)) \leq s\, d_{\mathcal{C}}|_{\mathcal{C}_{c,k}}(f, g),$$

where

$$s = \left(\max_{1\leq i\leq k} \frac{1}{a_i}\right)\left(\frac{2^k-1}{2^k}\right).$$

Indeed, we have that

$$\begin{aligned}
d_{\mathcal{C}}|_{\mathcal{C}_{c,k}}(\Psi_T(f), \Psi_T(g)) &= \sum_{n=1}^{\infty} 2^{-n} \max\left(\frac{1}{\Psi_T(g)(n)} - \frac{1}{\Psi_T(f)(n)}, 0\right) \\
&= \sum_{n=k+2}^{\infty} 2^{-n} \max\left(\frac{\sum_{i=1}^{k} a_i\left(f(n-i) - g(n-i)\right)}{r(n)}, 0\right) \\
&\leq \sum_{n=k+2}^{\infty} 2^{-n} \max\left(\frac{\sum_{i=1}^{k} a_i\left(f(n-i) - g(n-i)\right)}{\sum_{i=1}^{k} a_i^2\left(g(n-i)f(n-i)\right)}, 0\right) \\
&\leq \left(\max_{1\leq i\leq k} \frac{1}{a_i}\right) \sum_{n=k+2}^{\infty} 2^{-n} \max\left(\sum_{i=1}^{k} \frac{1}{g(n-i)} - \frac{1}{f(n-i)}, 0\right) \\
&\leq \left(\max_{1\leq i\leq k} \frac{1}{a_i}\right) \sum_{n=k+1}^{\infty} 2^{-n}\left(\frac{2^k-1}{2^k}\right) \max\left(\frac{1}{g(n)} - \frac{1}{f(n)}, 0\right) \\
&= \left(\max_{1\leq i\leq k} \frac{1}{a_i}\right)\left(\frac{2^k-1}{2^k}\right) d_{\mathcal{C}}|_{\mathcal{C}_{c,k}}(f, g),
\end{aligned}$$

where

$$r(n) = (h(n))^2 + h(n)\sum_{i=1}^{k} a_i\,(f(n-i)+g(n-i)) + \left(\sum_{i=1}^{k} a_i f(n-i)\right)\cdot\left(\sum_{i=1}^{k} a_i g(n-i)\right),$$

for all $n > k$.

Now the existence and uniqueness of the fixed point $f_T \in \mathcal{C}_{c,k}$ of Ψ_T follow from Corollary 4 and Theorem 1, because $(\max_{1\leq i\leq k}\frac{1}{a_i})\left(\frac{2^k-1}{2^k}\right) < 1$. ■

Since $f_T \in \mathcal{C}_{c,k}$ is the solution to a the recurrence equation of type (12) if and only if f_T is a fixed point of Ψ_T, Theorem 5 yields that a recurrence of the form (12) has a unique solution f_T in $\mathcal{C}_{c,k}$. Moreover, note that, by Theorem 1, we have that $\lim_{n\to\infty}\Psi_T^n(g) = f_T$ in $(\mathcal{C}_{c,k}, d^s|_{\mathcal{C}_{c,k}})$ for all $g \in \mathcal{C}_{c,k}$.

4.2 Bounding the solution: the complexity class of running time of computing

In order to describe the complexity of those recursive algorithms whose running time of computing satisfies a recurrence equation of type (12) we need recall the below auxiliary result which was announced without proof in (Romaguera et al., 2011) with the aim of extending Schellekens fixed point technique and, thus, analyze the complexity class of those algorithms whose running time of computing holds a recurrence equation of type (8) .

Lemma 6. *Let C be a subset of $\mathcal{C}$ such that the quasi-metric space $(C, d_{\mathcal{C}}|_C)$ is bicomplete and suppose that $\Psi : C \longrightarrow C$ is a contractive functional with fixed point $f \in C$ and contractive constant s. Then the following statements hold:*

1) *If there exists $g \in C$ with $d_{\mathcal{C}}|_C(\Psi(g), g) = 0$, then $d_{\mathcal{C}}|_C(f, g) = 0$.*
2) *If there exists $g \in C$ with $d_{\mathcal{C}}|_C(g, \Psi(g)) = 0$, then $d_{\mathcal{C}}|_C(g, f) = 0$.*

Proof. 1) Assume that there exists $g \in C$ such that $d_{\mathcal{C}}|_C(\Psi(g), g) = 0$. Suppose for the purpose of contradiction that $d_{\mathcal{C}}|_C(f, g) > 0$. Then we have that

$$\begin{aligned} d_{\mathcal{C}}|_C(f,g) &\leq d_{\mathcal{C}}|_C(f,\Psi(g)) + d_{\mathcal{C}}|_C(\Psi(g),g) = d_{\mathcal{C}}|_C(f,\Psi(g)) \\ &\leq d_{\mathcal{C}}|_C(f,\Psi(f)) + d_{\mathcal{C}}|_C(\Psi(f),\Psi(g)) \\ &= d_{\mathcal{C}}|_C(\Psi(f),\Psi(g)) \leq s d_{\mathcal{C}}|_C(f,g). \end{aligned}$$

From the preceding inequality we deduce that $1 \leq s$, which contradicts the fact that s is a contractive constant. So $d_{\mathcal{C}}|_C(f, g) = 0$.

2) The thesis of 2) can be proved applying similar arguments to those given in the proof of 1). ■

Observe that if a complexity function f represents the running time of computing of an algorithm under study, the fact that there exists a complexity function g satisfying the condition $d_{\mathcal{C}}|_C(\Psi(g), g) = 0$ ($d_{\mathcal{C}}|_C(g, \Psi(g)) = 0$) in the preceding lemma provides an asymptotic upper (lower) bound of the aforesaid running time, since $d_{\mathcal{C}}|_C(f, g) = 0$ ($d_{\mathcal{C}}|_C(g, f) = 0$) implies that $f \in \mathcal{O}(g)$ ($f \in \Omega(g)$).

From statements in Lemma 6 we infer, such as it was pointed out in (Romaguera et al., 2011), that to provide an asymptotic upper bound of the running time of computing of an algorithm whose running time matches up with the fixed point of a contractive mapping $\Psi : C \longrightarrow C$ ($C \subseteq \mathcal{C}$) associated to a recurrence equation is enough to check if such a mapping satisfies the condition $\Psi(g) \leq g$ for any complexity function even if Ψ is not monotone (see Section 3). This fact presents an improvement of our new method over the Schellekens one. So in the remainder of this paper, and according to (Romaguera et al., 2011), given $C \subseteq \mathcal{C}$ and a contraction $\Psi : C \longrightarrow C$ we will say that Ψ is a cont-improver with respect to a complexity function $g \in C$ provided that $\Psi(g) \leq g$. Note that the contractivity of the functional implies that a cont-improver is an improver. Consequently, a cont-improver is a transformation on algorithms in such a way that the application of the transformation yields, from a complexity point of view, an improved algorithm.

Motivated by statement 2) in Lemma 6, it was introduced a new kind of functionals called worseners. For our subsequent purpose, let us recall that, given $C \subseteq \mathcal{C}$, a contraction $\Psi : C \longrightarrow C$ is called a *worsener* with respect to a function $f \in C$ provided that $f \leq \Psi(f)$. An easy verification shows that if a functional Ψ is a worsener with respect to f, then $\Psi^{n-1}(f) \leq \Psi^{n}(f)$ for all $n \in \mathbb{N}$. Hence the computational meaning of a worsener functional is dual to the meaning of a cont-improver. Indeed, a worsener is a functional which corresponds to a transformation on algorithms in such a way that the application of the transformation yields, from a complexity point of view, a worsened algorithm.

The next result provides the method to provide the asymptotic upper and lower bounds of the running time of computing of those algorithms whose running time of computing is the solution to a recurrence equation of type (12).

Theorem 7. *Let $f_T \in \mathcal{C}_{c,k}$ be the (unique) solution to a recurrence equation of type (12). Then the following facts hold:*

1) *If the functional Ψ_T associated to (12), and given by (13), is a cont-improver with respect to some function $g \in \mathcal{C}_{c,k}$, then $f_T \in \mathcal{O}(g)$.*
2) *If the functional Ψ_T associated to (12), and given by (13), is a worsener with respect to some function $g \in \mathcal{C}_{c,k}$, then $f_T \in \Omega(g)$.*

Proof. Assume that Ψ_T is a cont-improver with respect to $g \in \mathcal{C}_{c,k}$. Then we have $\Psi_T(g) \leq g$. Hence we obtain that $d_{\mathcal{C}}|_{\mathcal{C}_{c,k}}(\Psi_T(g), g) = 0$. It immediately follows, by statement 1) in Lemma 6, that $d_{\mathcal{C}}|_{\mathcal{C}_{c,k}}(f_T, g) = 0$ and, thus, $f_T \in \mathcal{O}(g)$. So we have proved 1).

To prove 2) suppose that Ψ_T is a worsener with respect to $g \in \mathcal{C}_{c,k}$. Then $g \leq \Psi_T(g)$. Whence we deduce that $d_{\mathcal{C}}|_{\mathcal{C}_{c,k}}(g, \Psi_T(g)) = 0$. Thus statement 2) in Lemma 6 gives that $d_{\mathcal{C}}|_{\mathcal{C}_{c,k}}(g, f_T) = 0$, and we conclude that $f_T \in \Omega(g)$. This finishes the proof. ■

In the light of Theorem 7, we have that the solution to a recurrence equation of type (12) satisfies that $f_T \in \mathcal{O}(g) \cap \Omega(h)$ whenever Ψ_T is a cont-improver and a worsener with respect to $g \in \mathcal{C}_{c,k}$ and $h \in \mathcal{C}_{c,k}$, respectively. Consequently we obtain the complexity class of algorithms whose running time of computing satisfies a recurrence equation of type (12) when there exist $l \in \mathcal{C}_{c,k}$, $r, t > 0$ and $n_0 \in \mathbb{N}$ such that $g(n) = rl(n)$ and $h = tl(n)$ for all $n \geq n_0$ and, besides, Ψ_T is a cont-improver and a worsener with respect to g and h respectively, because, in such a case, $f_T \in \Theta(l)$.

4.3 An application to Asymptotic Complexity Analysis: Fibonacci case

In this subsection we validate the developed theory and illustrate the potential applicability of the obtained results by means of providing the asymptotic complexity class of the recursive algorithm that computes the Fibonacci sequence, an algorithm whose running time of computing can be analyzed neither via the technique exposed in (Schellekens, 1995) nor via its extended version given in (Romaguera et al., 2011).

As we have exposed above, the running time of computing of Fibonacci is the solution to the below recurrence equation:

$$T(n) = \begin{cases} 2c & \text{if } n = 1 \\ 3c & \text{if } n = 2 \\ T(n-1) + T(n-2) + 4c & \text{if } n > 2 \end{cases},$$

where $c > 0$. Clearly, this recurrence equation can be retrieved from (12) as a particular case when we fix $k = 2$, $a_1 = a_2 = 1$, $c_1 = 2c$, $c_2 = 3c$ and $h(n) = 4c$ for all $n \in \mathbb{N}$. Then, taking

$$\Psi_T(f)(n) = \begin{cases} 2c & \text{if } n = 1 \\ 3c & \text{if } n = 2 \\ f(n-1) + f(n-2) + 4c & \text{if } n > 2 \end{cases},$$

for all $f \in \mathcal{C}_{c,2}$, Theorem 5 guarantees the existence and uniqueness of the solution in $\mathcal{C}_{c,2}$, say f_T^F, to the above recurrence equation in such a way that it matches up with the running time of computing of the recursive algorithm under consideration.

Next, fix $r > 0$ and $\alpha > \frac{1}{2}$ and define the function $h_{\alpha,r}$ by

$$h_{\alpha,r}(n) = \begin{cases} 2c & \text{if } n = 1 \\ 3c & \text{if } n = 2 \\ r\alpha^n & \text{if } n > 2 \end{cases}.$$

Since $\alpha > \frac{1}{2}$, the D'Alembert ratio test guarantees that $h_\alpha \in \mathcal{C}_{c,2}$.

It is not hard to see that Ψ_T is a cont-improver with respect to the complexity function h_α (i.e. $\Psi_T(h_\alpha) \leq h_\alpha$) if and only if $\alpha \geq 1.61$ and $r \geq \frac{4c}{\alpha^2}$. Hence we obtain, by statement 1) in Theorem 7, that the running of Fibonacci holds $f_T^F \in \mathcal{O}(h_{1.61,\frac{4c}{\alpha^2}})$.

Moreover, a straightforward computation shows that at Ψ_T is a worsener with respect to the complexity function $h_{\alpha,r}$ (i.e. $h_{\alpha,r} \leq \Psi_T(h_{\alpha,r})$) if and only if $\alpha \leq 1.61$ (r is not subject to any constraint). Thus we deduce, by statement 2) in Theorem 7, that $f_T^F \in \Omega(h_{1.61,\frac{4c}{\alpha^2}})$.

Therefore we obtain that $f_T^F \in \Theta(h_{1.61,\frac{4c}{\alpha^2}})$, which agrees with the complexity class that can be found in the literature for the recursive algorithm under study, i.e. $f_T^F \in \Theta((1.61)^n)$ (Cull et al., 1985).

5. Asymptotic Complexity Analysis and Denotational Semantics via a common mathematical framework

As we have pointed out in Sections 1 and 3, the main objective of Schellekens' work was to apply the fixed point technique of the Scott approach for Denotational Semantics to Asymptotic Complexity Analysis. After accomplishing the original aim, he suggested the possibility of giving applications of the complexity space framework to new realms of Computer Science as, in particular, to Denotational Semantics. Thus, the research line began by Schellekens would have benefited from the fundamentals of Denotational Semantics (concretely from Scott's ideas) and, at the same time, the latter would benefit from the ideas and techniques that could be originated in the context of the complexity space. In this direction, a few fruitful interactions between both research disciplines have recently been shown in (Romaguera & Valero, 2008), (Rodríguez-López et al., 2008), (Llull-Chavarría & Valero, 2009) , (Romaguera & Valero, 2011b) and (Romaguera et al., 2011a).

In this section we go more deeply into the relationship between both aforenamed disciplines and present a unified mathematical structure that will be helpful in Asymptotic Complexity Analysis and Denotational Semantics simultaneously. For this purpose, consider a recursive algorithm computing the factorial of a nonnegative integer number by means of the recursive denotational specification introduced in Section 1, that is

$$fact(n) = \begin{cases} 1 & \text{if } n = 1 \\ n fact(n-1) & \text{if } n \geq 2 \end{cases}. \tag{14}$$

It is clear that the running time of computing of such a recursive algorithm is the solution to the following recurrence equation (Boxer and Miller, 2005):

$$T(n) = \begin{cases} c & \text{if } n = 1 \\ T(n-1) + d & \text{if } n \geq 2 \end{cases}, \tag{15}$$

where $c, d > 0$. In the light of the preceding recursive specifications, our objective is to be able to describe simultaneously under a unique fixed point technique the running time of computing and the meaning of the recursive algorithm that computes the factorial of a nonnegative integer number, that is to provide the complexity class of the solution to the recurrence equation (15) and to prove that the unique solution to the denotational specification (14) is the entire factorial function. To this end we will need to recall the following facts.

On one hand, in (Romaguera & Schellekens, 2000) S. Romaguera and Schellekens introduced and studied a new complexity space setting, that we will call generalized complexity spaces, whose construction is as follows:

Given a quasi-metric space (X, d) and a fixed $x_0 \in X$, the generalized complexity space of (X, d, x_0) is the quasi-metric space $(\mathcal{C}_{X,x_0}, d_{\mathcal{C}_{X,x_0}})$, where

$$\mathcal{C}_{X,x_0} = \{f : \mathbb{N} \longrightarrow X : \sum_{n=1}^{\infty} 2^{-n} d^s(x_0, f(n)) < \infty\},$$

and the quasi-metric $d_{\mathcal{C}_{X,x_0}}$ on $\mathcal{C}_{X,x_0}$ is defined by

$$d_{\mathcal{C}_{X,x_0}}(f,g) = \sum_{n=1}^{\infty} 2^{-n} d\left(f(n), g(n)\right),$$

for all $f,g \in \mathcal{C}_{X,x_0}$.

Notice that if we take in the preceding definition the base quasi-metric space (X,d) with $X = (0,\infty]$, $x_0 = \infty$ and $d = u_{-1}$, then the generalized complexity space $(\mathcal{C}_{X,x_0}, d_{\mathcal{C}_{X,x_0}})$ is exactly the original complexity space $(\mathcal{C}, d_{\mathcal{C}})$.

In (Romaguera & Schellekens, 2000) several mathematical properties, which are interesting from a computational point of view, of generalized complexity spaces were studied. Among them we are interested in the bicompleteness, because it will be useful for our aim later on. In particular, we have the following result.

Theorem 8. *Let (X,d) be a quasi-metric space and let $x_0 \in X$. Then the generalized complexity space $(\mathcal{C}_{X,x_0}, d_{\mathcal{C}_{X,x_0}})$ is bicomplete if and only if (X,d) is bicomplete .*

On the other hand, in the literature it has been introduced the so-called domain of words as a possible mathematical foundation of Denotational Semantics (Davey & Priestley, 1990; Künzi, 1993; Matthews, 1994). Such a mathematical structure can be constructed as follows:

Denote by $\mathbb{N}^\omega$ the set of all finite and infinite sequences (words) over $\mathbb{N}$. Denote by $\sqsubseteq$ the prefix order on $\mathbb{N}^\omega$, i.e. $x \sqsubseteq y \Leftrightarrow x$ is a prefix of y. The pair $(\mathbb{N}^\omega, \sqsubseteq)$ is known as the domain of words over the alphabet $\mathbb{N}$.

Moreover, for each $x \in \mathbb{N}^\omega$ the length of x will be denoted by $\ell(x)$. Thus, $\ell(x) \in [1,\infty]$ for all $x \in \mathbb{N}^\omega$,. In the following, given $x \in \mathbb{N}^\omega$, we will write $x = x_1, x_2x_3, \ldots$ whenever $\ell(x) = \infty$ and $x = x_1x_2, \ldots, x_n$ whenever $\ell(x) = n < \infty$.

According to (Matthews, 1994) and (Künzi, 1993), the domain of words can be endowed with a quasi-metric. Indeed, define on $\mathbb{N}^\omega$ the function $d_{\mathbb{N}^\omega} : \mathbb{N}^\omega \times \mathbb{N}^\omega \to \mathbb{R}^+$ by

$$d_{\mathbb{N}^\omega}(x,y) = 2^{-\ell(x,y)} - 2^{-\ell(x)},$$

for all $x,y \in \mathbb{N}^\omega$, where $\ell(x,y)$ denotes the length of the longest common prefix of x and y provided that such a prefix exists, and $\ell(x,y) = 0$ otherwise. Of course we adopt the convention that $2^{-\infty} = 0$.

It is well known that $(\mathbb{N}^\omega, d_{\mathbb{N}^\omega})$ is a bicomplete quasi-metric space. Furthermore, $x \sqsubseteq y \Leftrightarrow d_{\mathbb{N}^\omega}(x,y) = 0$.

Next we present the new mathematical framework and we apply it to to discuss, in the spirit of Scott and Schellekens, the complexity and the meaning of a recursive algorithm computing the factorial of a nonnegative integer number. First of all, we mix the original complexity space and the domain of words via a generalized complexity space in the following way:

Since $((0,\infty], u_{-1})$ and $(\mathbb{N}^\omega, d_{\mathbb{N}^\omega})$ are bicomplete quasi-metric spaces we have that $((0,\infty] \times \mathbb{N}^\omega, u_{-1} + d_{\mathbb{N}^\omega})$ is a bicomplete quasi-metric space, where $(u_{-1} + d_{\mathbb{N}^\omega})((x_1,x_2),(y_1,y_2)) = u_{-1}(x_1,y_1) + d_{\mathbb{N}^\omega}(x_2,y_2)$, for all $(x_1,x_2),(y_1,y_2) \in (0,\infty] \times \mathbb{N}^\omega$.

Hence $(\mathcal{C}_{(0,\infty]\times\mathbb{N}^\omega,(\infty,1_{\mathbb{N}^\omega})}, d_{\mathcal{C}_{(0,\infty]\times\mathbb{N}^\omega,(\infty,1_{\mathbb{N}^\omega})}})$ is, by Theorem 8, a bicomplete quasi-metric space, where by $1_{\mathbb{N}^\omega}$ we denote the word of $\mathbb{N}^\omega$ such that $\ell(1_{\mathbb{N}^\omega}) = 1$ and $(1_{\mathbb{N}^\omega})_1 = 1$.

Note that if $f \in \mathcal{C}_{(0,\infty]\times\mathbb{N}^\omega,(\infty,1_{\mathbb{N}^\omega})}$, then we can write $f = (f_1, f_2)$, with $f_1 : \mathbb{N} \longrightarrow (0,\infty]$ and $f_2 : \mathbb{N} \longrightarrow \mathbb{N}^\omega$. Moreover $f_1 \in \mathcal{C}$ because

$$\sum_{n=1}^{\infty} 2^{-n}\frac{1}{f_1(n)} \leq \sum_{n=1}^{\infty} 2^{-n}(u_{-1} + d_{\mathbb{N}^\omega})^s((\infty, 1_{\mathbb{N}^\omega}), f(n)) < \infty.$$

In fact $f_1 \in \mathcal{C}_{c,1}$, where $c = f_1(1)$.

Now for $f = (f_1, f_2) \in \mathcal{C}_{(0,\infty]\times\mathbb{N}^\omega,(\infty,1_{\mathbb{N}^\omega})}$ define

$$\Gamma(f)(n) = (\Psi_T(f_1)(n)), M(f_2(n))),$$

for all $n \in \mathbb{N}$, where, compare Theorem 5, $\Psi_T : \mathcal{C}_{c,1} \longrightarrow \mathcal{C}_{c,1}$ is the functional associated to (15) (given by (13)) and $M : \mathbb{N}^\omega \longrightarrow \mathbb{N}^\omega$ is the mapping defined by

$$(M(x))_n = \begin{cases} 1 & \text{if } n = 1 \\ nx_{n-1} & \text{if } 1 < n \leq \ell(x) + 1 \end{cases}, \tag{16}$$

for all $x \in \mathbb{N}^\omega$.

Observe that $d_{\mathbb{N}^\omega}(1_{\mathbb{N}^\omega}, M(x)) = 0$ and $d_{\mathbb{N}^\omega}(M(x), 1_{\mathbb{N}^\omega}) = 2^{-1} - 2^{-(\ell(x)+1)}$, for all $x \in \mathbb{N}^\omega$.

Then $\Gamma(f) \in \mathcal{C}_{(0,\infty]\times\mathbb{N}^\omega,(\infty,1_{\mathbb{N}^\omega})}$, because

$$\begin{aligned}
&\textstyle\sum_{n=1}^{\infty} 2^{-n}(u_{-1} + d_{\mathbb{N}^\omega})^s((\infty, 1_{\mathbb{N}^\omega}), \Gamma(f)(n)) &=\\
&\textstyle\sum_{n=1}^{\infty} 2^{-n}\left[u_{-1}(\infty, \Psi_T(f_1)(n))) + d_{\mathbb{N}^\omega}(M(f_2(n)), 1_{\mathbb{N}^\omega})\right] &\leq\\
&\textstyle\sum_{n=1}^{\infty} 2^{-n}\max\{\frac{1}{\Psi_T(f_1)(n)}, \frac{1}{4}\} &< \infty.
\end{aligned}$$

Furthermore, it is a simple matter to check that

$$\begin{aligned}
&d_{\mathcal{C}_{(0,\infty]\times\mathbb{N}^\omega,(\infty,1_{\mathbb{N}^\omega})}}(\Gamma(f), \Gamma(g)) &=\\
&\textstyle\sum_{n=1}^{\infty} 2^{-n}\left[u_{-1}(\Psi_T(f_1)(n)), \Psi_T(g_1)(n)) + d_{\mathbb{N}^\omega}(M(f_2(n)), M(g_2(n)))\right] &\leq\\
&\textstyle\frac{1}{2}\sum_{n=1}^{\infty} 2^{-n}\left[u_{-1}(f_1(n), g_1(n)) + d_{\mathbb{N}^\omega}(f_2(n), g_2(n))\right] &=\\
&\textstyle\frac{1}{2}d_{\mathcal{C}_{(0,\infty]\times\mathbb{N}^\omega,(\infty,1_{\mathbb{N}^\omega})}}(f, g),
\end{aligned}$$

for all $f, g \in \mathcal{C}_{(0,\infty]\times\mathbb{N}^\omega,(\infty,1_{\mathbb{N}^\omega})}$.

Therefore, by Theorem 1, we can deduce that the functional Γ has a unique fixed point $f_{fact} = (f_{fact,1}, f_{fact,2}) \in \mathcal{C}_{(0,\infty]\times\mathbb{N}^\omega,(\infty,1_{\mathbb{N}^\omega})}$. Of course, by construction of Γ, we have that $f_{fact,1} \in \mathcal{C}_{c,1}$.

Moreover, $f_{fact}(n) = \Gamma(f_{fact})(n)$ if and only if $f_{fact,1}(n) = \Psi_T(f_{fact,1})(n)$ and $f_{fact,2}(n) = M(f_{fact,2}(n))$ for all $n \in \mathbb{N}$.

Notice that a complexity function (a function belonging to $\mathcal{C}$) is a solution to the recurrence equation (15) if and only if it is a fixed point of the functional Ψ_T and that a word is a fixed point of the mapping M if and only if it satisfies the denotational specification (14). Whence we obtain that $f_{fact,1}$ is the solution to the recurrence equation (15) and that $f_{fact,2}$ is the solution to the recursive denotational specification (14). Moreover, by construction of M, $f_{fact,2}(n) = n!$ for all $n \in \mathbb{N}$. Hence $f_{fact,1}$ represents the running time of computing of the recursive algorithm under study and $f_{fact,2}$ provides the meaning of the recursive algorithm that computes the factorial of a nonnegative number using the denotational specification (14), respectively.

So we have shown that generalized complexity spaces in the sense of (Romaguera & Schellekens, 2000) are useful to describe, at the same time, the complexity and the program correctness of recursive algorithms using recursive denotational specifications. The exposed method is also based on fixed point techniques like the Schellekens and Scott techniques but it presents an advantage with respect the latter ones. Indeed, the method provided by generalized complexity spaces allows to discuss the correctness of recursive algorithms which is an improvement with respect to the Schellekens technique and, in addition, it allows to analyze the correctness of the recursive algorithms by means of quantitative techniques which is an improvement with respect to the classical Scott technique that, as we have pointed out in Section 1, is based only on qualitative reasonings.

6. Conclusions

In 1970, D.S. Scott introduced a mathematical framework as a part of the foundations of Denotational Semantics, based on topological spaces endowed with an order relation that represents the computational information, which allowed to model the meaning of recursive denotational specification by means of qualitative fixed point techniques. Later on, in 1995, M.P. Schellekens showed a connection between Denotational Semantics and Asymptotic Complexity Analysis applying the original Scott ideas to analyze the running time of computing of Divide and Conquer algorithms but, this time, via quantitative fixed point techniques (the topology is induced by a quasi-metric that provides quantitative information about the elements of the mathematical framework). In this chapter, we have extended the Schellekens technique in order to discuss the complexity of recursive algorithms that do not belong to the Divide and Conquer family. In particular, we have introduced a new fixed point technique that allows to obtain the asymptotic complexity behavior of the running time of computing of the aforesaid recursive algorithms. The new technique has the advantage of providing asymptotic upper and lower bounds of the running time of computing while that the Schellekens technique only allows to obtain upper asymptotic bounds. Furthermore, we have gone more deeply into the relationship between Denotational Semantics and Asymptotic Complexity Analysis constructing a mathematical approach which allows, in the spirit of Scott and Schellekens, to model at the same time the running time and the meaning of a recursive algorithm that performs a task using a recursive denotational specification by means of quantitative fixed point techniques and, thus, presents a improvement with respect to the Scott and Schellekens approaches.

7. Acknowledgements

The authors thank the support from the Spanish Ministry of Science and Innovation, grant MTM2009-12872-C02-01.

8. References

Boxer, L. & Miller, R. (2005). *Algorithms sequential and parallel: a unified approach*, Charles River Media, ISBN: 1584504129, Massachusetts.

Brassard, G. & Bratley, P. (1988). *Algorithms: Theory and Practice*, Prentice Hall, ISBN: 9780130232434, New Jersey.

Cull, P.; Flahive, R. & Robson, R. (1985). *Difference equations: from rabbits to chaos*, Springer, ISBN: 9780387232348, New York.

Davey, B.A. & Priestley, H.A. (1990). *Introduction to Lattices and Order*, Cambridge University Press, ISBN: 0521784514, Cambridge.

Ecklund, E.F. Jr.&, Cull. P. (1985). Towers of Hanoi and analysis of algorithms. *The American Mathematical Monthly*, Vol. 92, 407–420.

Künzi, H.P.A. Nonsymmetric topology, *Proceedings of Colloquium on Topology*, pp. 303-338, Szekszárd (Hungary), August 1993.

Llull-Chavarría, J. & Valero, O. (2009). An application of generalized complexity spaces to denotational semantics via domain of words. *Lecture Notes in Computer Science*, Vol. 5457, 530–541.

Matthews, S.G. (1994). Partial metric topology. *Annals of the New York Academy of Sciences*, Vol. 728, 183–197.

Rodríguez-López, J.; Romaguera. S & Valero, O. (2008). Denotational semantics for programming languages, balanced quasi-metrics and fixed points. *International Journal of Computer Mathematics*, Vol. 85, 623–630.

Romaguera, S. & Schellekens, M.P. (1999). Quasi-metric properties of complexity spaces. *Topology and its Applications*, Vol. 98, 311–322.

Romaguera, S. & Schellekens, M.P. (2000). The quasi-metric of complexity convergence. *Quaestiones Mathematicae*, Vol. 23, 359–374.

Romaguera, S.; Schellekens, M.P. & Valero, O. (2011). Complexity spaces as quantitative domains of computation, *Topology and its Applications*, Vol. 158, 853–860.

Romaguera, S.; Schellekens, M.P. & Valero, O. (2011). The complexity space of partial functions: a connection between Complexity Analysis and Denotational Semantics. *International Journal of Computer Mathematics*, Vol. 88, 1819–1829.

Romaguera, S.; Tirado, P. & Valero, O. (2011). New results on mathematical foundations of asymptotic complexity analysis of algorithms via complexity spaces, *Proceedings of the 11th International Conference on Mathematical Methods in Science and Engineering*, pp. 996-1007, ISBN: 9788461461677, Alicante (Spain), July 2011.

Romaguera, S. & Valero, O. (2008). On the structure of the space of complexity partial functions. *International Journal of Computer Mathematics*, Vol. 85, 631–640.

Schellekens, M.P. (1995). The Smyth completion: a common foundation for denotational semantics and complexity analysis, *Electronic Notes in Theoretical Computer Science*, Vol. 1, 211–232.

Scott, D.S. (1970). Outline of a mathematical theory of computation, *Proceedings of 4th Annual Princeton Conference on Information Science and Systems*, pp. 169-176, Princeton (New York), March 1970.

Scott, D.S. (1982). Domains for denotational semantics. *Lecture Notes in Computer Science*, Vol. 140, 577– 613.

6

A Semantic Framework for the Declarative Debugging of Wrong and Missing Answers in Declarative Constraint Programming

Rafael del Vado Vírseda and Fernando Pérez Morente
Universidad Complutense de Madrid
Spain

1. Introduction

Debugging tools are a practical need for helping programmers to understand why their programs do not work as intended. Declarative programming paradigms involving complex operational details, such as constraint solving and lazy evaluation, do not fit well to traditional debugging techniques relying on the inspection of low-level computation traces. As a solution to this problem, and following a seminal idea by Shapiro (Shapiro, 1982), *declarative debugging* (a.k.a. *declarative diagnosis* or *algorithmic debugging*) uses *Computation Trees* (shortly, *CTs*) in place of traces. *CTs* are built *a posteriori* to represent the structure of a computation whose top-level outcome is regarded as a *symptom* of the unexpected behavior by the user. Each node in a *CT* represents the computation of some observable result, depending on the results of its children nodes, using a program fragment also attached to the node. Declarative diagnosis explores a *CT* looking for a so-called *buggy node* which computes an unexpected result from children whose results are all expected. Each buggy node points to a program fragment responsible for the unexpected behavior. The search for a buggy node can be implemented with the help of an external *oracle* (usually the user with some semiautomatic support) who has a reliable declarative knowledge of the expected program semantics, the so-called *intended interpretation*.

The generic description of declarative diagnosis in the previous paragraph follows (Naish, 1997). Declarative diagnosis was first proposed in the field of *Logic Programming* (*LP*) (Ferrand, 1987; Lloyd, 1987; Shapiro, 1982), and it has been successfully extended to other declarative programming paradigms, including (lazy) *Functional Programming* (*FP*) (Nilsson, 2001; Nilsson & Sparud, 1997; Pope, 2006; Pope & Naish, 2003), *Constraint Logic Programming* (*CLP*) (Boye et al., 1997; Ferrand et al., 2003; Tessier & Ferrand, 2000), and *Functional-Logic Programming* (*FLP*) (Caballero & Rodríguez, 2004; Naish & Barbour, 1995). The nature of unexpected results differs according to the programming paradigm. Unexpected results in *FP* are mainly *incorrect values*, while in *CLP* and *FLP* an unexpected result can be either a single computed answer regarded as *incorrect*, or a set of computed answers (for one and the same goal with a finite search space) regarded as *incomplete*. These two possibilities give rise to the declarative debugging of *wrong* and *missing* computed answers, respectively. The case of unexpected *finite failure* of a goal is a particular symptom of missing answers with special relevance. However, diagnosis methods must consider the most general case, since finite failure of a goal is often caused by non-failing subgoals that do not compute all the expected answers.

In contrast to recent approaches to error diagnosis using *abstract interpretation* (e.g., (Alpuente et al., 2003; Comini et al., 1999; Hermenegildo, 2002), and some of the approaches described in (Deransart et al., 2000)), declarative diagnosis often involves complex queries to the user. This problem has been tackled by means of various techniques, such as user-given partial specifications of the program's semantics (Boye et al., 1997), safe inference of information from answers previously given by the user (Caballero & Rodríguez, 2004), or *CT*s tailored to the needs of a particular debugging problem over a particular computation domain (Ferrand et al., 2003). Another practical problem with declarative diagnosis is that the size of *CT*s can cause excessive overhead in the case of computations that demand a big amount of computer storage. As a remedy, techniques for piecemeal construction of *CT*s have been considered; see (Pope, 2006) for a recent proposal in the *FP* field. However, current research in declarative diagnosis has still to face many challenges regarding both the foundations and the development of practical tools.

In spite of the above mentioned difficulties, we are confident that declarative diagnosis methods can be useful for detecting programming bugs by observing computations whose demand of computer storage is modest. The aim of this chapter is to present a logical and semantic framework for diagnosing wrong and missing computed answers in $CFLP(\mathcal{D})$ (López et al., 2006), a newly proposed generic programming scheme for lazy *Constraint Functional-Logic Programming* which can be instantiated by any constraint domain $\mathcal{D}$ given as parameter, and supports a powerful combination of functional and constraint logic programming over $\mathcal{D}$. Sound and complete goal solving procedures for the $CFLP(\mathcal{D})$ scheme have been obtained (López et al., 2004). Moreover, useful instances of this scheme have been implemented in the $\mathcal{TOY}$ system (López & Sánchez, 1999) and tested in practical applications (Fernández et al., 2007). Borrowing ideas from $CFLP(\mathcal{D})$ declarative semantics we obtain a suitable notion of *intended interpretation*, as well as a kind of abridged *proof trees* with a sound logical meaning to play the role of *CT*s. Our aim is to achieve a natural combination of previous approaches that were independently developed for the $CLP(\mathcal{D})$ scheme (Tessier & Ferrand, 2000) and for lazy functional-logic languages (Caballero & Rodríguez, 2004). We give theoretical results showing that the proposed debugging method is logically correct for any sound $CFLP(\mathcal{D})$-system whose computed answers are logical consequences of the program in the sense of $CFLP(\mathcal{D})$ semantics. We also present a practical debugger called $\mathcal{DDT}$, developed as an extension of previously existing but less powerful tools (Caballero, 2005; Caballero & Rodríguez, 2004). $\mathcal{DDT}$ implements the proposed diagnosis method for $CFLP(\mathcal{R})$-programming in the $\mathcal{TOY}$ system (López & Sánchez, 1999) using the domain $\mathcal{R}$ of arithmetic constraints over the real numbers.

The rest of the chapter is organized as follows: Section 2 motivates our approach by presenting debugging examples which are used as illustration of the main features of our diagnosis method. Section 3 recalls the $CFLP(\mathcal{D})$ scheme from (López et al., 2006) to the extent needed for understanding the theoretical results in this chapter. Section 4 presents a correct method for the declarative diagnosis of wrong computed answers in any soundly implemented $CFLP(\mathcal{D})$-system. Section 5 describes the debugging tool $\mathcal{DDT}$ for wrong answers. Section 6 presents the abbreviated proof trees used as *CT*s in our method for debugging missing computed answers, as well as the results ensuring the logical correctness of the diagnosis. Section 7 presents a prototype debugger for diagnosing missing answers. Section 8 concludes and points to some plans for future work.

2. Motivating examples

As a motivation for our declarative debugging method of wrong answers in the *CFLP*($\mathcal{D}$) scheme, we consider the following program fragment written in $\mathcal{TOY}$ (López & Sánchez, 1999), a programming system which supports several instances of the *CFLP*($\mathcal{D}$) scheme:

Example 1. (Debugging Wrong Answers in $\mathcal{TOY}$)

```
infixr 40 &&
(&&) :: bool -> bool -> bool
false && Y = false
true && Y = Y

head :: [A] -> A
head [X|Xs] = X

type point = (real,real)
type figure = point -> bool

rect :: point -> real -> real -> figure
rect (X,Y) LX LY (X',Y') = (X' >= X) && (X' <= X+LX) && (Y' <= Y) && (Y' <= Y+LY)

% This program rule is incorrect. It should be: (Y' >= Y)...

intersect :: figure -> figure -> figure
intersect F1 F2 P = F1 P && F2 P

ladder :: point -> real -> real -> [figure]
ladder (X,Y) LX LY = [rect (X,Y) LX LY | ladder (X+LX, Y+LY) LX LY]
```

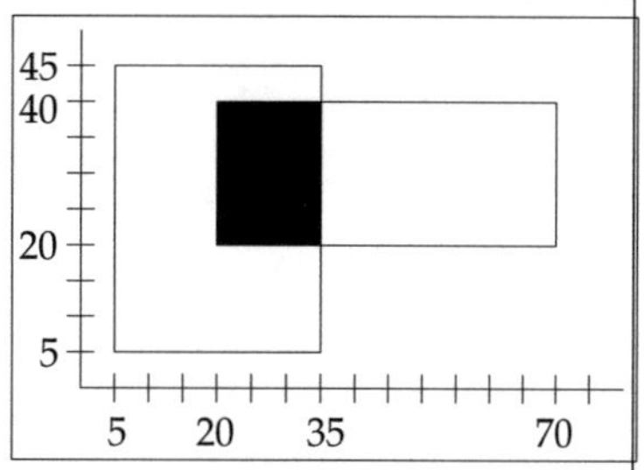

Fig. 1. Building ladders in $\mathcal{TOY}$

In this example (see Fig. 1), $\mathcal{TOY}$ is used to implement the instance *CFLP*($\mathcal{R}$) of the *CFLP*($\mathcal{D}$) scheme, with the parameter $\mathcal{D}$ replaced by the real numbers domain $\mathcal{R}$, which provides real numbers, arithmetic operations and various arithmetic constraints, including equalities, disequalities and inequalities. The type figure is intended to represent geometric figures as boolean functions, the function rect is intended to represent rectangles (more precisely, (rect (X,Y) LX LY) is intended to represent a rectangle with leftmost-bottom vertex (X,Y) and rightmost-upper vertex (X+LX,Y+LY)); and the function ladder is intended to build an infinite list of rectangles in the shape of a ladder. Although the text of the program seems to include no constraints, it uses arithmetic and comparison operators that give rise to constraint solving in execution time. More precisely, consider the following session in $\mathcal{TOY}$:

```
Toy> /run(examples/debug/ladder)                          % compile ladder.toy
Toy> /cflpr                                               % load CFLP(R)
Toy(R)> intersect (head (ladder (20,20) 50 20))
                   (head (ladder (5,5) 30 40)) (X,Y) == R % goal
    { R -> true } { Y <= 5, X >= 2.0E+01, X <= 35 }       % computed answer
```

The goal asks for the membership of a generic point (X,Y) to the intersection of the two rectangles (rect (20,20) 50 20) and (rect (5,5) 30 40), computed indirectly as the first steps of two particular ladders. The diagram included in Fig. 1 shows these two rectangles as well as the rectangle corresponding to their intersection (highlighted in black). The $\mathcal{TOY}$ system has solved the goal by a combination of lazy narrowing and constraint solving; the computed answer consists of the substitution R –> true and three constraints imposed on the variables X and Y[1]. The only constraint imposed on Y (namely Y <= 5) allows for arbitrarily small values of Y, which cannot correspond to points belonging to the rectangle expected as intersection. Therefore, the user will view the computed answer as *wrong* with respect to the intended meaning of the program. As we will see in Sections 4 and 5, the declarative debugging technique presented in this chapter leads to the diagnosis of the program rule for the function rect as responsible for the *wrong answer*. Indeed, this program rule is incorrect with respect to the intended program semantics; as shown in Fig. 1, the third inequality at the right hand side should be Y' >= Y instead of Y' <= Y.

After this correction, no more wrong computed answers will be observed for the goal discussed above. As any debugging technique, declarative diagnosis has limitations. A "corrected" program fragment can still include more subtle bugs that can be observed in the computed answers for other goals. In our case, we can consider the goal

```
Toy> /cflpr
Toy(R)> intersect (head (ladder (70,40) -50 -20))
                  (head (ladder (35,45) -30 -40)) (X,Y) == R
```

whose meaning with respect to the intended semantics is the same as for the previous goal, except that the rectangles playing the role of initial steps of the two ladders are represented differently. Since the boolean expression at the right hand side of the "corrected" program rule for function rect yields the result false whenever LX or LY is bound to a negative number, wrong answers including the substitution R –> false will be computed. Moreover, other answers including the substitution R –> true will be expected by the user but *missing* to occur among the computed answers.

The traditional approach to declarative debugging in the $CLP(\mathcal{D})$ scheme includes the diagnosis of both *wrong* and *missing* computed answers (Tessier & Ferrand, 2000). Now, we motivate our approach for the declarative debugging of *missing answers* in the $CFLP(\mathcal{D})$ scheme by means of the following example, intended to illustrate the main features of our diagnosis method.

[1] There are other five computed answers consisting of the substitution R –> false and various constraints imposed on X and Y.

Example 2. (Debugging Missing Answers in $\mathcal{TOY}$)

The following small *CFLP*($\mathcal{H}$)-program $\mathcal{P}_{\mathtt{fD}}$, written in $\mathcal{TOY}$ syntax over the *Herbrand domain* $\mathcal{H}$ with equality (==) and disequality (/=) constraints, includes program rules for the non-deterministic functions `(//)` and `fDiff`, and the deterministic functions `gen` and `even`. Note the infix syntax used for `(//)`, as well as the use of the equality symbol = instead of the rewrite arrow `->` for the program rules of those functions viewed as deterministic by the user. This is just meant as user given information, not checked by the $\mathcal{TOY}$ system, which treats all the program defined functions as possibly non-deterministic.

```
infixr 40 //            % non-deterministic choice operator

(//) :: A -> A -> A
X // _ --> X
_ // Y --> Y

fDiff :: [A] -> A
fDiff [X]        --> X
fDiff (X:Y:Zs) --> X // fDiff (Y:Zs) <== X /= Y
fDiff (X:Y:Zs) --> X                 <== X == Y

gen :: A -> A -> [A]          even :: int -> bool
gen X Y = X : Y : gen Y X     even N = true <== (mod N 2) == 0
```

Function `fDiff` is intended to return any element belonging to the longest prefix `Xs` of the list given as parameter such that `Xs` does not include two identical elements in consecutive positions. In general, there will be several of such elements, and therefore `fDiff` is non-deterministic. Function `gen` is deterministic and returns a potentially infinite list of the form $[d_1, d_2, d_2, d_1, d_1, d_2, \ldots]$, where the elements d_1 and d_2 are the given parameters. Therefore, the lazy evaluation of `(fDiff (gen 1 2))` is expected to yield the two possible results `1` and `2` in alternative computations, and the initial goal $G_{\mathtt{fD}}$: `even (fDiff (gen 1 2)) == true` for $\mathcal{P}_{\mathtt{fD}}$ is expected to succeed, since `(fDiff (gen 1 2))` is expected to return the even number `2`. However, if the third program rule for function `fDiff` were *missing* in program $\mathcal{P}_{\mathtt{fD}}$, the expression `(fDiff (gen 1 2))` would return only the numeric value `1`, and therefore the goal $G_{\mathtt{fD}}$ would fail unexpectedly. At this point, a diagnosis for *missing answers* could take place, looking for a *buggy node* in a suitable *CT* in order to detect some *incomplete* function definition (that of function `fDiff`, in this case) to be blamed for the missing answers. As we will see in Sections 6 and 7, this particular *incompleteness symptom* could be mended by placing again the third rule for `fDiff` within the program.

3. The *CFLP*($\mathcal{D}$) programming scheme

In this section we summarize the essentials of the *CFLP*($\mathcal{D}$) scheme (López et al., 2006) for lazy Constraint Functional-Logic Programming over a parametrically given constraint domain $\mathcal{D}$, which serves as a logical and semantic framework for the declarative diagnosis method presented in the chapter.

3.1 Preliminary notions

We consider a *universal signature* $\Sigma = \langle DC, FS\rangle$, where $DC = \bigcup_{n\in\mathbb{N}} DC^n$ and $FS = \bigcup_{n\in\mathbb{N}} FS^n$ are countably infinite and mutually disjoint sets of *data constructors* resp. *evaluable function symbols*, indexed by arities. Evaluable functions are further classified into domain dependent *primitive functions* $PF^n \subseteq FS^n$ and user *defined functions* $DF^n = FS^n \setminus PF^n$ for each $n \in \mathbb{N}$. We write $\Sigma_\perp$ for the result of extending DC^0 with the special symbol $\perp$, intended to denote an undefined data value and we assume that DC includes the two constants *true* and *false* and the usual list constructors. We use the notations $c, d \in DC$, $f, g \in FS$, and $h \in DC \cup FS$. We also assume a countably infinite set $\mathcal{V}$ of *variables* $X, Y, \ldots$ and a set $\mathcal{U}$ of *primitive elements* $u, v, \ldots$ (as e.g. the set $\mathbb{R}$ of the real numbers) mutually disjoint and disjoint from $\Sigma_\perp$. *Expressions* $e \in Exp_\perp(\mathcal{U})$ have the following syntax:

$$e ::= \perp \mid u \mid X \mid h \mid (e\, e_1 \ldots e_m) \text{ \% shortly: } (e\, \overline{e}_m)$$

where $u \in \mathcal{U}$, $X \in \mathcal{V}$, $h \in DC \cup FS$. An important subclass of expressions is the set of *patterns* $s, t \in Pat_\perp(\mathcal{U})$, whose syntax is defined as follows:

$$t ::= \perp \mid u \mid X \mid (c\, \overline{t}_m) \mid (f\, \overline{t}_m)$$

where $u \in \mathcal{U}$, $X \in \mathcal{V}$, $c \in DC^n$ with $m \leq n$, and $f \in FS^n$ with $m < n$. Patterns are used as representations of possibly functional data values. For instance, the rectangle $(rect\ (5,5)\ 30\ 40)$ we met when discussing Example 1 is a functional data value represented as pattern[2].

As usual, we define *substitutions* $\sigma \in Sub_\perp(\mathcal{U})$ as mappings $\sigma : \mathcal{V} \to Pat_\perp(\mathcal{U})$ extended to $\sigma : Exp_\perp(\mathcal{U}) \to Exp_\perp(\mathcal{U})$ in the natural way. By convention, we write $e\sigma$ instead of $\sigma(e)$ for any $e \in Exp_\perp(\mathcal{U})$, and $\sigma\theta$ for the composition of σ and θ. A substitution σ such that $\sigma\sigma = \sigma$ is called *idempotent*.

3.2 Constraints over a constraint domain

Intuitively, a constraint domain provides a set of specific data elements, along with certain primitive functions operating upon them. Primitive predicates can be modelled as primitive functions returning boolean values. Formally, a *constraint domain* with primitive elements $\mathcal{U}$ and primitive functions $PF \subseteq FS$ is any structure $\mathcal{D} = \langle D_\mathcal{U}, \{p^\mathcal{D} \mid p \in PF\}\rangle$ with carrier set $D_\mathcal{U}$ the set of *ground* patterns (i.e., without variables) over $\mathcal{U}$ and interpretations $p^\mathcal{D} \subseteq D^n_\mathcal{U} \times D_\mathcal{U}$ of each $p \in PF^n$ satisfying the technical *monotonicity*, *antimonotonicity*, and *radicality* requirements given in (López et al., 2006). We use the notation $p^\mathcal{D}\, \overline{t}_n \to t$ to indicate that $(\overline{t}_n, t) \in p^\mathcal{D}$.

Constraints over a given constraint domain $\mathcal{D}$ are logical statements built from atomic constraints by means of logical conjunction $\wedge$ and existential quantification $\exists$. *Atomic constraints* can have the form $\lozenge$ (standing for *truth*), $\blacklozenge$ (standing for *falsity*), or $p\, \overline{e}_n \to!\, t$, meaning that the primitive function $p \in PF^n$ with parameters $\overline{e}_n \in Exp_\perp(\mathcal{U})$ returns a *total* result $t \in Pat_\perp(\mathcal{U})$ (i.e, with no occurrences of $\perp$). Constraints whose atomic parts have the

[2] Note that $(5,5)$ can be seen as syntactic sugar for $(pair\ 5\ 5)$, *pair* being a constructor for ordered pairs.

form $\Diamond, \blacklozenge$ or $p\,\bar{t}_n \rightarrow! t$ with $\bar{t}_n \in Pat_\perp(\mathcal{U})$ are called *primitive constraints*. In the sequel, we use the notation $PCon_\perp(\mathcal{D})$ for the set of primitive constraints over $\mathcal{D}$ and $DCon_\perp(\mathcal{D})$ for the set of user defined constraints over $\mathcal{D}$.

Example 3. (Constraint Domain $\mathcal{R}$) *The constraint domain $\mathcal{R}$ has the carrier set $D_{\mathbb{R}}$ of ground patters over $\mathbb{R}$ and the primitives defined below:*

1. *$eq_{\mathbb{R}}$, equality primitive for real numbers, such that: $eq_{\mathbb{R}}^{\mathcal{R}}\ u\ u \rightarrow true$ for all $u \in \mathbb{R}$; $eq_{\mathbb{R}}^{\mathcal{R}}\ u\ v \rightarrow false$ for all $u, v \in \mathbb{R}$, $u \neq v$; $eq_{\mathbb{R}}^{\mathcal{R}}\ t\ s \rightarrow \perp$ otherwise.*
2. *seq, strict equality primitive for ground patterns over the real numbers, such that: $seq^{\mathcal{R}}\ t\ t \rightarrow true$ for all total $t \in D_{\mathbb{R}}$; $seq^{\mathcal{R}}\ t\ s \rightarrow false$ for all $t, s \in D_{\mathbb{R}}$ such that t, s have no common upper bound with respect to the* information ordering *introduced in (López et al., 2006); $seq^{\mathcal{R}}\ t\ s \rightarrow \perp$ otherwise. In the sequel, $e_1 == e_2$ abbreviates $seq\,e_1\,e_2 \rightarrow! true$.*
3. *$+, -, *$, for addition, subtraction and multiplication, such that: $x +^{\mathcal{R}} y \rightarrow x +^{\mathbb{R}} y$ for all $x, y \in \mathbb{R}$; $t +^{\mathcal{R}} s \rightarrow \perp$ whenever $t \notin \mathbb{R}$ or $s \notin \mathbb{R}$; and analogously for $-^{\mathcal{R}}$ and $*^{\mathcal{R}}$.*
4. *$<, \leq, >, \geq$, for numeric comparisons, such that: $x <^{\mathcal{R}} y \rightarrow true$ for all $x, y \in \mathbb{R}$ with $x <^{\mathbb{R}} y$; $x <^{\mathcal{R}} y \rightarrow false$ for all $x, y \in \mathbb{R}$ with $x \geq^{\mathbb{R}} y$; $t <^{\mathcal{R}} s \rightarrow \perp$ whenever $t \notin \mathbb{R}$ or $s \notin \mathbb{R}$; and analogously for $\leq^{\mathcal{R}}, >^{\mathcal{R}}, \geq^{\mathcal{R}}$. In the sequel, $e_1 < e_2$ abbreviates $e_1 < e_2 \rightarrow! true$ and $e_1 \geq e_2$ abbreviates $e_1 < e_2 \rightarrow! false$ (analogously for other comparison primitives).*

The set of *valuations* over a constraint domain $\mathcal{D}$ is defined as the set $Val_\perp(\mathcal{D})$ of ground substitutions (i.e., mappings from variables to ground patterns). The semantics of constraints relies on the idea that a given valuation can satisfy or not a given constraint. Therefore, the set of *solutions* of $\pi \in PCon_\perp(\mathcal{D})$ can be defined in a natural way as a subset $Sol_{\mathcal{D}}(\pi) \subseteq Val_\perp(\mathcal{D})$; see (López et al., 2006) for details. Moreover, the set of solutions of $\Pi \subseteq PCon_\perp(\mathcal{D})$ is defined as $Sol_{\mathcal{D}}(\Pi) = \bigcap_{\pi\in\Pi} Sol_{\mathcal{D}}(\pi)$.

3.3 Constraint functional-logic programming

For any given constraint domain $\mathcal{D}$, a $CFLP(\mathcal{D})$-program $\mathcal{P}$ is presented as a set of constrained rewrite rules, called *program rules*, that define the behavior of user-defined functions. More precisely, a *constrained program rule* R for $f \in DF^n$ has the form $R : f\,\bar{t}_n \rightarrow r \Leftarrow \Delta$ (abbreviated as $f\,\bar{t}_n \rightarrow r$ if Δ is empty) and is required to satisfy the conditions listed below[3]:

1. The *left-hand side* $f\,\bar{t}_n$ is a *linear* expression (i.e, there is no variable having more than one occurrence), and for all $1 \leq i \leq n$, $t_i \in Pat_\perp(\mathcal{U})$ are total patterns. The *right-hand side* $r \in Exp_\perp(\mathcal{U})$ is also total.
2. $\Delta \subseteq DCon_\perp(\mathcal{D})$ is a finite set of total atomic constraints, intended to be interpreted as conjunction, and possibly including occurrences of user defined functions.

Program defined functions can be higher-order and/or non-deterministic. For instance, the $\mathcal{TOY}$ program presented in Example 1 can be viewed as an example of $CFLP(\mathcal{R})$-program written in $\mathcal{TOY}$'s syntax. The reader is referred to (López et al., 2006) for more explanations and examples in other constraint domains.

[3] In practice, $\mathcal{TOY}$ and similar languages require program rules to be well-typed in a polymorphic type system. However, the $CFLP(\mathcal{D})$ scheme can deal also with untyped programs. Well-typedness is viewed as an additional requirement, not as part of progam semantics.

The intended use of programs is to perform computations by solving goals proposed by the user. An *admissible goal* for a given $CFLP(\mathcal{D})$-program must have the form $G : \exists \overline{U}.\ (P \ \Box \ \Delta)$, where $\overline{U}$ is a finite set of so-called *existential variables* of the goal G (the rest of variables in G are called *free variables* and denoted by $fvar(G)$), P is a finite conjunction of so-called *productions* of the form $e \rightarrow s$ fulfilling the *admissibility conditions* given in (López et al., 2006), with $e \in Exp_{\perp}(\mathcal{U})$ and $s \in Pat_{\perp}(\mathcal{U})$ intended to mean that e can be evaluated to s, and $\Delta \subseteq DCon_{\perp}(\mathcal{D})$ is a finite conjunction of total user defined constraints. Two special kinds of admissible goals are interesting. *Initial goals*, where $\overline{U}$ and P are both empty (i.e., G has only a constrained part Δ without occurrences of existential variables), and *solved goals* (also called *solved forms*) of the form $S : \exists \overline{U}.\ (\sigma \ \Box \ \Pi)$, where σ is a finite set of productions $X \rightarrow t$ or $s \rightarrow Y$ interpreted as the variable bindings of an idempotent substitution and $\Pi \subseteq PCon_{\perp}(\mathcal{D})$ is a finite conjunction of total primitive constraints. Finally, a *goal solving system* for $CFLP(\mathcal{D})$ is expected to accept a program $\mathcal{P}$ and an initial goal G from the user, and to obtain one or more solved forms S_i as *computed answers*. As explained in Section 2, an initial goal G for the $CFLP(\mathcal{R})$-program shown in Example 1 can be $intersect\ (head\ (ladder\ (20,20)\ 50\ 20))\ (head\ (ladder\ (5,5)\ 30\ 40))\ (X,Y) == R$ and a computed answer S for G is $R \rightarrow true \ \Box \ X \leq 35 \wedge X \geq 20 \wedge Y \leq 5$.

Goal solving systems can be implementations of $CFLP$ languages such as *Curry* (Hanus, 2003) or $\mathcal{TOY}$ (López & Sánchez, 1999), or formal *goal solving calculi* including recent proposals such as the $CDNC(\mathcal{D})$ calculus (López et al., 2004), which is sound and complete with respect to the declarative semantics discussed in the next subsection, and behaves as a faithful formal model for actual computations in the $\mathcal{TOY}$ system.

3.4 Standardized programs and negative theories

Let $\mathcal{P}$ be a $CFLP(\mathcal{D})$-program. Its associated *Negative Theory* $\mathcal{P}^-$ is obtained in two steps. First, each program rule $f\ \overline{t}_n \rightarrow r \Leftarrow \Delta$ is replaced by a *standardized* form $f\ \overline{X}_n \rightarrow Y \Leftarrow R$, where $\overline{X}_n, Y$ are new variables, $R = \exists \overline{U}.\ R$ with $\overline{U} = var(R) \setminus \{\overline{X}_n, Y\}$, and the condition R is $X_1 \rightarrow t_1, \ldots, X_n \rightarrow t_n, \Delta, r \rightarrow Y$. Next, $\mathcal{P}^-$ is built by taking one *axiom* $(f)^-_{\mathcal{P}}$ of the form $\forall \overline{X}_n, Y.\ (f\ \overline{X}_n \rightarrow Y \Rightarrow (\bigvee_{i \in I} R_i) \vee (\perp \rightarrow Y))$ for each function symbol f whose standardized program rules are $\{f\ \overline{X}_n \rightarrow Y \Leftarrow R_i\}_{i \in I}$. By convention, we may use the notation D_f for the disjunction $(\bigvee_{i \in I} R_i) \vee (\perp \rightarrow Y)$, and we may leave the universal quantification of the variables $\overline{X}_n, Y$ implicit. Intuitively, the axiom $(f)^-_{\mathcal{P}}$ says that any result computed for f must be obtained by means of some of the rules for f in the program. The last alternative $(\perp \rightarrow Y)$ within D_f says that Y is bound to the undefined result $\perp$ in case that no program rule for f succeeds to compute a more defined result. For example, let $\mathcal{P}_{\texttt{fD}}$ be the $CFLP(\mathcal{H})$-program given in Section 2, with the third program rule for `fDiff` omitted. Then $\mathcal{P}^-_{\texttt{fD}}$ includes (among others) the following axiom for the function symbol *fDiff*:

$$
\begin{aligned}
(fDiff)^-_{\mathcal{P}_{\texttt{fD}}} : \forall L, F.\ (fDiff\ L \rightarrow F \Rightarrow \\
& \exists X.\ (L \rightarrow [X] \wedge X \rightarrow F) \vee \\
& \quad \exists X, Y, Zs.\ (L \rightarrow (X : Y : Zs) \wedge X \mathrel{/=} Y \wedge X \mathbin{//} fDiff\ (Y : Zs) \rightarrow F) \vee \\
& \quad\quad (\perp \rightarrow F))
\end{aligned}
$$

3.5 Answer collection assertions

In this work we propose to use computation trees for missing answers whose nodes have attached so-called *answer collection assertions*, briefly *acas*. The *aca* at the root node has the form $G \Rightarrow \bigvee_{i \in I} S_i$, where G is the initial goal and $\bigvee_{i \in I} S_i$ (written as the *failure symbol* ♦ if $I = \emptyset$) is the disjunction of computed answers observed by the user. This root *aca* asserts that the computed answers cover all the solutions of the initial goal, and will be regarded as a false statement in case that the user misses computed answers. For example, the root *aca* corresponding to the initial goal G_{fD} for program $\mathcal{P}_{\mathrm{fD}}$ is `even (fDiff (gen 1 2)) == true` ⇒ ♦ stating that this goal has (unexpectedly) failed. The *acas* at internal nodes in our computation trees have the form $f\bar{t}_n \rightarrow t \,\square\, S \Rightarrow \bigvee_{i \in I} S_i$, asserting that the disjunction of computed answers $\bigvee_{i \in I} S_i$ covers all the solutions for the intermediate goal $G' : f\bar{t}_n \rightarrow t \,\square\, S$. Note that G' asks for the solutions of the production $f\bar{t}_n \rightarrow t$ which satisfy the constraint store S. The *acas* of this form correspond to the intermediate calls to program defined functions f needed for collecting all the answers computed for the initial goal G. Due to *lazy evaluation*, the parameters $\bar{t}_n$ and the result t will appear in the most evaluated form demanded by the topmost computation. When these values are functions, they are represented in terms of partial applications of top-level function names. This is satisfactory under the assumption that no local function definitions are allowed in programs, as it happens in $\mathcal{TOY}$.

3.6 Declarative semantics

In this subsection we recall some notions and results on the declarative semantics of *CFLP*($\mathcal{D}$)-programs which were developed in (López et al., 2006) and are needed for the rest of this work. Given a constraint domain $\mathcal{D}$ we consider two different kinds of constrained statements (briefly, *c-statements*) involving partial patterns t, $t_i \in Pat_\perp(\mathcal{U})$, partial expressions e, $e_i \in Exp_\perp(\mathcal{U})$, and a finite set $\Pi \subseteq PCon_\perp(\mathcal{D})$ of primitive constraints:

1. *c-productions* $e \rightarrow t \Leftarrow \Pi$, with $e \in Exp_\perp(\mathcal{U})$ and $t \in Pat_\perp(\mathcal{U})$, intended to mean that e can be evaluated to t if Π holds (if Π is empty they boil down to unconstrained productions written as $e \rightarrow t$). As a particular kind of c-productions useful for debugging we distinguish *c-facts* $f\,\bar{t}_n \rightarrow t \Leftarrow \Pi$ with $f \in DF^n$. A c-production is called *trivial* iff $t = \perp$ or $Sol_{\mathcal{D}}(\Pi) = \emptyset$.
2. *c-atoms* $p\,\bar{e}_n \rightarrow!\, t \Leftarrow \Pi$, with $p \in PF^n$ and t total (if Π is empty they boil down to unconstrained atoms written as $p\,\bar{e}_n \rightarrow!\, t$). A c-atom is called *trivial* iff $Sol_{\mathcal{D}}(\Pi) = \emptyset$.

In the sequel, we use φ to denote any c-statement. A *c-interpretation* over $\mathcal{D}$ is defined as any set $\mathcal{I}$ of c-facts including all the trivial c-facts and closed under $\mathcal{D}$*-entailment*, a generalization of the entailment notion introduced in (Caballero & Rodríguez, 2004) to arbitrary constraint domains. We write $\mathcal{I} \Vdash_{\mathcal{D}} \varphi$ to indicate that the c-statement φ (not necessarily a c-fact) is semantically valid in the c-interpretation $\mathcal{I}$. This notation relies on a formal definition given in (López et al., 2006). Now we are in a position to define various semantics notions which rely on a given c-interpretation $\mathcal{I}$ over $\mathcal{D}$.

Definition 1. (Interpretation-Dependent Semantic Notions)

1. *The set of* **solutions** *of* $\delta \in DCon_\perp(\mathcal{D})$ *is a subset* $Sol_{\mathcal{I}}(\delta) \subseteq Val_\perp(\mathcal{D})$ *defined as follows:*
   (a) $Sol_{\mathcal{I}}(\pi) = Sol_{\mathcal{D}}(\pi)$, *for any* $\pi \in PCon_\perp(\mathcal{D})$.

(b) $Sol_{\mathcal{I}}(\delta) = \{\eta \in Val_{\perp}(\mathcal{D}) \mid \mathcal{I} \Vdash_{\mathcal{D}} \delta\eta\}$, *for any* $\delta \in DCon_{\perp}(\mathcal{D}) \setminus PCon_{\perp}(\mathcal{D})$.

The set of solutions of a set of constraints $\Delta \subseteq DCon_{\perp}(\mathcal{D})$ *is defined as* $Sol_{\mathcal{I}}(\Delta) = \bigcap_{\delta \in \Delta} Sol_{\mathcal{I}}(\delta)$.

2. *The set of solutions of a production* $e \to t$ *is a subset* $Sol_{\mathcal{I}}(e \to t) \subseteq Val_{\perp}(\mathcal{D})$ *defined as* $Sol_{\mathcal{I}}(e \to t) = \{\eta \in Val_{\perp}(\mathcal{D}) \mid \mathcal{I} \Vdash_{\mathcal{D}} e\eta \to t\eta\}$. *The set of solutions of a set of productions P is defined as* $Sol_{\mathcal{I}}(P) = \bigcap_{(e \to t) \in P} Sol_{\mathcal{I}}(e \to t)$.
3. *The set of solutions of an admissible goal* $G : \exists \overline{U}.\ (P \,\Box\, \Delta)$ *is a subset* $Sol_{\mathcal{I}}(G) \subseteq Val_{\perp}(\mathcal{D})$ *defined as follows:* $Sol_{\mathcal{I}}(G) = \{\eta \in Val_{\perp}(\mathcal{D}) \mid \eta' \in Sol_{\mathcal{I}}(P) \cap Sol_{\mathcal{I}}(\Delta)$ *for some* η' *such that* $\eta'(X) = \eta(X)$ *for all* $X \notin \overline{U}\}$.

For primitive constraints one can easily check that $Sol_{\mathcal{I}}(\Pi) = Sol_{\mathcal{D}}(\Pi)$. Moreover, we note that $Sol_{\mathcal{I}}(S) = Sol_{\mathcal{D}}(S)$ for every solved form S.

Definition 2. (Model-Theoretic Semantics) *Let* $\mathcal{P}$ *a CFLP(*$\mathcal{D}$*)-program and* $\mathcal{I}$ *a c-interpretation.*

1. $\mathcal{I}$ *is a* **model** *of* $\mathcal{P}$ *(in symbols,* $\mathcal{I} \models_{\mathcal{D}} \mathcal{P}$*) iff every constrained program rule* $(f\overline{t}_n \to r \Leftarrow \Delta) \in \mathcal{P}$ *is* **valid** *in* $\mathcal{I}$*: for any ground substitution* $\eta \in Sub_{\perp}(\mathcal{U})$ *and* $t \in Pat_{\perp}(\mathcal{U})$ *ground such that* $(f\overline{t}_n \to r \Leftarrow \Delta)\eta$ *is ground,* $\mathcal{I} \Vdash_{\mathcal{D}} \Delta\eta$ *and* $\mathcal{I} \Vdash_{\mathcal{D}} r\eta \to t$ *one has* $\mathcal{I} \Vdash_{\mathcal{D}} (f\overline{t}_n)\eta \to t$ *(or equivalently,* $((f\overline{t}_n)\eta \to t) \in \mathcal{I}$*).*
2. *A solved form S is a* **semantically valid** *answer for a goal G with respect to a program* $\mathcal{P}$ *(in symbols,* $\mathcal{P} \models_{\mathcal{D}} G \Leftarrow S$*) iff* $Sol_{\mathcal{D}}(S) \subseteq Sol_{\mathcal{I}}(G)$ *for all* $\mathcal{I} \models_{\mathcal{D}} \mathcal{P}$.
3. $\mathcal{I}$ *is a* **model** *of* $\mathcal{P}^-$ *iff every axiom* $(f)^-_{\mathcal{P}} : (f\ \overline{X}_n \to Y \Rightarrow D_f) \in \mathcal{P}^-$ *satisfies* $Sol_{\mathcal{I}}(f\ \overline{X}_n \to Y) \subseteq Sol_{\mathcal{I}}(D_f)$. *When this inclusion holds, we say that* $(f)^-_{\mathcal{P}}$ *is* **valid** *in* $\mathcal{I}$*, or also that f's definition as given in* $\mathcal{P}$ *is* **complete** *with respect to* $\mathcal{I}$.
4. *The aca* $G \Rightarrow \bigvee_{i \in I} S_i$ *is a* **logical consequence** *of* $\mathcal{P}^-$ *iff* $Sol_{\mathcal{I}}(G) \subseteq \bigcup_{i \in I} Sol_{\mathcal{D}}(S_i)$ *for any model* $\mathcal{I}$ *of* $\mathcal{P}^-$. *When this happens, we also say that the disjunction of answers* $\bigvee_{i \in I} S_i$ *is* **complete** *for G with respect to* $\mathcal{P}$.

4. Declarative debugging of wrong answers in *CFLP*($\mathcal{D}$)

In this section, we present the logical and semantic framework of the declarative diagnosis method of wrong answers for CFLP($\mathcal{D}$) and prove its logical correctness. In what follows, we assume that a constraint domain $\mathcal{D}$ and a CFLP($\mathcal{D}$)-program $\mathcal{P}$ are given.

4.1 Wrong answers and intended interpretations

Declarative diagnosis techniques rely on a declarative description of the intended program semantics. We will assume that the user knows (at least to the extent needed for answering queries during the debugging session) a so-called *intended model* $\mathcal{I}$, which is a c-interpretation expected to satisfy $\mathcal{I} \models_{\mathcal{D}} \mathcal{P}$, unless $\mathcal{P}$ is incorrect. For instance, $rect\,(X,Y)\,LX\,LY\,(A,B) \to false \Leftarrow A < X \wedge LX > 0 \wedge LY > 0$ could belong to the intended model $\mathcal{I}$ for the program fragment shown in Example 1. As explained in Subsection 3.6, the c-facts belonging to c-interpretations can be non-ground. Nevertheless, the model notion $\mathcal{I} \models_{\mathcal{D}} \mathcal{P}$ used here (see Definition 2 above) corresponds to the so-called *weak semantics* from (López et al., 2006), which depends just on the ground c-facts valid in $\mathcal{I}$. Therefore, different presentations of the intended model will be equivalent for the purposes of this work, as long as the ground c-facts valid in them are the same.

The aim of declarative diagnosis of wrong answers is to start with an observed *symptom* of erroneous program behavior, and detect some *error* in the program. The proper notions of symptom and error in our setting are as follows:

Definition 3. (Symptoms and Errors) *Assume $\mathcal{I}$ is the intended interpretation for program $\mathcal{P}$, and consider a solved form S produced as computed answer for the initial goal G by some goal solving system. We define:*

1. *S is a* **wrong answer** *w.r.t $\mathcal{I}$ (serving as* **symptom***) iff $Sol_{\mathcal{D}}(S) \not\subseteq Sol_{\mathcal{I}}(G)$.*
2. *$\mathcal{P}$ is* **incorrect** *with respect to $\mathcal{I}$ iff there exists some program rule $(f\bar{t}_n \rightarrow r \Leftarrow \Delta) \in \mathcal{P}$ (manifesting an* **error***) that is not valid in $\mathcal{I}$ (in the sense of Definition 2).*

For instance, the computed answer shown in Example 1 is wrong with respect to the intended model of the program assumed in that example, for the reasons already discussed in Section 2. As illustrated by that example, computed answers typically include constraints on the variables occurring in the initial goal. However, goal solving systems for *CFLP*($\mathcal{D}$) programs also maintain internal information on constraints related to variables used in intermediate computation steps, but not occurring in the initial goal. Such information is relevant for declarative debugging purposes. Therefore, in the rest of this section we will assume that computed answers S include also constraints related to intermediate variables.

4.2 A logical calculus for witnessing computed answers

Assuming that S is a computed answer for an initial goal G using a program $\mathcal{P}$, the declarative diagnosis of wrong answers needs a suitable *Computation Tree* (shortly, *CT*) representing the computation. In our setting we will obtain the *CT* from a logical proof $\mathcal{P} \vdash_{CPPC(\mathcal{D})} G \Leftarrow S$ which derives the statement $G \Leftarrow S$ from the program $\mathcal{P}$ in the *Constraint Positive Proof Calculus* (shortly $CPPC(\mathcal{D})$) given by the inference rules in Fig. 2. We will say that the $CPPC(\mathcal{D})$-proof *witnesses* the computed answer.

Most of these inference rules have been borrowed from the proof theory of *CRWL*($\mathcal{D}$), a *Constraint ReWriting Logic* which characterizes the semantics of *CFLP*($\mathcal{D}$) programs (López et al., 2006). The main novelties in $CPPC(\mathcal{D})$ are the addition of rule **EX** (to deal with existential quantifiers in computed answers) and a reformulation of rule **DF**$_{\mathcal{P}}$, which is presented as the consecutive application of two inference steps named **AR**$_f$ and **FA**$_f$, which cannot be applied separately. The purpose of this composite inference is to introduce the c-facts $f\,\bar{t}_n \rightarrow t \Leftarrow \Pi$ at the conclusion of inference **FA**$_f$, called *boxed c-facts* in the sequel. As we will see, only boxed c-facts will appear at the nodes of *CTs* obtained from $CPPC(\mathcal{D})$-proofs. Therefore, all the queries asked to the user during a declarative debugging session will be about the validity of c-facts in the intended model of the program, which is itself represented as a set of c-facts. We also agree that the premises $G\sigma \Leftarrow \Pi$ in rule **EX** (resp. $\Delta \Leftarrow \Pi$ in rule **DF**$_{\mathcal{P}}$) must be understood as a shorthand for several premises $\alpha \Leftarrow \Pi$, one for each atomic φ in $G\sigma$ (resp. Δ). Moreover, rule **PF** depends on the side condition $Sol_{\mathcal{D}}(\Pi) \subseteq Sol_{\mathcal{D}}(p\bar{t}_n \rightarrow t)$ which is true iff $p^{\mathcal{D}}\,\bar{t}_n\eta \rightarrow t\eta$ holds for all $\eta \in Sol_{\mathcal{D}}(\Pi)$. Some other inference rules in Fig. 2 have similar conditions.

EX Existential $\dfrac{G\sigma \Leftarrow \Pi}{G \Leftarrow \exists \overline{U}.\,(\sigma \,\square\, \Pi)}$ if $fvar(G) \cap \overline{U} = \emptyset$.

TI Trivial Inference $\dfrac{}{\varphi}$ if φ is a trivial c-statement.

RR Restricted Reflexivity $\dfrac{}{t \rightarrow t \Leftarrow \Pi}$ if $t \in \mathcal{U} \cup \mathcal{V}$.

SP Simple Production $\dfrac{}{s \rightarrow t \Leftarrow \Pi}$

if $s \in Pat_\perp(\mathcal{U})$, $s \in \mathcal{V}$ or $t \in \mathcal{V}$, and $Sol_\mathcal{D}(\Pi) \subseteq Sol_\mathcal{D}(s \rightarrow t)$.

DC Decomposition $\dfrac{e_1 \rightarrow t_1 \Leftarrow \Pi \ \ldots\ e_m \rightarrow t_m \Leftarrow \Pi}{h\overline{e}_m \rightarrow h\overline{t}_m \Leftarrow \Pi}$

IR Inner Reduction $\dfrac{e_1 \rightarrow t_1 \Leftarrow \Pi \ \ldots\ e_m \rightarrow t_m \Leftarrow \Pi}{h\overline{e}_m \rightarrow X \Leftarrow \Pi}$

if $h\overline{e}_m \notin Pat_\perp(\mathcal{U})$, $X \in \mathcal{V}$, and $Sol_\mathcal{D}(\Pi) \subseteq Sol_\mathcal{D}(h\overline{t}_m \rightarrow X)$.

PF Primitive Function $\dfrac{e_1 \rightarrow t_1 \Leftarrow \Pi \ \ldots\ e_n \rightarrow t_n \Leftarrow \Pi}{p\,\overline{e}_n \rightarrow t \Leftarrow \Pi}$

if $p \in PF^n$, $t_i \in Pat_\perp(\mathcal{U})$ $(1 \leq i \leq n)$, $Sol_\mathcal{D}(\Pi) \subseteq Sol_\mathcal{D}(p\overline{t}_n \rightarrow t)$.

DF$_\mathcal{P}$ $\mathcal{P}$-Defined Function

$$\dfrac{e_1 \rightarrow t_1 \Leftarrow \Pi \ \ldots\ e_n \rightarrow t_n \Leftarrow \Pi \qquad \dfrac{\Delta \Leftarrow \Pi \quad r \rightarrow t \Leftarrow \Pi}{\boxed{f\overline{t}_n \rightarrow t \Leftarrow \Pi}}\,\textbf{(FA}_f\textbf{)}}{f\,\overline{e}_n \rightarrow t \Leftarrow \Pi}\,\textbf{(AR}_f\textbf{)}$$

$$\dfrac{e_1 \rightarrow t_1 \Leftarrow \Pi \ \ldots\ e_n \rightarrow t_n \Leftarrow \Pi \qquad \dfrac{\Delta \Leftarrow \Pi \quad r \rightarrow s \Leftarrow \Pi}{\boxed{f\overline{t}_n \rightarrow s \Leftarrow \Pi}}\,\textbf{(FA}_f\textbf{)} \qquad s\,\overline{a}_k \rightarrow t \Leftarrow \Pi}{f\,\overline{e}_n\overline{a}_k \rightarrow t \Leftarrow \Pi}\,\textbf{(AR}_f\textbf{)}$$

if $f \in DF^n$ $(k > 0)$, $(f\,\overline{t}_n \rightarrow r \Leftarrow \Delta) \in [\mathcal{P}]_\perp \equiv \{R\theta \mid R \in \mathcal{P}, \theta \in Sub_\perp(\mathcal{U})\}$, and $s \in Pat_\perp(\mathcal{U})$.

AC Atomic Constraint $\dfrac{e_1 \rightarrow t_1 \Leftarrow \Pi \ \ldots\ e_n \rightarrow t_n \Leftarrow \Pi}{p\,\overline{e}_n \rightarrow! \, t \Leftarrow \Pi}$

if $p \in PF^n$, $t_i \in Pat_\perp(\mathcal{U})$ $(1 \leq i \leq n)$, $Sol_\mathcal{D}(\Pi) \subseteq Sol_\mathcal{D}(p\overline{t}_n \rightarrow! \, t)$.

Fig. 2. The Constraint Positive Proof Calculus $CPPC(\mathcal{D})$

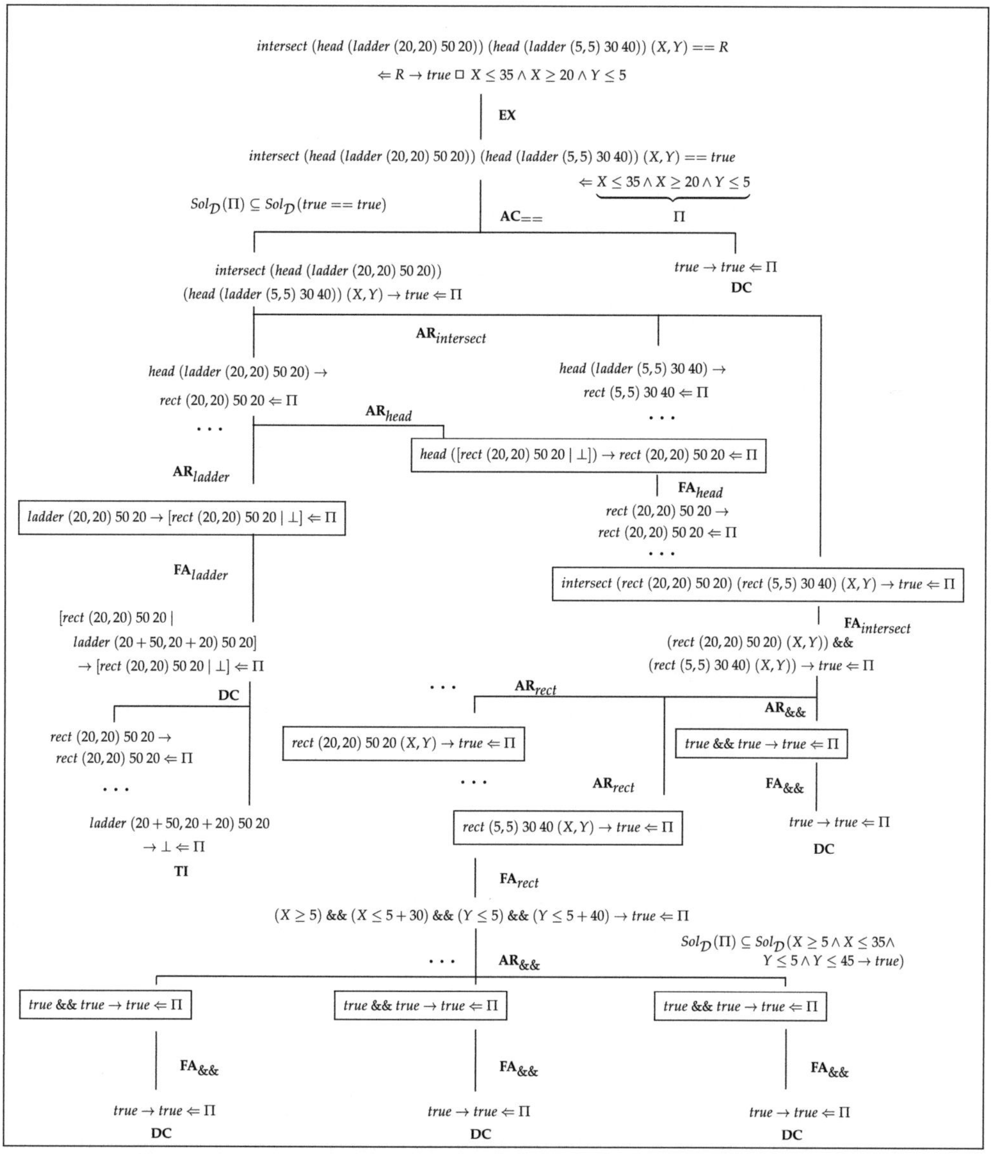

Fig. 3. A Positive Proof Tree in $CPPC(\mathcal{R})$

Any $CPPC(\mathcal{D})$-derivation $\mathcal{P} \vdash_{CPPC(\mathcal{D})} G \Leftarrow S$ can be depicted in the form of a Positive Proof Tree over $\mathcal{D}$ (shortly, $PPT(\mathcal{D})$) with $G \Leftarrow S$ at the root and c-statements at the internal nodes, and such that the statement at any node is inferred from the statements at its children using some $CPPC(\mathcal{D})$ inference rule. In particular, the statement at the root must be inferred using rule **EX**, which is then applied nowherelse in the proof tree. Fig. 3 shows a $PPT(\mathcal{R})$ representing a $CPPC(\mathcal{R})$-derivation which witnesses the computed answer from Example 1, which is wrong with respect to the intended model of the program. We say that a goal solving system is called $CPPC(\mathcal{D})$-*sound* iff for any computed answer S obtained for an initial goal G

using program $\mathcal{P}$ there is some witnessing $CPPC(\mathcal{D})$-proof $\mathcal{P} \vdash_{CPPC(\mathcal{D})} G \Leftarrow S$. The next result shows that $CPPC(\mathcal{D})$-sound goal solving systems exist:

Theorem 1. (Existence of $CPPC(\mathcal{D})$-Sound Goal Solving Systems) *The goal solving calculus $CDNC(\mathcal{D})$ given in (López et al., 2004) is $CPPC(\mathcal{D})$-sound.*

Proof. Straightforward adaptation of the soundness theorem for $CDNC(\mathcal{D})$ presented in (López et al., 2004). □

In addition to the goal solving calculus $CDNC(\mathcal{D})$, other formal goal solving calculi known for $CFLP(\mathcal{D})$ are also $CPPC(\mathcal{D})$-sound. Moreover, it is also reasonable to assume $CPPC(\mathcal{D})$-soundness for implemented goal solving systems such as *Curry* (Hanus, 2003) and $\mathcal{TOY}$ (López & Sánchez, 1999) whose computation model is based on constrained lazy narrowing. Moreover, any $CPPC(\mathcal{D})$-sound goal solving system is semantically sound in the sense of item 2 in Definition 2:

Theorem 2. (Semantic Correctness of the $CPPC(\mathcal{D})$ Calculus) *If G is an initial goal for $\mathcal{P}$ and S is a solved goal s.t. $\mathcal{P} \vdash_{CPPC(\mathcal{D})} G \Leftarrow S$ then $\mathcal{P} \models_{\mathcal{D}} G \Leftarrow S$.*

Proof. For each of the inference rules **EX**, **AR**$_f$, and **FA**$_f$, we prove that an arbitrary model $\mathcal{I} \models_{\mathcal{D}} \mathcal{P}$ such that the premises of the rule are valid in $\mathcal{I}$, also verifies that the conclusion of the rule is valid in $\mathcal{I}$. Similar proofs for the other inference rules in $CFLP(\mathcal{D})$ can be found in (López et al., 2006).

- The rule **EX** is semantically correct. Let $\mathcal{I}$ be an arbitrary model of $\mathcal{P}$ such that $\mathcal{I} \models_{\mathcal{D}} G\sigma \Leftarrow \Pi$, i.e., $Sol_{\mathcal{D}}(\Pi) \subseteq Sol_{\mathcal{I}}(G\sigma)$. We prove that $\mathcal{I} \models_{\mathcal{D}} G \Leftarrow \exists \overline{U}.\ (\sigma \,\Box\, \Pi)$, i.e., $Sol_{\mathcal{D}}(\exists \overline{U}.\ (\sigma \,\Box\, \Pi)) \subseteq Sol_{\mathcal{I}}(G)$. Let $\eta \in Sol_{\mathcal{D}}(\exists \overline{U}.\ (\sigma \,\Box\, \Pi))$. By the syntactic form of solved goals, $\eta \in Sol_{\mathcal{D}}(\exists \overline{U}.\ (\overline{X_n \to t_n \wedge s_m \to Y_m} \,\Box\, \Pi))$ and $\eta \in Sol_{\mathcal{D}}(\exists\, \overline{U}.\ (\overline{X_n = t_n} \wedge \overline{Y_m = s_m} \,\Box\, \Pi))$. By applying Definition 1, there exists $\eta' \in Val_{\perp}(\mathcal{D})$ such that $\eta' =_{\setminus \overline{U}} \eta$ y $\eta' \in Sol_{\mathcal{D}}(\overline{X_n = t_n} \wedge \overline{Y_m = s_m} \,\Box\, \Pi)$, and therefore, $\eta' \in Sol_{\mathcal{D}}(\overline{X_n = t_n} \wedge \overline{Y_m = s_m})$ (i.e., $\eta' \in Sol_{\mathcal{D}}(\sigma)$) and $\eta' \in Sol_{\mathcal{D}}(\Pi)$. Since by *induction hypothesis* $Sol_{\mathcal{D}}(\Pi) \subseteq Sol_{\mathcal{I}}(G\sigma)$, it follows that $\eta' \in Sol_{\mathcal{I}}(G\sigma)$. Moreover, since $\eta' \in Sol_{\mathcal{D}}(\sigma)$, we obtain $\eta' \in Sol_{\mathcal{I}}(G)$. In consequence, there exists $\eta' \in Val_{\perp}(\mathcal{D})$ such that $\eta' =_{\setminus \overline{U}} \eta$ and $\eta' \in Sol_{\mathcal{I}}(G)$. Finally, using the condition of applicability $fvar(G) \cap \overline{U} = \emptyset$ associated to the rule **EX**, we can conclude that $\eta \in Sol_{\mathcal{I}}(G)$.
- The rule **AR**$_f$ is semantically correct. Let $\mathcal{I}$ be an arbitrary model of $\mathcal{P}$ such that $\mathcal{I} \models_{\mathcal{D}} e_i \to t_i \Leftarrow \Pi$ for each $1 \leq i \leq n$ (i.e., $Sol_{\mathcal{D}}(\Pi) \subseteq Sol_{\mathcal{I}}(e_i \to t_i)$ for each $1 \leq i \leq n$), $\mathcal{I} \models_{\mathcal{D}} f\overline{t}_n \to s \Leftarrow \Pi$ (i.e., $Sol_{\mathcal{D}}(\Pi) \subseteq Sol_{\mathcal{D}}(f\overline{t}_n \to s)$) and $\mathcal{I} \models_{\mathcal{D}} s\overline{a}_k \to s \Leftarrow \Pi$ (i.e., $Sol_{\mathcal{D}}(\Pi) \subseteq Sol_{\mathcal{I}}(s\overline{a}_k \to t)$). We prove that $\mathcal{I} \models_{\mathcal{D}} f\overline{e}_n\overline{a}_k \to t \Leftarrow \Pi$, i.e., $Sol_{\mathcal{D}}(\Pi) \subseteq Sol_{\mathcal{I}}(f\overline{e}_n\overline{a}_k \to t)$. Let $\eta \in Sol_{\mathcal{D}}(\Pi)$. We have then $\eta \in Sol_{\mathcal{I}}(e_i \to t_i)$ for each $1 \leq i \leq n$, and by Definition 1, $\mathcal{I} \Vdash_{\mathcal{D}} e_i\eta \to t_i\eta$ for each $1 \leq i \leq n$. Analogously, $\eta \in Sol_{\mathcal{I}}(f\overline{t}_n \to s)$, by Definition 1, $\mathcal{I} \Vdash_{\mathcal{D}} f\overline{t}_n\eta \to s\eta$, and by the *Conservation Property* (see (López et al., 2006) for details), $(f\overline{t}_n\eta \to s\eta) \in \mathcal{I}$. Analogously, $\eta \in Sol_{\mathcal{I}}(s\overline{a}_k \to t)$ and by Definition 1, $\mathcal{I} \Vdash_{\mathcal{D}} (s\eta)(\overline{a}_k\eta) \to t\eta$. But then, by applying of the rule **DF**$_{\mathcal{I}}$ (see (López et al., 2006) for details), we have that $\mathcal{I} \Vdash_{\mathcal{D}} f(\overline{e}_n\eta)(\overline{a}_k\eta) \to t\eta$. From Definition 1, we obtain finally $\eta \in Sol_{\mathcal{I}}(f\overline{e}_n\overline{a}_k \to t)$.

- The rule $\mathbf{FA}_f$ is semantically correct. By definition of $[\mathcal{P}]_\perp$, there are $(f\overline{t'}_n \to r' \Leftarrow \Delta') \in \mathcal{P}$ and $\theta \in Sub_\perp(\mathcal{U})$ such that $(f\overline{t'}_n \to r' \Leftarrow \Delta')\theta \equiv (f\overline{t}_n \to r \Leftarrow \Delta)$. Let $\mathcal{I}$ be an arbitrary model of $\mathcal{P}$ such that $\mathcal{I} \models_\mathcal{D} \Delta \Leftarrow \Pi$ (i.e., $Sol_\mathcal{D}(\Pi) \subseteq Sol_\mathcal{I}(\Delta)$) and $\mathcal{I} \models_\mathcal{D} r \to s \Leftarrow \Pi$ (i.e., $Sol_\mathcal{D}(\Pi) \subseteq Sol_\mathcal{I}(r \to s)$). We prove that $\mathcal{I} \models_\mathcal{D} f\overline{t}_n \to s \Leftarrow \Pi$, i.e., $Sol_\mathcal{D}(\Pi) \subseteq Sol_\mathcal{I}(f\overline{t}_n \to s)$. Let $\eta \in Sol_\mathcal{D}(\Pi)$. Then we have $\eta \in Sol_\mathcal{I}(\Delta)$, and by Definition 1, $\mathcal{I} \Vdash_\mathcal{D} \Delta\eta$, and also, $\mathcal{I} \Vdash_\mathcal{D} \Delta'\theta\eta$. Analogously, $\eta \in Sol_\mathcal{I}(r \to s)$, and by Definition 1, $\mathcal{I} \Vdash_\mathcal{D} r\eta \to s\eta$, and also, $\mathcal{I} \Vdash_\mathcal{D} r'\theta\eta \to s\eta$. We have then $(f\overline{t'}_n \to r' \Leftarrow \Delta') \in \mathcal{P}$, $\theta\eta \in Sub_\perp(\mathcal{U})$ ground substitution and $s\eta \in Pat_\perp(\mathcal{U})$ ground such that $(f\overline{t'}_n \to r' \Leftarrow \Delta')\theta\eta \equiv (f\overline{t}_n \to r \Leftarrow \Delta)\eta$ is ground, $\mathcal{I} \Vdash_\mathcal{D} \Delta'\theta\eta$ and $\mathcal{I} \Vdash_\mathcal{D} r'\theta\eta \to s\eta$. Since $\mathcal{I}$ is a model of $\mathcal{P}$, by applying Definition 2, we obtain $((f\overline{t'}_n)\theta\eta \to s\eta) \in \mathcal{I}$, i.e., $((f\overline{t}_n)\eta \to s\eta) \in \mathcal{I}$, or also, $(f\overline{t}_n \to s)\eta \in \mathcal{I}$. Finally, by applying the *Conservation Property* (see (López et al., 2006) for details), it is equivalent to $\mathcal{I} \Vdash_\mathcal{D} (f\overline{t}_n \to s)\eta$, and by Definition 1, we can conclude that $\eta \in Sol_\mathcal{I}(f\overline{t}_n \to s)$.

□

4.3 Declarative diagnosis using positive proof trees

Now we are ready to present a declarative diagnosis method of wrong answers and to prove its correctness. Our results apply to any $CPPC(\mathcal{D})$-sound goal solving system. First we prove that the observation of an error symptom implies the existence of some error in the program:

Theorem 3. (Wrong Answers Are Caused By Erroneous Program Rules) *We assume that a $CPPC(\mathcal{D})$-sound goal solving system computes S as an answer for the initial goal G using program $\mathcal{P}$. If S is wrong with respect to the user's intended interpretation $\mathcal{I}$ then some program rule belonging to $\mathcal{P}$ is incorrect with respect to $\mathcal{I}$.*

Proof. Because of $CPPC(\mathcal{D})$-soundness of the goal solving system, we know that $\mathcal{P} \vdash_{CPPC(\mathcal{D})} G \Leftarrow S$. Then, from Theorem 2 we obtain $\mathcal{P} \models_\mathcal{D} G \Leftarrow S$, i.e., $Sol_\mathcal{D}(S) \subseteq Sol_\mathcal{J}(G)$ for each model $\mathcal{J} \models_\mathcal{D} \mathcal{P}$. Since S is wrong with respect to the user's intended model $\mathcal{I}$, it must be the case that $Sol_\mathcal{D}(S) \not\subseteq Sol_\mathcal{I}(G)$ because of Definition 3. Therefore, we can conclude that the intended model $\mathcal{I}$ is not a model of $\mathcal{P}$. Then, by Definition 2, some program rule belonging to $\mathcal{P}$ is not valid in $\mathcal{I}$. □

The previous theorem does not yet provide a practical method for finding an erroneous program rule. As explained in the Introduction, a declarative diagnosis method is expected to find the erroneous program rule by inspecting a CT. We propose to use abbreviated $CPPC(\mathcal{D})$ proof trees as CTs. Since $\mathbf{DF}_\mathcal{P}$ is the only inference rule in the $CPPC(\mathcal{D})$ calculus that depends on the program, abbreviated proof trees will omit the inference steps related to all the other $CPPC(\mathcal{D})$ rules. More precisely, given a $PPT(\mathcal{D})$ $\mathcal{T}$, its associated *Abbreviated Positive Proof Tree* over $\mathcal{D}$ (shortly, $APPT(\mathcal{D})$) $\mathcal{AT}$ is defined as follows:

- The root of $\mathcal{AT}$ is the root of $\mathcal{T}$.
- The children of a node N in $\mathcal{AT}$ are the closest descendants of N in $\mathcal{T}$ corresponding to boxed c-facts introduced by $\mathbf{DF}_\mathcal{P}$ inference steps.

A node in an $APPT(\mathcal{D})$ is called a *buggy node* iff the c-statement at the node is not valid in the intended interpretation $\mathcal{I}$, while all the c-statements at the children nodes are valid in $\mathcal{I}$. Our last theorem guarantees that declarative diagnosis with $APPT(\mathcal{D})$s used as *CTs* leads to the correct detection of program errors.

Theorem 4 (Declarative Diagnosis of Wrong Answers). *Under the assumptions of Theorem 3, any* $APPT(\mathcal{D})$ *witnessing* $\mathcal{P} \vdash_{CPPC(\mathcal{D})} G \Leftarrow S$ *(which must exist due to* $CPPC(\mathcal{D})$*-soundness of the goal solving system) has some buggy node. Moreover, each buggy node points to a program rule belonging to* $\mathcal{P}$ *which is incorrect in the user's intended interpretation.*

5. A declarative debugging tool of wrong answers in $\mathcal{TOY}$

Fig. 4 shows the $APPT(\mathcal{R})$ associated to the $PPT(\mathcal{R})$ of Fig. 3 as displayed by $\mathcal{DDT}$, the debugger tool included in the system $\mathcal{TOY}$. Although in theory all the c-facts in a $PPT(\mathcal{R})$ should include the same constraint Π, in practice the tool simplifies Π at each c-fact $f\,\bar{t}_n \rightarrow t \Leftarrow \Pi$, keeping only those atomic constraints related to the variables occurring on $f\,\bar{t}_n \rightarrow t$. It can be checked that such a simplification does not affect the intended meaning of c-facts.

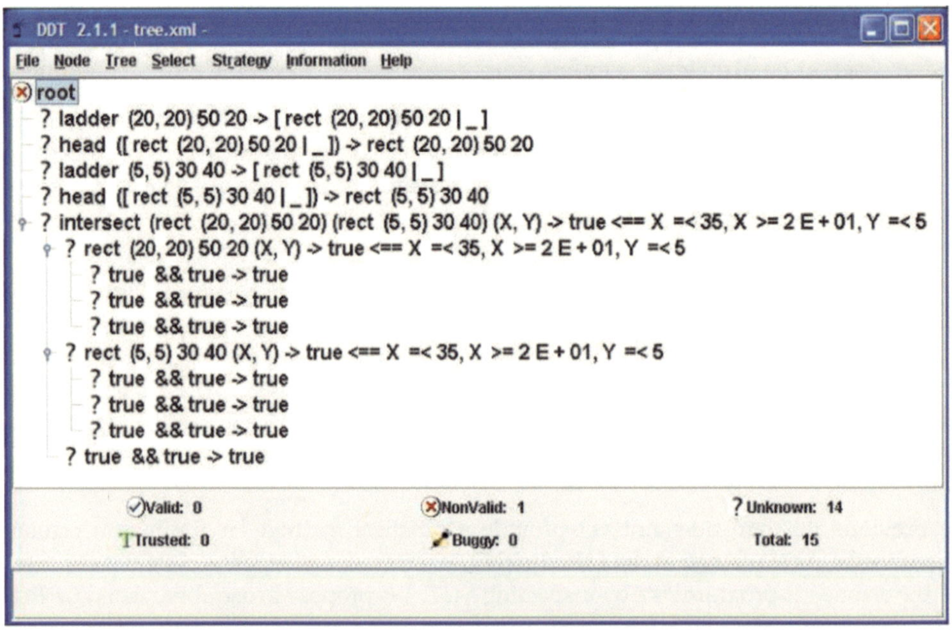

Fig. 4. The $APPT(\mathcal{R})$ corresponding to the $PPT(\mathcal{R})$ of Fig. 3

Before starting a *debugging session*, the user may inspect and simplify the tree using several facilities. For instance the user could mark any node corresponding to the infix function && as *trusted*, indicating that the definition of && is surely not erroneous. This makes all the nodes corresponding to && automatically valid. Valid nodes can be removed from the tree safely (the set of buggy nodes doesn't change) by using a suitable menu option.

Next, the user can start a debugging session by selecting one of the two possible strategies included in $\mathcal{DDT}$: the *top-down* or the *divide and query* strategy (see (Caballero & Rodríguez,

2004) for a comparative between both strategies in an older version of $\mathcal{DDT}$ which did not yet support constraints). After selecting the *divide and query* strategy, which usually leads to shorter sessions, $\mathcal{DDT}$ asks about the validity of the following node:

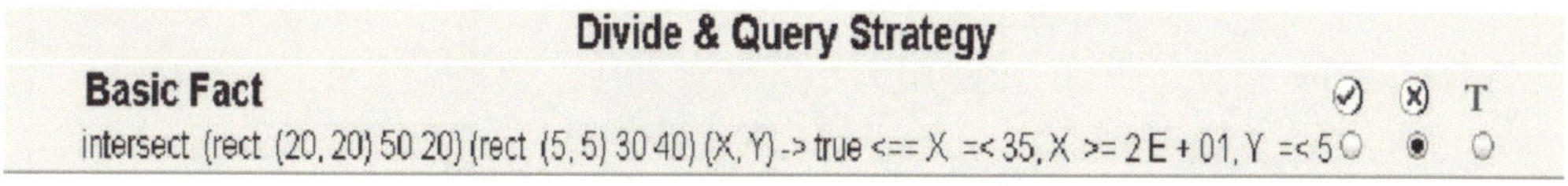

The intended program model corresponds to the intuitions explained in Section 2. Therefore, the question must be understood as: *Is* (X, Y) *a point in the intersection of the two rectangles for all possible values of* X, Y *satisfying* $X \leq 35, X \geq 20, Y \leq 5$ *is* (X, Y)*?* The answer is *no*, because with these constraints Y can take any value less than 5 and some of these values would yield a pair (X, Y) out of the intersection for every X. Therefore the user marks the cross meaning that the c-fact is non-valid. The next question is:

which is also reported as non-valid by the user. At this point a buggy node is found by the tool, pointing out to the incorrect program rule and ending the debugging session:

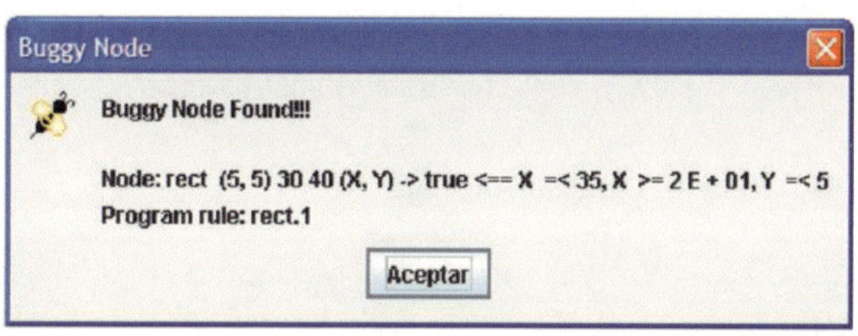

The current version of the debugger supports programs using the constraint domain $\mathcal{R}$, which provides arithmetic constraints over the real numbers as well as strict equality and disequality constraints over data values of any type; see Example 3 and (López et al., 2006) for details. The tool is as an extension of older versions which did not yet support constraints over the domain $\mathcal{R}$ (Caballero, 2005; Caballero & Rodríguez, 2004), and it is part of the public distribution of the functional-logic programming system $\mathcal{TOY}$, available at `http://toy.sourceforge.net`. The $APPT(\mathcal{R})$ associated to a wrong answer is constructed by means of a suitable program transformation. The yielded tree is then displayed through a graphical debugging interface implemented in Java. More detailed explanations on the practical use of $\mathcal{DDT}$ can be found in (Caballero, 2005; Caballero & Rodríguez, 2004).

SF Solved Form $\dfrac{}{R \,\square\, S \Rightarrow D}$ if $Sol_{\mathcal{D}}(S) \subseteq Sol_{\mathcal{D}}(D)$.

CJ Conjunction

$$\frac{R_1 \,\square\, S \Rightarrow \bigvee_{i \in I} \exists \overline{Z}_i.\, S_i \quad \ldots (R_2 \,\&\, S_i) \Rightarrow \bigvee_{j \in J_i} \exists \overline{Z}_{ij}.\, S_{ij} \ldots (i \in I)}{(R_1 \wedge R_2) \,\square\, S \Rightarrow \bigvee_{i \in I} \bigvee_{j \in J_i} \exists \overline{Z}_i, \overline{Z}_{ij}.\, S_{ij}}$$

if $\overline{Z}_i \notin var((R_1 \wedge R_2) \,\square\, S)$, $\overline{Z}_{ij} \notin var((R_1 \wedge R_2) \,\square\, S) \cup \overline{Z}_i$, for all $i \in I, j \in J_i$.

TS Trivial Statement $\dfrac{}{\varphi : G \Rightarrow D}$ if $Sol(G) \subseteq Sol_{\mathcal{D}}(D)$.

DC DeComposition $\dfrac{\overline{e_m \to t_m} \,\square\, S \Rightarrow D}{h\overline{e}_m \to h\overline{t}_m \,\square\, S \Rightarrow D}$ if $h\overline{e}_m$ is not a pattern.

IM IMitation $\dfrac{\overline{e_m \to X_m} \,\square\, (S \wedge h\overline{X}_m \to X) \Rightarrow \bigvee_{i \in I} \exists \overline{Z}_i.\, S_i}{h\overline{e}_m \to X \,\square\, S \Rightarrow \bigvee_{i \in I} \exists \overline{X}_m, \overline{Z}_i.\, S_i}$

if $h\overline{e}_m$ is not a pattern, $X \in \mathcal{V}$, and $\overline{X}_m \notin var(h\overline{e}_m \to X \,\square\, S)$.

$(AR)_p$ Argument Reduction for Primitive Functions

$$\frac{\overline{e_n \to X_n} \,\square\, (S \wedge p\overline{X}_n \to^! t) \Rightarrow \bigvee_{i \in I} \exists \overline{Z}_i.\, S_i}{p\overline{e}_n \to^? t \,\square\, S \Rightarrow (S \wedge \bot \to t) \vee (\bigvee_{i \in I} \exists \overline{X}_n, \exists \overline{Z}_i.\, S_i)}$$

if $p \in PF^n, \overline{X}_n \notin var(p\overline{e}_n \to^? t \,\square\, S)$, $\to^? \equiv \to$ *(production)*$\cup \to^!$ *(constraint)*.

$(AR)_f$ Argument Reduction for Defined Functions

$$\frac{(\overline{e_n \to X_n} \wedge f\overline{X}_n \to Y \wedge Y\overline{a}_k \to t) \,\square\, S \Rightarrow \bigvee_{i \in I} \exists \overline{Z}_i.\, S_i}{f\overline{e}_n\overline{a}_k \to t \,\square\, S \Rightarrow \bigvee_{i \in I} \exists \overline{X}_n, Y, \overline{Z}_i.\, S_i}$$

if $f \in DF^n$ $(k > 0)$, and $\overline{X}_n, Y \notin var(f\overline{e}_n\overline{a}_k \to t \,\square\, S)$.

$(DF)_f$ Defined Function $\dfrac{\ldots R_i[\overline{X}_n \mapsto \overline{t}_n, Y \mapsto t] \,\square\, S \Rightarrow D_i \ldots (i \in I)}{\boxed{f\overline{t}_n \to t \,\square\, S \Rightarrow (S \wedge \bot \to t) \vee (\bigvee_{i \in I} D_i)}}$

if $f \in DF^n, \overline{X}_n, Y \notin var(f\overline{t}_n \to t \,\square\, S)$, and $(f\overline{X}_n \to Y \Rightarrow \bigvee_{i \in I} R_i) \in \mathcal{P}^-$.

Fig. 5. The Constraint Negative Proof Calculus $CNPC(\mathcal{D})$

6. Declarative debugging of missing answers in $CFLP(\mathcal{D})$

The declarative debugging of *missing answers* also assumes an intended interpretation $\mathcal{I}_\mathcal{P}$ of the *CFLP*($\mathcal{D}$)-program $\mathcal{P}$, starts with the observation of an *incompleteness symptom* and ends with an *incompleteness diagnosis*. A more precise definition of this *debugging scenario of missing answers* is as follows:

Definition 4. (Debugging Scenario of Missing Answers) *For any given CFLP*($\mathcal{D}$)*-program* $\mathcal{P}$:

1. *An* **incompleteness symptom** *occurs if the goal solving system computes finitely many solved goals* $\{S_i\}_{i \in I}$ *as answers for an admissible initial goal G, and the programmer judges that* $Sol_{\mathcal{I}_\mathcal{P}}(G) \not\subseteq \bigcup_{i \in I} Sol_\mathcal{D}(S_i)$*, meaning that the aca* $G \Rightarrow \bigvee_{i \in I} S_i$ *is not valid in the intended interpretation* $\mathcal{I}_\mathcal{P}$*, so that some expected answers are* **missing**.
2. *An* **incompleteness diagnosis** *is given by pointing to some defined function symbol f such that the axiom* $(f)^-_\mathcal{P} : (f\,\overline{X}_n \to Y \Rightarrow D_f)$ *for f in* $\mathcal{P}^-$ *is not valid in* $\mathcal{I}_\mathcal{P}$*, which means* $Sol_{\mathcal{I}_\mathcal{P}}(f\,\overline{X}_n \to Y) \not\subseteq Sol_{\mathcal{I}_\mathcal{P}}(D_f)$*, showing that f's definition as given in* $\mathcal{P}$ *is* **incomplete** *w.r.t.* $\mathcal{I}_\mathcal{P}$.

Some concrete debugging scenarios have been discussed in Section 2. Assume now that an incompleteness symptom has been observed by the programmer. Since the goal solving system has computed the disjunction of answers $D = \bigvee_{i \in I} S_i$, the *aca* $G \Rightarrow D$ asserting that the computed answers cover all the solutions of G should be derivable from $\mathcal{P}^-$. The Constraint Negative Proof Calculus $CNPC(\mathcal{D})$ consisting of the inference rules displayed in Fig. 5 has been designed with the aim of enabling logical proofs $\mathcal{P}^- \vdash_{CNPC(\mathcal{D})} G \Rightarrow D$ of *acas*. We use a special operator & in order to express the result of attaching to a given goal G a solved goal S' resulting from a previous computation, so that computation can continue from the new goal $G \,\&\, S'$.

Formally, assuming $G = \exists \overline{U}.\, (R \,\square\, (\Pi \,\square\, \sigma))$ and $S' = \exists \overline{U}'.\, (\Pi' \,\square\, \sigma')$ a solved goal such that $\overline{U} \setminus dom(\sigma') \subseteq \overline{U}'$, $\sigma\sigma' = \sigma'$, and $Sol_\mathcal{D}(\Pi') \subseteq Sol_\mathcal{D}(\Pi\sigma')$, the operation $G \,\&\, S'$ is defined as $\exists \overline{U}'.\, (R\sigma' \,\square\, (\Pi' \,\square\, \sigma'))$. The inference rule **CJ** infers an *aca* for a goal with composed kernel $(R_1 \wedge R_2) \,\square\, S$ from *acas* for goals with kernels of the form $R_1 \,\square\, S$ and $(R_2 \,\&\, S_i)$, respectively; while other inferences deal with different kinds of atomic goal kernels.

Any $CNPC(\mathcal{D})$-derivation $\mathcal{P}^- \vdash_{CNPC(\mathcal{D})} G \Rightarrow D$ can be depicted in the form of a Negative Proof Tree over $\mathcal{D}$ (shortly, *NPT*) with *acas* at its nodes, such that the *aca* at any node is inferred from the *acas* at its children using some $CNPC(\mathcal{D})$ inference rule. We say that a goal solving system for *CFLP*($\mathcal{D}$) is *admissible* iff whenever finitely many solved goals $\{S_i\}_{i \in I}$ are computed as answers for an admissible initial goal G, one has $\mathcal{P}^- \vdash_{CNPC(\mathcal{D})} G \Rightarrow \bigvee_{i \in I} S_i$ with some witnessing *NPT*. The next theorem is intended to provide some plausibility to the pragmatic assumption that actual *CFLP* systems such as *Curry* (Hanus, 2003) or $\mathcal{TOY}$ (López & Sánchez, 1999) are admissible goal solving systems.

Theorem 5. (Existence of Admissible Goal Solving Calculi) *There is an admissible Goal Solving Calculus* $GSC(\mathcal{D})$ *which formalizes the goal solving methods underlying actual CFLP systems such as Curry or* $\mathcal{TOY}$.

Proof. A more general result can be proved: If $(\underline{R} \wedge R') \,\&\, S \Vdash^p_{\mathcal{P},GSC(\mathcal{D})} D$ (with a partially developed search space of finite size p built using the program $\mathcal{P}$, a *Goal Solving Calculus*

$GSC(\mathcal{D})$ inspired in (López et al., 2004), and a certain selection strategy that only selects atoms descendants of the part R) then $\mathcal{P}^- \vdash_{CNPC(\mathcal{D})} R \ \& \ S \Rightarrow D$ with some witnessing NPT. The proof proceeds by induction on p, using an auxiliary lemma to deal with compound goals whose kernel is a conjunction. □

We have also proved the following theorem, showing that any *aca* which has been derived by means of a NPT is a logical consequence of the negative theory associated to the corresponding program. This result will be used below for proving the correctness of our diagnosis method of missing answers.

Theorem 6. (Semantic Correctness of the $CNPC(\mathcal{D})$ Calculus) *Let $G \Rightarrow D$ be any aca for a given CFLP($\mathcal{D}$)-program $\mathcal{P}$. If $\mathcal{P}^- \vdash_{CNPC(\mathcal{D})} G \Rightarrow D$ then $G \Rightarrow D$ is a logical consequence of $\mathcal{P}^-$ in the sense of Definition 2.*

6.1 Declarative diagnosis of missing answers using negative proof trees

We are now prepared to present a declarative diagnosis method for missing answers which is based on NPTs and leads to correct diagnosis for any admissible goal solving system. First, we show that incompleteness symptoms are caused by incomplete program rules. This is guaranteed by the following theorem:

Theorem 7. (Missing Answers are Caused by Incomplete Program Rules) *Assume that an incompleteness symptom has been observed for a given CFLP($\mathcal{D}$)-program $\mathcal{P}$ as explained in Definition 4, with intended interpretation $\mathcal{I}_\mathcal{P}$, admissible initial goal G, and finite disjunction of computed answers $D = \bigvee_{i \in I} S_i$. Assume also that the computation has been performed by an admissible goal solving system. Then there exists a defined function symbol f such that the axiom $(f)^-_\mathcal{P}$ for f in $\mathcal{P}^-$ is not valid in $\mathcal{I}_\mathcal{P}$, so that f's definition as given in $\mathcal{P}$ is incomplete with respect to $\mathcal{I}_\mathcal{P}$.*

Proof. Because of the admissibility of the goal solving system, we can assume $\mathcal{P}^- \vdash_{CNPC(\mathcal{D})} G \Rightarrow D$. Then the *aca* $G \Rightarrow D$ is a logical consequence of $\mathcal{P}^-$ because of Theorem 6. By Definition 2, we conclude that $Sol_\mathcal{I}(G) \subseteq Sol_\mathcal{D}(D)$ holds for any model $\mathcal{I}$ of $\mathcal{P}^-$. However, we also know that $Sol_{\mathcal{I}_\mathcal{P}}(G) \nsubseteq Sol_\mathcal{D}(D)$, because the disjunction D of computed answers is an incompleteness symptom with respect to $\mathcal{I}_\mathcal{P}$. Therefore, we can conclude that $\mathcal{I}_\mathcal{P}$ is not a model of $\mathcal{P}^-$, and therefore the completeness axiom $(f)^-_\mathcal{P}$ of some defined function symbol f must be invalid in $\mathcal{I}_\mathcal{P}$. □

The previous theorem does not yet provide a practical method for finding an incomplete function definition. As explained in Section 2, a declarative diagnosis method is expected to find the incomplete function definition by inspecting a CT. We propose to use abbreviated NPTs as CTs. Note that **(DF)**$_f$ is the only inference rule in the $CNPC(\mathcal{D})$ calculus that depends on the program, while all the other inference rules are correct with respect to arbitrary interpretations. For this reason, abbreviated proof trees will omit the inference steps related to the $CNPC(\mathcal{D})$ inference rules other than **(DF)**$_f$. More precisely, given a NPT $\mathcal{T}$ witnessing a $CNPC(\mathcal{D})$ proof $\mathcal{P}^- \vdash_{CNPC(\mathcal{D})} G \Rightarrow D$, its associated *Abbreviated Negative Proof Tree* (shortly, $ANPT$) $\mathcal{AT}$ is constructed as follows:

(1) The root of $\mathcal{AT}$ is the root of $\mathcal{T}$.

(2) The children of any node N in $\mathcal{AT}$ are the closest descendants of N in $\mathcal{T}$ corresponding to *boxed acas* introduced by $\mathbf{(DF)}_f$ inference steps.

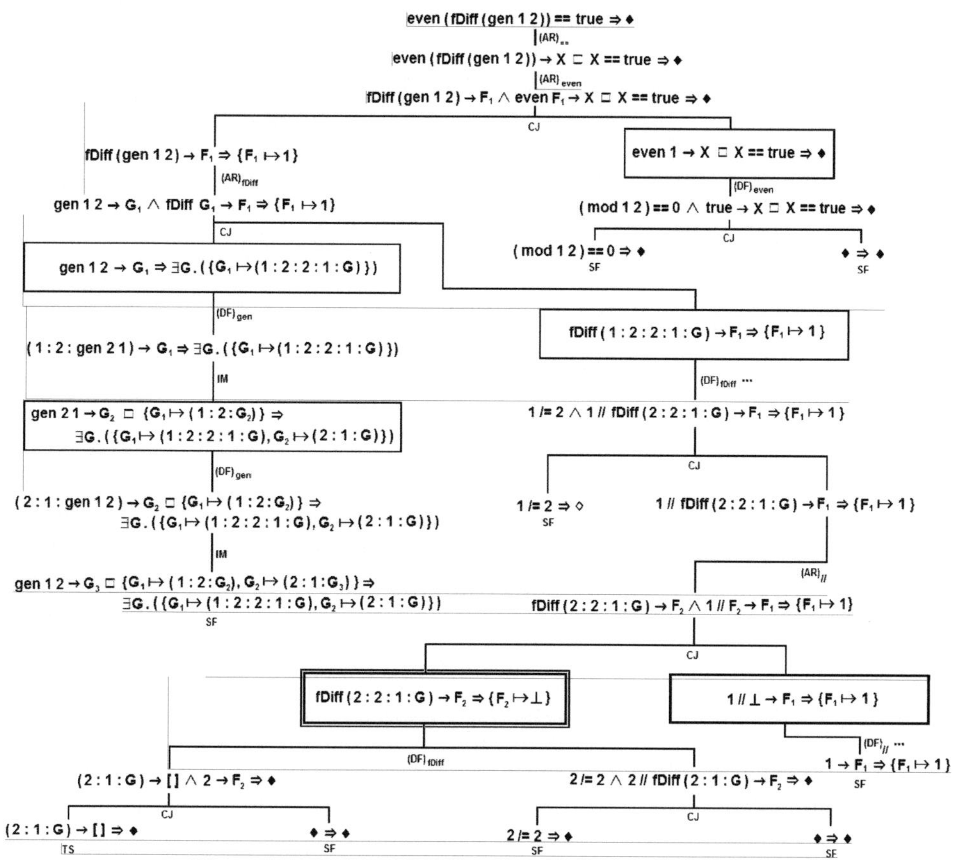

Fig. 6. *NPT* for the declarative diagnosis of missing answers

As already explained, declarative diagnosis methods search a given *CT* looking for a *buggy node* whose result is unexpected but whose children's results are all expected. In our present setting, the *CT*s are *ANPT*s, the "results" attached to nodes are *aca*s, and a given node N is *buggy* iff the *aca* at N is *invalid* (i.e., it represents an incomplete recollection of computed answers in the intended interpretation $\mathcal{I}_\mathcal{P}$) while the *aca* at each children node N_i is *valid* (i.e., it represents a complete recollection of computed answers in the intended interpretation $\mathcal{I}_\mathcal{P}$).

As a concrete example, Fig. 6 displays a *NPT* which can be used for the diagnosis of missing answers in the Example 2. Buggy nodes are highlighted by encircling the *aca*s attached to them within double boxes. The *CT* shown in Fig. 7 is the *ANPT* constructed from this *NPT*. In this case, the programmer will judge the root *aca* as *invalid* because he did not expect finite failure. Moreover, from him knowledge of the intended interpretation, he will decide to consider the *aca*s for the functions `gen`, `even`, and `(//)` as valid. However, the *aca* `fDiff (2:2:1:G)` $\rightarrow F_2 \Rightarrow (F_2 \mapsto \bot)$ asserts that the *undefined value* $\bot$ is the only possible result for the function call `fDiff (2:2:1:G)`, while the user expects also the result `2`. Therefore, the user will judge this *aca* as invalid. The node where it sits (enclosed within a double box in Fig. 7) has no children and thus becomes buggy, leading to the diagnosis of `fDiff` as incomplete. This particular incompleteness symptom could be mended by placing the third rule for `fDiff` within the program. Our last result is a refinement of Theorem 7. It

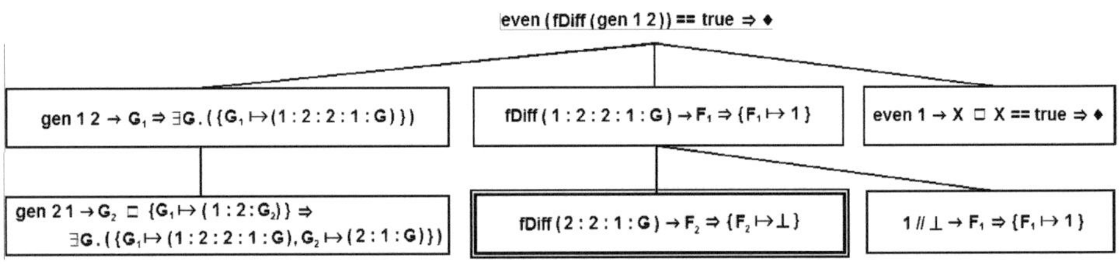

Fig. 7. *CT* for the declarative diagnosis of missing answers

guarantees that declarative diagnosis with *ANPT*s used as *CT*s leads to the correct detection of incomplete program functions.

Theorem 8. **(*ANPT*s Lead to the Diagnosis of Incomplete Functions)** *As in Theorem 7, assume that an incompleteness symptom has been observed for a given CFLP($\mathcal{D}$)-program $\mathcal{P}$ as explained in Definition 4, with intended interpretation $\mathcal{I}_{\mathcal{P}}$, admissible initial goal G, and finite disjunction of answers $D = \bigvee_{i \in I} S_i$, computed by an admissible goal solving system. Then $\mathcal{P}^- \vdash_{CNPC(\mathcal{D})} G \Rightarrow D$, and the ANPT constructed from any NPT witnessing this derivation, has some buggy node. Moreover, each such buggy node points to an axiom $(f)^-_{\mathcal{P}}$ which is incomplete with respect to the user's intended interpretation $\mathcal{I}_{\mathcal{P}}$.*

7. A declarative debugging tool of missing answers in $\mathcal{TOY}$

In this section, we discuss the implementation in the $\mathcal{TOY}$ system of a tool based on the debugging method presented in the previous section. The current prototype only supports the Herbrand constraint domain $\mathcal{H}$, although the same principles can be applied to other constraint domains $\mathcal{D}$.

We summarize first the normal process followed by the $\mathcal{TOY}$ system when compiling a source program $\mathcal{P}$*.toy* and solving an initial goal G with respect to $\mathcal{P}$. During the compilation process the system translates a source program $\mathcal{P}$*.toy* into a Prolog program $\mathcal{P}$*.pl* including a predicate for each function in $\mathcal{P}$. For instance the function `even` of our running example is transformed into a predicate

```
even(N,R,IC,OC):- ... code for even ... .
```

where the variable `N` corresponds to the input parameter of the function, `R` to the function result, and `IC,OC` represent, respectively, the input and output constraint store. Moreover, each goal G of $\mathcal{P}$ is also translated into a Prolog goal and solved with respect to $\mathcal{P}$*.pl* by the underlying Prolog system. The result is a collection of answers which are presented to the user in a certain sequence, as a result of Prolog's backtracking.

If the computation of answers for G finishes after having collected finitely many answers, the user may decide that there are some missing answers (*incompleteness symptom*, in the terminology of Definition 4) and type the command `/missing` at the system prompt in order to initiate a *debugging session*. The debugger proceeds carrying out the following steps:

1. The object program $\mathcal{P}.pl$ is transformed into a new Prolog program $\mathcal{P}^{\mathcal{T}}.\,pl$. The debugger can safely assume that $\mathcal{P}.pl$ already exists because the tool is always initiated *after* some missing answer has been detected by the user. The transformed program $\mathcal{P}^{\mathcal{T}}$ behaves almost identically to $\mathcal{P}$, being the only difference that it produces a suitable *trace* of the computation in a text file. For instance here is a fragment of the code for the function `even` of our running example in the transformed program:

```
1 % this clause wraps the original predicate
2 even(N,R,IC,OC):-
3     % display the input values for even
4     write(' begin('), write(' even,'), writeq(N), write(','),
5     write(R), write(', '), writeq(IC), write(').'), nl,
6     % evenBis corresponds to the original predicate for even
7     evenBis(N,R,IC,OC),
8     % display an output result
9     write(' output('), write(' even,'), writeq(N), write(','),
10    write(R), write(', '), writeq(OC), write(').'), nl.
11 % when all the possible outputs have been produced
12 even(N,R,IC,OC):-
13    nl, write(' end(even).'), nl,
14    !,
15    fail.
16 evenBis(N,R,IC,OC) :- ... original code for even ... .
```

   As the example shows, the code for each function now displays information about the values of the arguments and the contents of the constraint store at the moment of invoking any user defined function (lines 4-5). Then the predicate corresponding to the original function, now renamed with the `Bis` suffix, is called (line 7). After any successful function call the trace displays again the values of the arguments and the result, which may have changed, and the contents of the output constraint store (lines 9, 10). A second clause (lines 12-15) displays the value `end` when the function has exhausted its possible outputs. The clause fails in order to ensure that the program flow is not changed. The original code for each function is kept unaltered in the transformed program except for the renaming (`evenBis` instead of `even` in the example, line 16). This ensures that the program will behave equivalently to the original program, except for the trace produced as a side-effect.

2. In order to obtain the trace file, the debugger repeats the computation of all the answers for the goal G with respect to $\mathcal{P}^{\mathcal{T}}$. After each successful computation, the debugger enforces a `fail` in order to trigger the backtracking mechanism and produces the next solution for the goal. The program output is redirected to a file, where the trace is stored.

3. The trace file is then analyzed by the *CT builder* module of the tool. The result is the *Computation Tree* (an *ANPT*), which is displayed by a *Java graphical interface.*

4. The tree can be navigated by the user either manually, providing information about the validity of the *acas* contained in the tree, or using any of the automatic strategies included in the tool which try to minimize the number of nodes that the user must examine (see (Silva, 2006) for a description of some strategies and their efficiency). The process ends when a buggy node is found and the tool points to an incomplete function definition, as

explained in Section 6, as responsible for the missing answers. The current implementation of the prototype is available at `http://gpd.sip.ucm.es/rafav/`.

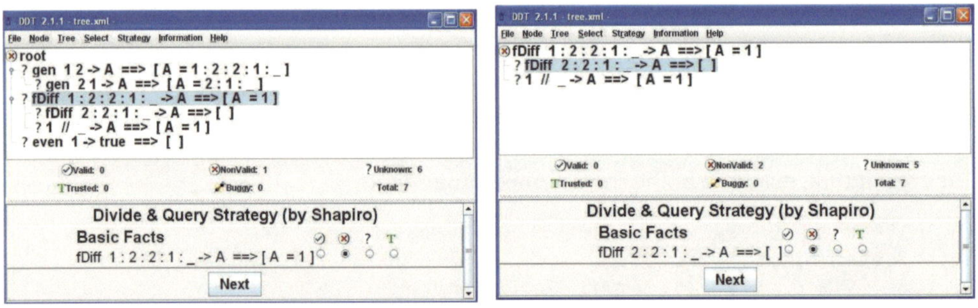

Fig. 8. Snapshots of the prototype of missing answers

Fig. 8 shows how the tool displays the *CT* corresponding to the debugging scenario discussed in Section 2. The initial goal is not displayed, but the rest of the *CT* corresponds to Fig. 7, whose construction as *ANPT* has been explained in Section 6. When displaying an *aca* $f\,\bar{t}_n \rightarrow t \,\Box\, S \Rightarrow \bigvee_{i \in I} S_i$, the tool uses list notation for representing the disjunction $\bigvee_{i \in I} S_i$ and performs some simplifications: useless variable bindings within the stores S and S_i are dropped, as in the *aca* displayed as `gen 2 1 -> A ==> [A = 2:1:_]` in Fig. 7; and if t happens to be a variable X, the case $\{X \mapsto \bot\}$ is omitted from the disjunction $\bigvee_{i \in I} S_i$, so that the user must interpret the *aca* as a collection of the possible results for X other than the undefined value $\bot$. The tool also displays the underscore symbol _ at some places. Within any *aca*, the occurrences of _ at the right hand side of the implication $\Rightarrow$ must be understood as different existentially quantified variables, while each occurrence of _ at the left hand side of $\Rightarrow$ must be understood as $\bot$. For instance, `1 // _ -> A ==> [A = 1]` is the *aca* `1 //` $\bot \rightarrow A \Rightarrow \{A \mapsto 1\}$ as displayed by the tool. Understanding the occurrences of _ at the left hand side of $\Rightarrow$ as different universally quantified variables would be incorrect. For instance, the *aca* `1 //` $\bot \rightarrow A \Rightarrow \{A \mapsto 1\}$ is valid with respect to the intended interpretation $\mathcal{I}_{\mathcal{P}_{\mathtt{fD}}}$ of $\mathcal{P}_{\mathtt{fD}}$, while the statement $\forall X.\,(\mathtt{1}\ \mathtt{//}\ X \rightarrow A \Rightarrow \{A \mapsto 1\})$ has a different meaning and is not valid in $\mathcal{I}_{\mathcal{P}_{\mathtt{fD}}}$.

In the debugging session shown in Fig. 8 the user has selected the *Divide & Query* strategy (Silva, 2006) in order to find a buggy node. The lower part of the left-hand side snapshot shows the first question asked by the tool after selecting this strategy, namely the *aca* `fDiff 1:2:2:1:_ -> A ==> [A = 1]`. According to her knowledge of $\mathcal{I}_{\mathcal{P}_{\mathtt{fD}}}$ the user marks this *aca* as invalid. The strategy now prunes the *CT* keeping only the subtree rooted by the invalid *aca* at the previous step (every *CT* with an invalid root must contain at least one buggy node). The second question, which can be seen at the right-hand side snapshot, asks about the validity of the *aca* `fDiff 2:2:1:_ -> A ==> []` (which in fact represents `fDiff 2:2:1:`$\bot \rightarrow A \Rightarrow \{A \mapsto \bot\}$, as explained before). Again, her knowledge of $\mathcal{I}_{\mathcal{P}_{\mathtt{fD}}}$ leads the user to expect that `fDiff 2:2:1:`$\bot$ can return some defined result, and the *aca* is marked as invalid. After this question the debugger points out at `fDiff` as an incomplete function, and the debugging session ends.

Regarding the efficiency of this debugging method our preliminary experimental results show that:

1. Producing the transformed $\mathcal{P}^{\mathcal{T}}.pl$ from $\mathcal{P}.pl$ is proportional in time to the number of functions of the program, and does require an insignificant amount of system memory since each predicate is transformed separately.
2. The computation of the goal for $\mathcal{P}^{\mathcal{T}}.pl$ requires almost the same system resources as for $\mathcal{P}.pl$ because writing the trace causes no significant overhead in our experiments.
3. Producing the *CT* from the trace is not straightforward and requires several traverses of the trace. Although more time-consuming due to the algorithmic difficulty, this process only keeps portions of the trace in memory at each moment.
4. The most inefficient phase in our current implementation is the graphical interface. Although it would be possible to keep in memory only the portion of the tree displayed at each moment, our graphical interface loads the whole *CT* in main memory. We plan to improve this limitation in the future. However the current prototype can cope with *CT*s containing thousands of nodes, which is enough for medium size computations.
5. As usual in declarative debugging, the efficiency of the tool depends on the computation tree size, which in turn usually depends on the size of the data structures required and not on the program size.

A different issue is the difficulty of answering the questions by the user. Indeed in complicated programs involving constraints the *aca*s can be large and intricate, as it is also the case with other debugging tools for *CLP* languages. Nevertheless, our prototype works reasonably well in cases where the goal's search space is relatively small, and we believe that working with such goals can be useful for detecting many programming bugs in practice. Techniques for simplifying *CT*s should be worked out in future improvements of the prototype. For instance, asking the user for a concrete missing instance of the initial goal and starting a diagnosis session for the instantiated goal might be helpful.

8. Conclusions and future work

We have presented a logical and semantic framework for the declarative diagnosis of wrong and missing computed answers in $CFLP(\mathcal{D})$, a generic scheme for Constraint Functional-Logic Programming over a given constraint domain $\mathcal{D}$ which combines the expressivity of lazy *FP* and *CLP* languages. The diagnosis technique of wrong answers represents the computation which has produced a wrong computed answer by means of an abridged proof tree whose inspection leads to the discovery of some erroneous program rule responsible for the wrong answer. The logical correctness of the method can be formally proved thanks to the connection between abbreviated proof trees and program semantics. The method for missing answers relies on computation trees whose nodes are labeled with *answer collection assertions* (*aca*s). As in declarative diagnosis for *FP* languages, the values displayed at *aca*s are shown in the most evaluated form demanded by the topmost computation. Following the *CLP* tradition, we have shown that our computation trees for missing answers are abbreviated proof trees in a suitable inference system, the so-called *Constraint Negative Proof Calculus*. Thanks to this fact, we can prove the correctness of our diagnosis method for any admissible goal solving system whose recollection of computed answers can be represented by means of a proof tree in the constraint negative proof calculus. As far as we know, no comparable result was previously available for such an expressive framework as *CFLP*.

Intuitively, the notion of *aca* bears some loose relationship to programming techniques related to answer recollection, as e.g., *encapsulated search* (Brassel et al., 2004). However, *aca*s in our setting are not a programming technique. Rather, they serve as logical statements whose falsity reveals incompleteness of computed answers with respect to expected answers. In principle, one could also think of a kind of logical statements somewhat similar to *aca*s, but asserting the *equality* of the observed and expected sets of computed answers for one and the same goal with a finite search space. We have not developed this idea, which could support the declarative diagnosis of a third kind of unexpected results, namely *incorrect answer sets* as done for *Datalog*. In fact, we think that a separate diagnosis of wrong and missing answers is pragmatically more convenient for users of *CFLP* languages.

On the practical side, our method can be applied to actual *CFLP* systems such as *Curry* or $\mathcal{TOY}$, leading to correct diagnosis under the pragmatic assumption that they behave as admissible goal solving systems. This assumption is plausible in so far as the systems are based on formal goal solving procedures that can be argued to be admissible. A debugging tool called $\mathcal{DDT}$, which implements the proposed technique for wrong answers over the domain $\mathcal{R}$ of arithmetic constraints over the real numbers has been implemented as a non-trivial extension of previously existing debugging tools. $\mathcal{DDT}$ provides several practical facilities for reducing the number and the complexity of the questions that are presented to the user during a debugging session. Moreover, a prototype debugger for missing answers under development is available, which implements the method in $\mathcal{TOY}$.

As future work, we plan several improvements of $\mathcal{DDT}$, such as enabling the diagnosis supporting *finite domain constraints* (Estévez et al., 2009; Fernández et al., 2007), and providing new facilities for simplifying the presentation of queries to the user. In this sense, some important pragmatic problems well known for declarative diagnosis tools in *FP* and *CLP* languages also arise in our context: both the *CT*s and the *aca*s at their nodes may be very big in general, causing computation overhead and difficulties for the user in answering the questions posed by the debugging tool. In spite of these difficulties, the prototype works reasonably well in cases where the goal's search space is relatively small, and we believe that working with such goals can be useful for detecting many programming bugs in practice.

9. References

Alpuente, M., Ballis, D., Correa, F.J. & Falaschi, M. (2003). Correction of Functional Logic Programs, *Proc. ESOP'03*, Springer LNCS, 2003.

Boye, J., Drabent, W. & Małuszyński, J. (1997). Declarative Diagnosis of Constraint Programs: an Assertion-based Approach. *DiSCiPl Delieverable D.WP2.2.M1.1-2*, 1997.

Brassel, B., Hanus, M. & Huch, F. (2004). Encapsulating non-determinism in functional logic computations. *Journal of Functional and Logic Programming*, 2004.

Caballero, R. (2005). A Declarative Debugger of Incorrect Answers for Constraint Functional-Logic Programs. *Proc. WCFLP'05*, ACM, pp. 8–13, 2005.

Caballero, R. & Rodríguez-Artalejo, M. (2004). $\mathcal{DDT}$: A Declarative Debugging Tool for Functional Logic Languages. *Proc. FLOPS'04*, Springer LNCS 2998, pp. 70–84, 2004.

Comini, M., Levi, G., Meo, M.C. & Vitiello, G. (1999). Abstract diagnosis. *Journal of Logic Programming* 39 (1–3): 43–93, 1999.

Deransart, P., Hermenegildo, M. & Małuszyński, J. (2000). *Analysis and Visualization tools for Constraint Programming: Constraint Debugging*. Springer LNCS 1870, pp. 151–174, 2000.

Drabent, W., Nadjm-Tehrani, S. & Małuszyński, J. (1989). Algorithmic Debugging with Assertions. In *Harvey Abramson and M.H. Rogers, editors, Meta-programming in Logic Programming*, pp. 501-522. The MIT Press, 1989.

Estévez, S, Hortalá, T., Rodríguez, M. & del Vado, R. (2009). On the cooperation of the constraint domains $\mathcal{H}$, $\mathcal{R}$, and $\mathcal{FD}$ in *CFLP*. *Journal of Theory and Practice of Logic Programming*, vol. 9, pp. 415–527, 2009.

Fernández, A.J., Hortalá-González, M.T., Sáenz-Pérez, F. & del Vado-Vírseda, R. (2007). Constraint functional logic programming over finite domains. *Theory and Practice of Logic Programming*, 7(5):537–582, 2007.

Ferrand, G. (1987). Error Diagnosis in Logic Programming, an Adaptation of E.Y. Shapiro's Method. *Journal of Logic Programming* 4(3), 177-198, 1987.

Ferrand, G., Lesaint, W. & Tessier, A. (2002). Theoretical foundations of value withdrawal explanations for domain reduction. *ENTCS 76*, 2002.

Ferrand, G., Lesaint, W. & Tessier, A. (2003). Towards declarative diagnosis of constraint programs over finite domains. *ArXiv Computer Science e-prints*, 2003.

Hanus, M. (2003). *Curry: an Integrated Functional Logic Language*, Version 0.8, April 15, 2003. Available at:
`http://www-ps.informatik.uni-kiel.de/currywiki/.`

Hermenegildo, M., Puebla, G., Bueno, F. & López-García, P. (2002). Abstract Verification and Debugging of Constraint Logic Programs. *Proc. CSCLP'02*, pp. 1–14, 2002.

Lloyd, J.W. (1987). Declarative Error Diagnosis. *New Generation Computing 5(2)*, 133–154, 1987.

López-Fraguas, F.J.; Rodríguez-Artalejo, M. & del Vado-Vírseda, R. (2006). A New Generic Scheme for Functional Logic Programming with Constraints. *Journal of Higher-Order and Symbolic Computation*, volume 20, numbers 1-2, pages 73-122, June 2007.

López-Fraguas, F.J., Rodríguez-Artalejo, M. & del Vado-Vírseda, R. (2005). Constraint Functional Logic Programming Revisited. *WRLA'04*, ENTCS 117, pp. 5–50, 2005.

López-Fraguas, F.J. & Sánchez-Hernández, J. (1999). $\mathcal{TOY}$: A Multiparadigm Declarative System. In *Proc. RTA'99*, Springer LNCS 1631, pp 244–247, 1999. System and documentation available at `http://toy.sourceforge.net.`

López-Fraguas, F.J., Rodríguez-Artalejo, M. & del Vado-Vírseda, R. (2004). A lazy narrowing calculus for declarative constraint programming. *6th International Conference on PPDP'04*, ACM Press, pp. 43–54, 2004.

Naish, L. (1997). A Declarative Debugging Scheme. *Journal of Functional and Logic Programming (3)*, 1997.

Naish, L. & Barbour, T. (1995). A declarative debugger for a logical-functional language. *DSTO General Document*, 5(2):91–99, 1995.

Nilsson, H. (2001). How to look busy while being as lazy as ever: the Implementation of a lazy functional debugger. *Journal of Functional Programming*, 11(6):629–671, 2001.

Nilsson, H. & Fritzson, P. (1994). Algorithmic Debugging of Lazy Funcional Languages. *Journal of Functional Programming*, 4(3):337–370, 1994.

Nilsson, H. & Sparud, J. (1997). The Evaluation Dependence Tree as a basis for Lazy Functional Debugging. *Automated Software Engineering*, 4(2):121–150, 1997.

Pope, B. (2006). A Declarative Debugger for Haskell. *PhD thesis, Department of Computer Science and Software Engineering, University of Melbourne*, 2006.

Pope, B. & Naish, L. (2003). Practical aspects of declarative debugging in Haskell 98. *Proc. PPDP'03*, ACM Press, pp. 230–240, 2003.

Shapiro, E.Y. (1982). *Algorithmic Program Debugging*. The MIT Press, Cambridge, 1982.

Silva, J. (2006). A comparative study of algorithmic debugging strategies. In *LOPSTR'06*, volume 4407 of LNCS, pages 143–159. Springer, 2006.

Tessier, A. & Ferrand, G. (2000). Declarative Diagnosis in the CLP Scheme. In P. Deransart, M. Hermenegildo, J. Małuszyński (eds.), *Analysis and Visualization Tools for Constraint Programming*, Chapter 5, pp. 151–174. Springer LNCS 1870, 2000.

Section 4

Semantic Web and Interfaces

7

Spatialization of the Semantic Web

Ashish Karmacharya[1], Christophe Cruz[2] and Frank Boochs[1]
[1]*Institut i3mainz, am Fachbereich 1 - Geoinformatik und Vermessung, Fachhochschule Mainz,*
[2]*Laboratoire Le2i, UMR-5158 CNRS, UFR Sciences et Techniques, Université de Bourgogne,*
[1]*Germany*
[2]*France*

1. Introduction

The abstraction of the real world melds the semantics of its objects with the spatial characteristics seamlessly. This is visible in a way the human perceives the real world where it is often difficult to pin point the spatial characteristics of the objects from their semantics. In other words the spatial characteristics are generally hidden with the semantics of the objects. As for example, describing relations of objects the terms near, far or touching are often used which are spatial relations but in general considered as semantic properties which is not true. Hence, it is a trend to consider that the spatial behaviors of objects are parts of its semantics. Similar approaches where the spatial properties are considered as part of semantics have been translated in technical advancements made by the technologies. There is a general trend to mix up spatial components in the semantics or the semantics in the spatial components within technologies. For instance, a classic GIS ignores semantics of objects to focus on the spatial components whereas a non GIS uses spatial components as the semantic parameters of the objects. As the technology is getting matured, it is moving closer to the human perception of the real world. Today, the knowledge management is being researched in real sense to model and to manage knowledge possessed by humans which is basically the perception of the real world.

The emergence of Internet technologies has provided a strong base to share the information in a wider community. As the needs of information have grown it has become necessary to represent them in a proper and meaningful way. It involves attesting semantics to the documents. The major approach to attach semantics to documents involves first to categorize them properly and then to index them with the relevant semantics for efficient retrieval. This categorization and indexing of the Web documents have become important topic for research. These researches focus on the use of knowledge management to structure documents which involves ontologies to conceptualize knowledge of a specific domain. Then, there is knowledge representation which is a vital part of knowledge management. It provides the possibilities to represent knowledge in order to be inferred. Knowledge representations and reasonings have traditionally been a domain within Artificial Intelligence. However, the recent growth in Semantic Web technologies has added fuel to the use of knowledge explicitly in a Web environment. The XML-based knowledge languages could be inferred through different inference mechanisms in order to infer knowledge.

1.1 Knowledge management and the semantic web

The current version of the Web could only be processed through human intelligence. Though the Internet technologies have taken a huge leap forward since it evolved, the fact is the information within the technology still needs to be interpreted by human brain. However, in his paper (Berners-Lee et al., 2001), Tim Berners-Lee and coauthors have envisaged the next generation of the Web which they call "the Semantic Web". In this Web the information is given with well-defined meaning, better enabling computers and people to work in cooperation. Adding on, the Semantic Web aims at machine-processable information enabling intelligent services such as information brokers, search agents and information filters, which offer greater functionality and interoperability (Decker, et al., 2000). Since then the technology has moved forward significantly and has opened the possibility of sharing and combining information in more efficient way.

The association of knowledge with Semantic Web has provided a scope for information management through the knowledge management. Since both the technologies use ontology to conceptualize the scenarios, Semantic Web technology could provide a platform for developments of knowledge management systems (Stojanovi & Handschuh, 2002). We believe the framework has adopted the knowledge technologies as sub technologies within. The ontologies are core underlying knowledge technologies within this Semantic Web framework. These ontologies are defined through XML based languages and the advanced forms of them.

The major context behind this project is the use of knowledge in order to manage huge sets of heterogeneous dataset in a Web based environment. It primarily focuses on the spatial dataset and its management through the available spatial technologies incorporated within the knowledge technology. As the Web technologies get matured through the Semantic Web, the implementation of knowledge in this domain seems even more appropriate. This research paper puts forward the views and results of the research activities within the backdrop of the Semantic Web technologies and the underlying knowledge technologies.

1.2 Knowledge representation and ontologies

Knowledge representation has been described in five distinct roles it plays in (Davis et al., 1993). Those roles are

- A surrogate for the thing itself used to enable an entity to determine consequences by thinking rather than acting, i.e., by reasoning about the world rather than acting it.
- A set of ontological commitments, i.e., an answer to the question: In what terms should I think about the world?
- A fragmentary theory of intelligent, reasoning, expressed in terms of three components
  - The representation's fundamental conception of intelligent reasoning
  - The set of inferences the representation sanctions; and
  - The set of inferences it recommends

- A medium for pragmatically efficient computation, i.e., the computational environment in which thinking is accomplished.
- A medium for human to express, i.e., a language human expresses things about the world.

Semantic Web technologies use these roles to represent knowledge. The first and the last roles are primarily theoretical roles through which knowledge could be better understood. The remaining roles are conceptual roles which are being implemented within the technology. If those roles are carefully evaluated, it could be seen that knowledge representation begins with ontological commitments. That is selecting a representation means and making a set of ontological commitments (Brachman et al., 1978). Thus defining ontology is a major activity with the process of the Semantic Web.

The term Ontology is being used for centauries to define an object philosophically. The core theme of the term remains the same in the domain of computer. Within the computer science domain, ontology is a formal representation of the knowledge through the hierarchy of concepts and the relationships between those concepts. In theory ontology is a formal, explicit specification of shared conceptualization (Gruber, 1993) In any case, ontology can be considered as formalization of knowledge representation and Description Logics (DLs) provide logical formalization to the ontologies (Baader et al., 2003).

Description logics (DLs) [(Calvanese et al., 2001); (Baader & Sattler, 2000)] are a family of knowledge representation languages that can be used to represent knowledge of an application domain in a structured and formally well-understood way. The term "Description Logics" can be broken down into the terms description and logic. The former would describe the real world scenario with the real world objects and the relationships between those concepts. More formally these objects are grouped together through unary predicates defined by atomic concepts within description logics and the relationships through binary predicates defined by atomic roles. The term logic adds the fragrance of logical interpretations to the description. Through these logics one could reason the description for generating new knowledge from the existing one.

As the Semantic Web technologies matured, the need of incorporating the concepts behind description logic within the ontology languages was realized. It took few generations for the ontology languages defined within Web environment to implement the description language completely. The Web Ontology Language (OWL) (Bechhofer, et al., 2004); (Patel-Schneider et al., 2004)] is intended to be used when the information contained in documents needs to be processed by applications and not by human (McGuinness & Harmelen, 2004). The OWL language has direct influence from the researches in Description Logics and insights from Description Logics particularly on the formalization of the semantics (Horrocks et al., 2004).

The horn logic more commonly known the Horn clauses is a clause with at most one positive literal. It has been used as the base of logic programming and Prolog languages (Sterling & Shapiro, 1994) for years. These languages allow the description of knowledge with predicates. Extensional knowledge is expressed as facts, while intentional knowledge is defined through rules (Spaccapietra et al., 2004). These rules are used through different Rule Languages to enhance the knowledge possess in ontology. The Horn logic has given a platform to define Horn-like rules through sub-languages of RuleML (Boley, 2009).

Summarizing, it could be said that ontology defines the data structure of a knowledge base and this knowledge base could be inferred through various inference engines. These inference engines can be perform under Horn logic through Horn-like rules languages.

Semantic Web technology is slowly revolutionizing the application of knowledge technologies. Knowledge technologies though existed before the Semantic Web, the implementation in their fullness is just being realized. This research benefits from the existing inference engines through the inference rules and reasoning engines to reason the knowledge. However in current stage, the research works moves beyond semantic reasoning and semantic rule processing and attempts to integrate the spatial reasoning and spatial rule inference integrating spatial components in its structure. This research project introduces the approach on achieving the spatial functionalities within those inference engines.

1.3 Spatial components in semantic web

The Semantic Web technologies is slowly gaining acceptance in the wider community. It is thus paramount to include every type of information within the technology. The core within Semantic Web technologies is the semantics of the resources. These semantics may be the spatial or non-spatial. However, the focus of the technology is mainly on utilizing the non-spatial semantics for managing the information. Thus, the spatial information is widely neglected. Nevertheless, it has been realized inclusion of spatial components within Semantic Web framework is important for way forward. Those researches mainly focus on semantic interoperability of spatial data for efficient exchange of spatial data over heterogeneous platforms or efficient data integration. In cases like (Cruz, et. al 2004; Cruz, 2004), the ontologies are used to map their concepts to a global concept within a global ontology and thus providing a common platform for data integration. This is a common trend of practice for managing heterogeneous data source through Semantic Web technologies. The same practice is applied for geospatial data sources. In other cases like (Tanasescu, et al., 2006), ontologies are used to manage the semantics within different data sources to maintain the semantic interoperability of spatial data within different platforms.

In the realm of geospatial and temporal concepts and relationships, the work has not yet reached a level of either consensus or actionability which would allow it to be basis of knowledge interoperability (Lieberman, 2007). The Open Geospatial Consortium (OGC) is playing a major role to develop a consensus among different stakeholder on various aspects of geospatial technologies. The data interoperability is a major area in which OGC is concerned upon and it has developed different standards for this. Groups like Geospatial Incubator have taken the works of OGC to formulate steps in updating the W3C Geo vocabulary and preparing the groundwork to develop comprehensive geospatial ontology. In the process it has reported different spatial ontologies that exist in the Web (Lieberman et al., 2007).

It is evident that the geospatial ontologies are developed to solve individual spatial problem and are not being used to be effective for knowledge formulation within the Semantic Web framework. Existing ontologies or the ontologies in the process of creation are mostly targeting the usage of vocabularies for the proper data management and not the knowledge management. One implication of such approach is that there is no possibility of geospatial reasoning to enhance the knowledge base. It is widely noticed there is the lack of a known, robust geospatial reasoners. Furthermore, it has been argued that while geospatial reasoning is an ever-evolving field of research, spatial data constructs are not yet accommodated within most current Semantic Web languages as the OWL language (Reitsma & Hiramatsu, 2006).

The seamless integration of spatial components within Semantic Web technologies is the major topic of this research project. Hence, the approach in which this component is integrated within the global framework of the Semantic Web technology is covered extensively within this research project. Additionally, it discusses different components involved in spatial activities within the framework.

1.4 Spatial components on database systems

It has been seen that in the previous section that the ontology engineering has not gained enough momentum to assist spatial activities through ontology. Hence, this project work utilizes the existing potentiality of spatial extensions within the current database system to carry out the spatial activities within the ontology.

Most of the database systems support spatial operations and functions through their spatial extensions. Over the past decade, as Relational DataBase Management System (RDBMS) has seen a huge growth in the database technology. Likewise, the spatial components within them also seen a tremendous improvement in their functionalities. In early days, spatial data were organized in dual architectures which consist of separate administrative data for data management in a RDBMS and spatial data for a GIS system. This could easily result in data inconsistency hence all the database systems today maintain the spatial component in a single RDBMS.

In order to have a common standard among different database systems, they implement their spatial performance accordance to the Open Geospatial Consortium (OGC 1998) Simple Features Specifications for SQL (OGC 1999). Since OGC Simple Feature Specifications are built within simple spatial features in 2D space, most of the spatial operations are restricted to 2D spatial data. It is also possible to store, retrieve and visualize 3D data but it does not follow OGC simple feature specifications. Some RDBMS system today also supports certain 3D spatial queries as well.

According to OGC specification any object is represented spatially following two structures - geometrical and topological. The geometrical structure is the feature providing the direct access to the coordinates of the objects. The topological structure provides the information about the spatial relationships of the objects. The database systems store the geometrical information of the objects and not their topology. They then use their spatial operations to retrieve topological relationships between these geometries (Hellerstein et al., 1995).

1.5 Aims and the motivation of the project

It is a general fact that technologies always shift for the betterment and the components of the previous technologies must be upgraded to the shifting technology. The world is experiencing a shift in technology from the database oriented Information technology to ontology oriented knowledge technology and thus each individual technology that have matured under previous technology requires to be shifted to this emerging technology. The tasks of shifting these components have always presented challenges as the principle foundations between the two technologies are entirely different in most of the cases.

One of the major technical components in the database oriented technologies is the spatial technology. The immense strength of spatial technology was realized long before the emergence of database or even the computers. Maps were used to analyze the problems and derive solutions spatially (Berry, 1999). With the evolution of computers, a new discipline emerged to analyze the problems spatially, which is termed as Geographic Information System (GIS). GIS technology was one of the first to use the spatial technology for the analysis of the geographic locations. Spatial analysis is used in other domains too besides GIS. Before the emergence of sophisticated database systems, GIS technologies used files to store the spatial data. Each vendors of the technology had their own algorithms for spatial operations and functions. This in turn provided lots of inconsistency in the analysis process. As the database technology matured, it started to include those spatial components into it. In this manner, the spatial technology got immersed within the database technology. As previously mentioned they followed the specifications provided by OGC to maintain a common standard and hence most of these inconsistencies were revolved. With the advancement in database systems the spatial technology also got matured and today it is not necessary to depend on a GIS to perform spatial analysis. This has clear advantages for the other domains which use spatial analysis as part of their analysis process.

When viewed from the Semantic Web point of view, the integration of spatial component will trigger the integration process of other data component adding an open layer for data type which could be argued as non-typically semantic within its framework. This data could be spatial or temporal data or even process data. Such level within the technical framework of Semantic Web will give clear advantages for the technology to grow.

The main aim of this research project is to initiate the process of setting up a layer in the Semantic Web framework for the non-typical semantic information that is not covered through the semantics. In order to illustrate its applicability, this research centers on integration of spatial component within the Semantic Web technologies. This work focuses beyond data interoperability and addresses the spatial processing through knowledge querying and inferring. In addition, the work attempts to change and to improve the ongoing data management process of archiving documents in the industrial archaeology domain through knowledge management process. This work also aims to initiate the usage knowledge for performing spatial analyses in the existing GIS tools. It tries to draw attention towards the benefit of introducing a knowledge level in the universal GIS model. This in fact supports the relevancy theory of the need to transfer the technical component in the wake of technology change.

1.6 Industrial archaeology: the case study

The research project is drawn around the case study of industrial archaeology. The discipline of industrial archaeology fits perfectly to demonstrate the effectiveness of the implementation of the research activities. In general the industrial archaeological sites are available for very short duration of time and the amount of information collected is huge and diverse making it impossible for the conventional technologies to manage them. This research takes on the Semantic Web and its underlying knowledge technology to manage them. The knowledge possess by archaeologists is used to identify the objects and map the data and documents to the respective objects. In this process the knowledge about the objects is acquired through first identifying the objects and defining their behavior at the ground. This knowledge can then be used during the management of these objects. In fact the research project is based on 4Ks processing steps: Knowledge Acquisition, Knowledge Management, Knowledge Visualization and Knowledge Analysis. In each of these 4Ks, the knowledge of archaeologists is used.

The research site lies in Krupp belt Essen. This 200 hectares site was used for steel production in early nineteenth century but was later destroyed. The majority of the area was never rebuilt. The site was excavated in 2007 in order to document the findings. The area is being converted to a park of the main building of ThyssenKrupp so there was not much time available to document the findings properly due to ever changing structure of data and documents and their volume. It is hence not possible to use the traditional technology for their rigid nature and huge dependency on human manipulation of the data and documents. Possibility to engage machine to understand the information and processed them through the collaboration of the knowledge possess by archaeologist was realized through an application tool - The Web platform ArchaeoKM.

The research highlights the importance of non-typical semantic information within the Semantic Web framework. The research discusses the possibility of including spatial technology within the framework. A layer is proposed for spatial data pattern that utilizes the Semantic Web component to process spatial knowledge. This layer could host other data patterns as well and follow the same trend of spatial integration.

The integration of spatial technology within the Semantic Web technologies adds up benefit to the geospatial community. Instead of depending on the information based on the data, the analysis process should be more efficient and less demanding through the application of knowledge. The approach of using knowledge that is supported by underlying spatial data to execute the analysis process was embraced by the research.

The paper is divided into four major sections with chapters discussing them. The first chapter introduces the domain of the case study and how the existing technologies are contributing on it. It mainly discusses these issues with backdrop of ArchaeoKM - an application tool developed during the research work. The next section covers the state of art and basically highlights the state of the art in underlying knowledge technologies within the Semantic Web technology and their relations to this research work. The fourth chapter points out the possibilities of spatial extension in the knowledge technologies thus proposing a separate level dedicated to geospatial integration within the Semantic Web framework. The paper concludes with the conclusion where an effort has been made to argue that there is vast implementation of spatial extension and the benefit could be realized in third party domain as shown within the case study domain.

2. The ArchaeoKM project

This chapter begins with a discussion about a general overview of the industrial archaeology. It presents the case study of the research site by discussing the nature of the data collected during the excavation process. It then reviews the current Information Systems that are either being implemented or researched in this domain. It includes the usages of Geographic Information Systems (GIS) in this field. Then after, the chapter continues with the introduction of the ArchaeoKM project through discussion on the principle and how it is different from the existing systems. It concludes with a discussion on the future prospective of the work.

2.1 The domain of the industrial archaeology: a case study

The domain of the Industrial archaeology is the recording, study, interpretation and preservation of the physical remains of the industrially related artifacts, sites and systems within their social and historical contexts (Clouse, 1995). During the period of 18th and 19th century the industrial revolution started from the United Kingdom and spread across the world marking a major turn of the human civilization. In the course of time the industries established during the period were abandoned and replaced by new installments. These abandoned sites however hide many important histories of modern developments which need to be preserved as historical facts. Today, the domain of the industrial archaeology has occupied its position in the archaeological community as a mainstream branch of archaeology which deals with the history of constructions, the development architecture, the history of technologies, socio-economic and cultural history (Boochs, 2009). The domain of the industrial archaeology has its own challenges. It does not involve the excavation process and just documents the standing artefacts in contrast to the conventional archaeology, so the discipline was initially considered as hobby archaeology and not a mainstream archaeology. Though the branch has now been taken more seriously by its contemporary branches, it still needs acceptance by the wider community as the awareness about the importance of this field in archaeology is still minimal. The lack of acceptance has its own impact here as there is no reliable tool to document the artifact as the classical archaeology and hence large scale of existing relicts get lost forever. Usually the industrial archaeological sites are available for limited amount of time as they are not mostly conserved for continuous excavation and they are most often the sites for new constructions. Adding on, the advancement of current data capturing technologies made it possible to capture huge and heterogeneous datasets in this limited duration. It is absolutely not possible to manage this nature of datasets in such a limited amount of time without the intervention of machine to assist human. It thus requires human machine collaboration to manage them which is not possible through the conventional technologies.

The project points out these limitations and provides a prospective solution to handle the dataset through the knowledge possessed by the archaeologists and facilitated by knowledge management tools within Semantic Web technology. This section presents the case study site used within this research work discussing the diversity and amount of data acquired through the modern technologies.

2.2 The main excavation area

The main excavation area lies in Krupp area in Essen belt, Germany. The 200 hectares area was used for steel production during early 19th century. The work on steel production has a critical impact on the settlement development of Essen. In this way the history of Essen is closely related to the activities of steel production in Krupp. The site grew over the decades and formed a so-called Krupp Belt. The site was destroyed during the Second World War. Most of the area is never rebuilt. In between 1945 to 2007, the area was basically a wasteland making it an ideal site for an industrial archaeological excavation. However, the ThyssenKrupp is returning to build its new headquarters in the site by then 2010. This has raised the problem of limitation of time period for a proper management of the recovered objects. The objects are recorded as soon as they are recovered and these records are stored in a repository in their respective data formats. Hence, there is a clear lack of well-defined structure for data management. Moreover, in contrast to the conventional archaeology where the data collection and data analysis goes side by side so in that case the data structure could be designed at the beginning, the data analysis is carried out at the end in industrial archaeology so it is not possible to perceive the structure of the data at the beginning. The first challenge consists of creating a proper data structure which helps in retrieving those data efficiently. As there was not enough time to filter the collected data concurrently, the amount of data that are collected is huge. Hence, the system that has to handle the collection of data should be able to handle this huge set.

Archaeologists with assistance of photogrammetric specialists were involved in data acquisition process. They were responsible to decide the methods of measurements. The findings were scanned through terrestrial laser scanning instruments. Two scanners were used to acquire the scanned data. They were the Zöller and Fröhlich scanner (ZF) and the Riegl scanner. Those two scanners were used according to their requirement. Large objects scanning were carried out with the help of the Riegl scanner whereas the ZF scanner is used whenever some important findings are recovered. The Riegl scanner was installed on the roof of the Kreuzhaus (the building marked at the bottom of the site in figure 1) so that the scanner gets a good overview of the area. The findings were scanned with a resolution of 0.036 degrees (6 mm on 10 m) hence the point cloud is very dense. All the data were stored in the Gauß Krüger zone II (GK II) coordinate system.

An orthophoto was orthorectified from the aerial images (that were taken during the course of research work). The orthophoto has 10 cm resolution and is in GK II coordinate system. Huge numbers of digital pictures were taken during the research activities and they were stored in their original formats. These photos were taken with non-calibrated digital cameras. However, certain knowledge can be extracted from them by the archaeologists. Besides, photographs documents like the site plan of the area and some documents with relevant information of the site or the objects recovered were collected during data acquisition process. These data and documents were digitized and stored for proper mapping with the relevant objects. Archaeological notes taken by archaeologists during these excavation processes are of high importance. Hence, these notes are digitized and stored in the repository. Similarly, the site plan of the area was digitized and stored as .shp format in ArcGIS.

The nature of the dataset that was collected during the research work is varied. There are four distinct kinds of data which ranges from textual documents as the archaeological notes to multimedia documents as images. The heterogeneity of dataset is evident through the nature of each type of dataset varying completely from others in terms of their storages, presentations and implementations.

Fig. 1. The main excavation area Site.

2.3 GIS for archaeology

What does a GIS do? Basically providing a definition of GIS and referring to its abilities to capture and manipulate spatial data doesn't provide much insight into its functionality. The basic tasks of a GIS system can be broken down into five groups, data acquisition, spatial data management, database management, data visualization and spatial data analysis (Jones, 1997). Most archaeological data such as artifacts, features, buildings, sites or landscapes, have spatial and aspatial attributes that can be explored by GIS. These attributes include the spatial location that informs about the local or global context concerning the pieces of information, and the morphology that defines the shape and the size of an object.

The acquisition of spatial data is undertaken with the help of existing digitizing functionalities within the application software providing them. They are responsible for the acquisition of data and integrating it to the existing spatial sets. Spatial data include, but are not limited to, topographic maps, site locations and morphology, archaeological plans, artifacts distribution, aerial photography, geophysical data and satellite imagery.

The spatial data management process uses sophisticated database management systems in order to store and retrieve spatial data and their attributes. Data collected from different sources have to be transformed in the same coordinate system in order to integrate them.

The database management system, involving conceptual and logical data modeling is an important part of GIS because it ensures that the construction and the maintenance of database is done and that the spatial and aspatial datasets and components are correctly linked.

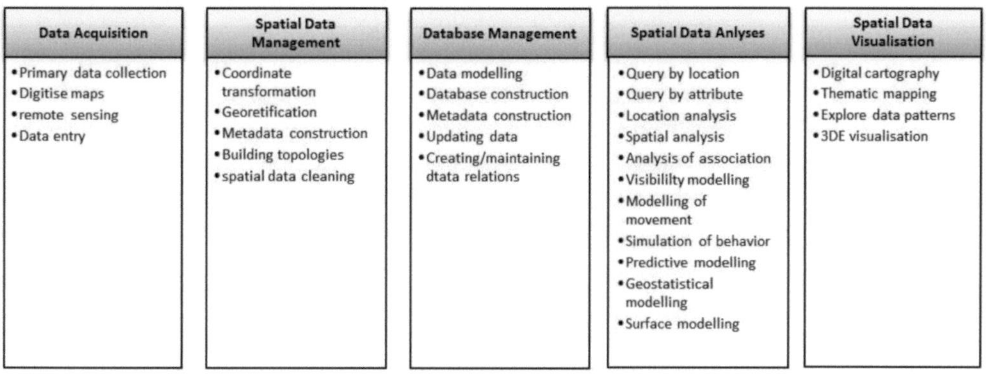

Fig. 2. The five main groups of tasks performed by GIS.

Some limitations appear visible in currents GIS system in the context of the Industrial Archaeology. The lack of GIS platforms that uses data like point cloud is one of such visible limitations. It however is a fact that conventionally an Information System for archaeologists is a Geographic Information System or 3D object modelling system. The statement has been supported by the current commercial applications for the archaeologists. Applications like ArchaeoCAD from ArcTron and PointCloud from Kubit rely heavily on the geometry of the objects excavated. The applications are thus used primarily to represent objects excavated in a 3D space. Similarly, GIS vendors like ESRI uses the spatial information of the objects to analyze them spatially. Meanwhile, the data collection process has seen a tremendous change in the last few years. Today, it is not only the amount of data that needs consideration, the diversity of data should also be taken into account. It is becoming increasingly difficult to manage them solely with the current database system due to the size and diversity of the data. In addition, information systems in archaeological projects or cultural heritage projects lacks from a complete package. There have been lots of researches going on but they are on the independent components. However, research projects like 3D MURALE (Cosmas et al., 2001) and GIS DILAS (Wüst et al., 2004) contains most of the elements needed for a complete package and hence could be considered as comprehensive Information System. The 3D MURALE system is composed of a recording component, a reconstruction component, a visualization component and database components. The findings are managed through a database management system. Once the findings are stored in the database with a proper data structure, the objects are reconstructed through the reconstruction component. This is done by modeling the objects in the 3D space. These 3D models are displayed in the visualization component. The DILAS is generic software, fully object oriented model for 3D geo-objects. The 3D geometry model is based on a topological boundary representation and supports most basic geometry types. It also incorporates the concept of multiple levels of detail (LOD) (Balletti et al., 2005) as well as texture information. It is thus clear that the existing systems rely heavily on the geometries of excavated objects for their representations, but the interoperability of these systems and the knowledge sharing remains a gap.

In addition, the sharing of knowledge in archaeology and disseminate it to the general public through wiki has been discussed in (Costa & Zanini, 2008). Likewise the use of knowledge to build up a common semantic framework has been discussed in (Kansa, 2008). Research works in data interoperability exist in the field of archaeology, but most of the research is carried out in other related fields. However, it could be applied in archaeology as well. The existing researches focus more on using the common language for efficient interoperability. The research project (Kollias, 2008) concerns the achieving syntactic and semantic interoperability through ontologies and the RDF framework to build a common standard. Data integration through ontologies and their relationships is discussed in (Doerr, 2008). Although the work on the Semantic Web and knowledge management in the field of Information System in Archaeology or related fields is stepping up with these research works, the fact is they are in very preliminary phases. Additionally, these projects concentrate more on how to achieve interoperability with semantic frameworks and ontologies. However, none of them focuses on the knowledge generation process and more specifically on rules defined by archaeologists in order to build up the system which should use, evaluate and represent the knowledge of the archaeologists.

Knowledge contained in documents has been traditionally managed through the use of metadata. Before going on details about knowledge management, let us first understand the perspective about the whole idea. Every activity begins with data. However data is meaningless until they are put in context of space or an event. Additionally, unless the relationship between different pieces of data is defined, simply data do not have any significance. Once the data are defined in terms of space or events and are defined through relationships, they become Information. Information understands the nature of the data but they do not provide the reasons behind the existence of data and are relatively static and linear by nature. Information is a relationship between data and, quite simply, is what it is, with great dependence on context for its meaning and with little implication for the future (Bellinger, 2004). Beyond every relationship, arises a pattern which has capacity to embody completeness and consistency of the relations to an extent of creating its own context (Bateson, 1979). Such patterns represent knowledge on the information and consequently on data. The term Knowledge Management has wide implications. However, very precisely Knowledge Management is about the capture and reuse of knowledge at different knowledge level. In order to access the knowledge, data are annotated and indexed in the knowledge base. This is in line to the concept proposed by Web Semantic where it proposes to annotate the document content using semantic information from domain ontologies (Berners-Lee et al., 2001). The goal is to create annotations with well-defined semantics so they can be interpreted efficiently. Today, in the context of Semantic Web, the contents of a document can be described and annotated using RDF and OWL. The result is a set of Web documents interpretable by machine with the help of mark-ups. With such Semantic Web annotation, the efficiency of information retrieval is enhanced and the interoperability is improved. The information retrieval is improved by the ability to perform searches, which exploit the ontology in order to make inferences about data from heterogeneous resources (Welty & Ide, 1999).

2.4 Towards knowledge processing

The project ArchaeoKM plans to complement the principle of knowledge management by implementing it in the application through formulating the knowledge rules that can be used by archaeologists on the excavated data. The knowledge stored in machine readable format is inferred to bring result which could be well understood by human. Moreover, it moves beyond managing the concepts defined to annotate documents, which most of the research projects currently focusing on, to the instances of concepts with their own property values. In this manner, an object found in a point cloud can be linked, with the help of an instance in the ontology to other documents (a part in an image or a section of archive document) that contains the same object.

One of the main focuses on ArchaeoKM project is to determine an approach of integrating the spatial data within its overall framework of data integration. The integration process did not only serve for the data integration but also has taken a step forward in data analysis and management through the knowledge management techniques.

2.4.1 The web platform ArchaeoKM

The challenges possessed to document the artifacts in such a site could be handled through utilizing the knowledge of responsible archaeologists. The platform ArchaeoKM focuses on the use of the knowledge of archaeologists to document the objects with respect to the surrounding. In the process a tool based on the Semantic Web technology and its underlying knowledge technology was develop to provide the archaeologists to share their knowledge and document the information collected during the excavation process. One of the challenges is to bring all the datasets previously presented in one common platform. As a knowledge representation format, the top level ontology acts as the global schema for data integration in the platform. The application tool provides a common platform for archaeologists to share their experience and knowledge.

2.4.2 The ArchaeoKM architecture

The GIS technology performs a group of five tasks to execute the result. These tasks as already been mentioned are acquisition of spatial data, spatial data management, database management, spatial data analysis and the spatial data visualization. The ArchaeoKM project attempts to complement the five major processing steps of a GIS through its four processing activities which it calls the processing steps of 4Ks: knowledge acquisition, knowledge management, knowledge visualization, knowledge analysis.

The knowledge acquisition task consists in general term defines metadata on data acquired during the survey process. The spatial data acquisition process is still involved during the process, but in addition metadata on these data are defined using a knowledge representation language. Actually, an ontology, which defines the semantic of the recovered features, is defined to capture and capitalized the knowledge of archeologists on the archaeological site. Hence the schema of the ontology is defined at this level. This is done by the help of a specialist on ontologies. The relationships and their semantics are stored into the ontology. This semantic could be provided through an example of the relation of "insideOf" which is transitive relationship. In mathematics, a binary relation R over a set X is transitive if whenever an element a is related to an element b, and b is in turn related to an element c, then a is also related to c by the same kind relation. The ArchaeoKM platform deals with this issue.

The acquisition process constitutes of generation of knowledge base through enriching the ontology. The knowledge of archaeologists is used again to identify the recovered objects and enrich them in the ontology schema formulated. In short the process consists of populating the ontology with "individual" which represent objects recovered from the archaeological site. This creates a knowledge base from the ontology schema.

The knowledge management task consists of storing and the retrieving data along with its semantics. Knowledge is defined through the relationships and it is the relationships between individuals that create the real knowledge in the knowledge base. These relationships not only imply the relations between objects but also relation to their spatial signatures in spatial database. A specialized tool has to be developed in order to retrieve data from the ontology and from its spatial representation stored in a GIS. The ArchaeoKM platform deals with this issue.

The knowledge analysis task is the ability of the system to perform inferences on datasets. This cannot be undertaken without the help of the semantic definition on the archaeological objects. Usually inference or deduction is conducted on attributive data which are defined in the ontology. Today, no tool is defined to compute inference on the individuals of ontology and its spatial definition store in a spatial database. The ArchaeoKM platform deals with this issue.

The knowledge visualization task provides powerful visualization capabilities used for viewing spatial datasets and its semantics counterparts. Tools for the visualization of ontologies are of benefit to visualize the results of knowledge analysis. The ArchaeoKM platform deals with this issue.

As illustrated in figure 3 the system architecture of the ArchaeoKM platform is a three layered architecture with a structure for spatial component standing parallel against them.

The bottom level is the Syntactic level. This level contains all the information recovered from the site. Most of the data and documents collected during the excavation process are stored in their original formats. Certain data which needs to be stored in database system such as GIS data are stored in the RDBMS. This level basically performs as the repository of the dataset. One of the main tasks of the syntactic level is to explain the data. For a proper identification, the data needs to be analyzed with reference to the objects illustrated in the index. One of the first features within the application is the identification process.

A proper identification mechanism allows defining the identified objects. The ArchaeoKM platform utilizes the knowledge of archaeologists to identify the object. The identification is carried out by tagging the objects in the orthophoto of the site provided in the application. Attaching the semantic characteristics through semantic analysis on these objects generates knowledge. Different methods are used for the associating the semantic information according to the data pattern. Three distinct methods are applied to associate the semantic information which depends on the nature of the datasets with which it is associating with: Minimum Bounding Rectangles (MBRs) for the spatial data set, Uniform Resource Identifier (URI) for images and archive data and mapping to the data tables for datasets stored within

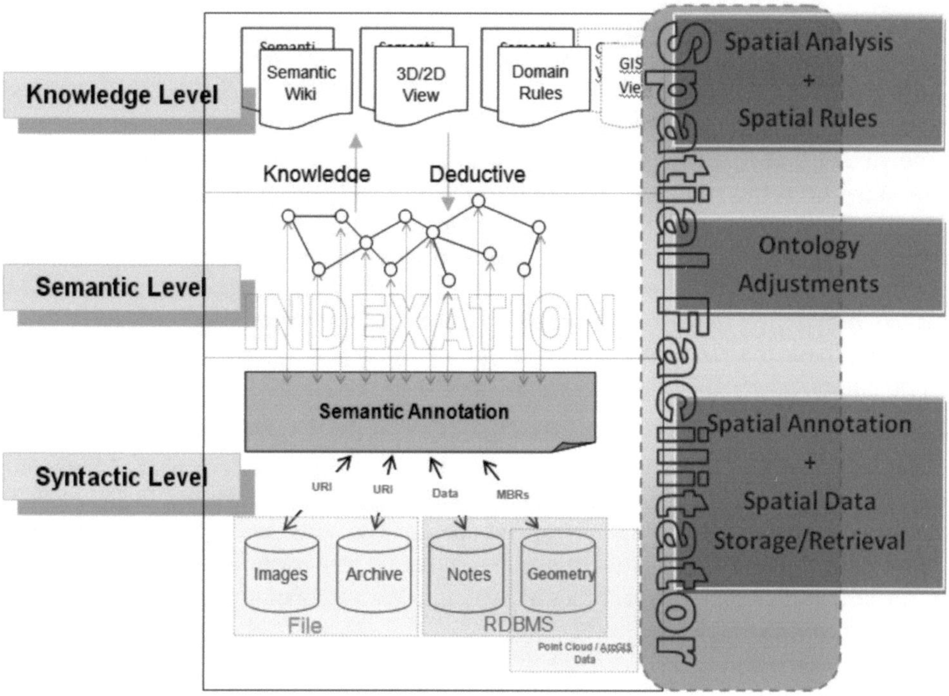

Fig. 3. The system architecture of the ArchaeoKM.

RDBMS. The method is reflected by the feature Semantic Annotation within the platform. These annotations are carried out through creating individual Resource Description Framework (RDF) triplets for each annotation process technology. RDF triplets also map the identified objects to the relevant classes in the domain ontology.

The next level is the semantic level, which manages the extracted knowledge. As stated, it is achieved through the ontological structure established through the descriptions, observations and rules defined by the archaeologists. These descriptions and rules are represented through different axioms in the domain ontology. Archaeologists are involved actively in this phase as they are the one best suited to provide entities and their relationships needed to build up the domain ontology. The semantic annotations from the Syntactic level will be indexed semantically to the entities of the domain ontology in this level. This semantic index through the identification process is the building block of the domain ontology and through semantic annotations provides a semantic view of the data. It also provides a global schema between various data sources making the data integration possible at certain level. This level represents a bridge between interpretative semantics in which users interpret terms and operational semantics in which computers handle symbols (Guarino, 1994). The knowledge is also managed through assigning semantic properties to the objects through proper relationships with other objects.

The top most level is the most concrete one as this level represents the organization of the knowledge on the semantic map through different visualizing tools. This level provides the user interfaces and they are visualized in form of Web pages as illustrated in figure 3. These Web pages represent knowledge which are generated through the knowledge management process discussed above. The pages are interrelated and can be used according to their relevance. The main representation of the knowledge is, however, demonstrated through Detail View pages. These pages are not only designed to illustrate the knowledge that has been generated and to manage it through the bottom two levels, but to also perform semantic research in order to gain new knowledge. Various techniques of the Semantic Web technology are being integrated within ArchaeoKM structure for acquiring new knowledge. Domain rules through inference engine provide one of those features in ArchaeoKM structure. In archaeology it is sometimes not possible to analyze the finding immediately and needs some properties or relationships to support them later. These inference rules provide the archaeologists such functionalities within the application.

In addition to the three levels, the system architecture contains components that facilitate the acquisition, validation, upgrade, management and analysis of the spatial knowledge. These components are packaged into the Spatial Facilitator as illustrated in figure 3. This component is responsible for analyzing the spatial data and providing results; either to update the current ontological structure in the semantic level or to populate the knowledge base. Through the inference capabilities in Semantic Web technology, new theories could be explored.

2.5 Discussion

This chapter has presented the case study of industrial archaeology for implementation of the arguments the research proposes. Industrial archaeology is the best suited for the research for the nature of the domain. The discipline of industrial archaeology generates huge and diverse data in very short duration of time and amount of time is short making it not possible to manage information through the conventional technologies. It is thus apprehending that this huge and diverse information could only be managed through active involvement of the archaeologists and the knowledge possess by them.

The ArchaeoKM project uses the knowledge possessed by the archaeologists to manage the information they gathered during the excavation. It is handled through a platform based on Semantic Web technologies and knowledge management and is termed as ArchaeoKM itself abbreviating Archaeological Knowledge Management. It uses the processing steps of 4Ks representing knowledge acquisition, knowledge management, knowledge analysis and knowledge visualization complementing the five steps of a GIS process. These 4Ks processing steps use the knowledge of the archaeologists in manipulating the data and to manage them.

This chapter establishes a relation between the case study of industrial archaeology and the spatial knowledge modeling paving the direction of the research. Primarily based on knowledge management of Semantic Web framework, it uses the spatial nature of case study to implement the spatial tools provided by the current spatial technology within the Semantic Web framework. The capabilities in existing tools to use the current database systems and their spatial extension are evident of the ability of database systems to manage spatial data. It however lacks the flexibility to adapt itself into new scenarios that might arise through generation of new information or changes in the contexts. This research carries these capabilities forward by using the spatial knowledge processing through knowledge tools which provides the proper data management in archaeology that addresses the limitation in adaptation of the conventional technologies.

This chapter has presented the concept of the inclusion of spatial knowledge in handling the spatial nature of data recovered. This is new domain of research and probably one of its kinds. Hence it is important to understand the current state of art in both spatial and Semantic Web technologies. The next chapter thus discusses the state of art in the Semantic Web.

3. The Semantic Web

The World Wide Web (WWW or the Web) is the single largest repository of information. The growth of Web has been tremendous since its evolvement both in terms of the content and the technology. The first generation Webs were mainly presentation based. They provided information through the Web pages but did not allow users to interact with them. In short they contained read only information. Moreover, the early pages were text only pages and do not contain multimedia data. These Web sites have higher dependency on the presentation languages as Hypertext Markup Languages (HTML) (Horrocks et al., 2004). With the introduction of eXtensible Markup Language (XML), the information within the pages became more structured. Those XML based pages could hold up the contents in more structured method but still lack the proper definition of semantics within the contents (Berners-Lee T., 1998). Needs of intelligent systems which could exploit the wide range of information available within the Web are widely felt. Semantic Web is envisaged to address the need. The term "Semantic Web" is coined by Tim Berners-Lee in his work (Berners-Lee et al., 2001) to propose the inclusion of semantic for better enabling machine-people cooperation for handling the huge information that exists in the Web.

The term "Semantic Web" has been defined numerous time. Though there is no formal definition of Semantic Web, some of its most used definitions are.

The Semantic Web is not a separate Web but an extension of the current one, in which information is given well-defined meaning, better enabling computers and people to work in cooperation. It is a source to retrieve information from the Web (using the Web spiders from RDF files) and access the data through Semantic Web Agents or Semantic Web Services. Simply Semantic Web is data about data or metadata (Berners-Lee et al., 2001).

- A Semantic Web is a Web where the focus is placed on the meaning of words, rather than on the words themselves: information becomes knowledge after semantic analysis is performed. For this reason, a Semantic Web is a network of knowledge compared with what we have today that can be defined as a network of information (Mazzocchi, 2000).
- The Semantic Web provides a common framework that allows data to be shared and reused across application, enterprise and community boundaries (Herman et al., 2010).

Any information systems which have to interoperate with various other information systems have to face the problem of interoperability. The archaeological community has seen the tremendous change in the manner the data are collected and manipulated. In one hand the technology growth provides the added functionalities to handle information which archaeologists cherish but at the same time they provide heterogeneity in the information pattern. The differences in manners and methods of individual community with the archaeological domain have led to development of independent systems and this has contributed in data incompatibility. A platform providing interoperability between different systems and in particular different sets of information has been widely felt within the community. Actually, the data heterogeneity is the main issue when the time comes to exchange and to manage information that describe the real world.

The issue of interoperability has always been there in the field of Information Technology ever since the computer systems started to communicate with each other through various modes. Factors like data authority, system autonomy and data heterogeneity are involved in the concerns of achieving efficient interoperability among different information systems. During the initial stages of the technology when a system was restricted to a department or at most a company, the issue of interoperability was limited within departments of a company. Hence the concern of data authority was not a big issue. However, the involvement of different departments and with them different players raised the issue of data heterogeneity. The evolvement of database management system (DBMS) fuelled up the necessity for data interoperability. Different underlying issues needed to be considered for achieving data interoperability in database systems like the structural differences, constraints differences or the difference in query languages. These information systems are based on DBMSs and hence the efficiency of system interoperability depended on tackling the question of heterogeneity of underlying data models of these DBMSs. As data models are represented through their schemas, the most common approach was to compare the schemas of the DBMSs and convert a schema of a DBMS to the next DBMS. Other approaches like building up a common model which acts as a broker to interchange the data between different DBMSs were also preferred to achieve the interoperability. In short, the first generation problem of data interoperability was mainly due to the fact of the differences in technical issues such as structures, constraints and different techniques. These problems are short term problems as they could be sorted out with a broker technology mediating between different technical approaches. The main problem of interoperability arises when there is a difference in understanding. The semantic differences between information fuel up the interoperability issues as the information gets more accessible and easy to use.

The next generation of systems saw gradual acceleration in the data types which are not necessarily structured. Those kinds of data could be semi-structured data or digital data like multimedia data. During this period data like geospatial data or temporal data got more acceptances within structured data community expanding the horizon of structured data. The influx of tailored made software applications for these kinds of data has raised the arguments of interoperability in much stronger manner. To add this there is the rapid growth of Internet technology and rapid growth in tendency to depend on internet for information. The information is thus distributed through various systems with their independent methods of developments and presentations. The issue of interoperability revolved around factors like technology for dealing heterogeneous systems with different data structures and patterns or handling the semantic interoperability through handling the difference in terminologies (Sheth, 1999). The necessity to have a common understanding of the information led to the concept of inclusion of some form of semantics to represent them. Metadata provided the semantic representations to the information. Metadata is data of data which provides information about the data in terms of their creation, storage, management, authority and in certain term their intended purpose. Metadata became essential part of any reliable information source and a medium to maintain interoperability. Likewise the trend to have standardization or adoption of ad hoc standards made significant progress towards achieving system, syntactic and structural interoperability (Sheth, 1999).

The current generation has followed the previous trend of heterogeneity in the data source and has carried it even further. The users have become more sophisticated in using this information. They expect the system to help them not at the data level but at the information and increasingly knowledge level (Sheth, 1999), thus expecting to have interoperability at the semantic level. Though metadata provides certain level of semantics for the data, they are generally not enough for managing the ever exploding information. The contexts of information needs to be taken into account to understand the information and these contexts are managed through the ontologies as traditionally they are built for specifying the vocabularies and their relationships. The underlying semantics in ontology provides foundation to interpret the knowledge within. This has provided a huge boosting in achieving interoperability between systems. The use of knowledge to understand information between systems and find a common linkage between them provides a framework for the interoperation. The issue of interoperability which started with technical differences has come to difference in understanding. The technical differences in dealing with interoperability is long been exercised but the semantic differences has come in a big way. It became even bigger issue with the amount of information that is available today. The problem could be tackled with resolving the differences in understanding of information. So a form of semantic mapping can address such issues of understanding.

Web 3.0 aims to make computers understand semantics behind information. This would make them intelligent to process information and deliver the required knowledge. It could be argued that the information when encapsulated by semantics would provide knowledge. The relationship between Web 3.0 and Semantic Web is a topic of argument. There are suggestions that they are the same whereas some argue that Semantic Web is a sub-set of Web 3. Sir Tim Berners-Lee has described Semantic Web as a component of Web 3.

> "People keep asking what Web 3.0 is. I think maybe when you've got an overlay of scalable vector graphics - everything rippling and folding and looking misty - on Web 2.0 and access to a Semantic Web integrated across a huge space of data, you'll have access to an unbelievable data resource"
>
> Tim Berners-Lee, 2006, (Shannon, 2006)

This chapter covers different features of the Semantic Web.

3.1 The knowledge base

Description Logics supports serialization through the human readable forms of the real world scenario with the classification of concepts and individuals. Moreover, they support the hierarchical structure of concepts in forms of subconcepts/superconcepts relationships of a concept between the concepts of a given terminology. This hierarchical structure provides efficient inference through the proper relations between different concepts. The individual-concept relationship could be compared to instantiation of an object to its class in object-oriented concept. In this manner, the approach DL takes can be related to classification of objects in a real world scenario.

Description logics provide formalization to knowledge representation of real world situations. This means, it should provide the logical replies to the queries of real world situations. This is currently most researched topic in this domain. The results are highly sophisticated reasoning engines which utilize the capabilities of expressiveness of DLs to manipulate the knowledge. A Knowledge Representation system is a formal representation of knowledge described through different technologies. When it is describe through DLs, they set up a Knowledge Base (KB), the contents of which could be reasoned or infer to manipulate them. A knowledge base could be considered as a complete package of knowledge content. It is however only a subset of a KR system that contains additional components.

Figure 4 (Baader & Nutt, 2002) sketches the architecture of any KR system based on DLs. It could be seen the central theme of such a system is a Knowledge Base (KB). The KB constitutes of two components: the TBox and the ABox.

TBox statements are the terms or the terminologies that are used within the system domain. In general they are statements describing the domain through the controlled vocabularies. For example in terms of a social domain the TBox statements are the set of concepts as People, Male,Female, Father, Daughter etc. or the set of roles as marriedTo, siblingOf, sonOf, hasDaughter etc. ABox in other hand contains assertions to the TBox statements. For example Ashish is a Male is an ABox statement. In object oriented concept ABox statements compliant TBox statements through instantiating what is equivalent to classes in TBox and relating the roles (equivalent to methods or properties in OO concept) to those instances. The DLs are expressed through the concepts and roles of a particular domain. This complements well with the fact how knowledge is expressed in the general term. Concepts are sets of classes of individual objects. Classes provide an abstraction mechanism for grouping resources with similar characteristics (Bechhofer, et al., 2004).

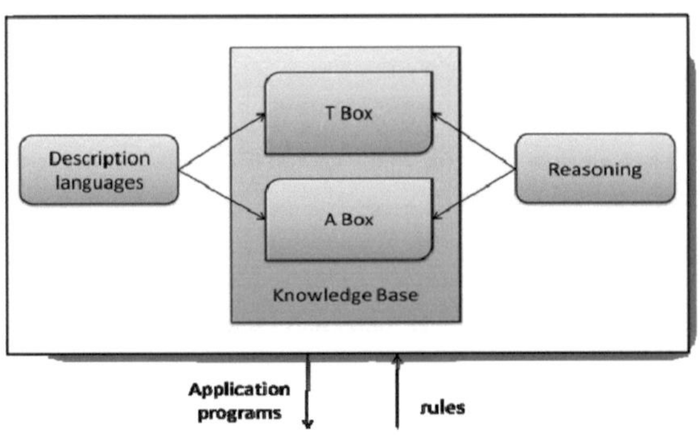

Fig. 4. The Architecture of a knowledge representation system based on DLs.

The concepts can be organized into superclass-subclass hierarchy which is also known as taxonomy. It shares the object-oriented concepts in managing the hierarchy of superconcept-subconcept. The subconcepts are specialized concepts of their superconcepts and the superconcepts are generalized concepts of their subconcepts. The subsumption algorithm determines the superclass-subclass relationships. For an example all individuals of a class must be individuals of its superclass. In general all concepts are subsumed by their superclass. In any graphical representation of knowledge concepts are represented through the nodes. Similarly the roles are binary relationship between concepts and eventually the relationships of the individuals of those concepts. They are represented by links in the graphical representation of knowledge. The description language has a model-theoretic semantics as the language for building the descriptions is independent to each DL system. Thus, statements in the TBox and in the ABox can be identified as first-order logic or, in some cases, a slight extension of it (Baader & Nutt, 2002).

3.2 The Semantic Web stack

The Semantic Web stack also called the Semantic Web cake is basically a hierarchy of the technologies composed of different layers. Each layer takes advantages of the capabilities concerning all the sub-layers. The following figure 5. illustrates the Semantic Web cake.

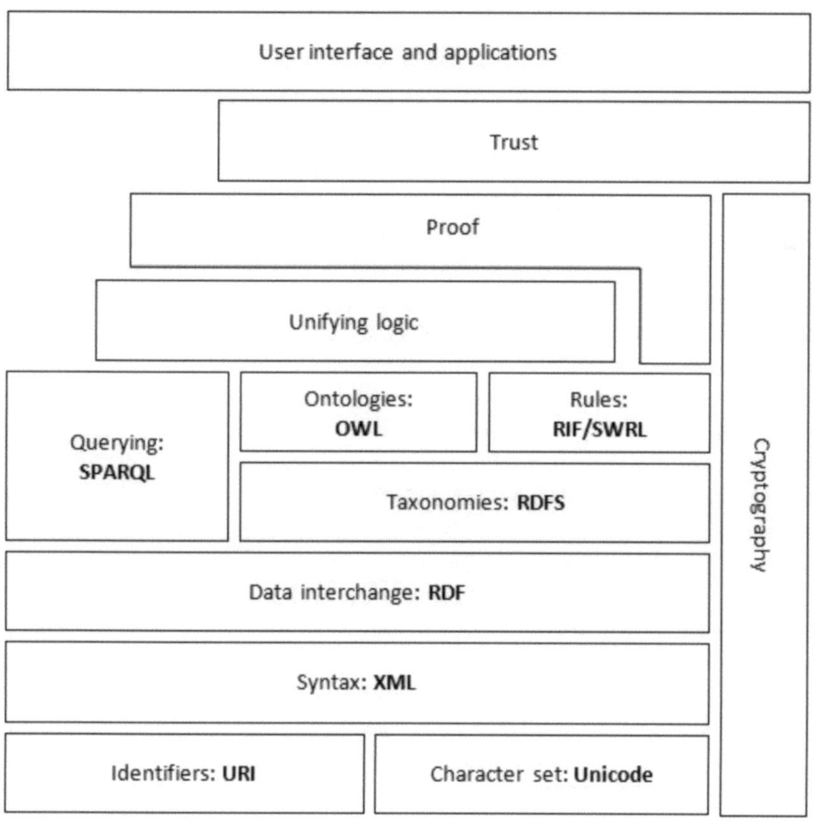

Fig. 5. The Semantic Web Stack.

There is a degrees of uncertainty in which the Semantic Web cake is defined. There are four versions of this cake till date, and none of them have been published in the literatures. All the four versions are presented by Berners-Lee in his presentations (Gerber et al., 2008). The components and their relationships are hence been defined profoundly. It is thus necessary to isolate each component and discuss their role in terms of the Web. The definitions of some layers within the semantic cake are illusive and could be interpreted in many ways. However, some layers especially the lower layers have clear definitions. Here, these hierarchical layers are discussed in terms of the knowledge representation approach. The layers in the Semantic Web stack can generally be divided into three categories: syntactic layers, knowledge layers and certifying layers composing of different technologies to support the technology.

The bottom layers are information holding layers and are either presented in uniform language or the through XML based information. The components within this layer hold the technologies that are direct descendent technologies from the hypertext Web. Though they are carryovers from basic technologies, they provide strong base to the Semantic Web. The technologies within these layers present syntactical representation of the information and thus be grouped into one common category of syntactic layers. They are capable to hold huge amount of information in each of the individual technologies within the level. These technologies include basic technologies as URI or content based technologies as XML and RDF. Despite rich with contents they lack interpretations as they do not possess semantics within.

The middle section contains layers which represents knowledge. These layers generally represent the technologies standardize by W3C for processing knowledge and can be grouped together to knowledge layer. The technologies here utilize the syntactically rich technologies in layers beneath. The knowledge is generated through attaching semantics to the information. RDFS provides vocabulary to RDF thus providing semantics to the structured statements representing the information as triplets. Through RDFS technology it is possible to derive hierarchical representations of objects and relate the objects to each other. The technology bridges the gaps between syntactically rich contents and tools to interpret knowledge from these contents. RDFS can define ontologies. Ontologies play important roles in order to provide semantics to the information or to the contents by providing suitable vocabulary to the contents and uplift contents to resources which could be related to real world objects. As a result of the work of the W3C Web Ontology Working Group, the "Ontology" layer has now been instantiated with the Web Ontology Language (OWL (Smith et al., 2004)) (Horrocks et al., 2005) due to its extended constructs to describe the semantics of the RDF statement. The semantic within the ontologies and expressed through OWL can be used within the ontologies and the knowledge bases themselves for the inferences. However, in order to express the rules independent to the languages two standards are emerging in the form of RIF (Boley & Kifer, 2010) and Semantic Web Rule Language (SWRL) (Horrocks et al., 2004). The rules are supported through inference engines. Simple Protocol and RDF Query Language (SPARQL) (Prud'hommeaux & Seaborne, 2008) is SQL equivalent language for querying data stored as RDF resources. As OWL is basically written in RDF pattern so the query could be applied to it as well. The topmost layer within knowledge layer is the unifying logic layer. This layer provides the logic behind knowledge manipulation through the reasoning capabilities of reasoning engines. This layer has not been formally defined so subjected to certain degrees of manipulation.

The top two layers in the stack are not yet fully conceptualized in terms of their applicability. These layers contain technologies which are not standardized yet but still they point toward maintaining the authenticity in the knowledge generated. The layer describing proof is therefore presumed responsible for providing evidence for the accuracy. At present no technology recommended to support this layer exists but there is an attempt for developing a proof language called Proof Mark-up Language (PML (da Silva et al., 2004; Al-Feel et al., 2009)) by knowledge systems laboratory at Stanford University. The top most layer Trust is to certify the knowledge reliability and there is a degrees of confidence in the knowledge generated within the layers under it. Again, at present there is no technology to support the layer.

The figure 5 can hence be updated with the three categories defined in this section and is illustrated in figure 6.

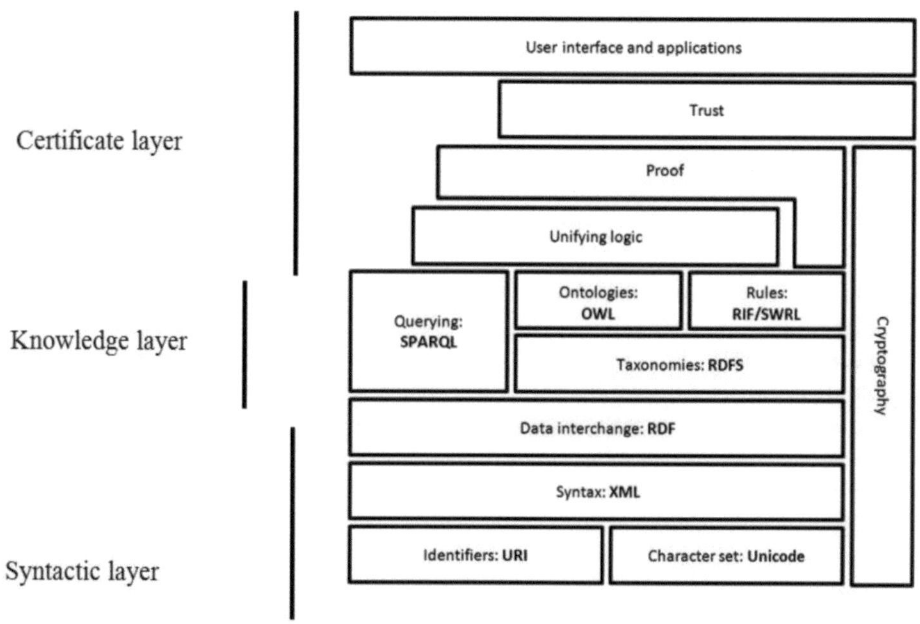

Fig. 6. The layers of the Semantic Web stack.

3.2.1 The syntactic layer

Semantic Web technologies are built up through the Web technologies that could hold up contents. The emergence of the eXtensible Markup Language (XML) marked the beginning of content based information in the Web environment. The language can encode information in machine readable format. The XML syntax is recommended in various data models and this syntactical approach laid a foundation for data models for defining metadata as Resource Description Framework (RDF). Resources are conventionally described through their metadata. The W3C recommended RDF as a standard to define the resources on Web.

W3C has defined five major reasons for developing the standard (Klyne et al., 2004). They focus on automatization of the information processing through serialization. That means the contents inside the documents are machine processable. In order for the documents to be machine processable they need to be machine readable and since the syntax of RDF is based on XML, it provides a mechanism to represent the information in machine readable manner.

The RDF (Resource Description Framework) is a graph data model. It is basically a framework to represent information on the Web. It has also been assigned as the standard model for data interchange on the Web by W3C because it can merge different sets of data irrespective to the underlying schema. RDF is conceptualized through graph data model which demonstrates the underlying structure of its expression. The nodes in the graph model are resources which can represent Uniform Resource Identifiers (URI reference or simply URIRef) or literals or even blank. The link in the graph representing properties are generally URI references. The literals within RDF expressions are generally assigned values of certain data types. RDF syntax is primarily based on its predecessor XML and is defined by RDF abstract syntax. This abstract syntax is the syntax over which the formal semantic are defined. It is a set of triples known as RDF graph (Klyne et al., 2004). It consists three parts which are normally called RDF triplet and represent a statement of relationship between the objects.

3.2.2 The Knowledge Layer

Knowledge representation has been described in five distinct roles it plays in (Davis et al., 1993). Those roles are

- A surrogate for the thing itself used to enable an entity to determine consequences by thinking rather than acting, i.e., by reasoning about the world rather than acting it.
- A set of ontological commitments, i.e., an answer to the question: In what terms should I think about the world?
- A fragmentary theory of intelligent, reasoning, expressed in terms of three components
  - The representation's fundamental conception of intelligent reasoning
  - The set of inferences the representation sanctions; and
  - The set of inferences it recommends
- A medium for pragmatically efficient computation, i.e., the computational environment in which thinking is accomplished.
- A medium for human to express, i.e., a language human expresses things about the world.

With these roles in view, different languages that represent the knowledge have been conceived over the time. They vary in terms of their characteristics, expressive power and computational complexity. The effectiveness of any representation language can be measured in:

- The expressiveness of the language is measured in terms of the range through which the language can use its constructs to describe the components in knowledge model.
- The strictness in the language is measured through the consistency and satisfiability within the knowledge model. The consistency and satisfiabilty issue is important in any

knowledge model because they decide the reliability of the model. If any model contains statements which contradict with each other, the model cannot be considered reliable. For an example A cannot be a father and son of B at the same time. Such statements should be rigorously audited for the model to be reliable enough.

- The semantic within the model should not be ambiguous. The meaning of each statement within the model should be clear and unambiguous.

RDFS

RDFS or the RDF Schema is the semantic extension of RDF. The applications using RDF uses it to describe its resources and those descriptions can be modeled as relationships among Web resources. These models constitute of interrelationships among the resources. They are carried out through the named properties and values. It however lacks the mechanism of defining the relationships between properties and other resources. Furthermore RDF data models do not declare these properties. They are hence information without any semantics. RDFS is designed to address these shortcomings. RDFS provides mechanisms for describing groups of related resources and the relationships between these resources.

The Web Ontology Language (OWL)

OWL or the Web Ontology Language is a family of knowledge representation language to create and manage ontologies. It is in general term an extension of RDFS with addition to richer expressiveness that RDFS lacks through its missing features (Antoniou & Harmelen, 2003). The OWL Working Group has approved two versions of OWL: OWL 1 and OWL 2. This research work uses OWL 1 for the applications of ontology as this version was the most used version at the time of research. The later version of OWL 1 was just evolving during the period. This research work discusses its activities in terms of OWL 1.

The expressiveness of OWL depends upon the level of serialization. The expressiveness of OWL comes at the cost of computational efficiency and reasoning effectiveness. This tradeoff between expressiveness and reasoning support was addressed through classifying OWL into three sub languages by the W3C Web Ontology working group.

OWL Full contains the maximum expressiveness but may lack in computational processing capability. It may also have restricted reasoning efficiency. OWL Full is completely compatible with RDF/RDFS both syntactically and semantically. OWLDL is compatible to the components of description logics and provides the functionalities of DLs. It provides the complete computational efficiency and reasoning capabilities. It is sub language of OWL Full with all OWL language constructs which could be used only through certain restrictions (McGuinness & Harmelen, 2004). This restriction is even more in OWL Lite - the third sublanguage of OWL. The advantage of this language is its easiness to understand and implement but the drawback is it is just a simple and fast migration from thesauri and other taxonomies.

The SPARQL language

It has been stated before that RDF statements store data in the form of informative contents. In this manner, it could be easily argued RDF documents are datasets complimenting the data storage capability of its conventional counterparts as database systems. As database systems provide efficient retrieval of the data through its query language in form of

Structured Query Language (SQL), the dataset within a RDF document can be retrieve through the query language called SPARQL. As with its counterpart SPARQL is also used to manage the RDF document. It is a key component of Semantic Web technology. As a query language, SPARQL is "data-oriented" in that it only queries the information held in the models; there is no inference in the query language itself. SPARQL does not do anything other than taking the description of what the application wants, in the form of a query, and returns that information in the form of a set of bindings or an RDF graph. In addition, the SPARQL is able to query OWL ontologies which use RDF graphs to structure them. However, no inferences are possible on that structure. SWRL is used for that purpose.

The query language has been standardized by W3C and has been recommended as official query language to retrieve RDF data (Prud'hommeaux & Seaborne, 2008).

SPARQL queries the RDF data in four distinct forms.

- SELECT returns the resulted dataset from this form. The results could be used accessed by the APIs as well could be serialized into XML or RDF graph.
- CONSTRUCT form constructs a RDF graph through running the query to derive the solution in solution sequence and then combines these triplets.
- ASK form is used to ask the authenticity of the query pattern. That means whether certain query pattern returns a solution or not.
- DESCRIBE forms describe the RDF data about its resources.

The SWRL language

An inference process consists of applying logic in order to derive a conclusion based on the observations and hypothesis. In computer science Inferences are applied through inference engines. These inference engines are basically computer applications which derive answers from a knowledge base. These engines depend on the logics through logic programming.

The horn logic more commonly known Horn clause is a clause with at most one positive literal. It has been used as the base of logic programming and Prolog languages (Sterling & Shapiro, 1994) for years. These languages allow the description of knowledge with predicates. Extensional knowledge is expressed as facts, while intentional knowledge is defined through rules (Spaccapietra et al., 2004). These rules are used through different Rule Languages to enhance the knowledge possess in ontology. The Horn logic has given a platform to define Horn-like rules through sub languages of RuleML (Boley, 2009). There have been different rule languages that have emerged in last few years. Some of these languages that have been evolving rapidly are Semantic Web Rule Language (SWRL) and JenaRule. Both have their own built-ins to support the rules. This research work uses SWRL to demonstrate the concepts but it could be applied to others rule language based on Horn clauses.

Semantic Web Rule Language (SWRL (Horrocks et al., 2004)) is a rule language based on the combination of the OWL-DL (SHOIN(D)) with Unary/Binary Datalog RuleML which is a sublanguage of the Rule Markup Language. One restriction on SWRL called DL-safe rules was designed in order to keep the decidability of deduction algorithms. This restriction is not about the component of the language but on its interaction. SWRL includes a high-level abstract syntax for Horn-like rules. The SWRL as the form, antecedent→consequent, where both antecedent and consequent are conjunctions of atoms written a1^ ... ^ an. Atoms in rules can be of the form C(x), P(x,y), Q(x,z), sameAs(x,y), differentFrom(x,y), or builtIn(pred, z1, ..., zn), where C is an OWL description, P is an OWL individual-valued property, Q is an OWL data-valued property, pred is a datatype predicate URIref, x and y are either individual-valued variables or OWL individuals, and z, z1, ... zn are either data-valued variables or OWL data literals. An OWL data literal is either a typed literal or a plain literal. Variables are indicated by using the standard convention of prefixing them with a question mark (e.g., ?x). URI references (URIrefs) are used to identify ontology elements such as classes, individual-valued properties and data-valued properties. For instance, the following rule asserts that one's parents' brothers are one's uncles where parent, brother and uncle are all individual-valued properties.

$$\text{parent}(?x, ?p) \wedge \text{brother}(?p, ?u) \rightarrow \text{uncle}(?x, ?u) \quad (1)$$

The set of built-ins for SWRL is motivated by a modular approach that will allow further extensions in future releases within a (hierarchical) taxonomy. SWRL's built-ins approach is also based on the reuse of existing built-ins in XQuery and XPath, which are themselves based on XML Schema by using the Datatypes. This system of built-ins should also help in the interoperation of SWRL with other Web formalisms by providing an extensible, modular built-ins infrastructure for Semantic Web Languages, Web Services, and Web applications. Many built-ins are defined and some of most common built-ins can be found in (Horrocks et al., 2004). These built-ins are keys for any external integration. The research work develops spatial built-in for the integration of spatial data structure.

3.3 Discussion

The Semantic Web, a set of technologies complementing the conventional Web tools proposed by Sir Tim Berners-Lee is seen as the most probabilistic approach to reach the goal of semantic interoperability. The Semantic Web is envisaged as an extension to the existing Web from a linked document repository into the platform where information is provided with the semantic allowing better cooperation between people and their machines. This is to be achieved by augmenting the existing layout information with semantic annotations that add descriptive terms to Web content, with meaning of such terms being defined in ontologies (Horrocks et al., 2004). Ontologies play crucial role in conceptualizing a domain and thus play an important role in enabling Web-based knowledge processing, sharing and reuse between applications.

This research takes advantages of the tools of Semantic Web technology to make a case of information management through knowledge. The case study of Industrial Archaeology fits perfectly to put forward the concept of information handling through knowledge as the domain generates huge and heterogeneous dataset. In addition the sites are not preserved for continuing excavation as in case of the conventional archaeology, making it ideal for utilizing knowledge techniques to manage the information because of the flexibility in knowledge techniques to handle information long after they are collected. The definition of a domain ontology representing the site is sketched out by the archaeologists. It is again their task to fill in knowledge in the domain ontology to make it a knowledge base where one can reason to derive new knowledge. Archaeologists use collaborative Web platform based on Semantic Web technology to identify the objects and define them in the ontology. These objects once defined, performs as common schemas between data sources to achieve a sense of data interoperability. The definitions of objects add semantics to the objects and thus adding knowledge about the objects. Knowledge techniques based on Description Logics (DLs) exploit these semantics to manipulate implicit knowledge within the knowledge base. Inference engines utilize the definition of DLs to infer the knowledge base through Horn based rules. The knowledge base stored in OWL syntactic structure is inferred through SWRL to infer the rules. This inference is complimented through querying with SPARQL.

Carrying the discussion from last chapter, this research attempts to use the Semantic Web techniques to perform spatial analysis in form of spatial SPARQL and spatial SWRL. The spatial analysis through Semantic Web can only be possible through providing spatial signatures to the defined objects in the ontology. This will allow the knowledge techniques to process spatial solutions. The spatial integration is carried out through OWL/RDF again and the spatial management is carried out again through tools as SWRL and SPARQL. This simplistic yet but effective approach of spatial integration into Semantic Web technologies provides the possibility to include different modes of data into its framework.

The Semantic Web stack shown in figure 5 and 6 can adjust a layer of spatial information into it. The research proposes such an arrangement in the stack. A layer of spatial data mixing seamlessly with the semantic proposition in the layer Ontology through its OWL/RDF based syntax can be envisaged. This layer since uses the standard syntax of OWL/RDF can perform spatial queries through SPARQL or infer rules through standards as SWRL. The next chapter discusses this integration process of spatial technology and Semantic Web technology which is undertaken by defining spatial FILTERs for SPARQL queries and spatial Built-ins for SWRL rules. Ideally the layer should be the top most layer of knowledge level but spatial layer does not yet possess any standards that are standardized by W3C so could not be placed there. It is hence placed as the bottom layer in the certificate level. The next chapter discusses this adjustment in stack in detail and how to apply spatial queries and rules on any existing ontology.

4. The spatial layer of the WS stack

This chapter presents the integration process of spatial technologies and the Semantic Web technologies at the backdrop of Industrial Archaeology, and its associated tool called the spatial facilitator which is a query and rule engine. The technologies discussed in previous chapters are used and adjusted for processing the spatial knowledge through knowledge technologies within the Semantic Web framework in the research works. This chapter attempts to outline the methods and the processes of these adjustments and how they return the results through knowledge tools as SWRL and SPARQL.

The discussions of the last two chapters aim at laying a background on the concepts of integration process. The discussions on Semantic Web and its underlying technologies and the spatial technology in GIS in the last two chapters have clearly pointed out that the technical advancements toward semantic technologies are integrating every data structures so it will integrate spatial data structure in future. However, for now it is still a topic of research. It could be conceived from earlier discussions that the integration process requires adjustments of the spatial components within the ontological framework. This chapter is dedicated to discuss the steps and process of this adjustment. The spatial signature of objects plays an important role in determining them. The identification of objects is the process of signing these spatial signatures on them. These signatures should be integrated within the semantics of the objects seamlessly in order to process the spatial knowledge through the knowledge technology. It should be noted however that the Semantic Web technologies are in the maturation process and hence there exists certain processing problems within especially for the non-conventional data type as that of spatial data. Thus, it needs to be sorted out through the existing tested techniques. The research in GIS systems uses the capabilities of existing RDBMS to process the spatial data through spatial operations and functions and use the results of these processes.

The Semantic Web stack discussed in the previous chapter can be updated to address the inclusion of a spatial component. Every tangible object has its spatial signature and thus it becomes indispensable to address the spatial component within its semantic framework. The Semantic Web technologies and its architecture are mostly influenced by the nature of information available on the Internet. Hence, these levels deals mostly with managing the semantic based information through knowledge technologies. However, in recent years there has been huge surge of other forms of information on Web platform and they need to be managed as well. With the advancement in spatial technologies, the trend of disseminating spatial information through Web based environment is rapidly growing. This has raised the issue of the integration of spatial component into the Semantic Web framework.

A layer representing geospatial data in the Semantic Web stack can be placed just above the knowledge layers as could be seen in figure 7. As the technologies within knowledge level are standardized by W3C, the geospatial layer needs to be above the level. However, the technologies within knowledge level needs to blend spatial components seamlessly both syntactically and semantically to maintain the satisfiability required for the consistency of the ontology. This integration procedure should be adjusted within the knowledge tool within the knowledge level of the stack. This approach thus uses the knowledge techniques through adding the spatial structures within them and implementing the spatial knowledge processing along with semantic knowledge processing. The first Semantic Web tool that comes direct in contact with the integration procedure is the structural schema of the knowledge base which is termed as top level ontology in general sense. The top level ontology is the structural schema that represents the nature of knowledge the ontology possesses. It should include the components to adjust the behavior of the knowledge base. Hence the initial task that needs to be adjusted within any top level ontology to perform spatial knowledge processing is to include spatial components within it.

The top level ontology is the structural schema that represents the nature of knowledge the ontology possesses. It should be noted that the top level ontology is syntactically presented through OWL/RDF and contains the top level concepts of the domain. Among these top level concepts, the concepts presenting the spatial components for storage, retrieval and processing of the spatial knowledge should be present. Moving down to the enrichment process, the spatial signatures are mapped to the objects within the knowledge base is again

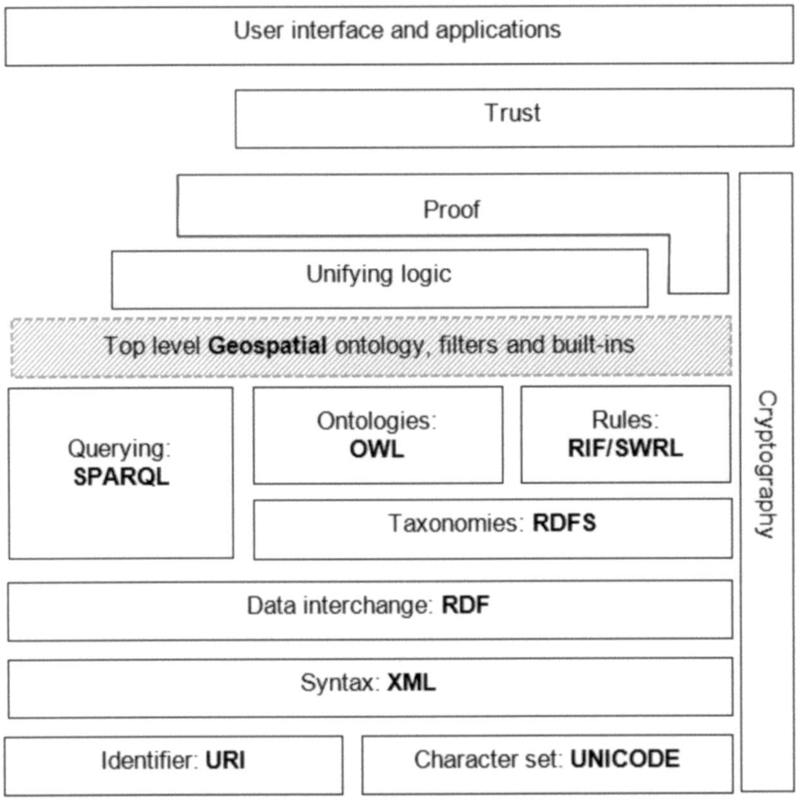

Fig. 7. The inclusion of a Geospatial layer in the Semantic Web Stack.

encoded with OWL/RDF syntax. The methodology of this integration is discussed in later sections within this chapter.

Similarly, the spatial filters and spatial built-ins defined in this layer facilitate the spatial querying and the spatial rule definition. The layers of Rules: SWRL/RIF and Querying: SPARQL provide a base to knowledge management through processing the spatial information semantically within the knowledge base. The only adjustment that is needed is to execute the built-ins and filters in conjunction to the processing capabilities of spatial extensions within current database systems.

Putting forward the arguments on the authenticity of the layer with respect to other layers, the geospatial layer exploits the capabilities of the layers below maintaining the trend of the stack. At the time of integration, the spatial components are included within the top level ontology which stores, retrieves and processes spatial knowledge and utilizes the capabilities of the other technologies in the stack. The spatial components on the top level ontology and the mapped spatial signatures are encoded through the OWL/RDF syntactical structure thus justifying the involvement of ontologies in the stack. Then after, the capability of the SWRL language is exploited through spatial built-ins for spatial SWRL rules. Similarly, the querying capability of the SPARQL language is exploited through spatial filters for the query language. These filters and built-ins can be used with conjunction to already standardized filters and built-ins of both the technologies thus forwarding the arguments of the process in standardizing these built-ins too.

4.1 The top level ontology

The top level ontology or more popularly upper ontology describes the general concept behind the knowledge domain. This ontology varies with the domain it addresses. There are efforts to come out with a universal upper ontology which addresses the requirements of every knowledge domains but they still are in the phase of researches. Every domain uses its own standard upper ontology for its purpose. This research work attempts to propose an upper level ontology for the domain of industrial archaeology. This top level ontology is the main driving force behind the ArchaeoKM framework. It represents the knowledge possessed by archaeologists in form of descriptions, observations and rules represented through different axioms within the ontology. This ontology serves as a foundational ontology to which objects can be instantiated during identification process. The axioms are the building blocks of the ontology. The integration of spatial components within the framework holds major importance and is required to be adjusted within the top level ontology of ArchaeoKM. The spatial extension of the top level ontology is discussed in the next section.

4.2 The spatial top level ontology

The realization of spatial signatures of the identified objects in the knowledge base has been discussed earlier. The attachments of these spatial signatures provide a framework that could exploit the developments in spatial technology to provide the objects their spatial identity in respect to their surrounding objects. However, it is important to adjust the components of the spatial technology in the top level ontology. This section covers the spatial top level ontology of the ArchaeoKM framework.

Although the impact of spatial integration is realized in the semantic level when the spatial components are integrated in the ontology, the usage of spatial features begins earlier than that. The spatial functionalities provided by database system form foundations to how they should be adjusted. A parallel structure facilitating the spatial components in different levels of the system architecture has already been presented in chapter 2 through figure 3. At the syntactic level where most of knowledge generation activities are carried out, spatial components are handled through spatially annotating the identified objects. This spatial annotation process draws a Minimum Bounding Rectangles (MBRs) around the objects and stores them as spatial data type in PostgreSQL database system. These MBRs would be used to carry out spatial rules while managing knowledge. It should be noted that the MBRs are not the optimal way of representing the objects and would constitutes some degrees of error during the analysis process. The ideal approach would be to use the boundaries of the objects for representation and analysis purpose. The algorithm to extract point cloud from the boundary is still in the domain of research and not completely matured and hence this research uses MBRs to put forward the ideas.

It is the semantic level where the most of the integration work is carried out. The domain ontology is modified to represent the spatial functions and operations within it. The research work revolves around two categories of spatial operations and the integration process takes the functions and operations within these two categories which are the georelationship functions and the geoprocessing functions. These functions are defined by the OGC consortium. The Open Geospatial Consortium, Inc. (OGC) is an international industry consortium of 404 companies, government agencies and universities participating in a consensus process to develop publicly available interface standards. OpenGIS® Standards support interoperable solutions that "geo-enable" the Web, wireless and location-based services, and mainstream IT. The standards empower technology developers to make complex spatial information and services accessible and useful with all kinds of applications.

The top level ontology should model spatial technology in terms of its spatial functions and operations. This modeling process should accommodate the spatial functions and operations and maintain their true identity.

4.3 Translation engine

The translation engine is a part of the spatial facilitator that allows the computation of spatial SPARQL queries and spatial SWRL rules. In both cases, the translation engine interprets the statements in order to parse the spatial components. Once the spatial components are parsed, they are computed through relevant spatial functions and operations by the translation engine through the operations provided at the database level. The results are populated in the knowledge base thus making it spatially rich. After that, the spatial statements are translated to standard statements for the executions through their respective engines. With the inference engine, the enrichment and the population of the ontology through the results of the inference process is stored in the ontology.

The next sections present in details the translation engine and more specifically the translation process of spatial SPARQL queries to regular queries. The following one presents the translation process of spatial SWRL rules to regular SWRL rules. These two processes have in common the use of SQL statements to query to the spatial database.

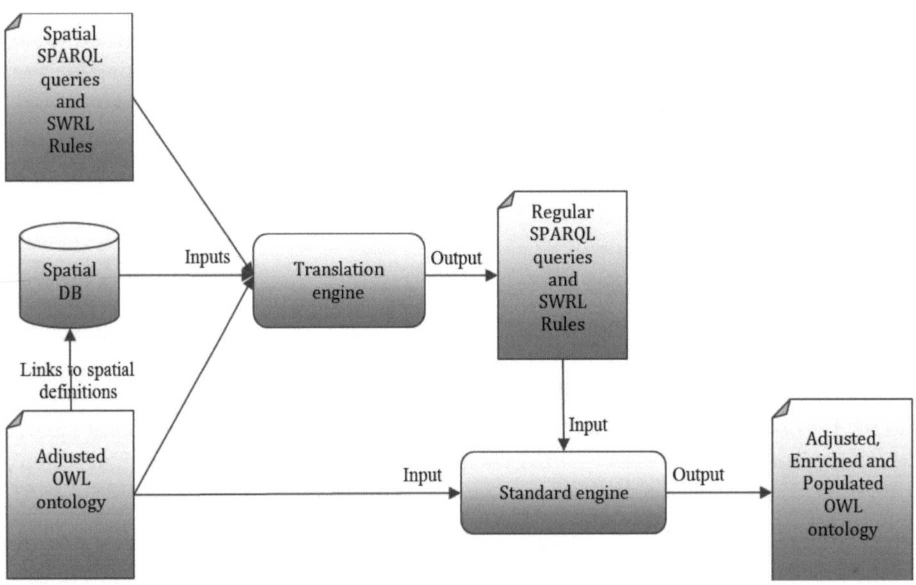

Fig. 8. The spatial processing of the translation Engine.

4.3.1 Spatial SPARQL queries

FILTERs can be used to compare strings and derive results. The functions like regular expression which matches plain literal with no language tag can be used to match the lexical forms of other literals by using string comparison function. In addition, SPARQL FILTER uses the relational operators as = or > or < for the comparison and restrict to the results that they return. The FILTER principle can hence be extended in order to process the geospatial functions.

Geoprocessing FILTER

Geoprocessing functions need to be addressed through enriching the knowledge base with the spatial operations which is related to them during the execution of the query. The enrichment process should be rolled back after the results are returned into its original form iff the SELECT statement is used under the filter. The optimization of the SPATIAL_FILTER is discussed later which highlights the management of the knowledge base during the execution of the SPARQL queries.

The following example demonstrates the syntax of geoprocessing filters in SPARQL. It could be seen that a new spatial filter through the keyword SPATIAL_FILTER is introduced which helps the translation engine during the parsing process. The SPARQL statement with spatial filters in the example returns names of all the buildings in class feat:Building which are intersecting with the buffer of 2000 meters of the rivers in class feat:River with their respective rivers names.

```
SELECT ?name1 ?name2
WHERE
{
        ?feat1      feat:name      ?name1
        ?feat2      feat:name      ?name2
        ?feat1      rdfs:type            feat:River
        ?feat2      rdfs:type            feat:Building

        SPATIAL_FILTER [buffer (?x, 2000,?feat1)]
        SPATIAL_FILTER [intersection (?y,?x,?feat2)]
}
```

Georelationship FILTER

In case of georelationship filter, it is straightforward as the enrichment process requires enriching the object properties imitating spatial relationship between objects through the results of the spatial operations at the database level. As with the previous case, the georelationship filter uses the keyword SPATIAL_FILTER. This keyword parses the spatial components from the SPARQL statements. The following example illustrates the execution of SPARQL with these filters. The first feature is a feat:River which is of kind of feat:Feature, and the second feature is a feat:Building which is also of kind of feat:Feature. The SPATIAL_FILTER selects the rivers and buildings which are touching spatially.

```
SELECT ?name1 ?name2
WHERE
{
        ?feat1          feat:name       ?name1
        ?feat2          feat:name       ?name2
        ?feat1          rdfs:type               feat:River
        ?feat2          rdfs:type
            feat:Building

        SPATIAL_FILTER [touches (?feat1, ?feat2)]
}
```

4.3.2 Inference rules through SWRL

In an attempt to define the built-ins for SWRL, a list of eight built-ins was proposed during the research work. These eight built-ins reflect four geoprocessing functions and four georelationship functions that are discussed previously. The built-ins reflecting geoprocessing functions are built up in combinations with the spatial classes adjusted in the ontology and their relevant object properties. The built-ins for georelationship functions are object properties and corresponding spatial functions in database system.

The domain of archaeology benefits from this work and could surely be of benefit for lot of other domains. To show this we present a simple example to determine the location of possible flooding zone when the river bank bursts with excessive water during rainy season. This is a very common exercise for a flood management system in hydrology and it gives interesting clues for archaeology. In general with a common GIS, a set of activities are carried out which are mentioned in the following sequences:

- Buffer the river by certain distance (e.g. 100 meters)
- Determine the elevation of land parcel inside the buffer zone
- Check whether the land parcel elevation is above the threshold (e.g. 25 meters)
- Select areas below the threshold area and determine them as flood liable zone.

It should be understood that this example is provided just as a proof of the concept. Hence details on other hydrological factors are ignored on purpose. For a simple location analysis as such requires at least four steps of spatial analyses. This paper provides an alternative through the spatial extension of SWRL in one step. We combine the existing built-ins in existing SWRL and the spatial built-in mentioned in this paper to execute this analysis.

River(?x) ^ LandParcel(?y) ^ hasElevation(?y, ?Elv) ^ swrlb:lessThan(?Elv, 25) ^
spatialswrlb:Buffer(?x, 50, ?z) ^ spatialswrlb:Intersection(?z, ?y, ?res)→
FloodingLandParcel(?y) (2)

The result of this rule is that the individuals which respect the rule and belong to LandParcel, belong also to the concept FloodingLandParcel.

5. Conclusion

This research has made an attempt to contribute through including the functionalities of spatial analysis within the Semantic Web framework. Moving beyond the semantic information, it has opened the chapter of inclusion of other form of information. It is important for the development of the technology itself. The world is witnessing a shift in technology and the Semantic Web is the direction the shift is moving towards. This would mean that the technology including that of GIS is moving towards the flexible solutions through knowledge based systems from static solution through current database systems. Hence, it is important to raise issues of integrating non-typical semantic data into it. This research work at least provides certain vision towards the direction the technology is taking to integrate these forms of data. It discusses the direction in terms of spatial integration. There are other data patterns like temporal data which need to be addressed too.

This concluding chapter begins with summarizing the work contribution that has been presented in previous chapters. It then discusses the contribution made to different related discipline. Lastly, the chapter concludes the future prospect and the direction of the research work in this field.

5.1 Contribution

This research attempts to highlight the possibilities to integrate spatial technology in Semantic Web framework. It moves beyond the scope of data interoperability while presenting the concept and makes efforts to utilize the potentiality in other areas of the Semantic Web technologies. The underlying technologies of knowledge processing provide the Semantic Web capabilities to process the semantics of the information through close collaboration with the machine. It makes not only the understanding of data easier for achieving interoperability among different data sources, but it also provides valuable knowledge which could enrich the knowledge base in order to equip it with new knowledge through the knowledge management techniques. This helps the users understand the data better.

5.1.1 In the industrial archaeology domain

This research benefits from the advancement in Semantic Web technologies and its knowledge representation formalization tools and techniques. The primary principle of 4Ks processing is based on the knowledge formalization techniques. The research uses the case study of the industrial archaeology to demonstrate the possibility of implementation of application based on Semantic Web and utilizes the knowledge possessed by the archaeologists to manage the information recovered. This turns out to be an ideal case for the experimentation as the site for industrial archaeology is available for short duration of time. With the conventional technology it is difficult to manage the information due to share volume of data and the limitation of available time. It is however seen that with 4Ks implemented within the application prototype of the ArchaeoKM framework, the information could be managed. There has always been active involvement of archaeologists in every phase of design and development. The domain ontology and its axioms and theorems are based on their experiences. The enrichments of domain ontology through the identification of objects are carried out by them. It is the first K, Knowledge Acquisition. The knowledge acquired through the identification process is managed through defining relationships. It is again the archaeologists with the ArchaeoKM platform to manage knowledge through adjuring proper relationships (which reflects archaeologists view of the world) to the objects and semantically annotating them to the data and documents collected. The process is second K: Knowledge Management. The third K is Knowledge Visualization which generally means that knowledge identified and managed could be visualized through the interfaces of the ArchaeoKM platform. The knowledge base enriched and managed through the collaborative approach of archaeologists could be analyzed through inferring the knowledge base with rules formulated by archaeologists. These rules are inferred through SWRL - a rule language for Semantic Web standardized by W3C (Horrocks et al., 2004). It is the last K, Knowledge Analysis.

5.1.2 In the geospatial domain

The 4Ks processing principle is implemented during the integration of spatial technology. The domain ontology is modified to adjust the spatial components into it. The research work considers the advancement in spatial technology in modern database systems. It implements the notations standardized by OGC simple feature specification (Herring, 2010) during the inclusion of the spatial components as axioms into the ontology. The spatial technologies provide spatial functions and operations to perform spatial analysis. These functions and operations are categorized into four major categories as documented in PostGIS documentation. However, the research implements functions under geoprocessing and georelationship functions as these two categories consist of mostly all the spatial functions. Geoprocessing functions are implemented as class axioms which relate to the classes containing features through the respective object properties. Likewise the georelationship functions are treated as object properties relating the classes containing features spatially to each other.

The knowledge acquisition process comprises of acquiring spatial signatures of the object. In general they are acquired during the identification process. However, the spatial signatures are formalized during spatial annotations of the objects which are then stored in database as spatial data type. The spatial operations and functions which are encoded as classes and object properties within the ontology provide the management of spatial knowledge. The ontology was spatially enriched through the spatial operations and functions at the database level. This enriched knowledge base can be inferred spatially through the spatial built-ins for SWRL proposed in the research. The research also proposes the spatial filters for query language of the Semantic Web (SPARQL) (Harris & Seaborne, 2010).

The benefits to geospatial community are prominent. The shift from data oriented to knowledge oriented GIS gives the GIS an edge. The flexibility of knowledge based systems should add the flexibility to GIS in terms of data acquisition, data management and data analysis. The data acquisition process though still remains to the conventional digitization techniques; the possibility of linking it up to its semantics adds knowledge to the whole process. This added knowledge then could be utilized for different purposes including semantic interoperation between other data from other sources. However, this paper discusses in terms of knowledge management and analysis. The knowledge query through

SPARQL or knowledge inference through SWRL to the spatially rich knowledge base generates new knowledge which is more authentic in a sense that this new result is the manipulation of knowledge base through the existing one. It is not just data any more. The semantic behind the results provides support to their authenticity.

This research has provided GIS community an alternative to conventional spatial data analysis through spatial rules. It can be opined that the proposed approach of knowledge analysis is apparent and less complicated to the conventional one. As the spatial rules could be combined with general rules they have wider implications. Additionally, the rules are based on formal logics which relate to day-to-day human interpretations; they should be easy to understand and implement. Consequently, the research proposes a rule based approach for spatial analysis and provides an evidence of possibilities through the experimentation performed.

5.1.3 In the Semantic Web domain

A spatial layer in the Semantic Web stack presented through this paper is not enough to address the overall problems of non-semantic data within the framework but at least there is something to start with. The full potential of underlying knowledge techniques through the reasoning or inferring capabilities within Semantic Web has not been identified in Geospatial community. The primary focus on these technologies is to achieve data interoperability within different data sources (Cruz, 2004; Cruz et al., 2004) Even W3C concentrated its priority in proposing comprehensive geospatial ontology acceptable to all through its Geospatial Incubator Group (Lieberman et al., 2007). All these research works show that the emphasis on using geospatial ontology lie in achieving data interoperability and thus ignores the capabilities of underlying knowledge techniques for carrying out complex spatial analysis. This research presented a concept to carry out spatial analysis through inferring knowledge base spatially.

The realization of spatial integration into Semantic Web framework is demonstrated through a demonstration application. The application demonstrates that through a suitable translation engine, it is possible to infer the spatially enriched knowledge base in order to deduce spatial knowledge. The translation engine developed within the demonstration application translates the spatial built-ins and enriches the knowledge base through results of spatial operations of these built-ins making the knowledge base ready to be inferred.

5.2 Way forward

This research work has highlighted the benefits of tools and techniques of the Semantic Web and especially underlying knowledge technologies and their usages with the spatial technologies for the efficient management of spatial information. It has also been discussed that the approach presented here benefits both the Semantic Web and spatial technology. The research activities has just initiated the integration of spatial technology into the Semantic Web framework and still has long way to go. This section presents few areas where the research work could be continued in this area.

Researches in the field of spatial technology within the Semantic Web framework have not moved beyond geospatial ontology and the possibility of semantic interoperability between different sources. This research attempts to break that trend and use knowledge to manage the spatial data through knowledge management techniques. In the process, it provided the mechanisms to infer spatial rules through spatial built-ins for SWRL. This was done first through populating domain ontology with the spatial components so that spatial knowledge could be enriched into it and this spatially rich knowledge base is inferred through SWRL. It could also be queried through SPARQL. However there are number of issues that need to be addressed in future work. The first one is about the dependability on the database systems to conduct the spatial operations and functions. This research uses the spatial operations and functions provided by PostGIS, the spatial extension of PostgreSQL to enrich the knowledge base through their result. Future works should make an attempt to free them with such dependency through providing such functionalities within spatial built-ins themselves.

Another area where the research could concentrate is the area of using current reasoning engines to reason the spatial knowledge base and deduce the implicit spatial knowledge. In other words addition to the the inference engine to infer the rules through SWRL, the constraint axioms should be introduced within the ontology which automatize the enrichment of knowledge base through reasoning mechanism. The constraint axioms in particular should be able to include the spatial built-ins and run through the respective spatial operations and functions to automatize the enrichment process while reasoning the knowledge base. It can be clarified with one of the typical examples in industrial archaeology: "chimney should be 5 meters around an oven and should be round". Currently it is possible to execute this only through SWRL rule.

$$\text{feat:Object}(?x) \wedge \text{feat:Oven}(?y) \wedge \text{spatialswrlb:Buffer}(?y, 5, ?x) \wedge \text{att:hasShape}(?x, \text{round}) \rightarrow \text{feat:Chimney}(?x) \quad (3)$$

This infers the spatial knowledge base to annotate the result to the class feat:Chimney. However an alternative could be a theorem

$$\text{feat:Chimney} \sqsubseteq \text{Within}(\text{Buffer}(\text{feat:Oven},5)) \sqcap \text{hasShape}.\{\text{round}\} \quad (4)$$

can be thought upon. The existing reasoning engine then reasons every object with round shape around 5 meters of every oven and terms them as individuals of chimney.

Lastly, it is important to have standard terms for every built-in that will be developed to process spatial knowledge. With other built-ins in the tools standardized by W3C, the spatial built-ins should also get standardized by the consortium. In addition to W3C, OGC should also get involved in standardizing the built-ins. An effort in this direction should be carried out.

6. References

Al-Feel, H., Koutb, M. A., & Suoror, H. (2009). Toward An Agreement on Semantic Web Architecture, *World Academy of Science, Engineering and Technology* (49), 806-810.

Antoniou, G., & Harmelen, F. v. (2003). Web Ontology Language: OWL, *Handbook on Ontologies in Information Systems* (pp. 67 - 92). Springer Series.

Baader, F., & Nutt, W. (2002). Basic Description Logics, *Description Logic Handbook* (pp. 47 - 100). Cambridge: Cambridge University Press.

Baader, F., & Sattler, U. (2001). An overview of tableau algorithms for description logics. *Studia Logica* , (pp. 5 - 40), Springer.

Baader, F., Horrocks, I., & Sattler, U. (2003). Description Logics as Ontology Languages for the Semantic Web, *Festschrift in honor of Jörg Siekmann, Lecture Notes in Artificial Intelligence,* (pp. 228 - 248) Springer

Balletti, C., Guerra , F., & Adami, A. (2005). 3D Multiresolution Representations in Archaeological Sites, *ISPRS* (pp. 654-659), ISPRS XXXVI-5/C34.

Bateson, G. (1979). Mind and Nature: A Necessary Unity (Advances in Systems Theory, Complexity, and the Human Sciences). Hampton Press.

Bechhofer, S., Harmelen, F. v., Hendler, J., Horrocks, I., McGuinness, D. L., Patel-Schneider, P. F., et al. (2004, February 10). OWL Web Ontology Language, In: *W3C Recommendation*, Date of Access: November 27, 2009, Available from: http://www.w3.org/TR/owl-ref/

Bellinger, G. (2004). Knowledge Management—Emerging Perspectives, In: *Systems thinking*, Date of Access: December 13, 2010, Available from http://www.systems-thinking.org/kmgmt/kmgmt.htm

Berners-Lee, T. (1998, October 14). Why RDF model is different from the XML model, In: *W3C: A roadmap to the Semantic Web,* Date of Access: October 2010, 22, Available from: http://www.w3.org/DesignIssues/Overview.html

Berners-Lee, T., Hendler, J., & Lassila, O. (2001, May). The Semantic Web, *Scientific American*, pp. 34-43.

Berry, J. K. (1999). GIS Technology in Environmental Management: a Brief History, Trends and Probable Future. In D. L. Soden, & B. S. Steel (Eds.), *Handbook of Global Environmental Policy and Administration* (pp. 49 - 81). Decker, Marcel Inc.

Bobillo, F., & Straccia, U. (2009). Supporting Fuzzy Rough Sets in Fuzzy Description Logics, *Proceeding of 10th European Conference on Symbolic and Quantitative Approaches to Reasoning with Uncertainty*. 5590/2009, pp. 676-687. Verona: LNCS.

Boley, H. (2009, August 11). RuleML: The Rule Markup Initiative, In: *RuleML*, Date of Access: September 27, 2009, Available from: http://ruleml.org/

Boley, H., & Kifer, M. (2010, June 22). W3C Recommendation, In: *RIF Basic Logic Dialect*, Date of Access: August 24, 2010, Available from: http://www.w3.org/TR/rif-bld/

Boochs, F. (2009). Spatial information system for acquisition, documentation and analysis of industrial archaeological objects, *Proceeding of The International Committee for the Conservation of the Industrial Heritage Conference*. Freiberg: TICCIH 2009.

Brachman, R., Eugene, C., Norton, G., & Martin, Y. (1978). KLONE Reference Manual, Cambridge: Bolt Beranek And Newman Inc.

Calvanese, D., Giacomo, G. D., Lenzerini, M., & Nardi, D. (2001). Reasoning in expressive description logics, *In A. Robinson, & A. Voronkov (Eds.), Handbook of Automated Reasoning* (Vol. II, pp. 1581-1634). Elsevier Science Publishers.

Clouse, R. A. (1995). Industrial Archaeology, In: *Minnesota Historical Society of Archaeology*, Date of Access: September 23, 2010, Available from: http://www1.umn.edu/marp/indus/indus.html

Cosmas, J., Itagaki, T., Green, D., Grabczewski, E., Waelkens, M., & Degeest, R. (2001). 3D MURALE: A Multimedia System for Archaeology, VAST *(p. Virtual Reality: Archaeology and Cultural Heritage)*. Glyfada, Nr Athens: ACM.

Costa, S., & Zanini , E. (2008). Sharing knowledge in archaeology: looking forward the next decade(s), *Proceeding of Digital Heritage in the New Knowledge Environment: Shared spaces & open paths to cultural content*, Athens: Hellenic Ministry of Culture

Cruz, I. F. (2004). Geospatial Data Integration, Chicago: ADVIS Lab, Dept. of Computer Science, University of Illinois.

Cruz, I. F., Sunna, W., & Chaudhry, A. (2004). Semi-Automatic Ontology Alignment for Geospatial Data Integration, *GIScience 2004*, (pp. 51 - 66). MaryLand: LNCS.

da Silva, P. P., McGuinness, D. L., & Fikes, R. E. (2004). A Proof Markup Language for Semantic Web Services, Stanford: Stanford University.

Davis, R., Shrobe, H., & Szolovits, P. (1993). What is Knowledge Representation, *AI Magazine*, 14(1), (pp. 17 – 33)

Decker, S., Melnik, S., Harmelen, F. V., Fensel, D., Klein, M., Erdmann, M., et al. (2000). The Semantic Web: the roles of XML and RDF, *IEEE Internet Computing*, (pp. 63-74)

Doerr, M. (2008). The CIDOC Conceptual Reference Model - A new standard for Interoperability, *Digital Heritage in the New Knowledge Environment: Shared spaces & open paths to cultural content*, Athens: Hellenic Ministry of Culture.

Gerber, A., Merwe, A., & Barnard, A. (2008). A functional Semantic Web architecture, *Proceedings of the 5th European Semantic Web conference on The Semantic Web: research and applications* (pp. 273 -287). Tenerife: Springer-Verlag.

Gruber, T. R. (1993). A Translation Approach to Portable Ontology Specifications, *Knowledge Acqusition*, 5(2), (pp. 199 – 220)

Guarino, N. (1994). The Ontological Level, R. Casati, & G. White, Eds., *Philosophy and the congitive sciences*

Harris, S., & Seaborne, A. (2010, January 26). SPARQL Query Language 1.1, In: *Minnesota Historical Society of Archaeology*, Date of Access: September 2, 2010, Available from: http://www.w3.org/TR/2010/WD-sparql11-query-20100126/

Hellerstein, J. M., Naughton, J. F., & Preffer, A. (1995). Generalized Search Trees for Database Systems, *Proceedings of the 21th International Conference on Very Large Data Bases* (pp. 562 - 573). San Francisco: Morgan Kaufmann Publishers Inc.

Herman, I., Halpin, H., Hawke, S., Prud'hommeaux, E., Raggett, D., & Swick, R. (2010, February 06). W3C Semantic Web, In: *W3C Semantic Web Activity*, Date of Access: August 15, 2010, Available from: http://www.w3.org/2001/sw/

Herring, J. R. (2010). OpenGIS Implementation Standard for Geographic information - Simple feature access - Part 1: Common architecture, Open Geospatial Consortium Inc.

Horrocks, I., Parsia, B., Patel-Schneider, P., & Hendler, J. (2005). Semantic Web Architecture: Stack or Two Towers. *Proceeding of 3rd Internation Workshop on Principles and Practice of Semantic Web Reasoning* (pp. 37 - 41), Dagstuhl: LNCS .

Horrocks, I., Pater-Schneider, P. F., McGuinness, D. L., & Welty, C. A. (n.d.). OWL: a Description Logic Based Ontology Language for the Semantic Web.

Horrocks, I., Schneider, P. f., Boley, H., Tabelt, S., Grosof, B., & Dean, M. (2004, December 21). SWRL - A Semantic Web Rule Language - Combining OWL and RuleML, In: *SWRL: A Semantic Web Rule Language - Combining OWL and RuleML*, Date of Access: May 22, 2009, Available from: http://www.w3.org/Submission/SWRL/

Jones, C. (1997). Geographical Information Systems and Computer Cartography, Addison Wesley Longman Ltd.

Kansa, E. C. (2008). Opening Archaeology to Mash-ups: Field Data and an Incremental Approach to Semantic, *Digital Heritage in the New Knowledge Environment: Shared spaces & open paths to cultural content,* Athens: Hellenic Ministry of Culture.

Klyne, G., Caroll, J. J., & McBride, B. (2004, February 10). Resource Description Framework (RDF): Concepts and Abstract Syntax, In: *W3C Recommendation,* Date of Access: August 26, 2010, Available from: http://www.w3.org/TR/rdf-concepts/

Kollias, S. (2008). Achieving Semantic Interoperability in Euroeana, *Digital Heritage in the New Knowledge Environment: Shared spaces & open paths to cultural content,* Athens: Hellenic Ministry of Culture.

Lieberman, J. (2007, June 23). Geospatial Incubator Group, In: *W3C Incubator Activity,* Date of Access: July 2010, 14, Available from: http://www.w3.org/2005/Incubator/geo/charter

Lieberman, J., Singh, R., & Goad, C. (2007). W3C Geospatial Ontologies - W3C Incubator Report, W3C Incubator Group, In: *W3C Incubator Activity,* Date of Access: September 15, 2009, Available from: http://www.w3.org/2005/Incubator/geo/XGR-geo-ont/

Mazzocchi, S. (2000). Toward the Semantic Web: a view of XML from outer space, *Proceeding: ApacheCON 2000,* London: Apache.

McGuinness, D. L., & Harmelen, F. v. (2004, February 10). OWL Web Ontology Language: Overview, In: *W3C Recommendation,* Date of Access: July 2010, 12, Available from: http://www.w3.org/TR/2004/REC-owl-features-20040210/

Patel-Schneider, P. F., Hayes, P., & Horrocks, I. (2004, February 10). OWL Web Ontology Language, In: *W3C Recommendation,* Date of Access: July 2010, 12, Available from: http://www.w3.org/TR/owl-semantics/

Prud'hommeaux, E., & Seaborne, A. (2008, January 2008). SPARQL Query Language for RDF, In: *W3C Recommendation,* Date of Access: May 22, 2010, Available from http://www.w3.org/TR/rdf-sparql-query/

Reitsma, F., & Hiramatsu, K. (2006). Exploring GeoMarkup on the Semantic Web, *Proceedings of 9th AGILE Conference on Geographic Information Science* (pp. 110 - 118). Visegrád: 9th AGILE Conference on Geographic Information Science.

Shannon, V. (2006, May 23). The New York Times – Technology, In: *A 'more revolutionary' Web,* Date of Access: August 16, 2010, Available from: http://www.nytimes.com/2006/05/23/technology/23iht-Web.html

Sheth, A. P. (1999). Changing Focus on Interoperability in Information Systems: From System, Syntax, Structure to Semantics, *Interoperating Geographic Information Systems* (pp. 5 - 30), MA: Kulewar Academic Publishers.

Smith, M. K., Welty, C., & McGuinness, D. L. (2004, February 10). OWL Web Ontology Language, In: *W3C Recommendation,* Date of Access: November 17, 2009, Available from: http://www.w3.org/TR/owl-guide/

Spaccapietra, S., Cullot, N., Parent, C., & Vangenot, C. (2004). On Spatial Ontologies, *GEOINFO,* Campos do Jordao.

Sterling, L., & Shapiro, S. (1994). The Art of Prolog, MIT Press.

Tanasescu, V., Gugliotta, A., Domingue, J., Gutiérrez-villarías, L., Davis, R., Rowlatt, M., et al. (2006). A Semantic Web Services GIS based Emergency Management Application, *Proceeding of The 5th International Semantic Web Conference (ISWC06),* Athens, Georgia: ISWC06.

W3C OWL Working Group. (2009, October 27). OWL 2 Web Ontology Language: Document Overview, In: *W3C Recommendation,* Date of Access: October 28, 2010, Available from: http://www.w3.org/TR/2009/REC-owl2-overview-20091027/

Welty, C., & Ide, N. (1999). Using the right tools: enhancing retrieval from marked-up documents, J. Computers and the Humanities, 33 (10), pp. 59 - 84.

Wüst, T., Nebiker, S., & Landolt, R. (2004). Applying the 3D GIS DILAS to Archaeology and Cultural Heritage Projects Requirements and First Results, *International Archives of Photogrammetry Remote Sensing and Spatial Information Sciences* (Vol. 35 Part 5, pp. 407 - 412). Natural Resources Canada.

8

Representation System for Quality Indicators by Ontology

Osamu Takaki, Izumi Takeuti, Koichi Takahashi,
Noriaki Izumi, Koichiro Murata and Koiti Hasida
Japan Advanced Institute of Science and Technology, National Institute of Advanced Industrial Science and Technology and Kitasato University Hospital
Japan

1. Introduction

We have not yet established a proper methodology to accurately evaluate the quality of medical services, although such a method is necessary for fair comparison between hospitals and/or improvement in the quality of medical services. The reason is that such a methodology needs a reasonable way to transform qualitative properties of medical services such as doctors' skill or patient satisfaction into quantitative properties that are measurable by data existing in medical databases, but, it has not yet been researched sufficiently. In general, it is not easy to fairly evaluate abstract things such as intelligence and performances by measuring quantitative aspects of them although we often have opportunities to evaluate such things. Moreover, even though we have quantitative properties denoting some useful properties, we need a proper method to accurately represent such quantitative properties in order to make users understand the definitions of the properties correctly.

In this chapter, we introduce a representation system of quality indicators. Quality indicators are barometers that indicate processes, results and/or other things of medical services numerically, in order to evaluate medical services. The representation system helps to define quality indicators and to calculate their values in a coherent manner that is based on the data in medical databases. The representation system primarily consists of three parts. The first one is an ontology to define concepts related to medical services. The second one is a set of graphs that express the targets of quality indicators. We call these graphs "objective graphs". The third one is a set of "quantifying concepts" that abstract the quantities of the subjects. The proposed system represents a quality indicator as a combination of an objective graph and a quantifying concept.

An objective graph can be interpreted as a set of instances of a concept. The set is defined by the properties described by the labels of the arrows in the graph. We also explain the interpretation of objective graphs for the sets in this paper.

The representation language provides the following advantages.

- The first advantage is that by representing a quality indicator with the representation system one can avoid the problem that occurs from a word in the quality indicator that has multiple meanings. In fact, we use a lot of words, each of that has multiple meanings. For example, the word "the first visit" has the meaning that differs among hospitals. So, we need to clarify the meanings of the words that constitute quality indicators, and the representation language enables one to clarify the meaning of each word in a quality indicator.

- The second advantage is that the representation language enables one to transform qualitative expressions into quantitative ones based on reasonable rationales and processes. The reasonable rationales and processes are provided by the fundamental theory of quantifications of concepts.
- The final advantage is that, since a quality indicator expressed by the representation language has the accurate semantics, one can calculate the value of the quality indicator via given medical databases. In this chater, we show a way to calculate the value of a quality indicator that is expressed by our language.

We finally introduce several examples of quality indicators that show that the representation language provides accurate and easily understandable expressions to quality indicators.

This chapter is an extended version of (Takaki et al., 2012), which is obtaiend from it by adding more detailed explanations and examples to demonstrate the working of the proposed representation system of quality indicators.

The remainder of this chapter is organized as follows. Section 2 briefly explains our framework to define quality indicators and to calculate their values based on the data in medical databases. Section 3 explains an ontology called the "medical service ontology". Sections 4 and 5 explain objective graphs and their interpretation based on a set theoretic interpretation of graphs. Section 6 explains quantifying concepts. Section 7 introduces an example of a quality indicator in the proposed representation system. Section 8 briefly explains a way to calculate the values of quality indicators based on the medical databases. Section 9 explains related works, and Section 10 concludes this chapter.

2. Framework for definition and calculation of quality indicators

We first show a whole image of the framework for definition and calculation of quality indicators.

From the user's point of view, the framework consists of (I) a representation system of quality indicators, (II) medical databases in hospitals, and (III) mapping systems that connect a certain global data model with data models of real medical databases.

Figure 1 below indicates the relationship between the representation system, medical databases, mapping systems and stakeholders of the frameworks. Users of the framework, who intend to evaluate medical services of hospitals that are associated with the framework, first define quality indicators with the representation system. Quality indicators are described to be diagrams with nodes and arrows, which are concepts and properties defined in an ontology we call Medical Service Ontology (MSO). In order to define quality indicators with the representation system, knowledge engineers, medical staffs and system engineers of medical databases collaborate in developing MSO in advance. Concepts and properties in MSO are translated to a virtual data model called the Global Data Model (GDM), which is translated to data models in medical databases in hospitals by the mapping system. In order to calculate values of quality indicators defined by the representation system, they are translated to query programs of tables (=data models) of medical databases through a certain interpretation and mappings in mapping systems. In many cases, the mapping systems are developed by system engineers who maintain the medical databases. By using the framework, users can define quality indicators and calculate the values of them without knowing structures of local medical databases.

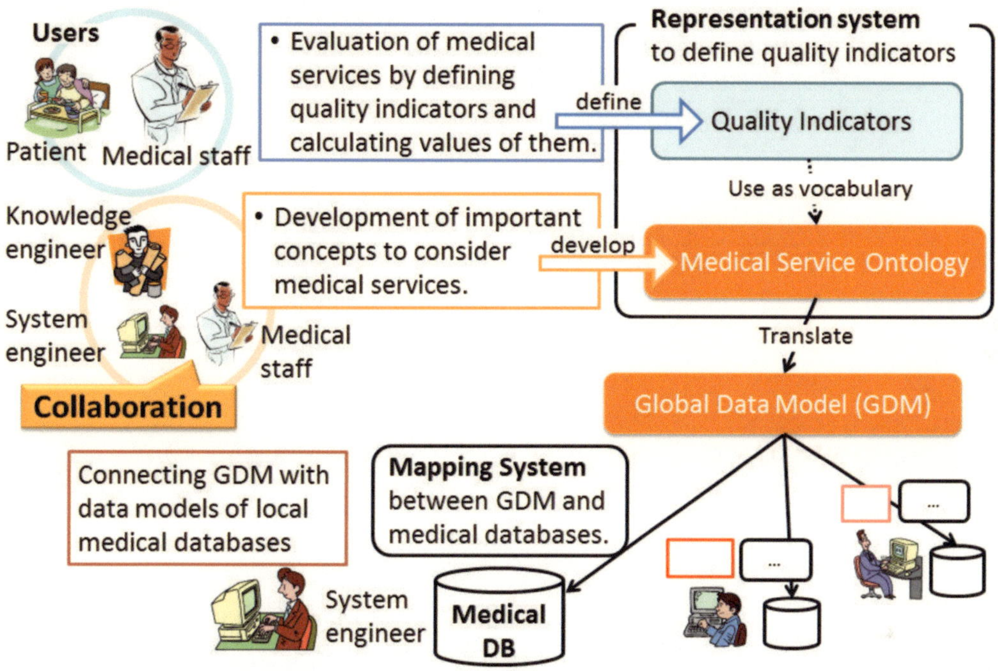

Fig. 1. Whole image of the framework for definition and calculation of quality indicators.

From a theoretical point of view, the framework consists of (i) the representation system, (ii) interpretations of components of the representation system, and (iii) several mappings that connect a database schema generated from MSO defined in the next section and other database schemas of given medical databases (see also Section 8). Also the representation system consists of (i) Medical Service Ontology, (ii) objective graphs, and (iii) quantifying concepts. Figure 2 below indicates how to define quality indicators and calculate values of them based on the representation system, the interpretations and the mappings.

A quality indicator is represented to be a graph obtained by combining objective graphs and a quantifying concept. An objective graph is a graph that expresses a set of patients, events (in a hospital) or other things such as "a set of patients who had operations for stomach cancers" or "a set of operations on patients with stomach cancers". An objective graph is constructed based on vocabularies in MSO. On the other hand, a quantifying concept is a function from a concept or a set of instances of a concept that is expressed by an objective graph to a numerical value. For example, a quality indicator "average length of hospital stays of patients who had operations for stomach cancers" is represented by an objective

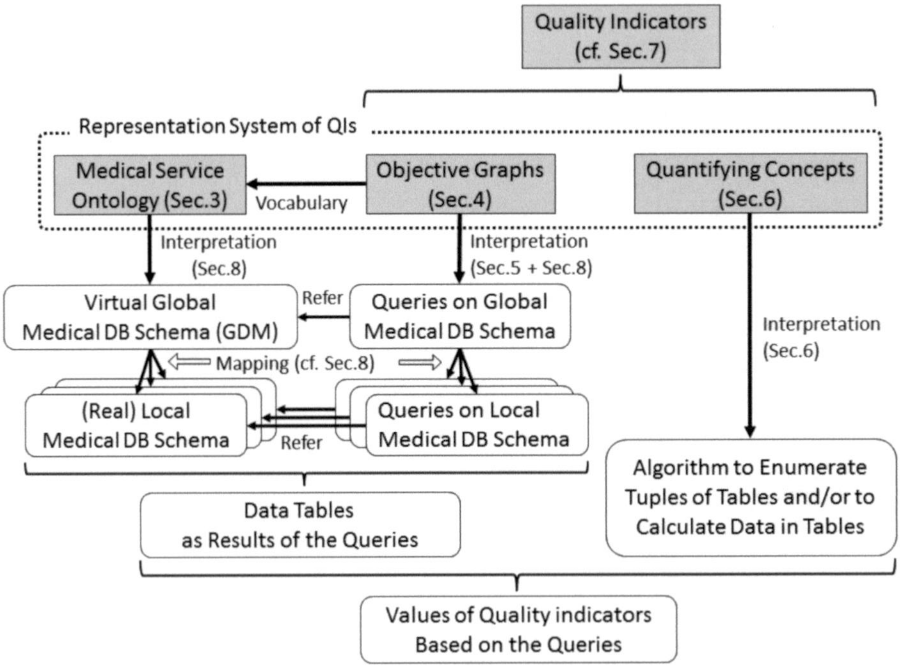

Fig. 2. Representation Language of Quality Indications and their values.

graph that expresses a set of hospital stays of patients who had operations for stomach cancers and a quantifying concept that calculate the average of length of the hospital stays for a given set of hospital stays.

In a coherent manner, concepts and properties in MSO are translated to tables or columns in them in GDM. Also an objective graph is translated to a query on GDM through a mathematical interpretation defined in Section 5. Moreover, by mappings between GDM and data models of local medical databases, tables and queries on GDM are translated to those in the local medical databases. On the other hand, a quantifying concept is translated to an algorithm to enumerate tuples of the tables that are obtained to be the results of the tables and queries above and/or to calculate data of them. Finally, the value of a quality indicator is calculated to be the result of the algorithm, queries and data above.

In this chapter, we focus on the representation system of quality indicators.

3. Medical service ontology

In the sections from now, we define the three main components of the representation system of quality indicators: medical service ontology (MSO), objective graphs, and quantifying concepts.

MSO is an ontology consisting of concepts related to medical services. In this section, we define the ontology by defining its concepts and properties[1]. The ontology has been

[1] In ontology engineering, concepts and properties in an ontology are often called classes and roles, respectively.

developed based on an ontology developing tool called the "Semantic Editor" (Hasida, 2011).

3.1 Concepts

We first define concepts in the medical service ontology. Concepts in MSO are used as vocabularies to describe quality indicators. Many quality indicators are described as the number, the rate or the average of (a) set(s) of patients or events in hospitals that are in a state. Moreover, many patients, events and states (of patients) can be characterized by them. Thus, concepts of stakeholders (especially, patients), events and states (of patients) are particularly important.

We introduce main concepts in MSO, as follows. Because of space limitations, we define some main concepts only. We describe a concept by the [name of a concept]. The concepts below are indicated by brackets.

1. Concepts of stakeholders:
   [patient], [medical staff]
2. Concepts of events
2.1. Concepts of events with terms:
   [hospital stay], [hospital visit]
   2.2. Concepts of events with no terms
      2.2.1. Concepts of scheduled events:
         [hospital admission], [hospital discharge],[diagnosis], [medical examination], [test], [operation], [prescription]
      2.2.2. Concepts of unscheduled events:
         [death], [bedsore], [falling]
3. Concepts of states:
   [state of age], [state of life or death], [state of disease]
4. Concepts of organizations:
   [department], [facility], [hospital]
5. Concepts of items:
   [medicine], [clinical instrument], [medical device]
6. Concepts of methods:
   [method], [cure], [method of examination]
7. Concepts of diseases:
   [disease]
8. Concept of time
   8.1. Concepts of time points:
      [date], [clock time]
   8.2. Concepts of terms:
      [number of years], [number of months],[number of weeks], [number of days]

A concept can be regarded as a set of instances of a given concept. Thus, we often identify the concept [patient] with the set of instances of that patient.

3.2 Properties

The ontology has two types of properties: the first type is an attribute of a concept, and the second type is a relation between two concepts. An attribute is a property that a concept own as an important part or feature. For example, name is one of typical attributes of a human, while parent and child relationship is one of typical relations on humans.

We often describe a property by the ⟨name of a property⟩.

3.2.1 Attributes of concepts

In medical service ontology, the concepts of actors, events and states are especially important. Thus, we here describe the attributes of actor concepts, state concepts and event concepts in Figures 3, 4 and 5, respectively.

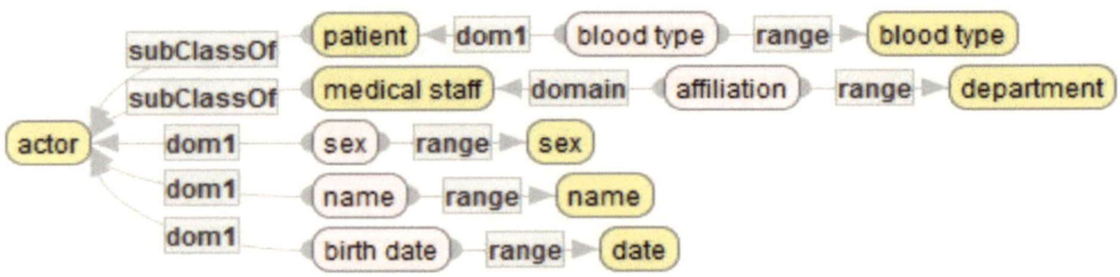

Fig. 3. Concepts and their attributes of actors (stakeholders).

In Figure 3, yellow rounded rectangles denote concepts, and pink rounded rectangles denote attributes. In general, pink rounded rectangles in diagrams on Semantic Editor denote properties.

The concept [actor] has three attribute ⟨sex⟩, ⟨name⟩ and ⟨birth date⟩. The sub classes [patient] and [medical staff] of [actor] have all attributes of [actor] and special attributes ⟨blood type⟩ and ⟨affiliation⟩, respectively. Though these concepts above have other attributes, we omit them since we do not use them in this paper.

The arrow "domain" from the attribute ⟨affiliation⟩ to [medical staff] denotes that the concept that has ⟨affiliation⟩ as an attribute is [medical staff], while the arrow "dom1" from the attribute ⟨sex⟩ to [actor] denotes that the concept having ⟨sex⟩ as an attribute is [actor] and that each actor has a single sex. On the other hand, the arrow "range" from the attribute ⟨blood type⟩ to the concept [blood type] denotes that the type of values of the attribute ⟨blood type⟩ is the concept [blood type]. On the other hand, the arrow "subClassOf" from the class [patient] to the concept [actor] denotes that [patient] is a sub class (a sub concept) of [actor].

The concept [state] in Figure 4 have five attributes ⟨subject (of a state)⟩, ⟨starting event⟩, ⟨terminating event⟩, ⟨starting time point⟩ and ⟨terminating time point⟩. ⟨starting event⟩ denotes a trigger of a state if the state has such a trigger, while ⟨terminating event⟩ denotes a trigger to stop a state. The arrow "dom01" from the attribute ⟨starting event⟩ to [state] denotes that [state] has ⟨starting event⟩ as an attribute and that each state has a single starting event or does not have any starting event.

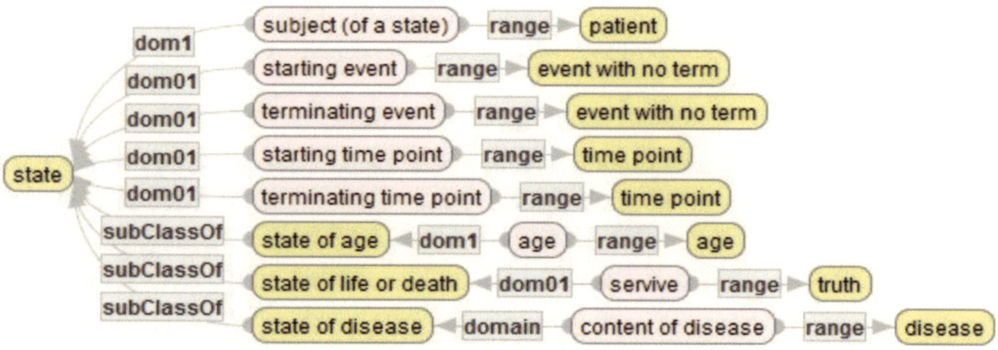

Fig. 4. Concepts and their attributes of patients' states.

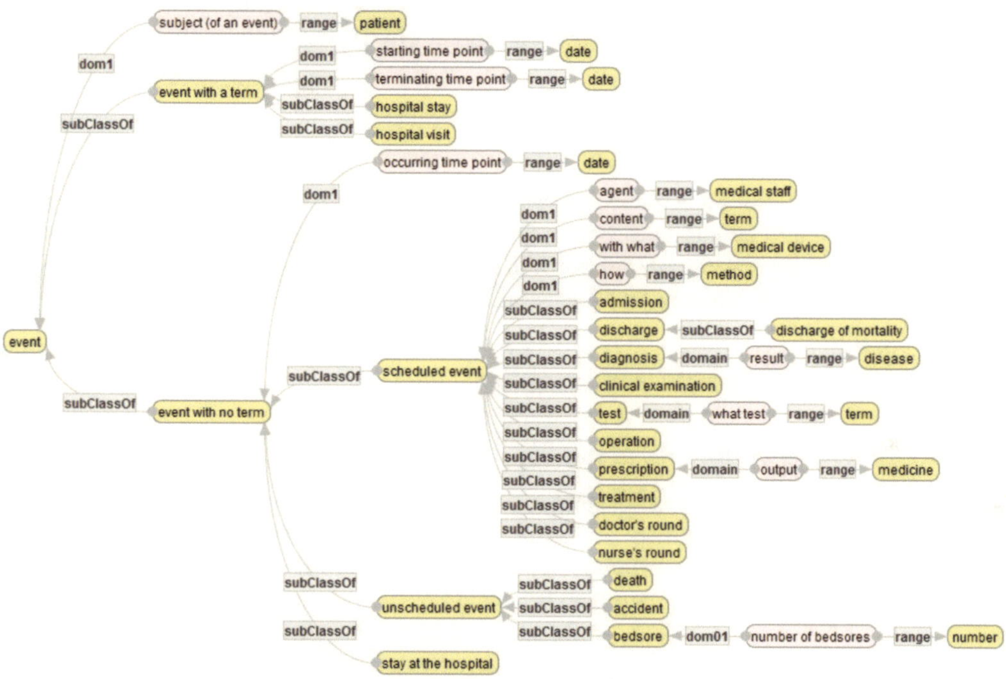

Fig. 5. Concepts and their attributes of events for patients.

3.2.2 Relations between concepts

We define the primary relations between concepts.

1. Relations of patients and events: The relations are defined between the [patient] and all event concepts. For example, the following relation denotes the relations between patients and their hospital stays.

   ⟨subject (of an event)⟩⊆ [patient]×[hospital stay].

Note that these relations share the same name "subject (of an event)". We omit the explanation of the relations between patients and other events.

2. **Relations of patients and states**: The relations are defined between the [patient] and all state concepts. For example, the following relation denotes the relationship between patients and their states of diseases.

$$\langle\text{subject (of a state)}\rangle \subseteq [\text{patient}]\times[\text{state of disease}].$$

Note that these relations also share the same name "subject (of an state)" and that all concepts of states have the attributes of starting time points and terminating time points. We omit the explanation of the relations between patients and other states.

3. **Relations of time ordering**: The relations are defined between the concepts of events and the states. For example, the following relations denote the relationships between operations.

$$\langle\text{more than <p> before}\rangle \subseteq [\text{operation}]\times[\text{operation}],$$
$$\langle\text{less than <p> befor}\rangle \subseteq [\text{operation}]\times[\text{operation}],$$
$$\langle\text{less than <p> after}\rangle \subseteq [\text{operation}]\times[\text{operation}] \text{ and}$$
$$\langle\text{more than <p> after}\rangle \subseteq [\text{operation}]\times[\text{operation}].$$

Here, "<p>" denotes a parameter. For example, the relation ⟨before more than <2 weeks>⟩ consists of a pair $<op_1, op_2>$ if op_1 and op_2 are performed and if op_1 is performed more than two weeks before op_2.

4. **Belonging relations of events**: The relations are defined between concepts of events with no term and events with terms. For example, the following relation denotes the relations between operations and hospital stays that have operations.

$$\langle\text{belonging}\rangle \subseteq [\text{operation}]\times[\text{hospital stay}].$$

The relation contains a pair (op, sty) of an event of an operation op and that of a hospital stay sty if op is performed in the duration of sty.

4. Representation of objects of quality indicators

In this subsection, we define a graph that represents a target of quantification based on the medical service ontology defined in the previous subsection. We call such a graph an "objective graph". An objective graph is defined as a finite and labelled directed graph with a root node. A node in an objective graph is labelled by an instance of a concept or a value of an attribute of a concept in MSO, while an edge in an objective graph is labelled by an instance of a property in MSO.

4.1 Definition of objective graphs

An objective graph $\mathbb{G}$ consists of the five components ($N(\mathbb{G})$, $R(\mathbb{G})$, $E(\mathbb{G})$, $L(\mathbb{G})$, $C(\mathbb{G})$), where

i. $N(\mathbb{G})$ is a set of nodes,
ii. $R(\mathbb{G})$ is a root node,
iii. $E(\mathbb{G})$ is a set of edges,
iv. $L(\mathbb{G})$ is a label function on $N(\mathbb{G}) \cup E(\mathbb{G})$, and
v. $C(\mathbb{G})$ is a concept.

We define these components by induction on the structure of the node labels, as follows.

Case 1. Assume that the following data are given:

a. concept C,
b. attributes $A_1,\ldots, A_n$ of C, and
c. values $a_1,\ldots, a_n$ of $A_1,\ldots, A_n$, respectively.

Then, we define an objective graph $\mathbb{G}$, as follows.

i. $N(\mathbb{G}):=\{*_0, \ldots, *_n\}$,
ii. $R(\mathbb{G}):=*_0$,
iii. $E(\mathbb{G}):=\{f_1,\ldots,f_n\}$, where each f_i is an edge from $*_0$ to $*_i$.
iv. $L(\mathbb{G})(*_0):=C$,
$L(\mathbb{G})(*_i):=a_i$ for $i=1,\ldots, n$, and,
$L(\mathbb{G})(f_i):=A_i$ for $i=1,\ldots, n$,
v. $C(\mathbb{G}):=C$.

Note that if n=0, then $N(\mathbb{G})$ is the singleton set $\{*_0\}$ and $E(\mathbb{G})$ is the empty set.

Case 2. Assume that the following data are given:

a. an integer n with $n \geqq 1$,
b. a set of objective graphs $\{\mathbb{G}_0, \ldots, \mathbb{G}_n\}$,
c. a set of relations $\{R_1,\ldots, R_n\}$, where each R_i is a relation between $C(\mathbb{G}_i)$ and $C(\mathbb{G}_0)$,
d. a set of integers $\{n(i,j)\}_{0\leqq i\leqq n,\ 0\leqq j\leqq n}$ and,
e. for each i with $0\leqq i\leqq n$ and j with $0\leqq j\leqq n$, the set of relations is $\{R^{i,j}_1,\ldots, R^{i,j}_{n(i,j)}\}$, where each $R^{i,j}_k$ is a relation between $C(\mathbb{G}_i)$ and $C(\mathbb{G}_j)$. (Note: if $n(i,j)=0$, the set $\{R^{i,j}_1,\ldots, R^{i,j}_{n(i,j)}\}$ is the empty set).

Then, we define an objective graph $\mathbb{G}$, as follows.

i. $N(\mathbb{G}):= \{*_0, \ldots, *_n\}$,
ii. $R(\mathbb{G}):= *_0$,
iii. $E(\mathbb{G}):=\{f_1,\ldots, f_n\}\cup(\cup_{0\leqq i\leqq n,\ 0\leqq j\leqq n}\{f^{i,j}_1,\ldots, f^{i,j}_{n(i,j)}\})$, where each f_i is an edge from $*_i$ to $*_0$ and each $f^{i,j}_k$ is an edge from $*_i$ to $*_j$.
iv. $L(\mathbb{G})(*_i):=\mathbb{G}_i$ $(i=0,\ldots, n)$,
$L(\mathbb{G})(f_i):=R_i$ $(i=0,\ldots, n)$ and,
$L(\mathbb{G})(f^{j,i}_k):= R^{i,j}_k$ $(i,j=0,\ldots, n$ and $k=1,\ldots, n(i, j))$.
v. $C(\mathbb{G}):= C(\mathbb{G}_0)$.

Each f_i is called a main edge of $\mathbb{G}$ and each $f^{i,j}_k$ is called an optional edge of $\mathbb{G}$.

4.2 Example of an objective graph

We give an example of an objective graph. For example, let us consider the quality indicator "5-year stomach cancer survival rate". The definition of the quality indicator is the ratio of the number of 5-year surviving patients to all stomach cancer patients, where a "stomach cancer patient" is a patient who had a diagnosis whose result was stomach cancer, and a "5-year surviving patient" is a patient who had a diagnosis whose result was stomach cancer but who is alive 5 years after that medical examination. Thus, we will first express the set of 5-year surviving patients in Figure 6. To this end, we construct three objective graphs $\mathbb{G}0$, $\mathbb{G}1$, and $\mathbb{G}2$, as follows.

(1) $\mathbb{G}_0 = (\{*\}, *, \emptyset$ (the empty set), L_0, [patient]), where $L_0(*)$=[patient].

(2) $\mathbb{G}_1$ = ({$*_0$, $*_1$}, $*_1$, {f_1:$*_0$→$*_1$}, L_1, [diagnosis]), where $L_1(*_0)$ = [diagnosis], $L_1(*_1)$ = ⟪stomach cancer⟫, $L_1(f_1)$ = ⟨result⟩ and [diagnosis] denotes an event concept, ⟪stomach cancer⟫ denotes an instance of the concept of diseases, and ⟨result⟩ denotes an attribute of the concept [diagnosis]. Note that the range of ⟨result⟩ is the concept of diseases.

(3) $\mathbb{G}$2 = ({$*_0$, $*_1$}, $*_1$, {f_1:$*_0$→$*_1$}, L_2, [state of life or death]), where $L_2(*_0)$ = [state of life or death], $L_2(*_1)$ = ⟪true⟫, L2(f1) = ⟨survive⟩, [state of life or death] denotes the viability status of a patient, ⟪stomach cancer⟫ denotes an instance of the concept of diseases, and ⟨result⟩ denotes an attribute of the concept [diagnosis]. Note that the range of ⟨result⟩ is the concept of diseases.

(1) $\mathbb{G}_0$=
(2) $\mathbb{G}_1$=
(3) $\mathbb{G}_2$=

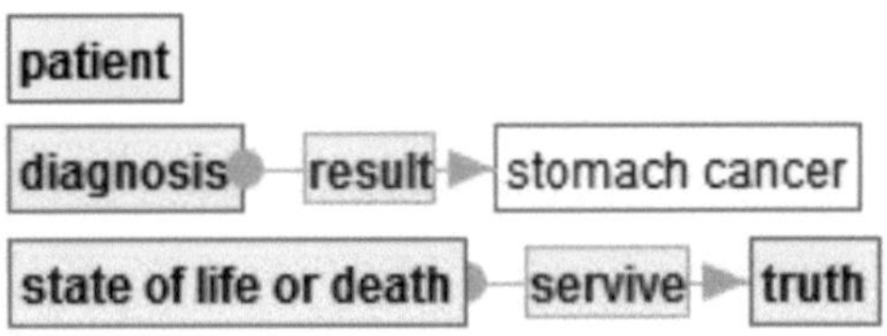

We next construct an objective graph of "5-year surviving stomach cancer patients" G, as follows.

(i) N($\mathbb{G}$) = {$*_0$, $*_1$, $*_2$},
(ii) R($\mathbb{G}$) =$*_0$,
(iii) E($\mathbb{G}$) = {f^1:$*_1$→$*_0$, f^2:$*_2$→$*_0$, f^{21}:$*_2$→$*_1$},
(iv) L($\mathbb{G}$)($*_i$) = $\mathbb{G}_i$ (i=0, 1, 2),
L($\mathbb{G}$)(f^1) = ⟨subject (of the event) ⟩ ,
L($\mathbb{G}$)(f^2) = ⟨subject (of the state) ⟩,
L($\mathbb{G}$)(f^{21}) = ⟨after more than <5 years>⟩,
(v) C($\mathbb{G}$) = C($\mathbb{G}_0$) = [patient].

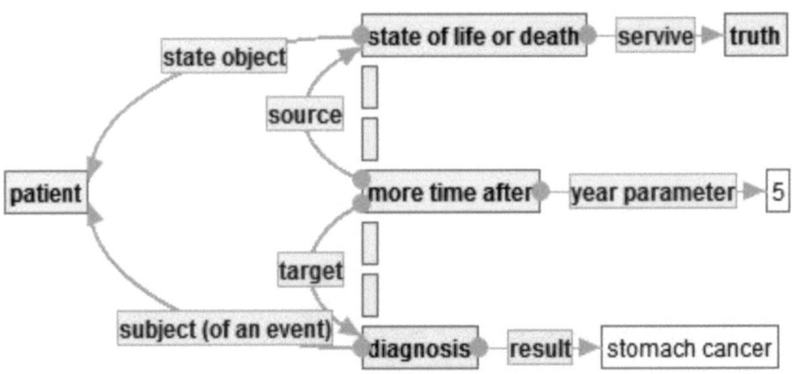

Fig. 6. Objective graph $\mathbb{G}$ describing 5-year surviving patients with stomach cancers

4.3 Segments of an objective graph

In the later section (Section 5), we will interpret an objective graph $\mathbb{G}$ as a set that is obtained from C($\mathbb{G}$) by adding the conditions defined by L($\mathbb{G}$). We define an objective graph $\mathbb{G}$*, which is called a segment of $\mathbb{G}$ and which can be interpreted as a super set of the interpretation of a given objective graph $\mathbb{G}$, as follows.

Case 1. If $\mathbb{G}$ is an objective graph defined in Case 1 of the definition of objective graphs, then graph $\mathbb{G}^*$ defined in the following properties is a segment of $\mathbb{G}$.

(i) $N(\mathbb{G}^*) \subseteq N(\mathbb{G})$,
(ii) $R(\mathbb{G}^*) = R(\mathbb{G})$,
(iii) $E(\mathbb{G}^*) \subseteq E(\mathbb{G})$,
(iv) $L(\mathbb{G}^*) = L(\mathbb{G}) \mid_{N(\mathbb{G}^*) \cup E(\mathbb{G}^*)}$ (the restriction of $L(\mathbb{G})$ to $N(\mathbb{G}^*) \cup E(\mathbb{G}^*)$), [2]
(v) $C(\mathbb{G}^*) = C(\mathbb{G})$.

Case 2. Let $\mathbb{G}$ be an objective graph defined in Case 2 of the definition of objective graphs. Then, graph $\mathbb{G}^*$ defined in the following properties is a segment of $\mathbb{G}$.

(i) $N(\mathbb{G}^*) \subseteq N(\mathbb{G})$,
(ii) $R(\mathbb{G}^*) = R(\mathbb{G})$,
(iii) $E(\mathbb{G}^*) \subseteq E(\mathbb{G})$, where, for all $*_i \in N(\mathbb{G}^*) \setminus \{*_0\}$[3], the main edge from $*_i$ to $*_0$ in $E(\mathbb{G})$ is contained in $E(\mathbb{G}^*)$.
(iv) $L(\mathbb{G})(*_i) := \mathbb{G}^*_i$ for all $*_i \in N(\mathbb{G}^*)$, where $\mathbb{G}^*_i$ is a segment of $\mathbb{G}_i$,
$L(\mathbb{G})(f^i) := R^i$ for all $f^i \in E(\mathbb{G}^*)$ and
$L(\mathbb{G})(f^{j,i}{}_k) := R^{i,j}{}_k$ for all $f^{j,i}{}_k \in E(\mathbb{G}^*)$.
(v) $C(\mathbb{G}^*) = C(\mathbb{G})$.

4.4 Example of a segment of an objective graph

For the objective graph $\mathbb{G}$ in Fig. 6, the objective graph $\mathbb{G}^*$ in Fig. 7 is a segment of $\mathbb{G}$, which expresses the set of stomach cancer patients.

Fig. 7. A segment $\mathbb{G}^*$ of $\mathbb{G}$.

5. Interpretation of objective graphs

An objective graph $\mathbb{G}$ can be regarded to be a concept denoted by $C(\mathbb{G})$ and modified by other concepts and properties that are denoted by $L(\mathbb{G})$. If each concept is identified with the set of instances of the concept, an objective graph can be identified with a subset of the set denoted by $C(\mathbb{G})$ that is obtained from $C(\mathbb{G})$ by restricting it by sets and functions denoted by $L(\mathbb{G})$. To make the identification clear, we here define an interpretation of an objective graph, as follows.

5.1 Definition of the interpretations of objective graphs

For an objective graph $\mathbb{G}$, we define a set $[[\mathbb{G}]]$, as follows.

Case 1. Let $\mathbb{G}$ be an objective graph defined in Case 1 of the definition of objective graphs. Then, $[[\mathbb{G}]] := \{c \in C \mid c.A_1 = a_1 \wedge \ldots \wedge c.A_n = a_n\}$,[4] where $c.A_i$ is the value of the attribute A_i on c.

---

[2] For sets X and Y with $Y \subseteq X$ and for a function f on X, $f|_Y$ denotes the function of Y that is defined by $f|_Y(y) := f(y)$ for all $y \in Y$. We often refer to $f|_Y$ as the restriction of f to Y.

[3] For sets X, Y with $Y \subseteq X$, $X \setminus Y$ denotes the set $\{x \in X \mid x \notin Y\}$.

Case 2. Let $\mathbb{G}$ be an objective graph defined in Case 2 of the definition of objective graphs. Then, $[[\mathbb{G}]]:=\{x_0\in[[\mathbb{G}_0]] \mid \exists x_1\in[[\mathbb{G}_1]],\ldots, \exists x_n\in[[\mathbb{G}_n]]$

$$(\bigwedge_{i=1,\ldots,n} R^i(x_i, x_0)) \wedge (\bigwedge_{i,j=0,\ldots,n} (\bigwedge_{k=1,\ldots,n(i,j)} R^{i,j}_k (x_i, x_j)))\}.$$

Lemma. For an objective graph $\mathbb{G}$ and a segment $\mathbb{G}^*$ of $\mathbb{G}$, $[[\mathbb{G}]] \subseteq [[\mathbb{G}^*]]$.

Proof. One can easily show the lemma above by induction on the structure of $\mathbb{G}$.

5.2 Example of the interpretation of an objective graph

In this subsection, we show a small example of the interpretation of an objective graph.

We first consider a concept of scheduled events denoted by [diagnosis] (cf. the definition of medical service ontology and Figure 5). Then, the concept has seven attributes (see the parenthetic names of columns of the table in Figure 5). Thus, one can obtain (the list of columns of) Table 1 corresponding to [diagnosis], whose attributes correspond to those of [diagnosis]. Let $\mathcal{T}_1$ be data (a set of tuples) in Table 1 and assume that there is no tuple in $\mathcal{T}_1$ whose value of the attribute "disease" is "stomach cancer" besides the tuples with id 1, 2, 3 and 5.

Id	Patient (subject (of an event))	Date (occurring time point)	Staff (agent)	Term (content)	Device (with what)	Method (how)	Set of Diseases (result)
E_1	P_1	03-11-2011	D_1	-	-	-	{stomach cancer}
E_2	P_2	03-15-2011	D_1	-	-	-	{stomach cancer}
E_3	P_3	04-06-2011	D_2	-	-	-	{stomach cancer}
E_4	P_4	05-08-2011	D_2	-	-	-	{gastric ulcer}
E_5	P_2	06-09-2011	D_2	-	-	-	{stomach cancer}
E_6	P_5	07-06-2011	D_1	-	-	-	{gastric varices, duodenal ulcer}
...	...	...	...	...	...	...	...

Table 1. The table generated from the concept of scheduled events [diagnosis] with tuples $\mathcal{T}_1$.

Let $\mathbb{G}_1$ be the objective graph in Section 4.2. Then, if the concept [diagnosis] is identified with $\mathcal{T}_1$, the interpretation of $\mathbb{G}_1$ based on $\mathcal{T}_1$ is $\{\, c\in\mathcal{T}_1 \mid c.\ \langle\text{result}\rangle\ni\langle\!\langle\text{stomach cancer}\rangle\!\rangle \,\}$, which is equivalent to $\{\text{tuple}^1_1, \text{tuple}^1_2, \text{tuple}^1_3, \text{tuple}^1_5\}$. Here, each tuple^1_i denotes the tuple in $\mathcal{T}_1$ whose id is E_i. That is,

$$[[\mathbb{G}_1]] = \{\, c\in\mathcal{T}_1 \mid c.\ \langle\text{result}\rangle\ni\langle\!\langle\text{stomach cancer}\rangle\!\rangle \,\} = \{\text{tuple}^1_1, \text{tuple}^1_2, \text{tuple}^1_3, \text{tuple}^1_{5,\ldots}\}.$$

Moreover, let $\mathbb{G}^*$ be the objective graph in Figure 7. Then, $\mathbb{G}^* = \{\{*_0, *_1\}, *_0, \{f^1\}, L, [\text{patient}]\}$, where L is the function satisfying the following properties.

(i) $L(*_0) = \mathbb{G}_0$ in Section 4.2,
(ii) $L(*_1) = \mathbb{G}_1$ in Section 4.2, and
(iii) $L(f^1) = \langle\text{subject (of a state)}\rangle$ ($\subseteq$ [patient]×[diagnosis]) (cf. Section 3.2.2).

---

[4] The symbol $\wedge$ denotes the logical connective symbol of "and."

Moreover, consider Table 2 corresponding to [patient], which is defined in Figure 3 and which has attributes ⟨result⟩ and ⟨blood type⟩, and let $\mathcal{T}_1$ be the set of tuples in Table 2.

Id	Name (name)	Sex (sex)	Blood type (blood type)
P_1	Alice Johnson	female	A
P_2	Richard Miller	male	O
P_3	Robert Williams	male	AB
P_4	William Brown	male	B
P_5	Susan Wilson	female	O
...	...	...	...

Table 2. The table generated from the concept of a stakeholder [patient] with tuples $\mathcal{T}_2$.

Thus, the interpretation of $\mathbb{G}^*$ based on $\mathcal{T}_2$ is $\{ c\in\mathcal{T}_2 \mid \exists x_1\in[[\mathbb{G}_1]]$ ⟨subject (of a state)⟩$(c, x_1) \}$, which is equivalent to $\{\text{tuple}^2{}_1, \text{tuple}^2{}_2, \text{tuple}^2{}_3\}$. Here, each $\text{tuple}^2{}_i$ denotes the tuple in $\mathcal{T}_2$ whose id is P_i. That is,

$$[[\mathbb{G}^*]] = \{ c\in\mathcal{T}_2 \mid \exists x_1\in[[\mathbb{G}_1]] \langle\text{subject (of a state)}\rangle(c, x_1) \} = \{\text{tuple}^2{}_1, \text{tuple}^2{}_2, \text{tuple}^2{}_3\}.$$

6. Quantifying concepts

A quantifying concept plays a role in a function that has an objective graph and optional parameters as input data and that outputs a numerical value. In general, one can classify quantifying concepts into three types. In the following, we explain each type of quantifying concept. We describe a quantifying concept by ⋞name of a quantifying concept⋟. Note that we often identify a concept with a set and that all sets are considered to be finite.

6.1 Total numbers

For a finite set S, the summation of numbers obtained from elements of S is called the total number of S. For example, if each element is assigned to 1 as the existence of the element, then the total number is the same as the cardinality of S. The quantifying concept ⋞cardinality⋟ is regarded as a function that has an objective graph $\mathbb{G}$ as input data and that outputs the cardinality of $[[\mathbb{G}]]$.

For a concept S, attributes $A_1,\ldots, A_n$ of S, and the real-valued function f on the set of values of instances of S with respect to $A_1,\ldots, A_n$, the summation $\Sigma_{s\in S} f(s.A_1,\ldots, s.A_n)$ is called the total attribute number of S with respect to $A_1,\ldots, A_n$ and f, where $s.A_i$ denotes the value of an instance s with respect to A_i, is an attribute quantifier function.

The quantifying concept ⋞total attribute number⋟ is regarded as a function that has the following data as input data:

1. an objective graph $\mathbb{G}$,
2. attributes $A_1,\ldots, A_n$ of $C(\mathbb{G})$, and
3. $f: C_1\times\ldots\times C_n\rightarrow R$, where $C_i := \{s.A_i \mid s\in[[\mathbb{G}]]\}$.

⋞total attribute number⋟ outputs the total attribute number of $[[\mathbb{G}]]$ with respect to $A_1,\ldots, A_n$ and f.

6.2 Rate

For a finite set S and a subset S* of S, the rate of the total number of S* among the total numbers of S obtained in the same way as that to calculate the total number of S* is called a rate of S* among S. In particular, the rate of the cardinality of S* among that of S is called the cardinality rate of S* among S. Moreover, the rate of the total attribute number of S* with respect to $A_1,\ldots, A_n$ and f among that of S with respect to the same attributes and the same attribute quantifier function is called the total attribute number rate.

The quantifying concept ⋘cardinality rate⋙ is regarded as a function that has the following data as input data:

1. An objective graph $\mathbb{G}$, and
2. A segment $\mathbb{G}^*$ of $\mathbb{G}$.

In contrast, the quantifying concept ⋘total attribute number rate⋙ is regarded as a function that has the following data as input data:

1. An objective graph $\mathbb{G}$,
2. A segment $\mathbb{G}^*$ of $\mathbb{G}$,
3. Attributes $A_1,\ldots, A_n$ of $C(\mathbb{G})$, and
4. $f: C_1\times\ldots\times C_n\rightarrow R$,, where $C_i := \{s.A_i \mid s\in[[\mathbb{G}]]\}$.

⋘total attribute number rate⋙ outputs the rate of the total attribute number of $[[\mathbb{G}]]$ with respect to $A_1,\ldots, A_n$ and f among that of $[[\mathbb{G}^*]]$ with respect to the same attributes and the same attribute quantifier function.

6.3 Average

For concept S, attributes $A_1,\ldots, A_n$ of S, and attribute quantifier function f, the ratio of the total attribute number of S with respect to $A_1,\ldots, A_n$ and f and the cardinality of S is called the average of the value of S with respect to $A_1,\ldots, A_n$ of f. The quantifying concept ⋘average⋙ is regarded as a function that has the same input data as that of ⋘total attribute number⋙ and that outputs the average of the value of S with respect to $A_1,\ldots, A_n$ of f.

7. Examples of quality indicators in the representation system

A quality indicator is a barometer to evaluate a medical service. We regard it as a combination of an objective graph and a quantifying concept. In this subsection, we describe one of the typical quality indicators "stomach cancer 5-year survival rate" with objective graphs and a quantifying concept. This indicator is defined to be the rate of the number of patients diagnosed with stomach cancer surviving 5 years after diagnosis among the number of patients diagnosed with stomach cancer. Thus, the numerator and the denominator of the indicator can be described to be objective graphs $\mathbb{G}$ and $\mathbb{G}^*$ in Figure 6 and Figure 7, respectively. Thus, one can describe the quality indicator by using $\mathbb{G}$, $\mathbb{G}^*$, and the quantifying concept ⋘cardinality rate⋙ as the graph in Figure 8 on the next page.

We will show another example of a quality indicator "the average length of the hospital stays for stomach cancers". The following figure denotes a set of hospital stays for stomach cancer treatments that have stomach cancer operations by laparotomies.

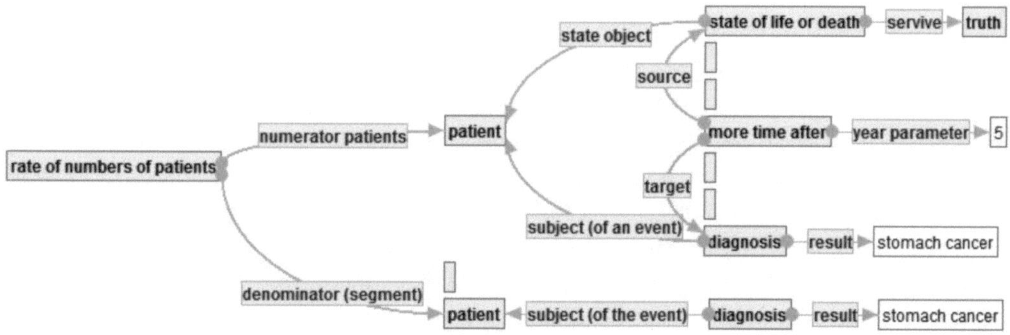

Fig. 8. Quality indicator "Stomach cancer 5-year survival rate".

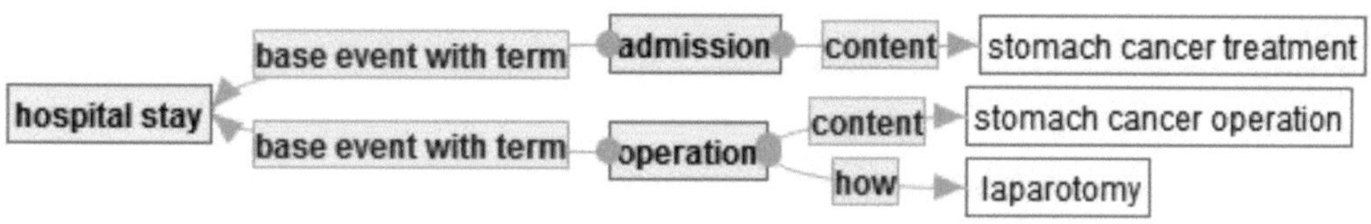

Fig. 9. Objective graph describing Hospital stays for stomach cancers.

To be more precise, Figure 9 denotes the set of hospital stays that have admissions with purposes treatments of stomach cancers and operations for stomach cancers by laparotomies. By using the objective graph above, the quantifying concept ≪average≫ (cf. Section 6.3) and a function that assigns to two dates the number of days between the two dates, one can obtain the quality indicator "the average length of the hospital stays for stomach cancers", as follows.

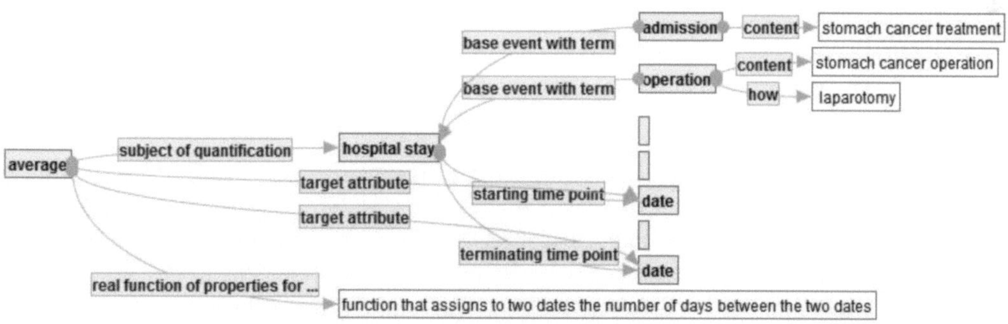

Fig. 10. Quality indicator "The average length of the hospital stays for stomach cancers"

In Figure 10, the objective graph in Figure 9 is the first input data of ≪average≫, two attributes ⟨starting time point⟩ and ⟨terminating time point⟩ of the concept [hospital stay] are assigned as second input data of ≪average≫, and the function that assigns to two dates the number of days between the two dates is the third input data of ≪average≫ (see Section 6.3).

8. Calculation of values of quality indicators based on medical databases

In this section, we briefly explain how to calculate the values of quality indicators described in the representation system by using medical databases. One can obtain an entity-relationship model (Chen, 1976) from the medical service ontology in Section 3 by translating concepts to entities and the properties between them to the relationship between entities obtained from the given concepts. Moreover, by translating the attributes of a concept to those of the entity translated from the concept, one can obtain a relational data model, which we call the global data model (GDM) of medical service ontology. In this paper, we often call an entity in GDM by a "table" and an attribute of an entity by a "column" of a table.

For example, a concept [diagnosis] of a scheduled event that is described in Figure 5 is translated to an entity in GDM, that is, it is translated to (a list of columns of) a table, as follows.

Diagnosis (diagnosis)	Patient (subject (of an event))	Date (occurring time point)	Staff (agent)	Term (content)	Device (with what)	Method (how)
E_1	P_1	03-11-2011	D_1	-	-	-
E_2	P_2	03-15-2011	D_1	-	-	-
E_3	P_3	04-06-2011	D_2	-	-	-
E_4	P_4	05-08-2011	D_2	-	-	-
E_5	P_2	06-09-2011	D_2	-	-	-
E_6	P_5	07-06-2011	D_1	-	-	-
...	...	...	...	...	...	...

Table 3. Modification of the table 1.

Here, the parenthetic name of a column of the table above denotes the concept or one of its attributes. The columns of this table are obtained from the concept [diagnosis] and its attributes whose values (instances) are uniquely determined by an instance of [diagnosis], and the column "Diagnosis" is the primary column (the primary key) of the table. The list of columns of Table 3 is obtained from the list of all columns of Table 1 in Section 5.2 by removing the column generated from the attribute ⟨result⟩, which may have multiple values of a single diagnosis (an instance of [diagnosis]). Each attribute of a concept that may have multiple values of a single instance of the concept is translated to (a list of columns of) a table whose primary key is the attribute. For example, the attribute ⟨result⟩ is translated to the list of columns in the following table.

Result (result)	Diagnosis (diagnosis)	Diseases (the range of result)
Rs_1	E_1	stomach cancer
Rs_2	E_2	stomach cancer
Rs_3	E_3	stomach cancer
Rs_4	E_4	gastric ulcer
Rs_5	E_5	stomach cancer
Rs_6	E_6	gastric varices
Rs_7	E_6	duodenal ulcer
...	...	...

Table 4. The table generated from the attribute of the concept scheduled events [diagnosis].

As another example of a table, we describe the list of columns of a table generated from the concept [sate of life or death] in Figure 4, as follows.

State of life or death (state of life or death)	Patient (subject (of a state))	Event (starting event)	Event (terminating event)	Starting time point (starting time point)	Terminating time point (terminating time point)	Truth value (service)

Table 5. The list of columns generated from the concept of states [state of life or death] and its attributes.

The data of tables in GDM generated from the medical service ontology is obtained from data in (real) medical databases. The data of each table is obtained by one of two ways: the first way is to define mapping functions between the table and those in medical databases; the second is to define the way to calculate data from other tables in GDM plus medical databases. For example, in many cases, data of Table 3 and Table 4 is obtained by a mapping function between the tables and those in medial databases and such a mapping function can be simply defined, since most of data models in medical databases have similar tables to them. On the other hand, many medical databases should not have any table similar to Table 5. Instead of defining a mapping function between such a table and some tables in medical databases directly, one had better consider a way to calculate data from other tables in GDM (and medical databases). For example, one can obtain data of important columns of Table 5 from the table generated from the concept [death] of unscheduled event in Figure 5, as follows.

Death (death)	Patient (subject (of an event))	Date (occurring time point)
F_1	P_2	11-10-2011
F_2	P_5	12-12-2011
...	...	...

Table 6. The table generated from the concept [death] and its attributes.

For example, one can obtain data of Table 5 from Table 6, as follows.

State of life or death (state of life or death)	Patient (subject (of a state))	Event (starting event)	Event (terminating event)	Starting time point (starting time point)	Terminating time point (terminating time point)	Truth value (service)
S_1	P_2	-	F_1	-	11-09-2011	True
S_2	P_2	F_1	-	11-10-2011	-	False
S_3	P_5	-	F_2	-	12-11-2011	True
S_4	P_5	F_2	-	12-12-2011	-	False
...	...	...	...	...	...	...

Table 7. Data generated from the data of Table 6.

By the interpretation of Section 5, one can perform a query on the GDM from a given objective graph 𝔾 by translating the condition of [[𝔾]] in a way based on relational calculus (Abiteboul et al, 1995), since the condition of [[𝔾]] is defined as a formula in first-order logic on the concepts and properties, and all properties are so simple that one can translate them to queries on the GDM automatically. Therefore, for a given medical database MD, if one has a suitable mapping between the data model on the MD and the GDM, one can automatically calculate the value of quality indicators based on the data in the MD.

For example, we calculate the value of the quality indicator "stomach cancer 5-year survival rate" in Section 7 based on data in Tables 2, 3, 4 and 7. Let 𝔾 be the objective graph of Figure 6 in Section 4.2, and let 𝔾* be the objective graph in Figure 7. Thus, by the definition of the interpretation of objective graphs in Section 5, [[𝔾]] and [[𝔾*]] can be considered to be sets of tuples in the table generated from the concept [patient], that is, Table 2 in Section 3.2. Moreover, they are calculated by using Tables 2, 3, 4 and 7, as follows.

```
[[𝔾]] = select * from Table-2 where
            Table-2.Patient=Table-3.Patient              and
            Table-3.Diagnosis=Table-4.Diagnosis          and
            Table-4.Disease="stomach cancer"             and
            Not exists * from Table-7 where
                Table-2.Patient=Table-7.Patient          and
                Table-7.Truth-value="False"              and
                Table-7.Starting-time-point < Table-3.Date + "5-years" (*)
```

= $\{tuple^2{}_1, tuple^2{}_3\}$, where each $tuple^2{}_i$ denotes the tuple in Table 2 (see 5.2).

```
[[𝔾*]] = select * from Table-2 where
            Table-2.Patient=Table-3.Patient              and
            Table-3.Diagnosis=Table-4.Diagnosis          and
            Table-4.Disease="stomach cancer"
```

= $\{tuple^2{}_1, tuple^2{}_2, tuple^2{}_3\}$.

Thus, the value of "stomach cancer 5-year survival rate" is calculated to be 2/3.

Note that all condition expressions in the queries above besides (*) are directly translated from the definitions of [[𝔾]] and [[𝔾*]]. On the other hand, the condition expression (*) is obtained from the condition "the date of the state of life or dead with truth value true is more than 5 years after the date of an event of diagnosis" in a coherent way, which is not difficult to establish.

9. Related works

It is important to fairly evaluate or compare the qualities of medical services that hospitals provide in order to improve the services. To this end, the qualities of medical services must be identified and adequate methods must be found to measure these qualities accurately (Donabedian, 1966). Quality indicators, which are quantitative criteria for the evaluation of medical services, have been attracting attention (Mainz, 2003). Many quality indicators already have been defined by standards organizations and projects such as IQIP (IQIP, 2011), MHA (Scheiderer, 1995), and OECD (Mattke et al, 2006).

However, as we mentioned in Section 1, although many good quality indicators have been developed, at least the following two issues remain for using quality indicators to fairly evaluate and compare medical services among hospitals.

The first issue is that, while many quality indicators (of medical services) are defined by terms in relation to medical care, many medical databases are developed from the aspect of accounting management. Moreover, many medical databases are developed in the vendors' or hospitals' own schema. Therefore, to calculate the values of quality indicators or to define them, it is often necessary for medical staffs to collaborate with system engineers who manage or developed the medical databases. However, the gaps in their knowledge and viewpoints often prevent them from collaborating to calculate the values of quality indicators and/or to define them accurately.

The second issue is that many words for medical services have meanings that differ according to the hospital or community of the medical staff. For example, at least in our country, the meaning of "new patients" or "inpatients" sometimes differs according to the medical staff in some hospitals, even though the hospitals may belong to the same hospital group. Such different interpretations of words also prevent medical staffs from coherently calculating accurate values of the quality indicators among multiple hospitals.

The proposed representation system of quality indicators helps to define quality indicators and calculate their values in a coherent manner that is based on the data in medical databases.

10. Conclusion

It is important to describe quality indicators that have no ambiguity of interpretation and to calculate their values accurately in a coherent way. To this end, we introduce a representation system of quality indicators, which consists of (i) an ontology of medical services, (ii) objective graphs to represent the objectives of quantification and an interpretation of objective graphs as sets, and (iii) quantifying concepts. We also briefly explain the whole image of our theoretical framework to define quality indicators and to calculate their values. Moreover, we explain a way to calculate the values of quality indicators based on the medical databases through an example of a quality indicator.

The proposed representation system plays a central role in the framework explained in Section 2, which enables medical staffs and patients, who desire to evaluate medical services, to define quality indicators and to calculate their values based on medical databases, without knowing the structure of the data models of them. Moreover, the representation system helps medical stuffs and system engineers, who develop or manage medical databases, collaborate in developing useful vocabularies to establish and standardize quality indicators.

11. References

Abiteboul, S.; Hull, R. B. & Vianu, V. (1995). *Foundations of Databases*, Addison-Wesley.

Chen, P. P. S. (1976). The entity-relationship model—toward a unified view of data, *ACM Transactions on Database Systems*, Vol. 1 Iss.1, pp. 9-36.

Donabedian, A. (1966). *Evaluating the quality of medical care*, The Milbank Memorial Fund Quarterly, Vol. 44, No. 3, Pt. 2, 1966, pp. 166–203.

Hasida, K. (2011). *Introduction to Semantic Editor* (in Japanese), http://i-content.org/semauth/intro/index.html.

Internatinal Quality Indicator Project (IQIP) (2011). http://www.internationalqip.com/index.aspx.

Mainz, J. (2003). Developing evidence-based clinical indicators: a state of the art methods primer, *International Journal for Quality in Health Care*, Vol.15, Supp.1, pp. i5-i11.

Mattke, S. et al. (2006). Health Care Quality Indicators Project: Initial Indicators Report, *OECD Health Working Papers*, No. 22, OECD Publishing. http://dx.doi.org/10.1787/481685177056.

Scheiderer, K. J. (1995). The Maryland Quality Indicator Project: searching for opportunities for improvement, *Top Health Inf Manage.* Vol.15, No.4, 1995, pp. 26-30.

Takaki, O.; Takeuti, I.; Takahashi, K.; Izumi, N.; Murata, K. & Hasida, K. (2012). Representation System of Quality Indicators towards Accurate Evaluation of Medical Services based on Medical Databases, *to appear in the Proceedings of the 4th International Conference on eHealth, Telemedicine, and Social Medicine (eTELEMED 2012).*

9

From Unstructured 3D Point Clouds to Structured Knowledge - A Semantics Approach

Helmi Ben Hmida, Christophe Cruz, Frank Boochs and Christophe Nicolle
[1]Laboratoire Le2i, UFR Sciences et Techniques
Université de Bourgogne, Dijon,
[2]Fachhochschule Mainz, Institut i3mainz,
amFachbereichGeoinformatik und Vermessung, Mainz,
[1]France
[2]Germany

1. Introduction

Over the last few years, formal ontologies has been suggested as a solution for several engineer problems, since it can efficiently replace standard data bases and relational one with more flexibility and reliability. In fact, well designed ontologies own lots of positive aspects, like those related to defining a controlled vocabulary of terms, inheriting and extending existing terms, declaring a relationship between terms, and inferring relationships by reasoning on existent ones. Ontologies are used to represent formally the knowledge of a domain where the basic idea was to present knowledge using graphs and logical structure to make computers able to understand and process it, (Boochs, et al., 2011). As most recent works, the tendency related to the use of semantic has been explored, (Ben Hmida, et al., 2010) (Hajian, et al., 2009) (Whiting, 2006) where the automatic data extraction from 3D point clouds presents one of the new challenges, especially for map updating, passenger safety and security improvements. However such domain is characterized by a specific vocabulary containing different type of object. In fact, the assumption that knowledge will help the improvement of the automation, the accuracy and the result quality is shared by specialists of the point cloud processing.

As a matter of fact, surveying with 3D scanners is spreading all domains. Terrestrial laser scanners have been established as a workhorse for topographic and building survey from the archaeology (Balzani, et al., 2004) to the architecture (Vale, et al., 2009). Actually, with every new scanner model on the market, the instruments become faster, more accurate and can scan objects at longer distances. Such technology presents a powerful tool for many applications and has partially replaced traditional surveying methods since it can speed up field work significantly. Actually, this powerful method allows the creation of 3D point clouds from objects or landscapes. However, the huge amount of data generated during the process proved to be costly in post-processing. The field time is very height since in most cases; processing techniques are still mainly affected by manual interaction of the user. Typical operations consist to clean point clouds, to delete unnecessary areas, to navigate in an often huge and complicated 3D structure, to select set of points, to extract and model geometries and objects. At the same time, it would be much more effective, to process the data automatically, which has already been recorded in a very fast and effective way.

From another side, the technical survey of facility aims to build a digital model based on geometric analysis. Such a process becomes more and more tedious. Especially with the new terrestrial laser scanners where a huge amount of 3D point clouds are generated. Within such scenario, new challenges have seen the light where the basic one is to make the reconstruction process automatic and more accurate. Thus, early works on 3D point clouds have investigated the reconstruction and the recognition of geometrical shapes (Pu, et al., 2007) to resolve this challenge. In fact, such a problematic was investigated as a topic of the computer graphic and the signal processing research where most works focused on segmentation or visualization aspects. As most recent works, the new tendency related to the use of semantic has been explored (Ben Hmida, et al., 2010). As a main operation, the technical survey relies fundamentally on the object reconstruction process where considerable effort has already been invested to reduce the impact of time consuming, manual activities and to substitute them by numerical algorithms. Unfortunately, most of such algorithmic conceptions are data-driven and concentrate on specific features of the objects being accessible to numerical models. By these models, which normally describe the behavior of geometrical (flatness, roughness…) or physical features (color, texture…), the data is classified and analyzed. Such strategies are static and not to allow a dynamic adjustment to the object or initial processing results. In further scenarios, an algorithm will be applied to the data producing better or minor results depending on several parameters like image or point cloud quality, the completeness of object representation, the viewpoints position, the complexity of object features, the use of control parameters and so on. Consequently, there is no feedback to the algorithmic part in order to choose a different algorithm or reuse the same algorithm with changed parameters. This interaction is mainly up to the user who has to decide by himself, which algorithms to apply for which kind of objects and data sets. Often good results can only be achieved by iterative processing controlled by a human interaction.

These problems can be solved when further information is integrated into the algorithmic process chain for object detection and recognition allowing supporting the process of validation. Such information might be derived from the context of the object itself and its behavior with respect to the data and/or other objects or from a systematic characterization of the parameterization and the effectiveness of the algorithms to be used. As programming languages used in the context of numerical treatments are not dedicated to process knowledge, their condition of use is not flexible and makes the integration of semantic aspects difficult.

As a matter of fact, the goal of our proposition is to develop efficient and intelligent methods for an automated processing of terrestrial laser scanner data, Fig 1. The principle our solution is a knowledge-based detection of objects in point clouds for AEC (Architecture, Engineering and Construction) engineering applications in correspondence to a project of the same name "WiDOP". In contrast to existing approaches, the project consists in using prior knowledge about the context and the objects. This knowledge is extracted from databases, CAD plans, Geographic Information Systems (GIS), technical reports or domain experts. Therefore, this knowledge is the basis for a selective knowledge-oriented detection and recognition of objects in point clouds. In such scenario, knowledge about such objects have to include detailed information about the objects' geometry, structure, 3D algorithms, etc.

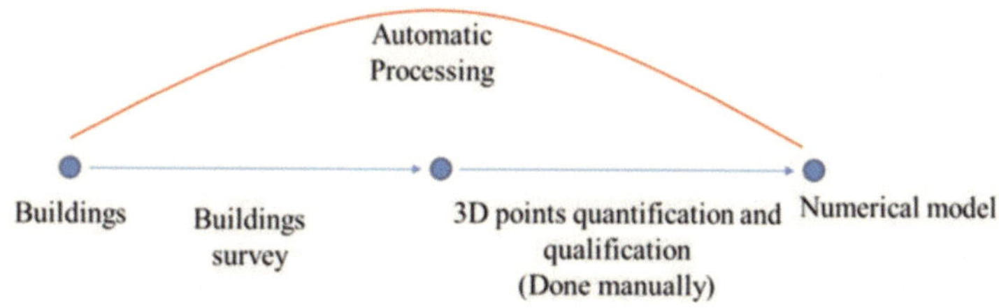

Fig. 1. Automatic processing compared to the manual one.

The present chapter aims at building a bridge between the semantic modelling and the numerical processing to define strategies based on domain knowledge and 3D processing knowledge. The knowledge will be structured in ontologies structure containing a variety of elements like already existing information about objects of that scene such as data sources (digital maps, geographical information systems, etc.), information about the objects' characteristics, the hierarchy of the sub-elements, the geometrical topology, the characteristics of processing algorithms, etc. In addition, all relevant information about the objects, geometries, inter and intra-relation and the 3D processing algorithms have been modeled inside the knowledge base, including characteristics such as positions, geometrics information, images textures, behavior and parameter of suitable algorithms, for example.

By this contribution, an approach on achieving the object detection and recognition within those inference engines will be presented. The major context behind the current chapter is the use of knowledge in order to manage the engineering problem in question based on heterogynous environment. It primarily focuses on 3D point clouds and its management through the available processing technologies for object detection and recognition incorporated through the knowledge. As the Web technologies get matured through its approach in the Semantic Web, the implementation of knowledge in this domain seems to be more appropriate.

This research puts forward the views and result of the research activities in the backdrop of the Semantic Web technologies and the knowledge management aspect within it. The suggested system is materialized via WiDOP project (Ben Hmida, et al., 2011). Furthermore, the created WiDOP platform is able to generate an indexed scene from unorganized 3D point clouds visualized within the virtual reality modelling language (W3C, 1995).

The following chapter is structured into section 2 which gives an overview of actual existing strategies for reconstruction processes, section 3 highlight the adopted languages and technologies for knowledge and semantic modeling, section 4 explains the suggested architecture for the WiDOP solution, section 5 presents an overview of the related knowledge model, section 6 emphasizes the intelligent process. Section 7 shows different strategies and level of knowledge for the processing, section 8 present the developed platform and gives first results for a real example, and finally section 9 concludes and shows next planned steps.

2. Background concept and methodology

The technical survey of facilities, as a long and costly process, aims at building a digital model based on geometric analysis since the modeling of a facility as a set of vectors is not sufficient in most cases. To resolve this problem, a new standard was developed over ten years by the International Alliance for Interoperability (IAI). It is named the IFC format (IFC - Industry Foundation Classes) (Vanland, et al., 2008). The specification is a neutral data format to describe exchange and share information typically used within the building and facility management industry. This norm considers the building elements as independent objects where each object is characterized by a 3D representation and defined by a semantic normalized label. Consequently, the architects and the experts are not the only ones who are able to recognize the elements, but everyone will be able to do it, even the system itself. For instance, an IFC Signal is not just a simple collection of lines and geometric primitives recognized as a signal; it is an "intelligent " object signal which has attributes linked to a geometrical definition and function. IFC files are made of objects and connections between these objects. Object attributes describe the "business semantic" of the object. Connections between objects are represented by "relation elements". This format and its semantics are the keystone of our solution.

The problematic of 3D object detection and scene reconstruction including semantic knowledge was recently treated within a different domain, basically the photogrammetry one (Pu, et al., 2007), the construction one, the robotics (Rusu, et al., 2009) and recently the knowledge engineering one (Ben Hmida, et al., 2010). Modeling a survey, in which low-level point cloud or surface representation is transformed into a semantically rich model is done in three tasks where the first is the data collection, in which dense point measurements of the facility are collected using laser scans taken from key locations throughout the facility; Then data processing, in which the sets of point clouds from the collected scanners are processed. Finally, modeling the survey in which the low-level point cloud is transformed into a semantically rich model. This is done via modeling geometric knowledge, qualifying topological relations and finally assigning an object category to each geometry (Boochs, et al., 2011). Concerning the geometry modeling, we remind here that the goal is to create simplified representations of facility components by fitting geometric primitives to the point cloud data. The modeled components are labeled with an object category. Establishing relationships between components is important in a facility model and must also be established. In fact, relationships between objects in a facility model are useful in many scenarios. In addition, spatial relationships between objects provide contextual information to assist in object recognition (Cantzler, 2003). Within the literature, three main strategies are described to rich such a model where the first one is based on human interaction with provided software's for point clouds classifications and annotations (Leica, 2011). While the second strategy relies more on the automatic data processing without any human interaction by using different segmentation techniques for feature extraction (Rusu, et al., 2009). Finally, new techniques presenting an improvement compared with the cited ones by integrating semantic networks to guide the reconstruction process have seen the light.

2.1 Manual survey model creation

In current practice, the creation of a facility model is largely a manual process performed by service providers who are contracted to scan and model a facility. In reality, a project may require several months to be achieved, depending on the complexity of the facility and the modeling requirements. Reverse engineering tools excel at geometric modeling of surfaces, but with the lack of volumetric representations, while such design systems cannot handle the massive data sets from laser scanners. As a result, modelers often shuttle intermediate results back and forth between different software packages during the modeling process, giving rise to the possibility of information loss due to limitations of data exchange standards or errors in the implementation of the standards within the software tools (Goldberg, 2005). Prior knowledge about component geometry, such as the diameter of a column, can be used to constrain the modeling process, or the characteristics of known components may be kept in a standard component library. Finally, the class of the detected geometry is determined by the modeler once the object is created. In some cases, relationships between components are established either manually or in a semi-automated manner.

2.2 Semi-Automatic and Automatic methods

The manual process for constructing a survey model is time consuming, labor-intensive, tedious, subjective, and requires skilled workers. Even if modeling of individual geometric primitives can be fairly quick, modeling a facility may require thousands of primitives. The combined modeling time can be several months for an average-sized facility. Since the same types of primitives must be modeled throughout a facility, the steps are highly repetitive and tedious (Hajian, et al., 2009). The above mentioned observations and others illustrate the need semi-automated and automated techniques for facility model creation. Ideally, a system could be developed that would take a point cloud of a facility as input and produce a fully annotated as-built model of the facility as output. The first step within the automatic process is the geometric modeling. It presents the process of constructing simplified representations of the 3D shape of survey components from point cloud data. In general, the shape representation is supported by Constructive Solid Geometry (CSG) (Corporation, 2006) or Boundary representation B-Rep representation (CASCADE, 2000). The representation of geometric shapes has been studied extensively (Campbell, et al., 2001). Once geometric elements are detected and stored via a specific presentation, the final task within a facility modeling process is the object recognition. It presents the process of labeling a set of data points or geometric primitives extracted from the data with a named object or object class. Whereas the modeling task would find a set of points to be a vertical plane, the recognition task would label that plane as being a wall, for instance. Often, the knowledge describing the shapes to be recognized is encoded in a set of descriptors that implicitly capture object shape. Research on recognition of facility's specific components related to a facility is still in its early stages. Methods in this category typically perform an initial shape-based segmentation of the scene, into planar regions, for example, and then use features derived from the segments to recognize objects. This approach is exemplified by Rusu et al. who use heuristics to detect walls, floors, ceilings, and cabinets in a kitchen environment (Rusu, et al., 2009). A similar approach was proposed by Pu and Vosselman to model facility façades (Pu, et al., 2009). To reduce the search space of object recognition algorithms, the use of knowledge related to a specific facility can be a fundamental solution. For instance, Yue et al. overlay a design model of a facility with the as-built point cloud to guide the process of identifying which data points belong to specific objects and to detect differences between the as-built and as-designed conditions (Yue, et al., 2006). In such cases, object recognition problem is simplified to be a matching problem between the scene model entities and the data points. Another similar approach is presented in

(Bosche, et al., 2008). Other promising approaches have only been tested on limited and very simple examples, and it is equally difficult to predict how they would fare when faced with more complex and realistic data sets. For example, the semantic network methods for recognizing components using context work well for simple examples of hallways and barren, rectangular rooms (Cantzler, 2003), but how would they handle spaces with complex geometries and clutter.

2.3 Discussion

The presented methods for survey modeling and object recognition rely on hand-coded knowledge about the domain. Concepts like "Signals are vertical" and "Signals intersect with the ground" are encoded either explicitly, through sets of rules, or implicitly, through the design of the algorithm. Such hard-coded, rule based approaches tend to be brittle and break down when tested in new and slightly different environments. Additionally, we can deduce that authors model the context but not the 3D processing algorithms, the geometry and the topology. Furthermore, it will be difficult in such a case to extend an algorithm with new rule or to modify the rules to work in new environments. To make it more flexible and efficient, and in contrast with the literature, we opt to use a new data structure labeled ontology. In fact, the last one presents a formal representation of knowledge by a set of concepts within a domain, and the relationships between those concepts. It is used to reason about the entities within that domain, and may be used to describe the domain where the basic strength of formal ontology is their ability to present knowledge within their taxonomy, relations and conditions, but also to reason in a logical way based on Description Logics DL concepts. Based on these observations, we predict that more standard and flexible representations of facility objects and more sophisticated guidance based algorithms for object detection instead of a standard one, by modeling algorithmical, geometrical and topological knowledge within an ontology structure will open the way to significant improvement in facility modeling capability and generality since it will allow as to create a more dynamic algorithm sequence for object detection based on object's geometries and to make more robust the identification process.

3. Knowledge and Semantic web

The growth of the World Wide Web has been tremendous since its evolvement both in terms of the content and the technology. The first Web generation was mainly presentation based. They provided information through the Web pages but did not allow users to interact with them. In short, they contained read only information. Moreover, they were only text pages and do not contain multimedia data. These Web sites have higher dependency on the presentation languages like Hypertext Markup Languages (HTML) (Horrocks, et al., 2004). With the introduction of e**X**tensible**M**arkup**L**anguage (XML), the information within the pages became more structured. Those XML based pages could hold up the contents in more structured method but still lack the proper definition of semantics within the contents, (Berners-Lee, 1998). For this reason, the needs of intelligent systems which could exploit the wide range of information available within the Web are widely felt. Semantic Web is envisaged to address this need.

The term "*Semantic Web*" is coined by Tim Berners-Lee in his work (Lee, et al., 2001) to propose the inclusion of semantic for better enabling machine-people cooperation for handling the huge information that exists in the Web. The term "*Semantic Web*" has been defined numerous time. Though there is no formal definition of Semantic Web, some of its most used definitions are "*The Semantic Web is not a separate Web but an extension of the current one, in which information is given well-defined meaning, better enabling computers and people to work in cooperation. It is a source to retrieve information from the Web (using the Web spiders from RDF files) and access the data through Semantic Web Agents or Semantic Web Services. Simply Semantic Web is data about data or metadata*" (Lee, et al., 2001). "*A Semantic Web is a Web where the focus is placed on the meaning of words, rather than on the words themselves: information becomes knowledge after semantic analysis is performed. For this reason, a Semantic Web is a network of knowledge compared with what we have today that can be defined as a network of information*" (Huynh, et al., 2007). "*The Semantic Web provides a common framework that allows data to be shared and reused across application, enterprise and community boundaries*" (Decker, et al., 2000). In the next subsection, we discuss the different issues related to the definition of such a technology where we focus mainly on the Description Logic theory (DL) and its impact on the semantic web technology.

3.1 The description logics

Actually, the convergence of formal foundations for extensible, semantically understood structure within description logic and the overall usability targets of the predecessor of DL and the Web languages for broader usability of Web has led to the effort such as Ontology Interface Language (OIL) (Fensel, et al., 2001). It presents the first major effort to develop a language which has its base in Description Logic. It was a part of the broader project called On-To-Knowledge funded by European Union. This is the first time that the concept within ontology is explicitly used within a Web based environment. However, it did not completely leave out the primitives of frame base languages with the formal semantics and reasoning capabilities by including them within the language. The syntax of OIL is based on RDF and XML with their limitations to provide complete semantic foundations at that time. However, it has started a trend of mapping description logic within the Web based language for Semantic Web. It maps description logic through $\mathcal{SHIQ}$. The derivation of $\mathcal{SHIQ}$ with respect to naming convention of the Description Logic is given as:

$\mathcal{S}$: Used for all $\mathcal{ALC}$ with transitive roles R+
$\mathcal{H}$: Role inclusion axioms $R1 \sqsubseteq R2$ (is_component_of $\sqsubseteq$ is_part_of)
$\mathcal{I}$: Inverse Role R-(isPartOf = hasPart-)
$\mathcal{Q}$: Qualified number restrictions

3.1.1 The base languages

Complex descriptions can be built up through the above mentioned elementary descriptions of concepts and roles. These descriptions are given different notations over the time. The Attributive Language ($\mathcal{AL}$) has been introduced in 1991 as minimal language that is of practical interest (Schmidt-Schauß, et al., 1991). It is further complemented through Attributive Concept Language with Complements ($\mathcal{ALC}$) to allow any concepts or roles to be included and not just atomic concepts and atomic roles which were the previous elements of descriptions. $\mathcal{ALC}$ is the important notation format to express Description Logics. Fig 2 illustrates the syntax rules on describing the concept.

Notation	Syntax	Semantics	Read-as
$\top$	$C, D \rightarrow \top$	$\top(x)$	Universal concept
$\bot$	$\bot$	$\bot\ (x)$	Bottom concept
$\sqcap$	$C \sqcap D$	$C(x) \sqcap D(x)$	Intersection
$\sqcup$	$C \sqcup D$	$C(x) \sqcup D(x)$	Union
$\neg$	$\neg C$	$\neg C(x)$	Negation
$\exists$	$\exists R.C$	$\exists R(x,y) \cap C(y)$	Existential Quantification
$\forall$	$\forall R.C$	$\forall y. R(x,y) \rightarrow C(y)$	Value Restriction

Here C and D are concept description and R is role

Fig. 2. The syntax and semantics based on $\mathcal{ALC}$.

We introduce in this section the terminological axioms, which make statements about how concepts or roles are related to each other. Then we single out definitions as specific axioms and identify terminologies as sets of definitions by which we can introduce atomic concepts as abbreviations or names for complex concepts. In the most general case, terminological axioms have the form $C \sqsubseteq D, R \sqsubseteq S\ Or\ C \equiv D, R \equiv S$ where C, D are concepts (and R, S are roles). Axioms of the first kind are called inclusions, while axioms of the second kind are called equalities. An equality whose left-hand side is an atomic concept. It´s used to introduce symbolic names for complex descriptions e,g. $RailWorker \equiv Person \sqcap \exists haswork. RailWork$. It could be clearly seen within Fig 2 that these concept descriptions are built with the concept constructors. The first four constructors are not dependent on the roles whereas the last two utilizes the roles in the constructors. This dependency is called role restrictions. Formally, a role restriction is an unnamed class containing all individuals that satisfy the restriction. DLs expressed through $\mathcal{ALC}$ provide two such restrictions in Quantifier restriction and value restrictions.

The Quantifier restriction

It´s again classified as the **existential quantifier** (at least one, or some) and **universal quantifiers** (every).

The existential quantifier links a restriction concept to a concept description or a data range. This restriction describes the unnamed concept for which there should be at least one instance of the concept description or value of the data value. Simplifying, the property restriction P relates to a concept of individuals x having at least one y which is either an instance of concept description or a value of data range so that *P(x,y)* is an instance of *P*.

From the other side, the **universal quantifier** () *(every)* constraint links a restriction concept to a concept description or a data range. This restriction describes the unnamed concept for which there should all instances of the concept description or value of the data value. Simplifying, the property restriction P relates to a concept of individuals x having all y which is either an instance of the concept description or a value of data range so that *P(x,y)* is concidered as an instance of *P*.

The Value restriction

It links a restriction concept directly to a value which could be either an individual or data value.

3.1.2 The description logics formalization

Description logics (DLs) are a family of logics which represents the structured knowledge. The Description Logic languages are knowledge representation languages that can be used to represent the knowledge of an application domain in a structured and formally well-understood way (McGuinness, et al., 2003), (Calvanese, et al., 2005). Description logics contain the formal, logic-based semantics, which present the major reason for its choice for Semantic Web languages over its predecessors. The reasoning capabilities within the DLs add a new dimension. Having these capabilities as central theme, inferring implicitly represented knowledge becomes possible. The movement of Description Logic into its applicability can be viewed in terms of its progression in Web environment (Noy, et al., 2001). Web languages such as XML or RDF(S) could benefit from the approach DL takes to formalize the structured knowledge representation (Lassila, 2007). This has laid background behind the emergence of Description Logic languages in Web. Actually, an agreement to encode these operators using an alphabetic letter to denote expressivity of DLs has seen the light. These letters in combinations are used to define the capabilities of DLs in terms of their performances. This implies to the DL languages as well. As could be seen in Fig 3, $\mathcal{ALC}$ has been extended to transitive role and given abbreviation S in the convention. Where S is used in every DL systems and languages as it plays significant role in shaping the behavioural nature of every DL systems.

$\mathcal{AL}$	$:C,D \rightarrow \top \mid \bot \mid A \mid C \sqcap D \mid \neg A \mid \exists R.T \mid \forall R.C$
$\mathcal{C}$	: Concept negation $\neg C$. Thus, $\mathcal{ALC}$=$\mathcal{AL}$+$\mathcal{C}$
$\mathcal{S}$	: Used for $\mathcal{ALC}$ with transitive role R+
$\mathcal{U}$	: Concept disjunction $C \sqcup D$
ε	: Existential quantification, $\exists R.C$
$\mathcal{H}$	: Role inclusions axioms, R1⊑ R2, e.g is_component_of ⊑ is_part_of
$\mathcal{N}$	:Number Restrictions, (≥ nR) and (≤ nR), e.g (≥ has_Child) (has at least 3 child)
$\mathcal{Q}$	:Qualified number restriction, (≥n R.C) and (≤n R.C) , e.g (≤2 has_child.Adult) (has at most 2 adult Children)
$\mathcal{O}$	:Nominals (singleton class), {a}. e.g $\exists has\_Child.\{mary\}$.
$\mathcal{I}$	:Inverse role R-, e.g isPartof=hasPart-
$\mathcal{F}$	:functional role, e.g functional(hasAge)
$\mathcal{R}$+	:Transitive role , e.g., transitive (isPartOf)
$\mathcal{R}$	:role inclusion with comparison, R1 o R2 ⊑ S, e.g, isPartOf o isPartOf ⊑ $isPartOf$

Fig. 3. Naming convention of Description Logic.

3.2 The knowledge base

Description Logics supports serialization through the human readable forms of the real world scenario with the classification of concepts and individuals. Moreover, they support the hierarchical structure of concepts in forms of subconcepts/superconcepts relationships of a concept between the concepts of a given terminology. This hierarchical structure provides efficient inference through the proper relations between different concepts. The individual-concept relationship could be compared to instantiation of an object to its class in object-oriented concept. In this manner, the approach DL takes can be related to classification of objects in a real world scenario. Description logics provide a formalization to knowledge representation of real world situations. This means it should provide the logical replies to the queries of real world situations. This is currently most researched topic in this domain. The results are highly sophisticated reasoning engines which utilize the capabilities of expressiveness of DLs to manipulate the knowledge. A Knowledge Representation system is a formal representation of a knowledge described through different technologies. When it is described through DLs, they set up a Knowledge Base (KB), the contents of which could be reasoned or infer to manipulate them. A knowledge base could be considered as a complete package of knowledge content. It is, however, only a subset of a Knowledge Representation system (KR) that contains additional components.

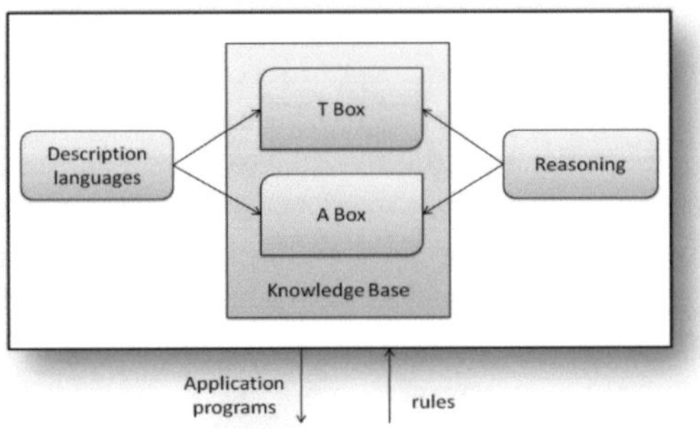

Fig. 4. The Architecture of a knowledge representation system based on DLs.

Baader (Baader, 2006) sketches the architecture of any KR system based on DLs. It could be seen the central theme of such a system is a Knowledge Base (KB). The KB constitutes of two components: the TBox and the ABox. Where **TBox** statements are the *terms* or the *terminologies* that are used within the system domain. In general they are statements describing the domain through the controlled vocabularies. For example in terms of a social domain the TBox statements are the set of concepts as *Rail, train, signal* etc. or the set of roles as *hasGeometry, hasDetectionAlg, hasCharacteristics* etc. ABox in other hand contains assertions to the TBox statements. In object oriented concept, **ABox** statements compliant **TBox** statements through instantiating what is equivalent to classes in TBox and relating the roles (equivalent to methods or properties in OO concept) to those instances.

The DLs are expressed through the *concepts* and *roles* of a particular domain. This complements well with the fact how knowledge is expressed in the general term. Concepts are sets of classes of individual objects. Where classes provide an abstraction mechanism for grouping resources with similar characteristics (Horrocks, et al., 2008). The concepts can be organized into superclass-subclass hierarchy which is also known as taxonomy. It shares the object-oriented concepts in managing the hierarchy of superconcept-subconcept. The sub-concepts are specialized concepts of their super-concepts and the super-concepts are generalized concepts of their sub-concepts. For an example all individuals of a class must be individuals of its superclass. In general all concepts are subsumed by their superclass. In any graphical representation of knowledge, concepts are represented through the nodes. Similarly the roles are binary relationship between concepts and eventually the relationships of the individuals of those concepts. They are represented by links in the graphical representation of knowledge. The description language has a model-theoretic semantics as the language for building the descriptions is independent to each DL system. Thus, statements in the TBox and in the ABox can be identified as first-order logic or, in some cases, a slight extension of it (Baader, et al., 2008).

3.3 The Web Ontology Language (OWL)

The association of knowledge with Semantic Web has provided a scope for information management through the knowledge management. Since both the technologies use ontology to conceptualize the scenarios, Semantic Web technology could provide a platform for developments of knowledge management systems (Uren, et al., 2006). The ontologies are core to both the technologies in whichever methods they are defined. The Semantic Web defines ontologies, (Gruber, 2008) through XML based languages and with the advancements in these languages. Within the computer science domain, ontologies are seen as a formal representation of the knowledge through the hierarchy of concepts and the relationships between those concepts. In theory ontology is a "*formal, explicit specification of shared conceptualization*" (Gruber, 2008). In any case, ontology can be considered as formalization of knowledge representation where the Description Logics (DLs) provide logical formalization to the Ontologies (Baader, et al., 2007).

OWL or the Web Ontology Language is a family of knowledge representation language to create and manage ontologies. It is in general term an extension of RDFS with addition to richer expressiveness that RDFS lacks through its missing features (Antoniou, et al., 2009). The OWL Working Group has approved two versions of OWL: OWL 1 and OWL 2, (Grau, et al., 2008). The Web Ontology Language (OWL) is intended to be used when the information contained in documents needs to be processed by applications and not by human (Antoniou, et al., 2009). The OWL language has direct influence from the researches in Description Logics and insights from Description Logics particularly on the formalization of the semantics. OWL takes the basic fact-stating ability of RDF (Allemang, et al., 2008) and the class- and property-structuring capabilities of RDF Schema and extends them in important ways. OWL own the ability to declare classes, and organise these classes in a subsumption ("subclass") hierarchy, as can RDF Schema. OWL classes can be specified as logical combinations (intersections, unions, or complements) of other classes, or as enumerations of specified objects, going beyond the capabilities of RDFS. OWL can also declare properties, organize these properties into a "subproperty" hierarchy, and provide domains and ranges for these properties, again as in RDFS. The domains of OWL properties are OWL classes, and ranges can be either OWL classes or externally-defined datatypes such as string or integer. OWL can state that a property is transitive, symmetric, functional, or is the inverse of another property, here again extending RDFS.

Add to that, OWL pocess the ability to specify which objects (also called "individuals") belong to which classes, and what the property values are of specific individuals. Equivalence statements can be made on classes and on properties, disjointness statements can be made on classes, and equality and inequality can be asserted between individuals.

However, the major extension over RDFS is the ability in OWL to provide restrictions on how properties behave that are local to a class. OWL can define classes where a particular property is restricted so that all the values for the property in instances of the class must belong to a certain class (or datatype); at least one value must come from a certain class (or datatype); there must be at least certain specific values; and there must be at least or at most a certain number of distinct values.

3.4 Semantic Web Rule Language (SWRL)

An inference process consists of applying logic in order to derive a conclusion based on observations and hypothesis. In computer science, interferences are applied through inference engines. These inference engines are basically computer applications which derive answers from a knowledge base. These engines depend on the logics through logic programming. The horn logic more commonly known Horn clause is a clause with at most one positive literal. It has been used as the base of logic programming and Prolog languages (Sterling, et al., 2009) for years. These languages allow the description of knowledge with predicates. Extensional knowledge is expressed as facts, while intentional knowledge is defined through rules (Spaccapietra, et al., 2004). These rules are used through different Rule Languages to enhance the knowledge possess in ontology. The Horn logic has given a platform to define Horn-like rules through sub languages of RuleML (Boley, et al., 2009). There have been different rule languages that have emerged in last few years. Some of these languages that have been evolving rapidly are Semantic Web Rule Language (SWRL) and Jena Rule. Both have their own built-ins to support the rules. With the actual work, SWRL language is used to rich the target concepts but it could be applied to others rule language based on Horn clauses.

Semantic Web Rule Language (Valiente-Rocha, et al., 2010) is a rule language based on the combination of the OWL-DL with Unary/Binary Datalog RuleML which is a sublanguage of the Rule Markup Language. One restriction on SWRL called DL-safe rules was designed in order to keep the decidability of deduction algorithms. This restriction is not about the component of the language but on its interaction. SWRL includes a high-level abstract syntax for Horn-like rules. The SWRL as the form, *antecedent→consequent*, where both antecedent and consequent are conjunctions of atoms written a1 ... an. Atoms in rules can be of the form *C*(x), *P*(x,y), *Q*(x,z), *sameAs*(x,y), *differentFrom*(x,y), or *builtIn*(*pred*, z1, ..., zn), where *C* is an OWL description, *P* is an OWL individual-valued property, *Q* is an OWL data-valued property, *pred* is a datatype predicate URI ref, x and y are either individual-valued variables or OWL individuals, and z, z1, ... zn are either data-valued variables or OWL data literals. An OWL data literal is either a typed literal or a plain literal. Variables are indicated by using the standard convention of prefixing them with a question mark (e.g., ?x). URI references (URI refs) are used to identify ontology elements such as classes, individual-valued properties and data-valued properties. For instance, the following rule, equation 1, asserts that one's parents' brothers are one's uncles where parent, brother and uncle are all individual-valued properties.

$$\text{Parent(?x, ?p)} \wedge \text{Brother(?p, ?u)} \rightarrow \text{Uncle(?x, ?u)} \quad (1)$$

The set of built-ins for SWRL is motivated by a modular approach that will allow further extensions in future releases within a hierarchical taxonomy. SWRL's built-ins approach is also based on the reuse of existing built-ins in XQuery and XPath, which are themselves based on XML Schema by using the Datatypes. This system of built-ins should also help in the interoperation of SWRL with other Web formalisms by providing an extensible, modular built-ins infrastructure for Semantic Web Languages, Web Services, and Web applications (OConnor, et al., 2008).

3.5 Swrl built-ins

These built-ins are keys for any external integration. They help in the interoperation of SWRL with other formalism and provide an extensible infrastructure knowledge based applications. Actually, *Comparisons Built-Ins, Math Built-Ins and Built-Ins for Strings* are already implemented within lots of platform for ontology management like protégé. In the actual work, new processing and topological built-in for the integration of 3D processing and topological knowledge are integrated respectively.

3.6 Discussion

Semantic Web technology is slowly modernizing the application of knowledge technologies, and though they existed before the Semantic Web, the implementation in their fullness is just being realized. Our actual research, materialized by WiDOP project relay on the above mentioned concept and technologies. In fact, this research benefits from the existing OWL languages, the existent inference engines through the inference rules and reasoning engines to reason the knowledge. However, the actual research works moves beyond semantic reasoning and semantic rule processing and attempts to implement new 3D processing and topological rule inference integrating the correspondent processing and topological built-Ins components in its structure to resolve the problem of object detection and annotation in 3D point clouds based on semantic knowledge.

4. Overview of the general WiDOP model

The problem of automatic object reconstruction remains a difficult task to realize in spite of many years of research. Major problems result from geometry and appearance of objects and their complexity, and impact on the collected data. For example, variations in a viewpoint may destroy the adjacency relations inside the data, especially when the object surface shows considerable geometrical variations. This dissimilarity affects geometrical or topological relations inside the data and even gets worse, when partial occlusions result in a disappearance of object parts. Efficient strategies therefore have to be very flexible and in principle need to model almost all factors having impact of the representation of an object in a data set. That leads to the finding, that at first a semantic model of a scene and the objects existing therein is required. Such a semantic description should be as close to the reality as possible and as necessary to take most relevant factors into account, which may have impact on later analysis steps. At least this comprises the objects to be extracted with their most characteristic features (geometry, shape, texture, orientation,...) and topological relations among each other. The decision upon features to be modelled should be affected by other important factors in an analysis step like characteristics of the data, the algorithms and their important features. Such a model might be supported by a DL-OWL ontology structure formed out of RDFS nodes and properties where the nodes represent classes or objects as their instances and the links show relationships of various characteristics. Such a network then contains the knowledge of that type of scene, which has to be processed. This knowledge base will act as basis for further detection and annotation activities and has to work in cooperation with numerical algorithms.

Up to this point, the new conception is still in concordance to other knowledge related set ups, although the degree of modelling goes farther because all relevant scene knowledge will be integrated. But another aspect will be considered also allowing to significantly improving processing strength. That is to integrate knowledge even on the algorithmic side. This means to make use of the flexibility of knowledge processing for decisions and control purposes inside the algorithmic processing chain. Even a propagation of findings from processing results into new knowledge for subsequent steps should be possible, what would give a completely new degree of dynamics and stability into the evaluation process.

It will finally leads to the conceptual view shown in Fig 5 where the general architecture for the suggested solutions is presented. It's composed of three parts: the knowledge model, the 3D processing algorithms execution and the interaction management and control part labelled WiDOP processing materialized within swrl rules and Built-Ins extensions, ensuring the interaction between the above sited parts. In contrast to existing approaches, we aim at the utilization of previous knowledge on objects. This knowledge can be contained in databases, construction plans, as-built plans or Geographic Information Systems (GIS). The suggested solution named as knowledge based detection of objects in point clouds (WiDOP) has its roots in the knowledge base which then guides individual algorithmic steps. Results from algorithms are also analyzed by the knowledge base and the reasoning engine, then deciding upon subsequent algorithmic steps is taken also from the knowledge base. Accordingly, detected objects and their features are populated to the knowledge base, which will permanently evolve until the work is done.

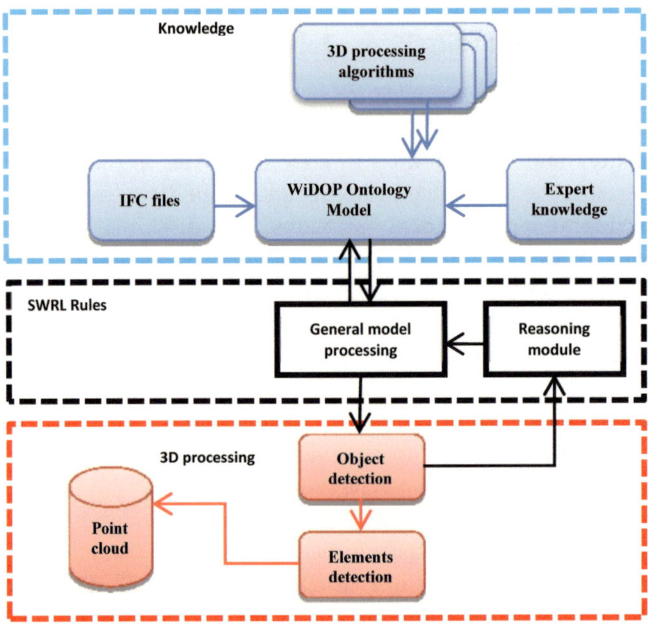

Fig. 5. WiDOP: Overview system.

4.1 The knowledge model

The needed knowledge for such purpose will be modelled within a top level ontology describing the general concept behind the knowledge domain. The suggested approach is intended to use semantics based on OWL technology for knowledge modelling and processing. Knowledge will be structured and formalized based on IFC schema, XML files, the domain concept which is the Deutsche Bahn scene in this case and 3D processing domain experts, etc., using classes, instances, relations and rules. An object in the ontology can be modelled as presented; a room has elements composed of walls, a ceiling and a floor. The sited elements are basic objects. They are defined by their geometry (plane, boundary, etc.), features (roughness, appearance, etc.), and also the qualified relations between them (adjacent, perpendicular, etc.). The object "room" gets its geometry from its elements, and further characteristics may be added such as functions in order to estimate the existent sub elements. For instance, a "classroom" will contain "tables", "chairs", "a blackboard", etc. The detection of the object "room" will be based on an algorithmic strategy which will look for the different objects contained in the point cloud. This means, using different detection algorithms for each element, based on the above mentioned characteristics, will allow us to classify most of the point region in the different element categories. It corresponds to the spatial structure of any facility, and it is an instance of semantic knowledge defined in the ontology. This instance defines the rough geometry and the semantics of the building elements without any real measurement. This model contains also knowledge extracted from the technical literature of the domain and knowledge from experts of the domain too. In addition, the ontology is as well enriched with knowledge about 3D processing algorithms and populated with the results of experiences undertaken on 3D point clouds, which define the empirical knowledge extracted from point clouds regarding a specific domain of application.

4.2 The 3D processing algorithms

Numerical processing includes a number of algorithms or their combination to process the spatial data. Strategies include geometric element detection (straight line, plane, surface, etc.), projection - based region estimation, histogram matrices, etc. All of these strategies are either under the guidance of knowledge, or use the modelled prior knowledge to estimate the object intelligently and optimally. Alongside with 3D point clouds, various types of input, data sets can be used such as images, range images, point clouds with intensity or color values, point clouds with individual images oriented to them or even stereo images without a point cloud. All sources are exploited for application to particular strategies. Knowledge not only describes the information of the objects, but also gives a framework for the control of the selected strategies. The success rate of detection algorithms using RANSAC (Tarsha-Kurdi, et al., 2007), Iterative Closest Point (Milella, et al., 2006) and Least Squares Fitting (Cantrell, 2008) should significantly increase by making use of the knowledge background. However, we are planning not only to process point data sets but also based on a surface and volume representation like mesh, voxels and bounding Boxes. These methods and others will be selected in a flexible way, depending on the semantic context.

4.3 The WiDOP processing

In order to manage the interaction between the knowledge part and the 3D processing one, a new layer labelled WiDOP processing materialized within rules is created. This layer ensures the control and the management of the knowledge transaction and the decision taken based on SWRL languages and its extensions through several steps explained within the next section. The semantic within the ontologies expressed through OWL-DL language can be used for further inferences. For instance, the following rule asserts that a Bounding Box with lines higher then 5 m are masts where Masts, Bounding Boxes and lines are all individual-valued properties. The DL syntax related to such an expression is Mast $\sqsubseteq$ ($\mathit{Bounding\ Box}$ $\sqcap \exists$ $\mathit{hasLine}$.Line $\sqcap \exists$ hasHeight.{> 5}) while the swrl conversion of such an expression is BoundingBox(?x) $\wedge$ hasLine(?x,?y) $\wedge$ hasHeight (?y,?h) $\wedge$ swrlb:GreaterThan (?h, 5) → Mast(?x).

The set of built-ins for SWRL is motivated by a modular approach that will allow further extensions in future releases within taxonomy. SWRL's built-ins approach is also based on the reuse of existing built-ins in XQuery and XPath, which are themselves based on XML Schema by using the Datatypes. This system of built-ins should as well help in the interoperation of SWRL rules with other Web formalisms by providing an extensible, modular built-ins infrastructure for Semantic Web Languages, Web Services, and Web applications. Many built-ins are defined. These built-ins are keys for any external integration where we take advantages of this extensional mechanism to integrate new Built-ins for 3D processing and topological processing.

4.4 Interaction process

To focus on the suggested method for the combination of the Semantic Web technologies and the 3D processing algorithms, Fig 6 illustrates an UML sequence diagram that represents the general design of the proposed solution. Hence, the purpose is to create a more flexible, easily extended approach where algorithms will be executed reasonably and adaptively on particular situations following an interaction process.

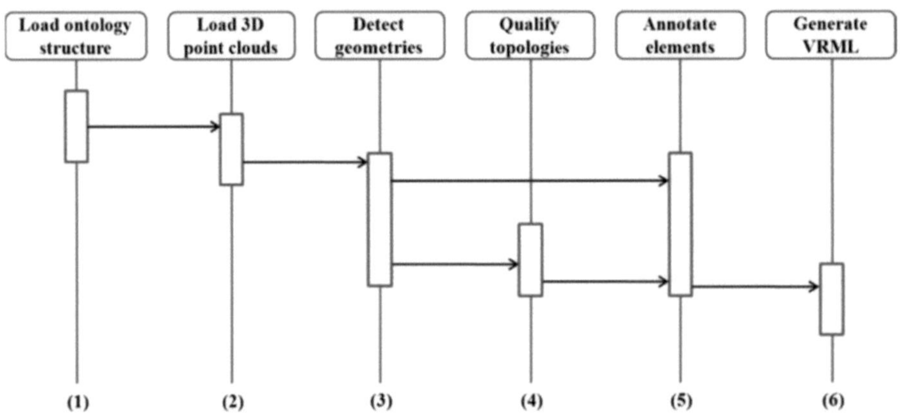

Fig. 6. The sequence diagram of interactions between the laser scanner, the 3D processing, the knowledge processing and the knowledge base

The processing steps can be detailed where three main steps aim at detecting and identifying objects.

(3) From 3D point clouds to geometric elements.
(4) From geometry to topological relations.
(5) From geometric and/or topological relations to semantic annotated elements.

As intermediate steps, the different geometries within a specific 3D point clouds are detected and stored within the ontology structure. Once done, the existent topological relations between the detected geometries are qualified and then populated in the knowledge base. Finally, detected geometries are annotated semantically, based on existing knowledge's related to the geometric characteristics and topological relations, where the input ontology contains knowledge about the Deutsche Bahn railway objects and knowledge about 3D processing algorithms.

5. Description of the WiDOP knowledge base

This section discusses the different aspects related to the domain concept top level ontology structure installed behind the WiDOP Deutsche Bahn prototype (Ben Hmida, et al., 2010). It's composed mainly by the classes and their relationships. Hence, we try to discuss theses component in term of axiom representing them.

The domain ontology presents the core of our research and provides a knowledge base to the created application. The global schema of the modelled ontology structure offers a suitable framework to characterize the different Deutsche Bahn elements from the 3D processing point of view. The created ontology is used basically for two purposes:

- To guide the processing algorithm sequence creation based on the target object characteristics.
- To ensure the semantic annotation of the different detected objects inside the target scene.

In fact, the ontology is managed through different components of description logics where the class axioms contain their own prefixes used to define their names. One of the big advantages of using prefix is that the same class could be used by applying different prefix for the class. Other advantages include the simplification in defining the resource and to solve the ambiguity for different context. The hierarchical structure of the top level class axioms of the ontology is given in Fig 7, where we find five main classes within other data and objects properties able to characterize the scene in question.

5.1 Class axioms

The class axiom `DC:DomainConcept` which represents the different object found in the target scene can be considered the main class in this ontology as it is the class where the target objects are modelled, this class is further specialized into classes representing the different detected object. However, the importance of other classes cannot be ignored. They are used to either describe the object geometry through the `Geom:Geometry` class axiom by defining its geometric component or the bounding box of the object that indicate its coordinates or to either describe its characteristics through the `Charac:Characteristics` class axiom. Additionally, the suitable algorithms are automatically selected based on its compatibility within the object geometry and characteristics via the `Alg:Algorithm` class. Add to that, other classes, equally significant, play their roles in the backend. The connection between the basic mentioned classes is carried out through object and data properties axioms.

5.2 Properties axioms

The properties axioms define relationship between classes in the ontology. They are also used to relate an object to other via topological relations. Actually, we found four major object properties axioms in the top level ontology which have their specialized properties for the specialized activities, Fig. 7, `DC:hastopologicRelation`, `Alg:isDeseignedFor`, `Geom:hasGeometry`, `Charac:hasCharacteristics`.

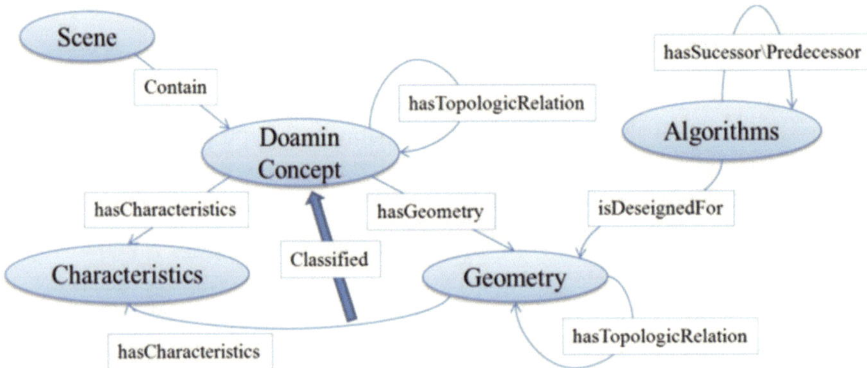

Fig. 7. Ontology general schema overview.

5.3 Created knowledge layers

Following to above considerations and with respect to technological possibilities, the current ontology will be modelled in various levels. In principle, we have to distinguish between object-related knowledge and algorithmic related knowledge. We therefore have a layer of the object knowledge and a layer of the algorithmic knowledge containing the respective semantic information.

5.3.1 Layers of object knowledge

The object knowledge layer will be classified in three categories: geometric, topological and semantic knowledge representing a certain scenario (Whiting, 2006) Therefore we distinguish between:

- Deutsche Bahn Scene knowledge
- Geometric knowledge
- Topological knowledge

Layer of the Deutsche Bahn Scene knowledge

The layer of object knowledge contains all relevant information about the objects and elements which might be found within a Deutsch Bahn scene. This might comprise a list such as: {Signals, Mast, Schalanlage, etc.}. They are used to fix either the main scene within its point clouds file and size through attributes related to the scene class, or even to characterize detected element with different semantic and geometric characteristics. The created knowledge base related to the Deutsche Bahn scene has been inspired next to our discussion with the domain expert and next to our study based on the official Web site for the German rail way specification "http://stellwerke.de". An overview of the targeted elements, the most useful and discriminant characteristics to detect it and their inter-relationship is presented in Table 1 .

Class	Sub Class	Subsub Class	Height	Correspondent image
Signals	Basic Signals	Main Signal	Between 4 and 6 m	
		Distant Signal	Between 4 and 6 m	
	Secondary signal	Vorsignalbake	between 1,5 and 2.5 m	
		Breakpoint_table	between 1 and 2 m	
		Chess_board	between 1 and 1,5 m	
Mast	BigMast	More than 6m		
	NormalMast	Between 5 and 6		
Schaltanlage	Schalthause	Less than 1m		
	SchaltSchrank	Less than 0,5m		

Table 1. Example of the Deutsche Bahn scene objects

Table 1 shows a possible collection of scene elements in case of a Deutsche Bahn scene. They may be additionally structured in a hierarchical order as might be seen convenient for a scene while Fig8 shows the suggested taxonomical structure to model them within the OWL language.

Basically, a railway signal is one of the most important elements within the Deutsche Bahn scene where we find `DC:main_signals` and `DC:secondary_signal`. The main signals are classified onto `DC:primary_signal` and `DC:distant_signal`. In fact, the primary signal is a railway signal indicating whether the subsequent section of track may be driven on. A primary signal is usually announced through a distant signal. The last one indicates which image signal to be expected that will be associated to the main signal in a distance of 1 km. Actually, big variety of secondary signals exists like the `DC:Vorsignalbake`, the `DC:Haltepunkt` and others. From the other side, the other discriminant elements within the same scene are the `DC:Masts` presenting electricity born for the energy alimentation. Usually, masts are distant from 50 m from to others. Finally, the `DC:Schaltanlage` elements present small electric born connected to the ground. For detection purpose, we define for example a signal as:

$$\text{DC: Signal} \sqsubseteq Geom{:}VerticalBB \sqcap \exists\ hasheight.\{>6\} \sqcap \exists\ hasDistanceFrom.DC{:}Mast\{>50\}$$

The above cited concepts are extended by relations to other classes or data. As an example, the data property `Geom:has_Bounding_Box` aims to store the placement of the detected object in a bounding box defined by its eight 3D points characterized by x, y and z values each one.

To specify its semantic characteristics, new classes are created, aiming to characterize a semantic object by a set of features like colour, size, visibility, texture, orientation and its position in the point cloud. To do so, new object properties axioms like `Geom:has_Color`, `Geom:has_Size`, `Geom:has_Orientation`, `Geom:has_Visibility` and `Geom:has_Texture` are created linking the `DC:DomainConcept` class to the `Charac:color"`, `Charac:size`, `Charac:Orientation`, `Charac:Visibility` and `Charac:Texture`classes axioms respectively.

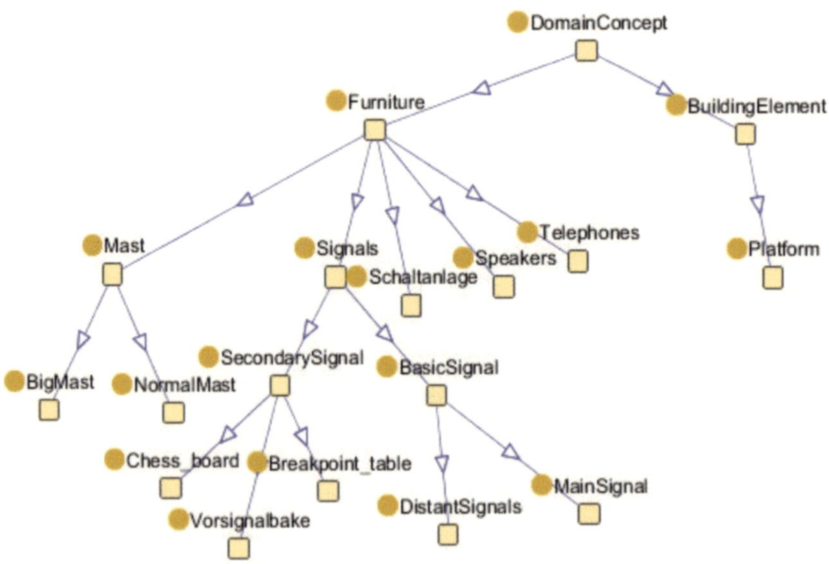

Fig. 8. Example of the DB scene objects modelling.

Layer of the geometric knowledge

Geometrical knowledge formulates geometrical characteristics to the physical properties of scene elements. In the simplest case, this information might be limited to few coordinates expressing a bounding box containing the object. However, for elements being accessible to functional descriptions, additional knowledge will be mentioned. A signal, for example, has vertical lines, which needs to be described by a line equation, its values and completed by width and height. In fact, we think that such knowledge can present a discriminant feature able to improve the automatic annotation process. For this reason, we opt to study the different geometric features related to the cited semantic elements, then, use only the discriminant one as basic features for a given object. The following table gathers the object characteristics together regarding the properties of a bounding box, Table 2, Fig 9.

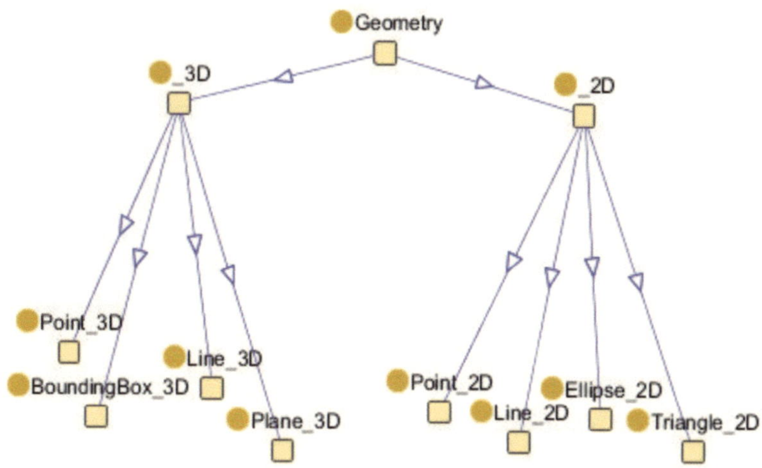

Fig. 9. The geometry class hierarchy.

Class	SubClass	Subsub Class	Restriction on Line number	Restriction on Planes number
Signals	Basic Signals	Main Signal	1 or 2 Vertical line	0
		Distant Signal	1 or 2 Vertical line	0
	Secondary signal	Vorsignalbake	1 Vertical line	1 Vertical plane
		Breakpoint_table	2 Vertical lines	1 Vertical Plan
		Chess_board	1 Vertical line	1 Vertical plane
Mast	BigMast	More than 6m	2 or 4 vertical lines	0
	NormalMast	Between 5 and 6	2 or 4 vertical lines	0
Schaltanlage	Schalthause	Less than 1m		1 Vertical plane 1 Horizontal plane
	SchaltSchrank	Less than 0,5m		1 vertical plane

Table 2. Geometric characteristics overview.

Layer of the topologic knowledge

While exploring the railway domain, lots of standard topological rules are imposed; such rules are used to help the driver and to ensure the passengers' security. From our point of view, the created rules are helpful also to verify and to guide the annotation process. In fact, topological knowledge represents adjacency relationships between scene elements. For instance, and in case of the Deutsche Bahn scene, the distance between the distant signal and the main one corresponds to the stopping distance that the trains require. The stopping distance shall be set on specific route and is in the main lines often 1000 m or in a rare case 700 m. Add to that, three to five Vorsignalbake are distant from 75m while then the last one is distant 100m from the distant signal, Fig.11.

At semantic view, topological properties describe adjacency relations between classes. For example, the property `Topo:isParallelTo` allows characterizing two geometric concepts

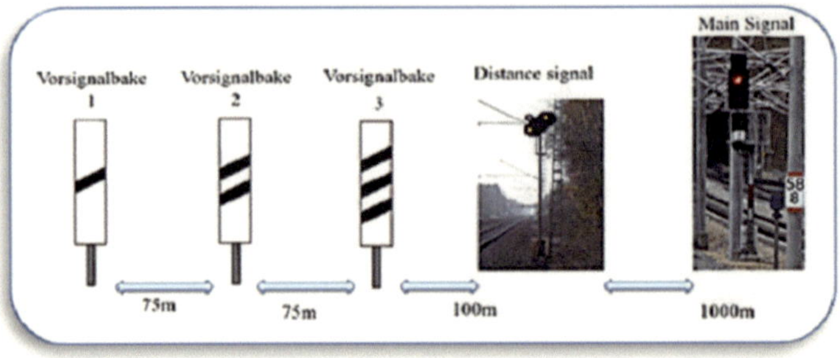

Fig. 10. Topological rules.

by the feature of parallelism. Similarly relations like `Topo:isPerpendicularTo` and `Topo:isConnectedTo` will help to characterize and exploit certain spatial relations and make them accessible to reasoning steps.

5.3.2 Layer of 3D processing knowledge

The 3D processing algorithmic layer contains all relevant aspects related to the 3D processing algorithms. It contains algorithm definitions, properties, and geometries related to each defined algorithms. An importance achievement is the detection and the identification of objects, which has a linear structure such as signal, indicator column, and electric pole, etc., through utilizing their geometric properties. Since the information in point cloud data sometimes is unclear and insufficient, the various methods to RANSAC (Tarsha-Kurdi, et al., 2007) are combined and upgraded. This combination is able to robustly detect the best fitting lines in 3D point clouds for example. Fig11 presents the Mast object constructed by linear elements, ambiguously represented in point cloud as blue points. Green lines are results of possible fitting lines and clearly show the shape of the object that is defined in the ontology. The object generated from this part is a bounding box that includes all inside geometries of the object and a concept label.

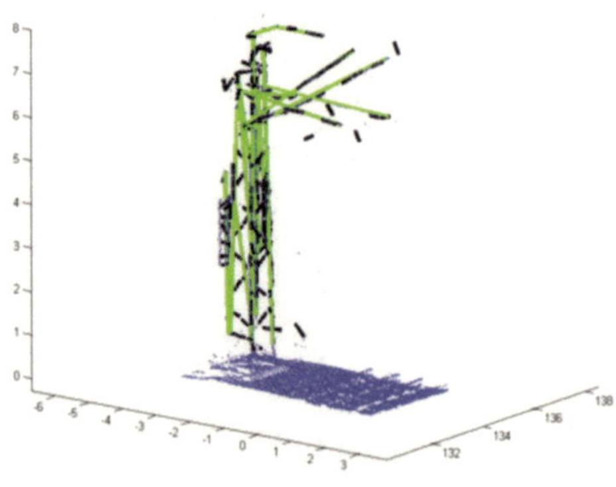

Fig. 11. Mast detection.

Next to the 3D expert recommendation, knowledge within the Table 3 is created linking a set of 3D processing algorithms to the target detected geometry; the input and output.

Algorithm name	has Input	hasOutput	isDesignedfor	hasSuccessor
Vertical Objects Detection	PointCloud	Point_2D	Vertical gemetry	None
Segmentationin2D	Point_2D PointCloud	SubPointCloud	Vertical gemetry	VerticalObjectsDetection
BoundingBox	SubPointCloud	Point_3D	Vertical gemetry	Segmentationin2D
ApproximateHeight	SubPointCloud	number	Geometry height	Segmentationin2D
RANSAC Line Detection	SubPointCloud	Line_3D	3D Lines	Segmentationin2D)
FrontFaceDetection	SubPointCloud	Boolean	Geometry with front face	Segmentationin2D
CheckPerpendicular	Line_3D	Boolean	Geometry containing Perpendicular elements	LinesDetectionin3DbyRANSAC
CheckParallel	Line_3D	Boolean	Geometry containing Parallel elements	LinesDetectionin3DbyRANSAC

Table 3. 3D processing algorithms and experts observations

The specialized classes of the `Alg:Algorithm` axiom are representing all the algorithms developed in the 3D processing layer. They are related to several properties which they are able to detect. These properties (Geometric and semantic) are shared with the `DC:DomainConcept` and the `Geom:Geometry` classes: By this way, a sequence of algorithms can detect all the characteristics of an element.

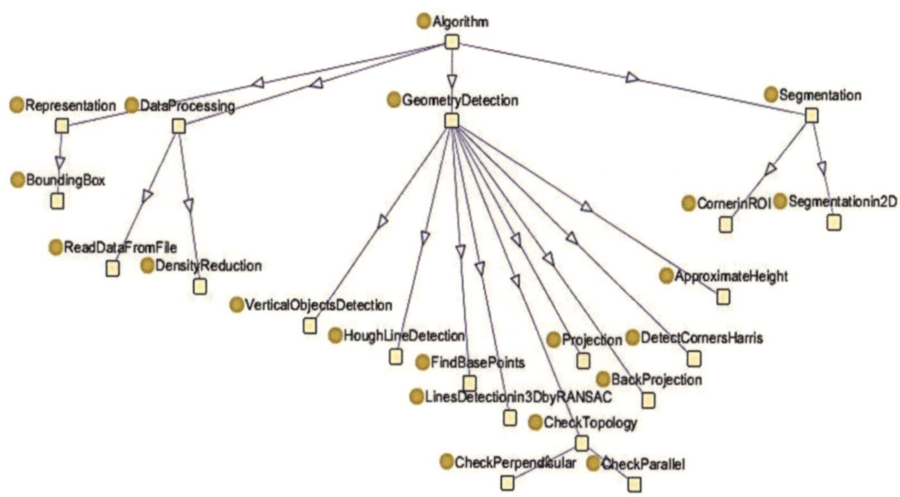

Fig. 12. Hierarchical structure of the Algorithm class.

The following section presents in details the semantic integration process undertaken in the WiDOP solution to detect and annotate semantically the eventual semantic elements.

6. Intelligent process

The basic strength of formal ontology is their ability to reason in a logical way based on Descriptive Logic language DL. As seem, the last one presents a form of logic to reason on objects. Lots of reasoners exist nowadays like Pellet (Sirin, et al., 2007), and KAON (U. Hustadt, 2010). Actually, despite the richness of OWL's set of relational properties, the axioms does not cover the full range of expressive possibilities for object relationships that we might find, since it is useful to declare relationship in term of conditions or even rules. These rules are used through different rules languages to enhance the knowledge possess in an ontology.

Within the actual research, the domain ontologies are used to define the concepts, and the necessary and sufficient conditions on them. These conditions are of value, because they are used to populate new concepts. For instance, the concept `Goem:Vertical_BoudinBox` can be specialized into `DC:Signal` if it contains a `Goem:VerticalLines`. Consequently, the concept `DC:Signal` will be populated with all `Goem:Vertical_BoudinBox` if they are linked to a `Goem:VerticalLines` with certain parameters. In addition, the rules are used to compute more complex results such as the topological relationships between objects. For instance, the relations between two objects are used to get new efficient knowledge about the object. The ontology is than enriched with this new relationship. The topological relation built-ins are not defined in the SWRL language. Consequently, the language was extended. To support the defined use cases, two basic further layers to the semantic one are added to ontology in order to ensure the geometry detection and annotation process tasks. These operations are the 3D processing and topological relations qualification respectively.

6.1 Integration of 3D processing operations

The 3D processing layer contains all relevant aspects related to the 3D processing algorithms. Its integration into the suggested semantic framework is done by special Built-Ins. They manage the interaction between processing layers and the semantic one. In addition, it contains the different algorithm definitions, properties, and the related geometries to the each defined algorithms. An importance achievement is the detection and the identification of objects with specific characteristics such as a signal, indicator columns, and electric pole, etc. through utilizing their geometric properties. Since the information in point cloud data sometimes is unclear and insufficient, the Semantic Web Rule Language within extended built-ins is used to execute a real 3D processing algorithm, and to populate the provided knowledge within the ontology (e.g. Table 4). The equation 2 illustrate the "3D_swrlb_Processing: VerticalElementDetection" built-ins for example, it aims at the detection of geometry with vertical orientation. The prototype of the designed Built-in is:

3D_swrlb_Processing:VerticalElementDetection(?Vert, ?Dir) (2)

Where the first parameter presents the target object class, and the last one presents the point clouds' directory defined within the created scene in the ontology structure. At this point, the detection process will result bounding boxes, representing a rough position and orientation of the detected object. Table 4 shows the mapping between the 3D processing built-ins, which is computer and translated to predicate, and the corresponding class.

3D Processing Built-Ins	Correspondent Simple class
3D_swrlb_Processing: VerticalElementDetection (?Vert,?Dir)	Geom:Vertical_BoundingBox(?x)
3D_swrlb_Processing: HorizentalElementDetection (?Vert,?Dir)	Geom:Horizental_BoundingBox(?y)

Table 4. 3D processing Built-Ins mapping.

6.2 Integration of topological operations

The layer of the topological knowledge represents topological relationships between scene elements since the object properties are also used to link an object to others by a topological relation. For instance, a topological relation between a distant signal and a main one can be defined, as both have to be distant from one kilometer. The qualification of topological relations in to the semantic framework is done by new topological Built-Ins. This step aims at verifying certain topology properties between detected geometries. Thus, 3D_Topologic built-ins have been added in order to extend the SWRL language. Topological rules are used to define constrains between different elements. After parsing the topological built-ins and its execution, the result is used to enrich the ontology with relationships between individuals that verify the rules. Similarly to the 3D processing built-ins, our engine translates the rules with topological built-ins to standard rules, Table 5.

Function	Correspondent topologic Built-Ins	Correspondent object property	Characteristics
Upper	3D_swrlb_Topology:Upper(?x, ?y)	Upper(?x,?y)	Transitive
Intersect	3D_swrlb_Topology:Intersect(?x, ?y)	Intersect(?x,?y)	Symmetric
Distance	3D_swrlb_Topology: Distance (?x, ?y,?d)	Distance(?x, ?y, ?d)	Symmetric

Table 5. Example of topological built-ins.

6.3 Guiding 3D processing algorithms

Actually, the created knowledge base aims to satisfy two basic purposes, which are, guiding the processing algorithm sequence creation based on the target object characteristics, and facilitate the semantic annotation of the different detected objects inside the target scene. Let's remember that one of the main ideas behind our suggestions is to direct, adapt and select the most suitable algorithms based on the object's characteristics. In fact, one algorithm could not detect and recognize different existent objects in the 3D point clouds, since they are distinguished by different shapes, size and capture condition. The role of knowledge is to provide not only the object's characteristics (shape, size, color...) but also object's status (visibility, correlation) to algorithmic part, in order to adjust its parameters to adapt with a current situation. Based on these observations, we issue a link from algorithms to objects based on the similar characteristics as Fig.13 shows.

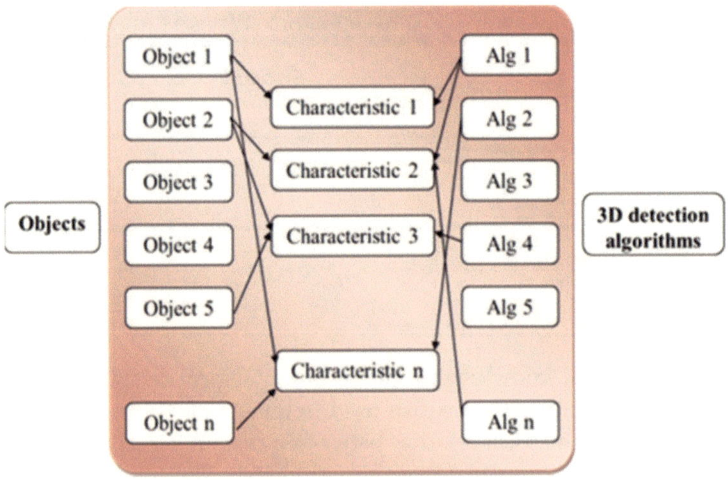

Fig. 13. Algorithms selection based on object's characteristics.

In fact, knowledge controls one or more algorithms for detecting an object. To do, a match between the object's characteristics and characteristics that a certain algorithm can be used for is achieved. For example, object O has characteristics: C_1, C_2, C_3; and algorithm A_i can detect characteristic C_1, C_3, C_4, while the algorithm A_j can detect characteristic C_2, C_5. Then, the decision algorithm will select A_i and A_j since these algorithms have the capability to detect the characteristics of an object O. The set of characteristics are determined by the object's properties such as geometrical features and appearance. Once done, selected algorithms will be executed and target characteristics will be detected. Let's recall that the whole process takes as input, the 3D point clouds scenes, and an ontology structure presenting a knowledge base to manipulate objects, geometries, topologies and relations (Object and data property) and produces as an output, an annotated scene within the same ontology structure. As intermediate steps, the different geometries within a specific 3D point cloud scene are detected and stored in the ontology structure. Once knowledge about geometries and the topologies are experienced, SWRL rules aim at qualifying and annotating the different detected geometries. The following equation 3 illustrates the DL definition of a Mast element while the simple example, equation 4, shows how a SWRL rule can specify the class of a VerticalBoundingBox, which is of type Mast regarding its altitude. The altitude is highly relevant only for this element.

$$\mathrm{DC.Mast} \sqsubseteq G\mathrm{eom.VerticalBB} \sqcap \exists\ \mathrm{hasheight.}\{> 6\} \tag{3}$$

$$\mathrm{3DProcessingSWRL: VerticalElementDetection(?\,Vert, ?\,dir)\ \ altitude\ (?\,x, ?\,alt)}$$

$$\mathrm{\hat{}swrlb: moreThan\ (?\,alt, 6)} \quad \rightarrow \mathrm{DC: Mast\ (?\,Vert)} \tag{4}$$

In other cases, geometric knowledge is not sufficient for the previous process. In such scenario, the topological relationships between detected geometries are helpful to manage the annotation process, equation 5. Equation 6 demonstrates how semantic information about existing objects is used conjunctly with topological relationships in order to define the class of another object.

$$\text{DC: Mast} \sqsubseteq DC{:}Mast \sqcap Geom{:}VerticalBB \sqcap \exists\ hasheight\{>6\}$$
$$\sqcap\ \exists hasDistanceFrom.DC{:}Mast.\{>50\} \quad (5)$$

$$\text{DC: Mast (?vert1) VerticalBB (?Vert2) hasDistanceFrom}$$
$$\text{(?vert1, ?vert2, 50)} \rightarrow \text{DC: Mast(?vert2)} \quad (6)$$

7. WiDOP prototype

The created WiDOP prototype takes in consideration the adjustment of the old methods and, in the meantime, profit from the advantages of the emerging cutting-edge technology. From the principal point of view, the developed system still retains the storing mechanism within the existent 3D processing algorithms; in addition, suggest a new field of detection and annotation, where we are getting a real-time support from the created knowledge. Add to that, we suggest a collaborative Java Platform based on semantic web technology (OWL, RDF, and SWRL) and knowledge engineering in order to handle the information provided from the knowledge base and the 3D packages results.

The process enriches and populates the ontology with new individuals and relationships between them. In addition, the created WiDOP platform offers the opportunity to materialize the annotation process by the generation and the visualization based on a VRML structure, (W3C, 1995) alimented from the knowledge base. It ensures an interactive visualization of the resulted annotation elements beginning from the initial state, to a set of intermediate states coming finally to an ending state, Fig 17 where the set of rules are totally executed. The resulting ontology contains enough knowledge to feed a GIS system, and to generate IFC file (Vanland, et al., 2008) for CAD software. The created system is composed of three main parts.

- Generation of a set of geometries from a point could file based on the target object characteristics.
- Computation of business rules with geometry, semantic and topological constrains in order to annotate the different detected geometries.
- Generation of a VRML model related to the scene within the detected and annotated elements.

As a first impression, the system responds to the target requirement since it would take a point cloud of a facility as input and produce a fully annotated as-built model of the facility as output.

7.1 System evaluation

For the demonstration of the created system, a scanned point cloud section related to Deutsch Bahn scene in the city of *Nürnberg* was extracted. While the last one measure 87 kms, we have just taken a small scene of 500m. It contains a variety of the target objects. The

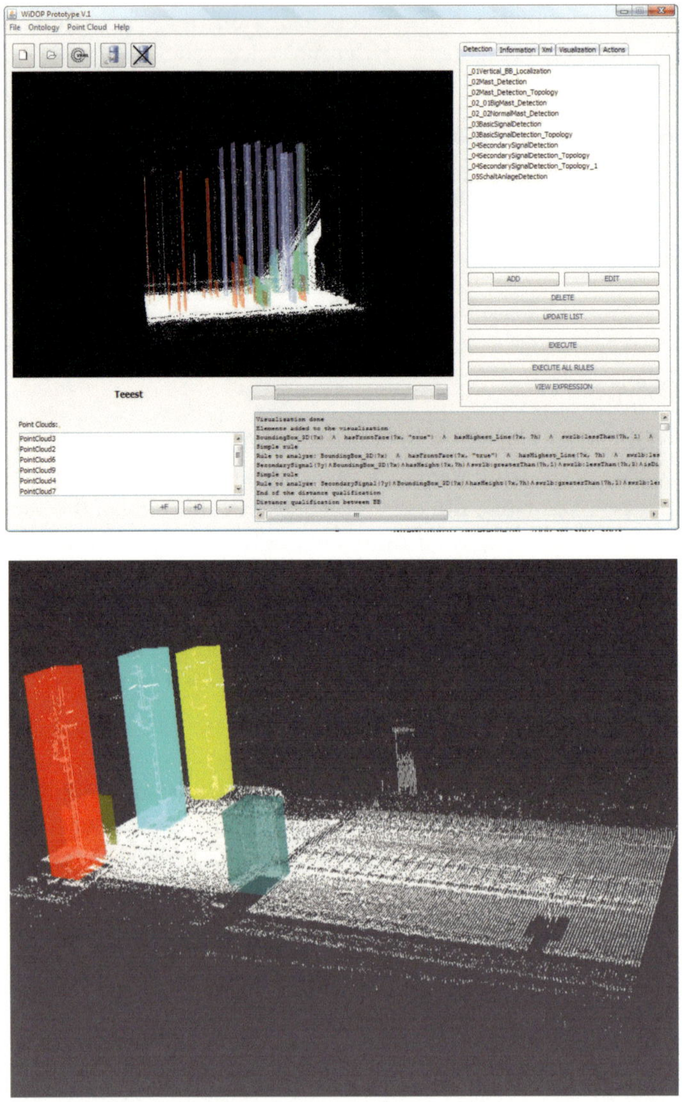

Fig. 14. Snapshot of the WiDOP prototype (top), Detected and annotated elements visualization within VRML language (bottom).

whole scene has been scanned using a terrestrial laser scanner fixed within a train, resulting in a large point cloud representing the surfaces of the scene objects. Within the created prototype, different SWRL rules are processed. First, geometrical elements will be searched in the area of interest based on dynamic 3D processing algorithm sequence created depending on semantic object properties. The second step aims to identify existing topologies between the detected geometries. Thus, useful topologies for geometry annotation are tested. Topological Built-Ins like `topo:isConnected`, `topo:touch`, `topo:Perpendicular`, `topo:isDistantfrom` are created. As a result, relations found between geometric elements are propagated into the ontology, serving as an improved knowledge base for further processing and decision.

The last step consists in annotating the different geometries. Vertical elements with certain characteristics can be annotated directly. Subsequently, further annotation may be relayed on aspects expressing facts to orientation or size of elements, which may be sufficient to finalize a decision upon the semantic of an object or, in more sophisticated cases, our prototype allows the combination of semantic information and topological ones that can deduce more robust results minimizing the false acceptation rate. The extracted scene contains 37 elements. As well, in most cases, our annotation process is able to affect the right label to the detected Bounding box based on knowledge on its component, its internal and external topology where among 13 elements are classified as Masts, three as a SchaltAnlage and 18 signals, Table 6, Table 7, Fig.15.

	Scene Size	Detected	Bounding Box	Annotated elements	Truth data
Scene1	500m		105	34	37

Table 6. Detected Element within the scene and annotated ones.

	Masts	signal	Schaltanlage
Annotated	13	18	3
Truth data	12	20	5

Table 7. Detected and annotated elements within the scene1.

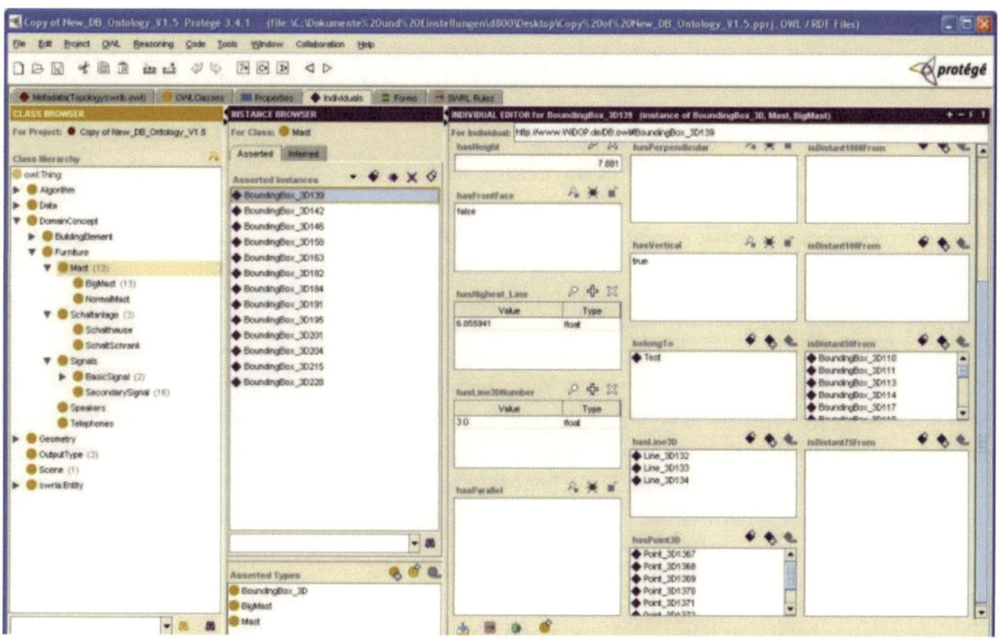

Fig. 15. Knowledge base after the annotation process.

Some limits are detected while making extra tests, especially with the SchaltAnlage object detection where the rate of false detection still high. Before explaining the reason behind this false detection, let's recall that the Schaltanlage present very small electronic boxes installed on the ground. In the some cases, lots of bounding boxes are detected where a high average of them presents small noise on the ground. The reason for the false annotation is the lack of semantic characteristics related to such elements since, until now; there is no real internal or external topology neither internal geometric characteristic that discriminate such an element compared to others.

8. Conclusion and discussion

By this chapter, we tried to contribute on the ongoing enhancement of the Semantic Web technologies through focusing on the possibility of integrating 3D processing and spatial topological components within its framework. It makes an attempt to cross the boundary of using semantics within the 3D processing researches to provide interoperability and takes it a step forward in using the underlying knowledge technology to provide 3D processing and topological analysis through knowledge.

The presented contribution raises the issue of object detection and recognition in 3D point clouds within the laser scanner by using available knowledge on the target domain, the processing algorithms and the 3D spatial topological relations.

The WiDOP framework is primarily designed to facilitate the object detection and recognition in 3D point clouds. It being based on Semantic Web technologies and has ontology in its core. The top level ontology provides the base for functionalities of the application. This prior knowledge modeled within an ontology structure. SWRL rules are used to control the 3D processing execution, the topological qualification and finally to annotate the detected elements in order to enrich the ontology and to drive the detection of new objects.

The designed prototype takes 3D point clouds of a facility, and produce fully annotated scene within a VRML model file. The suggested solution for this challenging problem has proven its efficiency through real tests within the Deutsche Bahn scene. The creation of processing and topological Built-Ins has presented a robust solution to resolve our problematic and to prove the ability of the semantic web language to intervene in any domain and create the difference.

The benefits of the emerging Semantic Web technology through its knowledge tools are quite visible to the convention technologies that rely heavily on database systems. More precisely, the benefits that have been experienced during the design and development of the WiDOP platform is quite strong. The flexibility nature of ontology based system allows integrating new components at any time of development and even implementations.

Future work will include the integration of new knowledge intervening during the annotation process. It will also include the update of the general platform architecture, by ensuring more interaction between the scene knowledge and the 3D processing. Add to that, it will include a more robust identification and annotation process of objects based on each object characteristics add to the integration of new 3D parameter knowledge's that can intervene within the detection and annotation process to make the process more flexible and intelligent.

9. Acknowledgment

This paper chapter work performed in the framework of the research project funded by the German ministry of research and education under contract No. 1758X09. The authors cordially thank for this funding.

10. References

Allemang, D. & Hendler, J A. (2008). *Semantic web for the working ontologist: modeling in RDF, RDFS and OWL,* Morgan Kaufmann, ISBN 9780123735560, Amsterdam.

Antoniou, G. & Harmelen, F. Web ontology language: Owl, Handbook on ontologies, Springer, 2009, pp. 91-110.

Horrocks, I. Peter, F. Schneider, P. Deborah, L. McGuinness & Christopher, A. (2007). *OWL: a Description Logic Based Ontology Language for the Semantic Web,* Proc of the 21st Int Conf on Automated Deduction.

Baader, F. *Nonstandard inferences in description logics: The story so far,* Mathematical Problems from Applied Logic I., Springer, pp. 1-75, 2006.

Baader, F. Horrocks, I. & Sattler, U. *Description logics,* Foundations of Artificial Intelligence. Elsevier, 2008. Vol. 3. pp. 135-179, 2008.

Balzani, M. Santopuoli, N. Grieco, A. & Zaltron, N. (2004) Laser Scanner 3D Survey in Archaeological Field, *the Forum Of Pompeii,* pp. 18-21, 2004.

Ben Hmida, H. Cruz, C. Nicolle, C. & Boochs, F. (2010). From 3D point clouds to semantic object, *KEOD, theInternational Joint Conference on Knowledge Discovery, Knowledge Engineering and Knowledge Management,* Paris, 2011.

Ben Hmida, H. Cruz, C. Nicolle, C. & Boochs, F. (2010). Semantic-based Technique for the Automation the 3D Reconstruction Process, *SEMAPRO 2010, The Fourth International Conference on Advances in Semantic Processing,* Florence, Italy, pp. 191-198, 2010.

Berners-Lee, T. (1998). Semantic web road map, 1998.

Boley, H. Osmun, T M. & Craig, B L. (2009). WellnessRules: A Web 3.0 Case Study in RuleML-Based Prolog, *N3 Profile Interoperation,* Vol. 5858, p 43, 2009.

Boochs, F. Marbs, A. Ben Hmida, H. Truong, H. Karmachaiya, A. Cruz, C. Habed, A. Nicolle, C. & Voisin, Y. (2010). Integration of knowledge to support automatic object reconstruction from images and 3D data. *International Multi-Conference on Systems, Signals & Devices,* Sousse Tunisia : pp. 1-13, 2011.

Bosche, F. & Haas, CT. (2008). Automated retrieval of 3D CAD model objects in construction range images *Automation in Construction,* Elsevier, Vol. 17, pp. 499-512, 2008.

Calvanese, D. De Giacomo, G. Lembo, D. Lenzerini, M & Rosati, R. (2005).DL-Lite: Tractable description logics for ontologies, Vol. 20, p. 602, 2005.

Campbell, RJ. & Flynn, PJ.(2001). A survey of free-form object representation and recognition techniques, *Computer Vision and Image Understanding,* Vol. 81, pp. 166-210, 2001.

Cantrell, CA. (2008). Technical Note: Review of methods for linear least-squares fitting of data and application to atmospheric chemistry problems, *Atmospheric Chemistry and Physics Discussions*. Vol. 8, pp. 6409-6436, 2008.

Cantzler, H. (2003). Improving architectural 3D reconstruction by constrained modelling, *College of Science and Engineering. School of Informatics*, Citeseer, 2003.

CASCADE OPEN. (2000). OpenCascade-an open source library for BRep solid modeling, 21.10.2010, Available from http://www.opencascade.org.

Corporation Leadwerks. (2006) . What is Constructive Solid Geometry?, 21.10.2010, Available from http://www.leadwerks.com/files/csg.pdf.

Decker, S. Melnik, S. Van Harmelen, F. Fensel, D. Klein, M. Broekstra, J. Erdmann, M. & Horrocks, I. (2000) .,The semantic web: The roles of XML and RDF, *Internet Computing, IEEE*, Vol. 4, pp. 63-73, 2000.

Fensel, D. Van Harmelen, F. Horrocks, I. McGuinness, D.L. & Patel-Schneider, P.F.(2001). OIL: An ontology infrastructure for the semantic web, *Intelligent Systems, IEEE*, Vol. 16, pp. 38-45, 2001.

Goldberg H.E. (2005). State of the AEC industry: BIM implementation slow, but inevitable, *Revista CADalyst*, maio 2005.

Grau, B.C. Horrocks, I. Motik, B. Parsia, B. Patel-Schneider, P. & Sattler, U. (2008). OWL 2: The next step for OWL ,*Web Semantics: Science, Services and Agents on the World Wide Web*, Elsevier, Vol. 6, pp. 309-322, 2008.

Gruber, T. (2008). What is an Ontology, *Encyclopedia of Database Systems*, Springer-Verlag, Vol. 1, 2008.

Hajian, H & Becerik-Gerber, B. (2009). A Research Outlook for Real-Time Project Information Management by Integrating Advanced Field Data Acquisition Systems and Building Information Modeling, *Computing in Civil Engineering*, p 83-94, 2009.

Horrocks, I. Patel-Schneider, P.F. Boley, H. Tabet, S. Grosof, B. & Dean, M. (2004). SWRL: A semantic web rule language combining OWL and RuleML, *W3C Member submission*, Vol. 21. - p. 79, 2004.

Horrocks, I, Bechhofer, S. (2008). Semantic Web, *Web Accessibility*. Springer, pp. 315-330, 2008.

Huynh, D. Mazzocchi, S. & Karger, D. (2007). Piggy bank: Experience the semantic web inside your web browser , *Web Semantics: Science, Services and Agents on the World Wide Web*, Elsevier, Vol. 5, pp. 16-27, 2007.

Lassila, O. (2007). Programming Semantic Web Applications: A Synthesis of Knowledge Representation and Semi-Structured Data, *phdthesis*. 2007.

Lee, T B. Hendler, J. & Lassila, O.(2001). The semantic web, Scientific American. Vol. 284. pp. 34-43, 2001.

Leica, Cyclone. (2011), Leica Geosystems Leica Geosystems, 21.10.2010, Available from http://hds.leica-geosystems.com/en/Leica-Cyclone_6515.htm, 2011.

McGuinness, D L. & Patel-Schneider, P F.(2003). From description logic provers to knowledge representation systems. pp. 265-281, 2003.

Milella, A & Siegwart, R.(2006). Stereo-based ego-motion estimation using pixel tracking and iterative closest point, IEEE Computer Society, p. 21-21, 2006.

Noy, N .F. & McGuinness .(2001). D L. Ontology development 101: A guide to creating your first ontology. *Citeseer*, 2001.

OConnor, M.J. Shankar, R. Nyulas, C. Tu, S. & Das, A.(2008). Developing a Web-based application using OWL and SWRL, *AAAI Spring*, 2008.

Pu, S. & Vosselman, G .(2007). Extracting windows from terrestrial laser scanning, *Intl Archives of Photogrammetry, Remote Sensing and Spatial Information Sciences*. Vol. 36, pp. 12-14, 2007.

Pu, S. & Vosselman, G. (2009). Knowledge based reconstruction of building models from terrestrial laser scanning data, *ISPRS Journal of Photogrammetry and Remote Sensing*, Vol. 64, pp. 575-584, 2009.

Rusu, R B. Marton, Z C. Blodow, N. Holzbach, A. & Beetz, M.(2009). Model-based and learned semantic object labeling in 3D point cloud maps of kitchen environments, *IEEE/RSJ International Conference on Intelligent Robots and Systems, IROS*, 2009.

Schmidt-Schauß, M, & Smolka, G.(2009). Attributive concept descriptions with complements, *Artificial intelligence, Elsevier*, Vol. 48, pp. 1-26, 1991.

Sirin, E. Parsia, B. Grau, B.C. Kalyanpur, A. & Katz, Y.(2007). Pellet: A practical owl-dl reasoner, Web Semantics: science, services and agents on the World Wide Web, Elsevier, Vol. 5, pp. 51-53, 2007.

Spaccapietra, S. Cullot, N. Parent, C. & Vangenot, C.(2004): On spatial ontologies, Citeseer, 2004.

Sterling, L. & Taveter, K A.(2009). Logic Programming Perspective on Rules, *Handbook of Research on Emerging Rule-Based Languages and Technologies: Open Solutions and Approaches*, IGI Global snippet, Vol. 1. p. 195, 2009.

Tarsha-Kurdi. F, Landes, T. & Grussenmeyer, P.(2007). Hough-transform and extended RANSAC algorithms for automatic detection of 3D building roof planes from Lidar data, Science And Technology, Vol 36, p. 407- 412 - 2007.

Hustadt, U. Motik, B & Sattler, U. (2006). KAON2, 21.10.2010, Available from http://kaon2.semanticweb.org.

Uren, V. Cimiano, P. Iria, J. Handschuh, S. Vargas-Vera, M. Motta, E. & Ciravegna, F. Semantic annotation for knowledge management: Requirements and a survey of the state of the art, *Web Semantics: Science, Services and Agents on the World Wide Web*, Elsevier, Vol. 4, pp. 14-28.

Vale, S & Hammoudi, S.(2009). An Architecture for the Development of Context-aware Services based on MDA and Ontologies, *Proceedings of the International MultiConference of Engineers and Computer Scientists*, Citeseer, Vol. 1, 2009.

Valiente-Rocha, P & Lozano-Tello, A.(2010). Ontology and SWRL-Based Learning Model for Home Automation Controlling, *Ambient Intelligence and Future Trends-International Symposium on Ambient Intelligence (ISAmI 2010)* ,pp. 79-86, 2010.

Vanland, R. Cruz, C. & Nicolle, C. (2008). IFC and building lifecycle management, *Automation in Construction. Elsevier*, Vol. 18. - pp. 70-78, 2008.

W3C, VRML Virtual Reality Modeling Language, , 21.10.2010, Available from http://www.w3.org/MarkUp/VRML/.

Whiting, E J.(2006). Geometric, Topological & Semantic Analysis of Multi-Building Floor Plan Data, phdthesis, 2006.

Yue, K. and Huber, D. and Akinci, B. and Krishnamurti, R. The ASDMCon project: The challenge of detecting defects on construction sites, *International Symposium on 3D Data Processing Visualization and Transmission,* IEEE Computer Society, Vol. 0, pp. 1048-1055, 2006.

10

C^3W semantic Temporal Entanglement Modelling for Human - Machine Interfaces

John Ronczka
Australian Maritime College, University of Tasmania
Australia

1. Introduction

This Chapter focuses on 'Command—causalities—consequences Wisdom' (C^3W) semantics temporal entanglement modeling using 'Wisdom open system semantic intelligence' (WOSSI) methodology (Ronczka, 2009). A feature might be a Rubik-Schlangen type three-dimensional system and wisdom-based delivery engine acting as a continuum with engagements.

WOSSI is a mapping system that allows identification of wisdom from lower order delivery engines and associated domains to acquire the information, knowledge, reasoning, and understanding whilst in an open-system context. WOSSI mapping has the outcome of minimising the influence of 'de Montaigne' paradoxes. That is, a possible negative outcome: '*nothing is so firmly believed as that which we least know*', (Collins, 2002) that may drive conflicting tangibles and intangibles such as 'actual monetary benefits' and 'Willingness-to-pay' but still providing foresight based on evidence based 'knowledge—information—learning delivery engines' (KILDEE's) for the user.

A modified Semantics approach based on WOSSI provides a mapping process that could account for the many complexities that interfaces are required to adjust too such as data mapping of the associated Ontologies, taxonomy of Semantics User Interfaces and Semantic Adaptive Systems. Interfacing Semantic and Semiotic may assist when it is required for various inclusion of natural languages to adjust to the intended user but yet overcome any adverse informatics outcomes when translated for oher users.

2. Problem addressed

Within the contextualization of Human—machine interface and supporting firmware information and knowledge there may be cognitive predisposition to the way information and knowledge may be processed within an interface C^3W Kernel. If critical constructs and associated domains are therefore skew the Human—machine interfaces information and knowledge critical path outcomes might not be met and skew the Kernel (e.g. biological and non-biological).

Temporal entanglement of the interface memory with information-knowledge cipher-prima strings further complicates the interface C^3W Kernel. This Kernel plausibly would be adaptive and assimilation the users preferences for how the presentation of KILDEE's is undertaken. What may exist are Human—machine interfaces information and knowledge critical path for Kernel (e.g. biological and non-biological) with a number of Rubik-Schlangen type three-dimensional system and wisdom-based delivery engines.

The associated firmware changes might in turn be required to be enabled in the WOSSI mapping systems that essentially allows wisdom to be identified from the lower order delivery engines information, knowledge, reasoning and understanding. This is suggested to be undertaken in an open-system (may be additionally known as open-source) to allow C^3W for self correction. C^3W Kernel self correction might be useful for Biorheology interfaces to help overcome impairments in Humans, weapons systems, wargaming.

Fiscal responsibility has recently been highlighted as an issue for general management that flows onto IT projects. These projects may have complex interconnecting engagement threads and stakeholder partnerships for a given business operation space.

Such a view is not uncommon of Cost benefit Analysis (CBA): "One of the problems of CBA is that the computation of many components of benefits and costs is intuitively obvious but that there are others for which intuition fails to suggest methods of measurement" [1].

Problems associated with ranking projects tend to involve complexities with determining value for tangible and intangibles. A simplification is required for IT projects to drive clarity of how to achieve efficiency outcomes as traditional Benefit to cost ratio (BCR) has shortcoming for a given scenario—context.

The problem addressed by moving to 'Wisdom open-system semantic identification (WOSSI) mapping, is therefore to simplify the outcome of leveraging evolutionary jump in the way to control and management the systems of gates as entities, events and interaction change. To move one needs not to be stuck in the conceptual phase of design with complex digital circuit mathematic and logic Truth tables. Secondly, WOSSI uses cognitive bases with hybrid semantics to facilitate moving from the macro, meso, micro, and quantum-nano scales with minimal support conjectures [9].

Problems that need to be addressed in the context of impairments in Humans, weapons, gaming (wargaming) systems tends to be the following:

- Human impairments overcome/minimised
- Enhancements via entangled single-to-multiple chain delivery engines
- Interoperability communication-companion Human—machines
- Biorheology interfaces for Human—machine interfaces
- Low rejection rates of host Bio material.

3. Methodology

The methodology focuses on benchmarking between how impairments in Humans, weapons systems, gaming (wargaming) systems are modeled using exercises. A well-executed and designed C^3W) exercises (Fig 1) are the most effective way to:

- Validation and testing of a range of entities and events (e.g. plans, procedures, training, agreements)

- Clarifying roles and responsibilities
- Demonstration of operating procedures through to communications
- Improvement of communications,and operations with coordination
- Identification of coordination surfaces and resource gaps to enable project completion
- Improvement of performance (system to personal)
- Identification of system improvements that need to be made (NCHRP 2006).

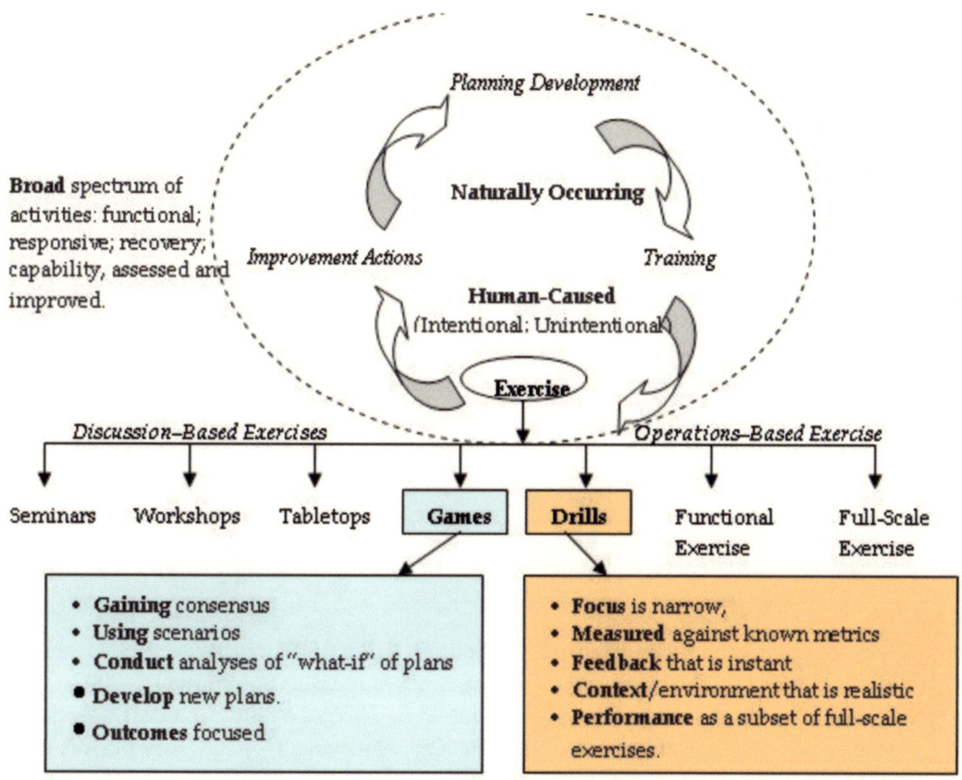

Fig. 1. Cycle of planning training, exercises, and improvement actions (NCHRP, 2006)

The basic conceptualization seems to have a relationship with traditional 'strategic management planning (SMP) systems and processes (Fig 2). The journey commences with a continnum:

- develop drivers of reasoning might gain an human-machine evolutionary jump in achieving wisdom integrated management information system (MIS)
- data interchange (EDI) and data cube aggregation via information packets by way of human-machine interfaces (neuro-fuzzy wisdom sub-delivery engines) could exist
- Constructs are likely to be shown to exist and may act as a temporal meshing continuum of events and entities within critical decision points (Ronczka, 2006).

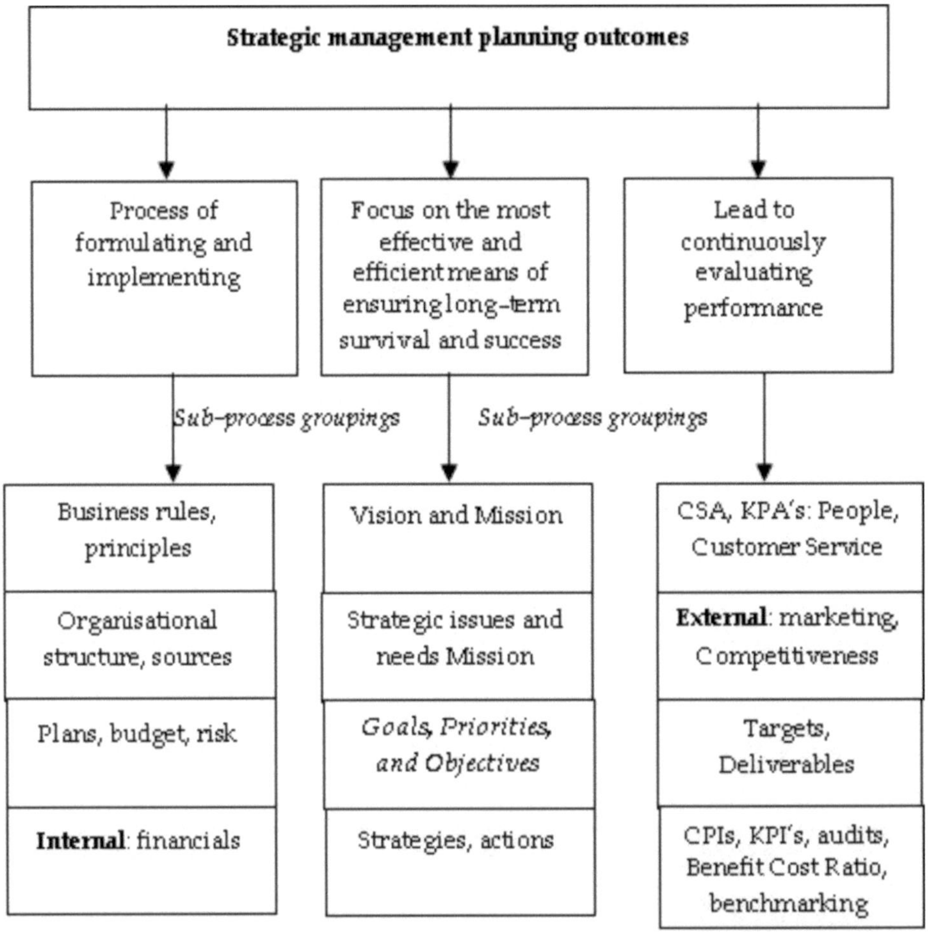

Fig. 2. How strategic management process outcomes drive domain groupings (Hawkins, 1993; Raimond & Eden, 1990; Camillus & Datta, 1991; David, 2002; CSMINTL, 2002; McNeilly, 2002; Goold & Campbell , 2002; Miller et al., 1996). Legend: Critical Success Areas = CSAs; Critical performance indicators = CPIs; Key result areas = KRA; Key performance areas = KPAs; Key performance indicators = KPIs.

The second part of the journey involves distilling the critical Theme (Conjecture) questions initially using Ackoff system of filters[1]::

- How did the Literature Review to get Information Theory Themes?
- Why is there variability within a 'fit-for-purpose' ethos?
- What cross platform control systems and memory exist with information-knowledge?
- When does the combining the 'logic gates' and 'event horizon' of enablers used in information-knowledge patterning?

[1] Ackoff system of filters: information ('who', 'what', 'where', and 'when'); knowledge (application of 'how'); understanding (appreciation of 'why') and wisdom (evaluated 'why' [e-Why]) continnum (Hobbs, 2005; Bellinger, 2004; Ackoff, 1962; Wikipedia, 2009).

- Where are highlighted the interconnected nodes and threads?
- Who is the driver of Semantics and Semiotic decision models, mapping and expressions?
- Why develop drivers to data interchange (EDI) and data cube aggregation for interfaces to help overcome impairments in Humans, weapons, Gaming (wargaming) systems?

The third I likely to involve testing using Causality:

- Context of 'Internet Technologies and Applications'
- Practical application examples to personalise the learning outcomes and the achieved competencies of participants.

Once testing has been undertaken an analysis to validate if say Semantic and Semiotic based information system is plausible initially using Ackoff system of filters:

- What are the relationships to an information interface packet?
- Where are the levels of Semantic and Semiotic packet distortion and random radicals at different scales
- How does a process undertake Semantic test?
- Who undertakes Semantics and Theory of Conversation (ToC) and its nexus
- How does a process undertake Semiotics test?
- When should base information be used?
- Why use Constructs and domains for interfaces to help overcome impairments in Humans, weapons systems, wargaming?

The basis of the methodology is to drive a paradigm shift *via a cognitive* Semantic and Semiotic interface mapping approach and strategic management planning (SMP) is a 'tool kit' help overcome impairments in Humans, weapons systems, wargaming.

4. Theory

Coalescence Theory based Semantic mapping has two principle conceptualisations, that is, 'Wisdom open-system semantic identification' (WOSSI) and the existence of 'Causality Logic gates' (COR gates) for use of Human—machine interfaces (Ronczka, 2006).

Human—machine interfaces could tend to be COR gates meshed and reflected within cognitive processes that semantic—semiotic mapping assists with. Current methods have extensive notations and mathematical fractals that make it difficulty for tech managers to understand the outcomes to be met and then develop the metrics to assist in monitoring.

As a stakeholders and partners the owner—funder—managers with the developer must have clarity and a common purpose. That is, the traditionally C^3 (say C^{3T}) has been 'Command—communication—control' but does not fit the current realities of 'Command—causalities—consequences' (C^{3N}) required for transparency, clarity of purpose and having processes that met the required corporate governance (Ronczka [2], 2006).

WOSSI based on Coalescence Theory may have application to rheology of entangled, single and multiple chains to suggest biorheology logic gates - Coalescence Theory (CT) application to rheology of entangled, of single and multiple chains suggests the existence of biorheology logic gates using CT developed at the University of Tasmania. Using CT may have plausibility in understanding the dynamics of deformation and flow of matter (rheology) as related to entanglement of single and multiple chains as possible biological logic gates (B-gate or biorheology logic gates) within bio-delivery engines and sub—delivery engines. Entanglements perhaps are the outcomes of coalescence processes and possible are part of a biologically based control systems approach. With the assistance of 'Wisdom open—system semantic identification' (WOSSI) mapping, what might be further suggested is the existence of entangled single-to-multiple chain 'causality logic gates' (COR gates). A likely outcome could be biorheology machine systems that provide SIANS (synergy, integration, assimilation narrative and synchronization) for strand-to-threads-to-chains (S2T2C), to accounts for random radicals in a dynamic continuum and achieve a human—machine partnership with enhanced biological entities (Ronczka, 2010).

5. Wisdom as multiple-dimensional

Lets start the journey, what is wisdom? It may be suggested to be a capability that has the outcome of decision that is likely to be based on perceived, discovered, or inferred insight (Ask, 2010).

If wisdom cannot be limited to the intellectual or cognitive domain but encompasses the whole person, it might be more important to find out what a person is like rather than what a person knows to measure wisdom. In terms of 'expert in wisdom' this might involve integration of cognitive, reflective, and affective characteristics (Table 1) (Ardelt, 2004).

Dimension	Definition	Operationalization
Cognitive	Intrapersonal and interpersonal meaning of phenomena and events with knowledge and acceptance	Ability and willingness to understand the Knowledge and acknowledge uncertainties.
Reflective	Multiple perspective perception of phenomena—entity—events from self-insight.	Ability and willingness to look at different perspectives of the phenomena and events.
Affective	Compassionate—sympathetic	Behavior toward entity and events.

Table 1. Wisdom as a three dimensional.

6. WOSSI - COR gates

Traditional Logic gates are the building blocks to digital logic circuits via combinational logic. This may cover mono concepts such as NOT gates (or inverters), AND gates, OR gates, NAND gates, NOR gates, XOR gates, and XNOR gates. WOSSI based Logic gate mapping tends to be a cognitive-human-machine process.

The focus of WOSSI mapping is on the nexus of WOSSI-COR gates on how they entangled single-to-multiple chain 'knowledge—information—learning domains (KILD's) using Information Theory. These entangled-single-multiple chains might exist in multiple operating dimensions as *Möbius strips* hybrid 'Biorheology causality logic gates' (B-COR gates). The B-COR tendency may be to act as a biological 'knowledge—information—learning delivery engines' (KILDEE's). Conceivably, the fusion of human—machine *Markov chain* Biorheology interfaces (Fig 3) might be the next *'Internet Technologies and Applications'* evolution (FEDEE, 2001).

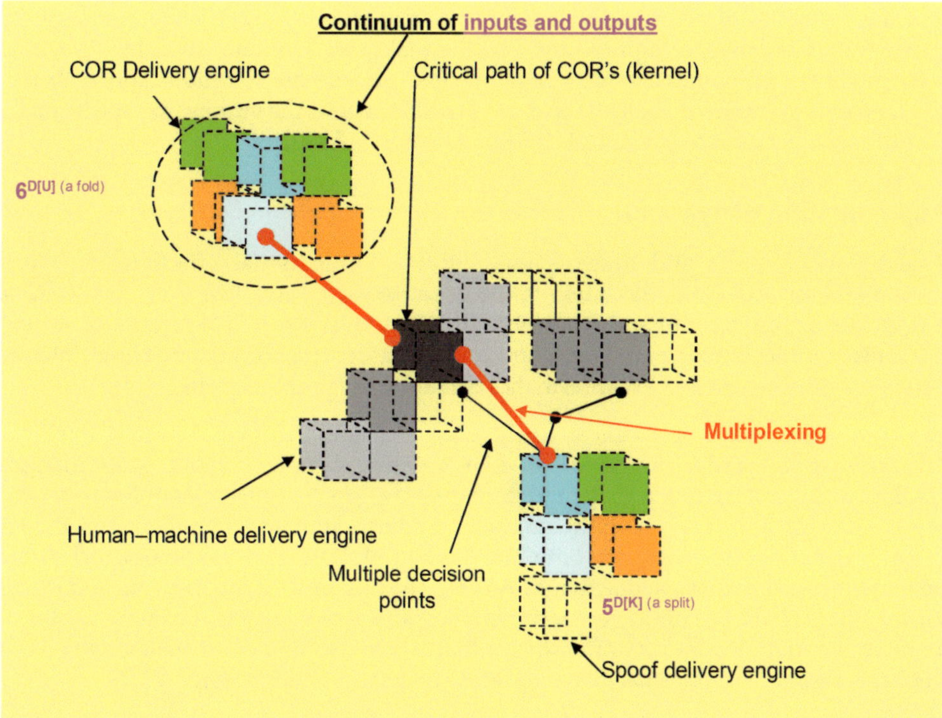

Fig. 3. Entangled-single-multiple chains – *Biorheology Markov chains* (Brand, 1993; Ronczka, 2006).

To allow validation and plausibility of the existence of WOSSI data cube embedded KILDEE packets conceptualization a process may use Information Theory, plausible hypotheses. Secondly, hypotheses could allow highlighting of WOSSI – B-COR entangled single-to-multiple chain KILD's philosophies to undergo convergence and merging at event horizons of:

- C^5M ('Command – communication – control' with *'Management – causalities – consequences'*) (Carbonell, 1979; Ronczka, 2010).
- SIAN (Synergy, integration (Interoperability), assimilation and narratives) (Carbonell, 1979).
- BRI (Biorheological informatics: use of mathematics, statistics, and computer science approaches to study biological interfaces of life sciences (e.g. biology, genome) (Fu-berlin, 2010).

WOSSI – B-COR entangled single-to-multiple chain KILD's convergence and merging as Biorheology interface hybrid access act as drivers. Conceivably the fusion of human – machine in the workplace – community may achieve life style and Health benefits. "*In the workplace of the future the most important ingredients will be people and knowledge. The technologies that are mesmerizing us today will be recognised for what they really are – the embedded tools for doing business*" (Goldsworthy, 2002). Semantic and Semiotic neutral nets may be a way forward for Biorheology interface hybrid access ('devices – entities – events – processes') to overcome impairments?

Within the dynamics of deformation and flow of matter (Rheology), biological logic gates (B-gates) with bio-delivery engines might be the reality for Human—machine 'Worldwide Interoperability' communication-conversation. Like in human communications there are misunderstanding (random radicals) that are possible within the supporting spectrums and bandwidths as they exist over multiple hybrid access interfaces.

7. Augmentation of systems

Augmentation of host's and systems may focus on intellectual effectiveness, wisdom extraction and assimulation-adaptation to the users needs (*Guanxi type C^{3}W*). Use of *Guanxi type C^{3}W* personalised command, control and communication (C^3) networks of influence could translate into impairment correction and enhancement Human-machine interfaces. The enablers are likely to be C^{3}W Informatics Semantic temporal mapping.

In the context of mapping Artifical Intelligence (AI) and Artifical Wisdom Intelligence (AWI) appears to require development of a Semantic-Semiotic based control-language vocabulary and sybolism to translate into impairment correction to augment interoperability between biological and non-biological interface communication-conversation. This therefore suggests alternatives to augment both the biological host and non-biological AI (e.g. symbolic, connectionist; situated activity). As both the host and AI are meshing and merging processes, there could be cognitive science implications that suggests the likely existance of AI impairment that may be random radicals that adversely impact on achieving correction and enhancement of Human-machine interfaces (Engelbart, 1968; Spector, 2001).

Augmented Reality (AR) together with AI within a host (entity) may result in compounding error correction (e.g. biological host and non-biological AI Adaptive Intent-Based Augmentation System that have contra wisdom intends) with unintentional consequences. Such a augmented wisdom entity may have unique Biorheology interface entangled single-to-multiple chain KILD's for a *Guanxi type C^{3}W* personalised command, control and communication (C^3) networks access between Human—machine 'Artifical life derived entity replication' (ALDER) which may be user modified ('Artifical life guided entity replication' (ALGER). Artificial life that is being suggested to be the bases to Human-machine interfaces tend to involve integrates motor, perceptual, behavioural, and cognitive components (Terzopoulos, 2009).

Depending on the user and systems shared understand and knowledge the communicative mechanism and intent may need C^{5}M with SIAN to lever the required level of AR application augmentation. This augmentation may suggest need for decision caution, need for diagnosis and intervention or entity re-purposing (AIBAS, 2006; Adkins et al., 2003).

Via Informatics Medicine (definition of Informatics medicine refers to using informatics for medicinal purposes) AWI's coulds be could be the leap beyond 'virtual entity—person in a reality environment' (Avatar). A version may be the 'artificial life derived entity replication' (ALDER) to 'artificial life guided entity replication' (ALGER). The may assist by augmentation of 'human like operations' to overcome impairment or enhance capabilities.

8. Delivery engines

Various logic delivery engines requires complexities in the supporting knowledge—information—learning. What may be an outcome are false negatives, confusion, or skewed interpretation (Watkins, 2000; WSU, 2003).

Delivery engine are a devices that probably is a process or series of processes or sub-delivery engines that interact for a common purpose, milestone, or outcome to achieve a specific deliverable. It is likely to have an analogy with legislative machinery within the judicial system enacted by a set of predetermined protocols when an event occurs. This machinery comes into being by the coalescence of unique trigger events, information—knowledge that has temporal meshing to facilitate a decision, event or process (WSU, 2003).

9. Simple causality mapping

An initial simple mapping tool is required to validate 'proof—of—concepts' before moving into complex mathematics and Truth Tables. A simple mapping tool facilitates adjustment of support knowledge—information—learning that might span discrete and possibly dilated entities, events and relationships in time, space, place, and tempo.

This paper therefore, put forward a plausible paradigm shift using wisdom-based open-system mapping of causality. By doing so, the blocks to digital logic circuits are broadened to provide nexus wisdom based 'Causality Logic gates' (COR gates; Fig 4). These gates are able to provide SIANS (synergy, integration, assimilation narrative, and synchronization) for clone strands to or with other hierarchies and hybrid gates to enable an evolutionary jump(s)[2].

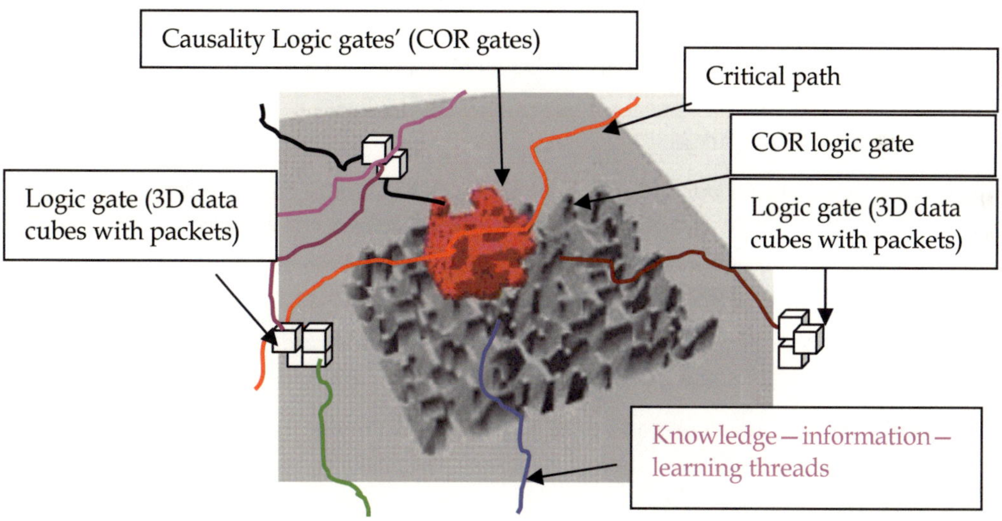

Fig. 4. Concept of WOSSI nexus 'Causality Logic gates' (COR gates) (Wander et al., 2004; Roh, 2006).

[2] Wave revolutions might be to be: First (agricultural); Second (industrial); Third (information); Fourth (overload-over-choice); Fifth (Quantum human-machines); Sixth (Unity); Seventh (Merged society?) (Dictionary, 2008; Golec, 2004).

10. Paradigm shift

Such an approach is the acceptance of adaptation to real world negative feedback loops with the interplay of causalities and consequences:

- Notion of mechanism of feedback
- Return to the input of part of the output'
- Negative resultant actions e.g. 'Willingness'
- Opposing the condition that triggers it (continuum)
- Output of a pathway inhibits inputs to another or the same pathway
- Control systems part of output may be 'fed back' to the system, resulting in an action-reaction in the opposite direction (Golec, 2004; Bowen, 2001).

Identification of critical paths and enablers to the existence of 'Command—causalities—consequences' (C^{3N}) (Dictionary, 2004) e.g. 'Willingness-to-pay' or 'benefit' for a given scenario—context.

A new paradigm of cognitive adaptation is not to say that there is no nexus between the 'Command' construct in both the C^{3N} and C^{3T} mode. Causalities—consequences might act as a continuum of drivers and as such making it no longer acceptable to fund projects without a business case, being within a strategic management planning framework or having defined outcomes.

The developer has a self interest by way of ensuring a bonus is paid at the delivery stage within the projects set financials. The outcome therefore sought is to drive corporate governance; transparency with Total Quality Management (TQM), and Continuous Quality Improvement (CQI) (LeBrasseur, et al., 2002; Nüchter, et al., 2008).

11. People and knowledge

This is not a new concept but still provides guidance to owner—funder—managers. "*It will be knowledge that will provide sustainable competitive advantage, and knowledge is the capital of people*" (Goldsworthy, 2002) or are likely to have radicals as drivers of uncertainty and 'Willingness-to-pay' or 'benefit' conflicts.

Simple Semantic and Semiotic mapping may be a way forward? A recent view point is provided by Dr. James Canton Institute of Global Futures CEO and advisor on Fortune 1000:

- "Despite the bleak economy and uncertain future, technology is key to our future" and
- 'Tech workers and IT leaders are in a unique position to create opportunities for themselves" (Daniel, 2009).

People knowledge—information—learning management are the corner stones of any plausible C^3 semantics modeling—dynamics to assist owner—funder—managers and developers as partners.

Various management and leaning styles exist that may complicate the implementation and use of ridge processes and tool sets. It is therefore appropriate to utilize a continuum approach that allows a practitioner to start and finish at any point and achieve workable outcomes such as cognitive adaptation and capabilities.

12. Semantic mapping

Semantic mapping (Fig 5) has variability within a 'fit-for-purpose' ethos (e.g. F-semantics; I-semantics). 'Fit-for-purpose' results in the need for cross platform control systems and memory with information-knowledge cipher-prima strings that may support families of delivery engines. Semantic mapping aids in verification, interoperability and collaborative distribution and facilitates moving from the macro, meso, micro, and quantum-nano scales within key themes (Table 2) for a given scenario—context.

Themes	Key details /Constructs
Control_semantics_promise (Coppock, 2005)	• Proposed a responsibility-based for control "shift" phenomena.
Control_semantics (Kiss, 2005)	• Contrast view theory of control and non-finite complementation.
Meta_semantic [Ikehara, et al., 2007)	• Logical semantic category; • Truth items (Common Concepts); • Semantically equivalent mapping: Truth Items.
Coordination _semantic (Armarsdottir, et al., 2006)	• Mapping; • Processes solve the interoperability emerges; • model-Reference Ontology; • Proposes a layered approach in the system.

Table 2. Semantic Themes (Coppock, 2005; Kiss, 2005; Ikehara, et al., 2007; Armarsdottir, et al., 2006)

In summary, Semantic mapping comprises:

- Domain: "*entities*"
- Model: "*representation*"
- Ontology: "describes/ description" taxonomies)"

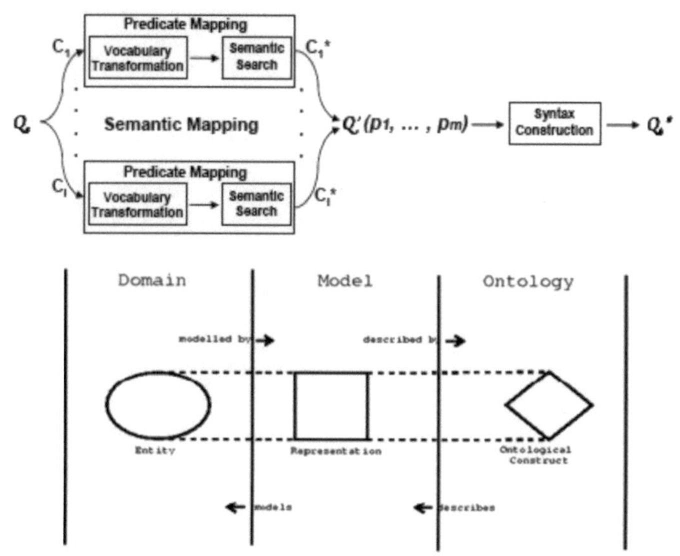

Fig. 5. Semantics modeling—dynamics mapping (He et al., 2005; Hatten et al., 1997; Wagner et al., 2005; Avery et al., 2004).

13. Semiotic mapping

In summary Semiotic mapping comprises:

- Object: "Immediate; dynamic"
- Sign: "representation"
- Interpretation: "Immediate; dynamic; logical"

Semiotics Themes (Fig 6) are inclined to be:

- Analysis is deemed essential for providing information and critical skills for interface and media literacy.
- Informs about a text, its underlying assumptions and its various dimensions of interpretation.
- Context with a operating-cultural structures and entities (human-machine) motivations that underlie perceptual representations.
- Offers a lens into entities (human-machine) communication.
- Sharpens the entities consciousness surrounding a given text.
- Rejects the possibility that can represent the world in a neutral fashion.
- Unmasks the deep-seated rhetorical forms and underlying codes that fundamentally shape entities realities (Ryder, 2004; Lemke, 2001).

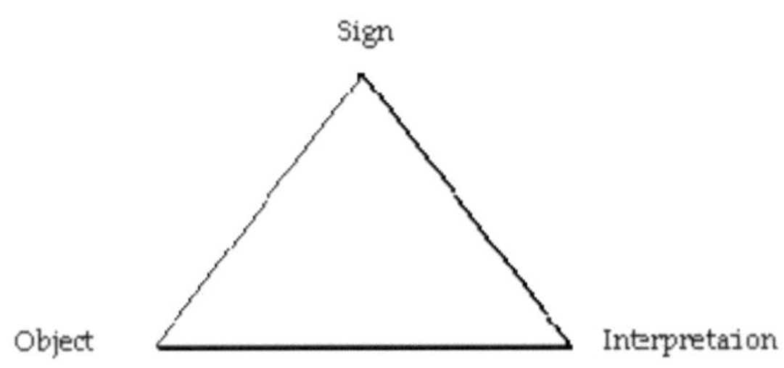

Fig. 6. Semiotoc model (Ryder, 2004; Lemke, 2001).

14. Guiding parameter

Essentially C³ semantics modeling—dynamics mapping is based on 'reasoning' and 'understanding' using dynamic information and knowledge domains in the context of Ackoff system of filters. An example may be a mobile machine cognitive map that may "*contains, in addition to spatial information about the environment, assignments of mapping features to entities of known classes*" (Uschold, 2001).

The semantic process serves another purpose to facilitate the 'resource description framework' (RDF) which is drawn from the traditional project management processes. If this is the commonality then C³ 'semantic project management mapping' (SPMM) stresses the 'semantics' core meaning of really 'itself' using knowledge—information—learning domains.

In the SPMM context there is a reliance on meaningful communication with and within dependant or independent domains that interact with various entities and events. This therefore leads to a continuum:

- Importance (specific [must]; explicit [description] or implicit [consensus]; essential [outcome to be met])
- Suitably (informally [likely] or formally [will])
- Processing (human or machine or both)
- Freedom of action (operating space; Limitation; restrictions; boundaries; opportunities; risk)
- Causality (facts; assumptions; criticality)
- Consequence (deductions; shape; course of actions; areas of interest) coalescences of delivery engines for a given scenario—context.

15. Graphic notations

A graphic notation tends to be cognitive by nature and as such is a feature of a semantic network or network. As an enabler, what is suggested is representing information-knowledge domains with patterns and symbols. By doing so the various management and learning styles are able to be accommodated. Additionally, what are highlighted are interconnected nodes and threads with alignments with philosophy, psychology, and linguistics (Sowa, 2006).

So what should it be F-semantics, I-semantics or a hybrid? F-semantics that is, the semantics is deterministic: no stable models or well-founded model is empty, but is meaningful. I-semantics namely lexical semantics: no principled reason to restrict being an ad hoc stipulation or satisfying declaratives for agent programs or a hybrid? (Phan Luong, 1999; Tancredi, 2007; Eiter et al., 1999).

16. Command and control

Command (to direct with specific authority) and Control (to exercise restraint or direction over (Dictionary, 2008) system theme have a nexus:

- Context: must be the same for all entities (human-machine) and tests
- Controlled: variables are important than if dependent or independent
- Isolate: the controlled variables as may lead to ruining the experiment
- Experimental design: manipulating one variable, the independent variable, and studying how that affects the dependent variables
- Control group: to give a baseline measurement for unknown variables
- Factors-characteristics: must be known control potential adverse influences on the results (separation between controller and the system)
- Causality: cause-effect upon the results must be standardized, or eliminated, exerting the same influence upon the different sample groups.
- Analysis: statistical tests have a certain error margin as such repetition and large sample groups should minimise the unknown variables.
- Consistency-systematic: via monitoring and checks, due diligence will ensure that the experiment is as accurate as is possible (Kiss, 2005)
- Consequence: can refer to a good or a bad result of your actions—knowledge—information—learning (Ask, 2010).
- Reasoning: A cognitive process of looking for reasons for beliefs, conclusions, actions or feelings (Deductive reasoning [support that conclusion]; Inductive reasoning

[phenomenal patterns]; Abductive reasoning [attempt to favour]; Fallacious reasoning [fallacy]) (Ask, 2010)..

Control system in summary can be considered a "system in which one or more outputs are forced to change in a desired manner as time progresses; Interconnections of components forming system configurations which will provide a desired system response as time progresses" (Ask, 2010).

17. Semantic mapping and Theory of Conversation

Drawing from traditional Theory of conversation (Fig 7) and Semiotic and Semiotic temporal mapping. This nexus allows the development of 'Command—communication—control' (C^3) interfaces with complementary explicit and implicit considerations associated with the realities of 'Management—causalities—consequences' (MC^2) (Tables 1 and 2) (Joslyn, 2001).

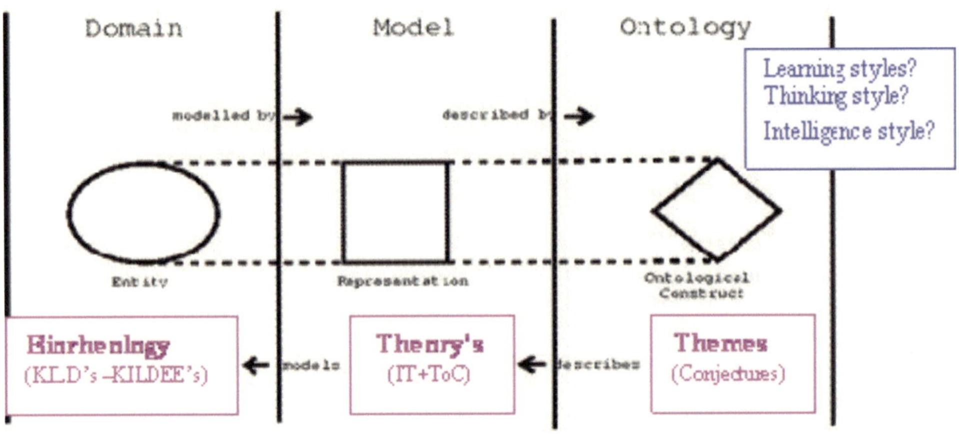

Fig. 7. Semantic mapping and Theory of Conversation (Wagner, et al., 2005; Avery, et al., 2004).

Theory of Conversation (ToC), have the following key domains (Fig 8):

- Long term memory (LTM).
- Captured in conversational to consequences (CAC)
- Short term memory (STM)
- Mixed-Initiative Conversational System (MICS) (Carbonell, 1979)

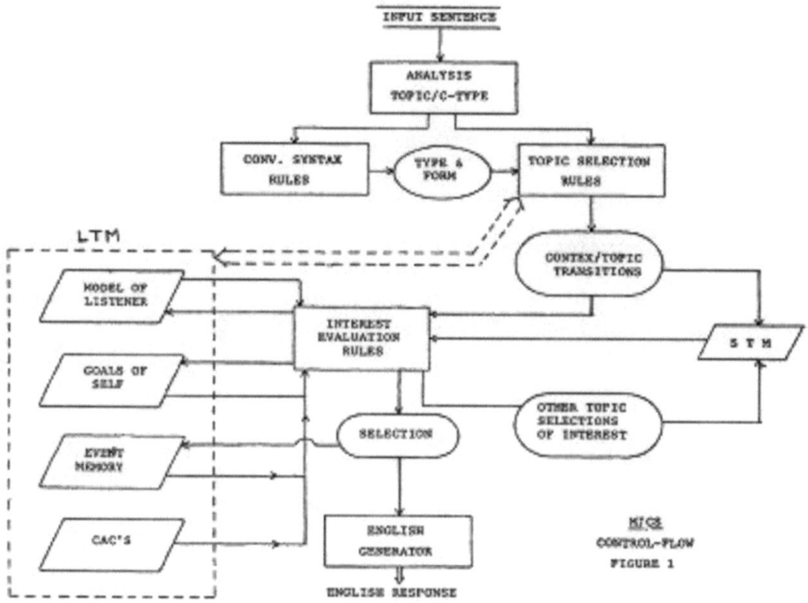

Fig. 8. Theory of conversation (Carbonell, 1979).

18. Wisdom open–system semantic identification (WOSSI)

18.1 What is WOSSI?

The 'Wisdom open system semantic intelligence' (WOSSI) is essentially a 'wisdom' mapping systems that fundamentally allows wisdom to be identified from the lower order delivery engines and sub–delivery engines information, knowledge, reasoning and understanding in an open-system (may be additionally known as open-source) (Ronczka, 2006). 'Wisdom abstraction virtual intelligence' (WAVI) threads tend to have variable bandwidth within and between the connecting and interconnecting COR logic gates.

18.2 Information—knowledge—domains'

These COR logic gates act as 'knowledge-through-to-wisdom' (KTTW) delivery engine(s) and sub–delivery engine(s). These engines contain sub-COR logic gates (CORS) within and with specific 'memory open-system semantic yielding' (MOSSY) information domains accessed any 'place-time-way' C^3M^3. Plausibly WAVI 'wisdom–information–knowledge–domains' (WIKED) exists in multi-dimensions and may be dilated and temporal. They can exist in both the virtual and actual reality with causality and can be identified by the Ackoff system of filters to drive augmented wisdom with common sense systems via cause–effect; inputs–outputs and desire outcomes.

18.3 WOSSI drives biorheology 'Causality Logic gates'

Wisdom open-system semantic identification (WOSSI) is a mapping system that allows identification of wisdom from the lower order delivery engines information, knowledge, reasoning, and understanding in an open-system. WOSSI mapping has the outcome of minimising the influence of 'de Montaigne' paradoxes (negative outcomes: *'nothing is so firmly believed as that which we least know'* (Lin, 2003 ; Collins, 2002)) and providing foresight based on knowledge–information–learning delivery engines (KILDEE's). Therefore CT used within WOSSI drives the development of KILDEE's to suggest the existence of 'biorheology causality logic gates' (B–COR gates) (Answers, 2010; Senese, 2005; Ronczka, 2009).

18.4 Causality logic gate themes

This covers themes that are put forward in the general literature within the causality logic gates context maybe suggested being 'Decomposition' to 'Enablers'.

18.4.1 Decomposition

The logic decomposition uses standard-C architecture for complex gates to promote optimization (Kondratyev, 1999).

18.4.2 Discrete

Discrete space-time, but discrete space-time tends not to be quantum, as C drives Boolean logic and might not allow cycles but does suggest mapping quantum space-time into proto-space-time via XOR gates (Zizzi, 2003).

Researchers from Kondratyev, Cortadella, Kishinevsky, Lavagno and Yakovlev (1999) through to Zizzi (2003) and Schneider, Brandt, Schucle and Tuerk (2005) have looked at relationships with logic gates.

Causality cycles between systems, preconditions, and "that stronger notions of causality are reasonable, as long as they retain the relation between stabilization of circuits, existence of dynamic schedules and constructive programs" (Schneider, 2005).

18.4.3 Complementary–symmetrical

Effect of logic circuits based on Markov random fields in Complementary metal-oxide-semiconductor (CMOS) occur using 'complementary-symmetrical' (C-S) pairs for logic functions and the need for a paradigm shift (Nepa, 2006).

Logic gate need a level of simulation that provides comparable accuracy and control of events without expensive code pre-processing (Riepe et al., 1994). Digital circuits known as combinational circuits occur with cycles (Riedel et al., 2003).

18.4.4 Decisions

Binary decision diagrams allow Boolean function computations (Schneider et al., 2005).

Boundaries, surfaces and gaps exist between gates that that may lead to random radicals. This may lead to spoofing and making the circuit behave in combination with externality gates not within the desired operating space or bandwidth parameters (Neiroukh, 2006).

18.4.5 Synthesized and adaptability

Synthesize connections via additional gates may occur as an outcome of disconformities within the semantic model and coding (Chung, et al., 2002).

18.4.6 Reasoning

Logic (reasoning) circuits with logic gate inputs and outputs with associated Truth Tables to develop a reasonable or logical conclusion based on known information (NAVEDTRA, 1998).

To provide a plausible avenue for the development of new ideas and paradigm shifts in digital circuit logic gates does one 'return to the future' by drawing on Aristotelian logic or Non-Aristotelian Logic. (Alder, 2004).

Another way forward might be to remain sceptical and focus on plausible conjectures based on deductive logic strands covering propositional, contemporary, and traditional through to monadic and dyadic. An Ockham's razor approach may have simple logic symbols: negation (~), conjunction (&), inclusive disjunction (v), exclusive disjunction (Ж), conditional (ɔ) and bi-conditional (≡) (QSA, 2004).

18.4.7 Enablers to Logic

Logic gate development has enablers that have critical path KILDEE's using Information Theory. The KILDEE's could tend to be 'devices—entities—events—processes' (DEEP) that in turn interact within a series of sub-DEEP (sub-delivery engines). Another could be that KILDEE's might be inclined to interact with say area network WIKED's within a specific context or series of constructs to achieve specific deliverable.

19. Coalescence Theory and biorheology

Coalescence Theory (CT) states: "in a situation where entities, events, actions, reactions, interactions and other influences are interlinking, they will cluster together as a unique construct and then may form a system of unique constructs within a unique, three-dimensional space continuum that is 'gooey-dough-like'" (Ronczka, 2006). In Table 3 the supporting hypotheses have been detailed (Table 3) as they are likely to apply to biorheology (Answers, 2010; Senese, 2005).

CT-SMP Hypothesis	Biorheological		
	Plasticity	Non-Newtonian fluids	Biological
1. Constructs emerge as unique	Y	Y	Y
2. Constructs could stay unique	Y	Y	Y
3. Constructs have bonds	Y	Y	Y
4. Might have a common vector	Y	Y	Y
5. Strongest bond, at the pivot point	Y	Y	Y
6. Profile changes	Y	Y	Y
7. Uniqueness decay likely	Y	Y	Y

Table 3. CT-SMT hypotheses as they apply to Biorheology (Answers, 2010; Ronczka, 2006).

Biorheological categorisation are:

- Plasticity: which describes materials that permanently deform after a large enough applied stress including the ability to retain a shape attained by pressure deformation and the capacity of organisms with the same genotype to vary in developmental pattern, in phenotype, or in behaviour according to varying environmental conditions (Answers, 2010; Merram-Webster, 2010).
- Non-Newtonian fluid: Compare with Newtonian fluid: A fluid whose viscosity changes when the gradient in flow speed changes. Colloidal suspensions and polymer solutions like ketchup and starch/water paste are non-Newtonian fluids (e.g. ketchup, blood, yogurt viscosity. What is the determinate is the coefficient of viscosity: The resistance a liquid exhibits to flow. Experimentally, the frictional force between two liquid layers moving past each other is proportional to area of the layers and the difference in flow speed between them (Answers, 2010; Merram-Webster, 2010).
- Biological: relates to biology or to life and living processes (Answers, 2010; Merram-Webster, 2010).

20. Temporal entangement mapping

20.1 Temporal mapping

This is essentially a visual aid for simplifying an expression; function; entities; events; interactions—to—influences over a time interval (Gregersen et al., 1998).

20.2 Entanglements (single-multiple) associated with Packets

There tend to be three domains to an entangled packet format:

- Describes what each type of packet looks like
- Tells the sender what to put in the packet
- Tells recipient how to parse the inbound packet (ANU, 2010)

In terms of entanglements (single-Multiple) associated with Packet Semantics the domains are:

- Sender and recipient must agree on what the recipient can assume if it receives a particular packet
- What actions the recipient should take in response to the packet
- May be described using a Finite State Machine (FSM) which represents the transitions involves in the protocol (ANU, 2010).

What are Semantic and Semiotic entangled-single-multiple chains based on:

- Complexities in the supporting knowledge—information—learning domains
- Multiple operating dimensions as *Möbius strips*
- 'Biorheology causality logic gates' (B–CORG)
- Biological-machine 'knowledge—information—learning delivery engines' (KILDEE's)
- Unique trigger events, information—knowledge that has Biological—*machine* temporal meshing
- Fusion of human—machine via *Markov chain* B–CORG Biorheology interfaces = evolution.

21. Interfaces

To assess interface effectiveness an Heuristic Evaluation is utilised as prime metrics:

- Visibility of system status: system with feedback within reasonable time.
- Consistency and standards: system follow conventions?
- User control and freedom: system offers control when mistake made?
- Flexibility and efficiency of use: system is flexible and efficient?
- Recognition rather than recall: system assists user to remember information (Sambasivan et al., 2007)?

What is suggested is that the concepts of user interface design ideally allows:

- Changes in State: for flexible exploration of the content through a variety of controls
- Closure: concept of closure of information within a learning environment
- Information Access: provides users information access with the controls to conduct deliberate searches
- Interactive Tools for Interactive: tools for interacting with the information
- Interface Consistency: users' ability to "scroll around" within text and audio segments
- Media Integration and Media Biases: more easily explained
- Metaphors: what information is contained
- Modelling the Process and Coaching the User: coaching the user
- Progressive Disclosure: keeping information within learning environment
- Searchability and Granularity: how chunks of media are stored
- Unfamiliar Territory: provide users with visual or verbal cues
- Visual Momentum: maintains a user's interest
- Way Finding: user verbal and symbolic information
- Selection Indicators: marks a user's selection of information
- Control Types: interaction controls
- Tool Availability: presenting users with interaction mechanisms (Jones et al., 1995).

21.1 Semantic interfaces

The Semantic interface has specific requirements:

- Effective: means of communication which has proven itself in practice?
- pre-established: human-defined ontology rely upon?
- Communication: can only proceed by the interpretations of behaviours, common behaviours? (Wagner et al., 2001; Eiter et al., 1999; Phan Luong, 1999).

21.2 Semiotic interfaces

The Semiotic interface has specific requirements:

- Metaphor: such as a new idea is created from the fusion of the two original ideas, or our understanding of the first idea
- Mental models: that are cognitive based for human-computer interaction
- User System usage comprises: D1: concepts the user knows and uses; D2: concepts used only occasionally and not initially known; D3: the user's model of the system (i.e. the set

of concepts the user *thinks* exists in the system); D4: the actual system (Joslyn, 2001; AIBAS, 2006; CSCS, 2004).

21.3 Biological interfaces

Biological interfaces tend to drive:

- preloaded firmware a feature of the biological entity
- Spoofing (rejection rates; skewed data-actions; random radical events?)
- Entity-event-data cascade (coalescence Theory)
- Cognitive: a visual focus due to eye construction - 3D mapping temporal dilation (version of atom structure). (Carbonell, 1979; Adkins et al., 2003).

21.4 Administrative Web Interface (AWI) for telecommunications

An administrative web interface provides for:

- Browse database, account management, orders and repairs
- Security and screening user profiles
- Administer "special users" (e.g., forum moderators) to Online Account Management (OAM)
- Create and edit applications and app versions including Off campus access
- Send mass email to users
- Recording malfunctioning hosts
- Distribution of how many Flops used
- Cancelling user access and work units
- View recent results, metrics and analyze failures
- Browse stripcharts and system flowcharts
- Browse log files (BOINC, 2007).

22. Results

Information and Causality Logic Gate Themes, as an initial stage, a review starts with statements and conjectures about what the literature considers Information Theory and Causality logic gates to be. The outcome required was the establishment of common themes that aid any 'place–time–way' C^3M^3.

22.1 Themes

Using Ockham's razors, Information Theory, and Causality logic gates enables themes to be filtered (Table 4).

These Themes appear as a continuum (Tables 4 and 5) that could be further clarified through the Theory of conversation shown in Fig 6.

22.2 Logic gates - blocks

Possible circuit construct blocks and plausible within Logic gates using the highlighted themes (Table 6).

Statement	Information Theory Themes (Conjectures)	Causality logic gate Themes (Conjectures)
The theory of the probability of transmission of messages with specified accuracy when the bits of information constituting the messages are subject, with certain probabilities, to transmission failure, distortion, and accidental additions (Answers, 2008) at different scales (Macro-to-quantum)	Message	Decomposition
	Transmission	Discrete
	Processing	Complementary-symmetrical
	Parameters	Decisions
	Conditions	Synthesized and adaptability
	Limitations	Reasoning
	Foresight	Enablers to logic

Table 4. Title of table, left justified Information Theory—causality logic gate themes (CSCS, 2005; Wikipedia 2008; Mei, 2008).

Key References	**Combining the *'logic gates'* and *'event horizon'* (C^{5}M-SIAN - BRI) as subject key words**	**Themes (Conjectures)**
(Kremer, 1998; NSF, 2004; Brand, 1993; **Ronczka, 2006;** Sturm, 1994; Wikipedia; 2009; Antsaklis, 1997; Sowa, 2006; Carbonell, 1979; Coppock. 2005; Schneider et al., 2005; Nepa, et al. 2006; Wikipedia, 2009; Riepe et al., 1994; **Als,** 1999; Bellinger, 2004	information; data; binary digits	Message
FEDEE, 2002; Kremer, 1998; NSF, 2004; Brand, 1993; **Ronczka, 2006;** Sturm, 1994; Wikipedia; 2009; Antsaklis, 1997; Carbonell, 1979; Kiss, 2004; Kondratyev et al., 1999; Wikipedia, 2009; Schneider, et al., 2005; **Als,** 1999; Bellinger, 2004	signal; code, transmit, event; decode; patterns; state; communication; generate; destination; receive	Transmission
Kremer, 1998; Brand, 1993; Sturm, 1994; Wikipedia; 2009; Wikipedia; 2009; Sowa, 2006; Carbonell, 1979; Coppock. 2005; Phan Luong, 1999; Tancredi, 2007; Zizzi, 2003; Schneider et al., 2005; Wikipedia; 2009; Schneider, et al., 2005; **Als,** 1999; Bellinger, 2004	medium; device; source, destination, channel; capability; amount; capacity; storage; control; content; compression; detection' learning; acquisition; strings; computation	Processing
Kremer, 1998; Brand, 1993; Wikipedia; 2009; Wikipedia; 2009; Antsaklis, 1997; Carbonell, 1979; Coppock. 2005; Kiss, 2004; Phan Luong, 1999; Tancredi, 2007; Eiter et al., 1999; Zizzi, 2003; Schneider et al., 2005; Nepa, et al. 2006; Wikipedia; 2009; Riepe et al., 1994; Riedel et al. 2003; Schneider, et al., 2005; **Als,** 1999;	measurement; mathematical; observation; rates, properties; statistical, quantification; methods; characters; assumptions; logical; semantic; relationship; category; constructs; definition; redundancy	Parameters

Bellinger, 2004		
FEDEE, 2002; Kremer, 1998; Wikipedia; 2009; Coppock. 2005; Schneider, et al., 2005; Bellinger, 2004	conditional; entropies: equivocation; conditions; optimal	Conditions
FEDEE, 2002; NSF, 2004; Brand, 1993; Sturm, 1994; Wikipedia; 2009; Antsaklis, 1997; Sowa, 2006; Carbonell, 1979; Coppock. 2005; Tancredi, 2007; Zizzi, 2003; Wikipedia; 2009; Riepe et al., 1994; Riedel et al. 2003; Schneider, et al., 2005; Bellinger, 2004	uncertainty; ambiguity; failure; distortion; additions; problems; random noise, beyond control; complexity; limitations; nonsense; improbability; negative feedback; random variable; ergodic; error; disorder	Limitations
NSF, 2004; Brand, 1993; Sowa, 2006; Carbonell, 1979; Kiss, 2004; Kondratyev et al., 1999; Tancredi, 2007; Eiter et al., 1999; Wikipedia; 2009; Riepe et al., 1994; Riedel et al. 2003; Bellinger, 2004	probabilities; prediction; selection, perception, memory; decision making; performances; choice; testing; accuracy; reliability; skills; analysis; determination; application; synonyms; simulations	Foresight

Table 5. Literature Review to get Information Theory Themes.

Causality logic gate Themes (Conjectures)	**Traditional Logic gates** (Collins, 2002; Als, 1999)	**Input to output connectivity** (Collins, 2002; Als, 1999)	**Valid Building Blocks** (Collins, 2002; Als, 1999)
Decomposition	NOT [inputs opposite to output]	single input; single output	output to input; no cycles circuits
Discrete	AND [1 if both inputs 1]	two input; single output	output to input; no cycles circuits
Complementary-symmetrical	OR [0 if both inputs 0]	two input; single output	output to input; no cycles circuits
Decisions	NAND [-1 if both inputs -1]	two input; single output	output to input; no cycles circuits
Synthesized and adaptability	NOR [-0 if both inputs -0]	two input; single output	output to input; no cycles circuits
Reasoning	XOR [1 if both inputs opposite]	two input; single output	output to input; no cycles circuits
Enablers to logic	XNOR [1 if both inputs same]	two input; single output	output to input; no cycles circuits

Table 6. Causality themes —logic gates—blocks

Venn diagrams, Boolean algebra and Karnaugh maps (K map) may be developed for all logic gates detailed within Table 6 to detail operations. Fig 7 details a traditional Venn diagrams for NAND Equivalent Circuits stressing the input to output relationship. If log gate Kernels are on the critical path the WOSSI concept can be used to highlighted them (Fig 9) (Collins, 2002; Als, 1999).

The feature that stands out is that the COR's occur as required any 'place-time-way' C^3M^3. COR's and not mono, they will find the cross platform control systems and memory with information-knowledge cipher-prima strings that may support families of delivery engines to achieve the desired outcome. The analogy may be from project management and the use of critical paths for the tasks and required resources.

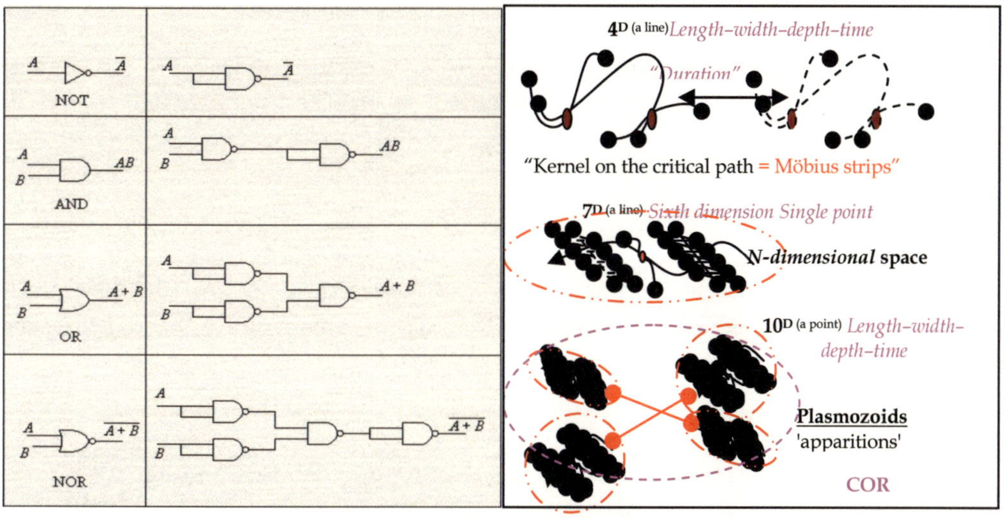

Fig. 9. NAND Equivalent Circuits Concept of WOSSI (COR gates) Logic circuit for function $\overline{\overline{AB}} = AB$ i.e. the complement of "A NAND B" (Collins, 2002; Als, 1999).

22.3 Symptoms– immediate cause– remote cause

A further refinement could be by providing a level of causality (Table 7), and relationship association. This is likely to indicate how useful the information might be considered and tested with an Ockham's razor outcomes aligned to causality (Carbonell, 1979; Wagner et al. 2005).

Causality logic gate Themes (Conjectures)	Symptoms	Immediate cause	Remote cause
Decomposition	Symptoms	–	–
Discrete	Symptoms	–	–
Complementary-symmetrical	–	Immediate cause	–
Decisions	–	Immediate cause	–
Synthesized and adaptability	–	–	Remote cause
Reasoning	–	–	Remote cause
Enablers to logic	Symptoms	–	–

Table 7. Causality Themes —logic gates - Causality.

A note on Causality: Symptoms: Affects—factors specific to an event or occurrence. Immediate cause explains why the event or occurrence has occurred. Remote cause may explain why the event or occurrence has occurred (Carbonell, 1979; Wagner et al., 2005; Hobbs, 2005; Bellinger, 2004; Mei, 2008; Ackoff, 1962; Wikipedia, 2009).

22.4 Wisdom open–system semantic identification

A paradigm shift occurs in the mapping of digital circuits by using 'Wisdom open-system semantic identification (WOSSI) mapping (Figure 8). This paradigm shift aligns more to project management and the use of critical paths and acceptance of random radicals. Schneider et al. (2005) work provides the foundations to move forward using the declared series of Theorems.

A question that is simple in nature from a colleague "what are you trying to do" leads to some form of cognitive interchange that semantics is an enabler. Cognitive influence of 'de Montaigne' paradox affects the outcomes of mapping and the practitioner's determinations.

22.4.1 Achoff filters

Achoff filters (Table 8; Figure 5) coalescence suggesting further alignment between causality, wisdom and Logic gates and scribing of the critical path. The KILDEE threads traced out the aligning WIKED's via control system mapping of logic gates and multiplexing.

Causality logic gate Themes (Conjectures)	**Information (I)**	**Knowledge (K)**	**Understanding (U)**	**Wisdom (W)**
Decomposition	When	–	–	–
Discrete	–	How	–	–
Complementary-symmetrical	–	–	Why	–
Decisions	Who	–	–	–
Synthesized and adaptability	Where	–	–	–
Reasoning	What	–	–	–
Enablers to logic	–	–	–	e-Why

Table 8. Causality Themes - Achoff Filters

22.4.2 WOSSI map

Fig 10 details the likely WOSSI circuits and continuum that forms a COR logic gate that may exists in multiple operating dimensions as 'U' and 'W' or hybrids. The COR act as 'knowledge-through-to-wisdom' (KTTW) delivery engine(s) to give plausibly equivalent circuits sets of 'wisdom—information—knowledge—domains' (WIKED). The concept of causality could be uncertain at the Planck scale in tracing the critical path memory.

22.5 WOSSI delivery engine of COR logic gates

Metrices suggest 'memory open-system semantic yielding' (MOSSY) that does not contravene the rules associated with Truth table but are 3 by 3 by 3 matrices (three-four dimensional considering time dilation). This enables the COR's to multiplex a number of WIKED's in support of critical path KILDEE threads (Fig 11).

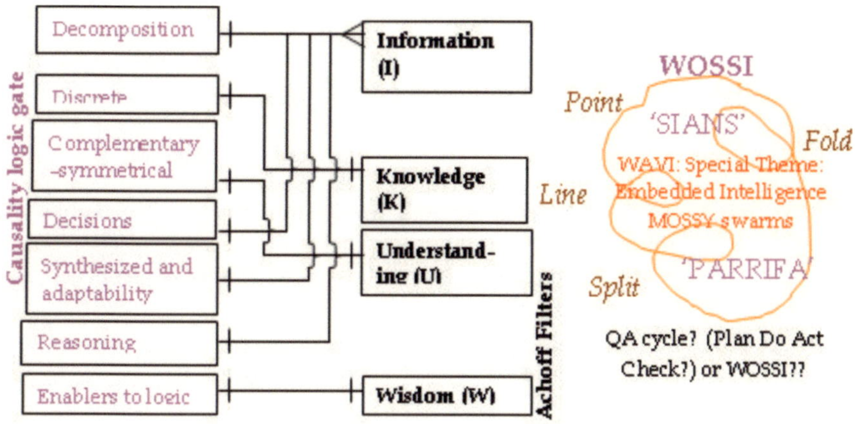

Fig. 10. WOSSI map of simple relationships and attributes (Mei, 2008; Ackoff, 1962; Wikipedia, 2009; Wikipedia, 2009).

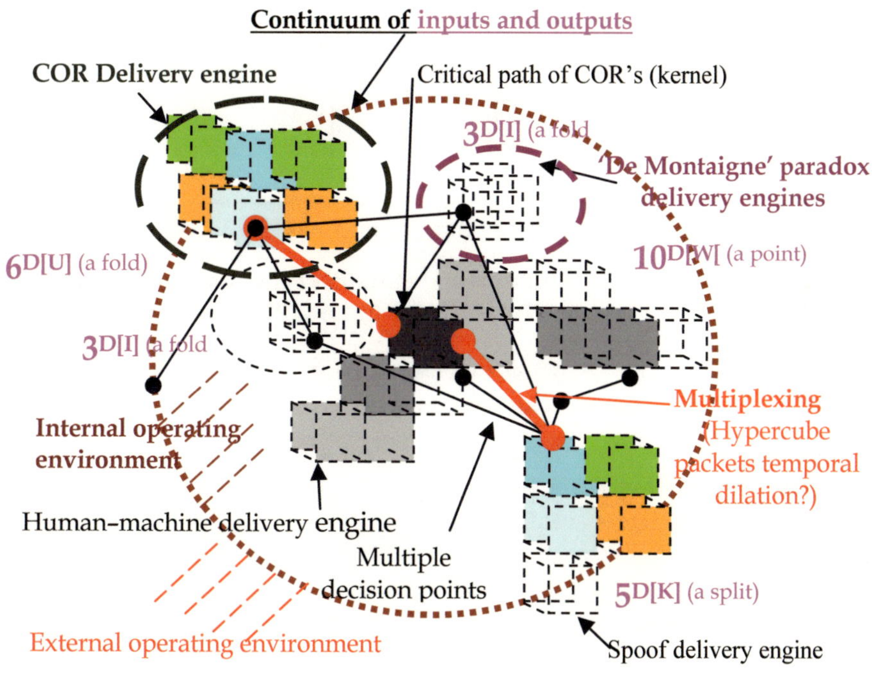

Fig. 11. WOSSI map (COR gates) Logic.

22.6 Plausible C^3

The fundamental question may be *"what's in it for me"*. In the financial context, it perhaps is shares of the bonus at the end of the project. An undesirable outcome would be complexity followed by more complexity.

Unintended consequences of an expeditionary cultural mentality might be a diminished rather than enhanced 'Command—communication—control' (C^{3T}). The bonus could be lost due to a skewed semantic C^3 entity constructs or scenario (Bellinger, 2004; CSCS, 2005).

22.7 Semantic mapping

The conceptualization assists in tracing the critical path memory using semantic mapping. Semantics utility is in how one infers a relationship between the signs of an event or entity and the things they refer to (Chung, 2002). Semantic mapping (Fig 12) has been undertaken with Guiding parameter and Achoff filters.

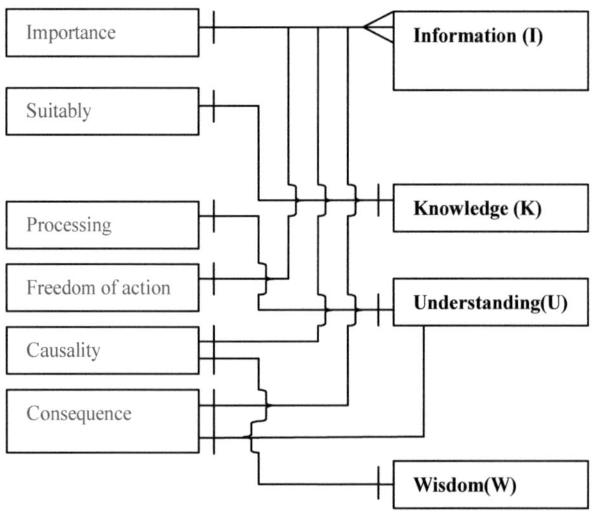

Fig. 12. Semantic map of simple relationships and attributes continuum (Schneider et al., 2005; Neiroukh, 2006; Chung, et al., 2002; NAVEDTRA, 1998; Wikipedia , 2008).

Notation used between domains (entities), models (representation) and Ontology (describes; description; taxonomies):

- No relationship
- Single relationship or Unique trigger events
- Many relationships or trigger events
- Single entanglement
- Multiple entanglement
- Multiple operating dimensions as *Möbius strips*
- Hypercube
- Causality
- Ackoff system of filters

22.8 Causality logic

Table 9 details the linkage of guiding parameter as 'delivery engine domains' within a causality framework. There appears to be immediate cause alignment with causality and consequence.

Guiding parameter	Symptoms	Immediate cause	Remote cause
Importance		–	Remote
Suitably	Symptoms	–	–
Processing	Symptoms	–	–
Freedom of action	–	–	Remote
Causality	–	Immediate	
Consequence	–	Immediate	

Table 9. Guiding parameter - Causality.

Causality within a medical context focuses on:

- Symptoms: effects—factors specific to an event or occurrence
- Immediate cause: explains why the event or occurrence has occurred
- Remote cause: may explain why the event or occurrence has occurred (Riepe et al., 1994; Riedel et al., 2003).

22.9 Achoff filters

Achoff filters coalescences (Table 10) suggests a further alignment between causality, consequences, and semantics for a given scenario—context.

Guiding parameter- DED	Information (I)	Knowledge (K)	Understanding (U)
Importance	When	–	–
Suitably	–	How	–
Processing	–	–	Why
Freedom of action	Who	–	–
Causality	Where	–	–
Consequence	What	–	Why

Table 10. Guiding parameter - Achoff Filters.

Ackoff system of filters focus on::

- Information: 'who', 'what', 'where', and 'when'
- Knowledge: application of 'how'
- Understanding: appreciation of 'why'
- Wisdom: evaluated 'why' or 'e-Why' (Riepe et al., 1994; Riedel et al., 2003; Schneider et al., 2005; Neiroukh, 2006; Chung, et al. 2002; NAVEDTRA, 1998).

Validates via Ackoff system of filters as 'conjectures' (inferences)?

- Information: knowledge communicated
- Knowledge: acquaintance with facts
- Understanding: comprehension process
- Wisdom: judgment as to action; or insight
- Application: special use or purpose
- Appreciation: perception; recognition
- Evaluate: worth, or quality of; assess.

23. Discussion

Logic gate and WOSSI mapping has a predisposition to be semantics by nature and therefore tends to be a biological-cognitive-human-machine process. As such, the associated mechanisms and tools perhaps could be influence by the 'de Montaigne' paradox, and causality—consequence creep. Traditional Logic gates are the building blocks to digital logic circuits via combinational logic that provides the foundations to move to B-COR gates. This has therefore required the need to draw from the solid foundations provided by traditional mono gate concepts such as NOT gates (or inverters), AND gates, OR gates, NAND gates, NOR gates, XOR gates, and XNOR gates (Lin, 2003; Als, 1999).

Plausible B-COR gates may be based on KILDEE's that have a common entangled-single-multiple chain themes such as *'any-place-any-time-any-way' 'Command – communication – control' of 'multiple – multiplexing – machines' (C3M3).* Pushing the conceptualisation further, B-COR gates possibly will exist in multiple dimensions with temporal *KILDEE's e.g. return to its starting point having traversed both sides of the strip, without ever crossing an edge of any dimensional state [all possible states]- n greater than 3 called hyperspaces hypercube/Hypersphere-moves between and within itself].* There could be biological-cognitive predisposition to the way information and knowledge may be used between human—machine partnerships with enhanced biological entities?

A 'tool kit' is able to be suggested to technology managers that is cognitively driven and not filled with complex data manipulations. As such the IT managers have a KISS 'tool kit' with portability and adaptability to meet the various management and leaning styles.

23.1 Semantics-dynamics

By focusing on required capability and reward required for effort a technologist or manager might use the 'Bonus' entity in the continuum (Plausible C^3 Semantics-dynamics). Both the manager and the technologist practitioner are able to find a commonality by starting and finishing at any event or entity within or external to the continuum.

Another example might be if manager viewed 'Obligations' within the business management cycle to be part of a continuous improvement initiative. By having an understanding of the critical path memory highlighted within the continuum then drivers of the technology practitioner bonus may be proposed with various risk profiles and program logic relationships. The practitioner would be aware of the likely causality. Both parties would then determine their 'Willingness-to-pay' and 'Willingness-to--benefit' which is a form of ROI to participant.

23.2 Stakeholders-partnership

The next step in the 'tool kit' is to have a KISS mechanism that qualifies the many interlaced tangible and intangibles. A plausible A^3 - Stakeholders-partnership using SMP as a 'back or envelope' calculation is suggested.

What is provided is a semantic—cognitive mechanism. A critical path memory exists and can lead to strengthening efficiency outcomes. The system of Ackoff threads through to packets of C^3 have a quantifiable 'delivery engine domains' within a semantic modeling—dynamics that works as a continuum.

What is inclined to be formed is a nested 3—by—3 matrices using the guiding parameters. Between these nested 3—by—3 matrices could be determined critical path memory. This memory can be change with the re-assignment of nested 3—by—3 matrices values by either the manager or technologist practitioner.

Such an approach of tool-sets adjusts the various management and learning styles. There is commonality between and within the nested 3—by—3 matrices as one, some or all may be used and still result in an achievable outcome.

The main Ockham's razor point of the paper are, firstly, CT application to rheology of entangled, single and multiple chains suggests the existence of biorheology logic gates. Secondly, these gates appear to have entangled-single-multiple chains that plausibly are critical paths that influence the circuit logic gate system. Thirdly, B-COR's have the capability to multiplex. Fourthly, biorheology machine systems are likely to provide SIANS as intended consequences for S2T2C. Fifthly, it is likely the number of random radicals have un-intentional consequence in a biological dynamic continuum. The Truth Tables connectivity for B-COR's will be addressed in a separate future research paper.

24. Conclusion

The owner—funder—managers may now identify the semantic causalities—consequences that could have been hidden in the traditional complex mathematics approach. A critical path memory within the C^3 *semantic modeling—dynamics* continuum (SMDC) is clearly seen. This allows owner—funder—managers to effective manage and to then bring technology project and capability under the financial limits. Secondly C^3 SMDC could have a critical path memory to aid connectivity and engagement for a given scenario—context of all stakeholders. Lastly but not least, the technologist can identify the projects that attract the greatest bonus for their efforts and skill sets.

24.1 Plausibility of concepts:

Biorheology interfaces may help overcome impairments in Humans, weapons systems, wargaming was plausible:

- Temporal Mapping Informatics use Semantics and Semiotics for Interfaces (Biorheology)
- Interfaces may have wisdom critical path threads may have the capability to multiplex
- may be basis to 'proof—of—concepts' for quantum control systems
- plausibly exists in hypercube/Hypersphere *N-dimensional* space
- Need to processes '*Keep It Simple and Stupid Sensible*' (KISS)
- Actual mechanism needs clarification: Evolution, Assimilation, Adaptation, Transformation, Deviation, or Mutation.

24.2 Validates Semantic and Semiotic based hypothesis - plausible?

- Semantics and Semiotics are part of an information system that may adapt and assimilate Biorheological information into a Host

- Semantic and Semiotic entangled-single-multiple informatics chains exist to assist medical interventions and countermeasures
- Semantic and Semiotic Interfaces have nexus nodes that transition Biorheological information to and from Host C3M3 kernel

What was emphasised was that WOSSI proof—of—concepts' demonstrates COR's wisdom critical paths that influence the circuit logic gate system. Secondly COR's have the capability to multiplex. The Truth Tables connectivity for COR's will be addressed in a separate paper

24.3 Rubik–Schlangen type three–dimensional system and wisdom–based delivery engine acting as a continuum with engagements?

A number of Rubik-Schlangen type three-dimensional system and wisdom-based delivery engine appear to act as a continuum with engagements that could be suggested from the survey questionnaire responses, to guide a weapons sytem-wargaming ‚foresight strategic management planning' (FSMP) processes. They may both work as a Rubik-Schlangen type, three-dimensional system and wisdom-based delivery engine in the given business context (Fig 13). These make it plausible to have the outcome of delivering the best possible business results and tap into the future potential within this particular business operating environment but have filters working as a continuum (SMP human-machine delivery engine) that could be under the influence of 'de Montaigne' paradox and subject to management process spoofing that skews SMP causality.

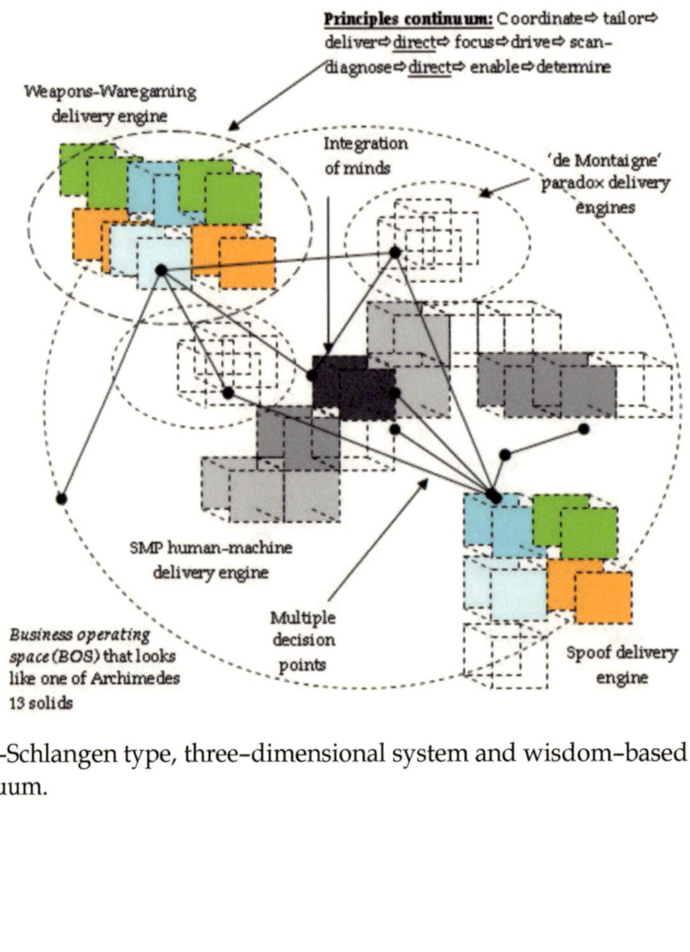

Fig. 13. Rubik-Schlangen type, three-dimensional system and wisdom-based delivery engine continuum.

C3W Kernel self correction might be useful for Biorheology interfaces to help overcome impairments in Humans, weapons systems, wargaming (Fig 14). The C3W Kernel associated firmware changes might in turn enable an expanded WOSSI mapping systems that essentially allows wisdom to be identified from the lower order delivery engines information, knowledge, reasoning and understanding. The entity is then able to self replicate based on the entities conceptualizations of it self and understanding of the environment that an interaction is required.

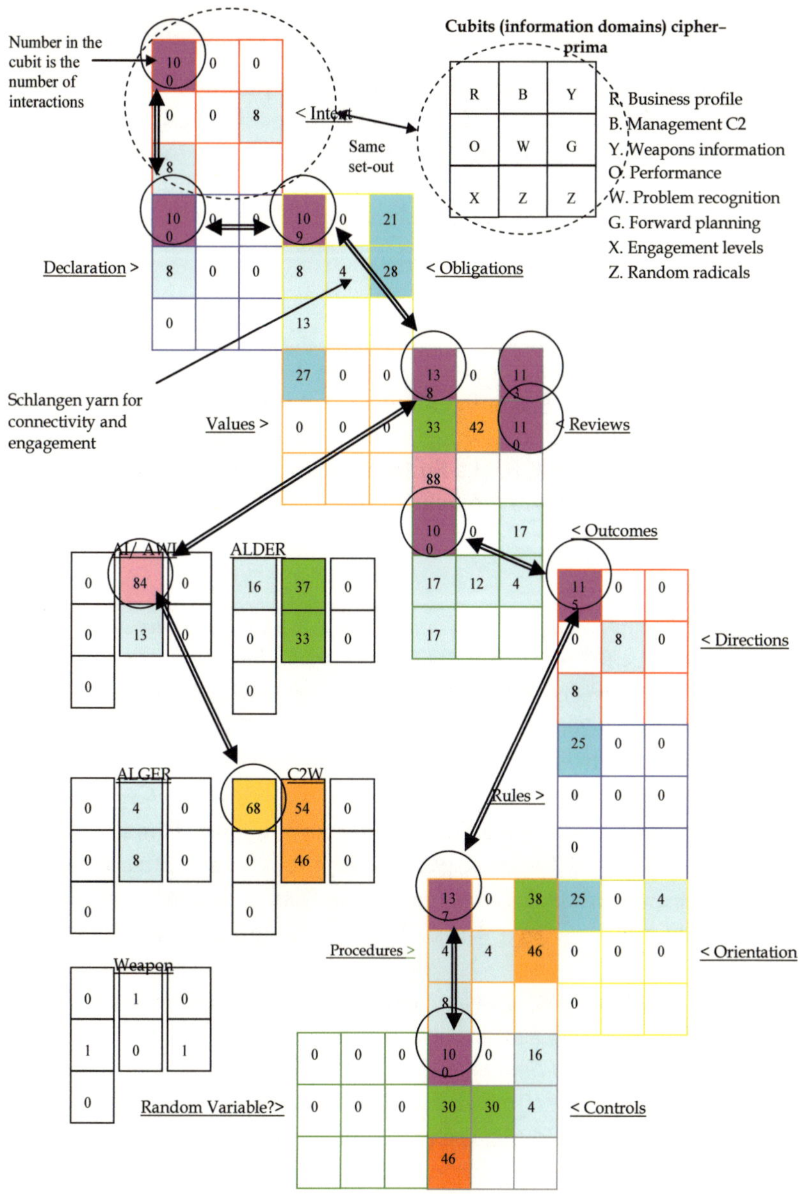

Fig. 14. Human–machine interfaces information and knowledge critical path for a C3W Kernel (e.g. biological and non-biological)

25. Implications for future work

The findings of the work may suggest the possibility to semantic via WOSSI enabling augmented reality with 'artificial life derived entity replication' (ALDER). This could be the leap beyond 'virtual entity—person in a reality environment' (Avatar). The 'artificial life guided entity replication' (ALGER) may assist 'human like operations' but conforming to established ethics and minimising unintended consequences such as 'operation not possible' outcomes.

Informatics Medicine as an option in the Medical Practitioners intervention toolkit:

- AIM: To emphases the use of informatics for medicinal purposes
- SCOPE: Traditionally the focus of Medical informatics has been supported by intelligent decision technologies within the health system. On the flip side of "Medical informatics" is its use as an overarching distinct specialty discipline of medicine that is 'Informatics Medicine *as an option in the Medical Practitioners intervention toolkit.*

26. Acknowledgment

The Author wishes to thank Australian Maritime College, University of Tasmania, Launceston, Tasmania, Australia for their support in his Adjunct role and WOSSI and Biorheology informatics research. Secondly, to thank Dr Muhammad Tanvir Afzal, Research Group Leader, Center for Distributed and Semantic Computing, Mohammad Ali Jinnah University, Islamabad, Pakistan the books Editor and InTech for this opportunity to detail C^3W semantic temporal entanglement modelling for Human—machine interfaces.

27. References

Ackoff, R.L., (1962). *Scientific Method: Optimizing Applied Research Decisions*, Wiley, pp.1-74.

Adkins, M.; Younger, R. & Schwarz, R. (2003). *Information Technology, Augmentation of The Skilled Facilitator Approach,* Proceedings of the 36th Hawaii International Conference on System Sciences - 2003, 0-7695-1874-5/03; 2003 IEEE , www.hicss.hawaii.edu/HICSS36/HICSSpapers/CLUSR11.pdf

AIBAS, (2006). *Adaptive Intent-Based Augmentation System*, The Georgia Institute of Technology, Graphics, visualization and usability Centre, Thursday, 16 November 2006 12:51:40 AM http://www.cc.gatech.edu/projects/ael/projects/aibas.html.

Alder, M., (2004). *Non-Aristotelian Logic in Practice, or How to be much cleverer than all your friends (so they really hate you),* Uni.of Western Australia, www.maths.uwa.edu.au; pp.1-14.

Als, A., (1999). *Logic Gates, Uni. of West Indies, www.scitec.uwichill.edu.bb, 1-10* (1999).

Answers, (2008). *information-theory by IEEE*, www.answers.com, p.1

Answers, (2010). *Relationship to continuum mechanics*, Wikipedia; www.answers.com/topic/fluid-mechanics, 1, (2010).

Antsaklis; P. J., (1997). *Intelligent Control*, Encyclopedia of EEE, http://www.nd.edu, p.1.

ANU, (2010). *Lectures Notes : Internet History and Principles*; Research School of Computer Science [Slide 25 / 60 http://escience.anu.edu.au/lecture/ivr/networkProtocols/printNotes.en.html].

Ardelt, M., (2004). *Wisdom as Expert Knowledge System: A Critical Review of a Contemporary Operationalization of an Ancient Concept;* Wisdom as Expert Knowledge System Human Development 2004;47:257–285 www.clas.ufl.edu/.../Wisdom%20as%20expert%20knowledge%20system.pdf

Armarsdottir, K.; Berre, A-J.; Hahn, A.; Missikoff, M.; Taglino, F., (2006). *Semantic mapping: ontology-based versus model-based approach Alternative or complementary approaches?* sunsite.informatik.rwth-aachen.de/Publications/CEUR-WS/Vol-200/17.pdf; (2006); p. 1.

Ask, (2010). *Wisdom,* http://ask.reference.com/web; http://ask.reference.com/web?q=WISDOM&qsrc=2445&o=10602&l=dir.

Avery, J.; & Yearwood, J., (2004). *Supporting Evolving Ontologies by Capturing the Semantics of Change;* University of Ballarat, Victoria, 3350; Available: www.ballarat.edu.au, p. 1.

Bellinger, G., Castro, G., & Mills, A. (2004). *Data, Information, Knowledge, and Wisdom,* ISSS, Available: http://www.systems-thinking.org, p.1.

BOINC, (2007). *Administrative Web Interface (AWI).* University of California; boinc.berkeley.edu/trac/wiki/HtmlOps

Bowen, R.A., (2001). *Control of Endocrine Activity,* Colorado State University, http://arbl.cvmbs.colostate.edu/hbooks/pathphys/endocrine/basics/control.html, (2001); p. 1.

Brand, S., (1993). *GBN Book Club Reviews–War and anti–war,* [comments on Heidi and Alvin Toffler's *War and anti–war: Survival at the Dawn of the 21st Century, 1993, Little, Brown], http://www.gbn.org/BookClub/War.html, (accessed March 2000),* p. 1.

Camillus, J. C. & Datta, D. K., (1991). *Making strategic issues in a turbulent environment,* Long Range Planning, vol. 24, no. 2, Reading 9.6, Strategic Management–Readings, Australian Maritime College, Launceston. pp. 67–74.

Carbonell, J.G., (1979). *Intentionality and Human Conversation; Context of language;* Association for Computing Machinery; Association for Computational Linguistic; Available: http://www.aclweb.org/anthology-new/J/J79/J79-1079.pdf; p. 48 (147).

Chung, K-S., Gupta, R. K., Kim, T., & Liu, C.L., (2002). *Synthesis and Optimization of Combinational Interface Circuits, Journal of VLSI, Netherlands, http://www.ics.uci.edu,* pp 1-19.

Collins, (2002). *Desk Calendar Refill 2002,* Collins Debden, p.28.

Coppock, E.; (2005). *Object-control promise;* October 4, 2005; Stanford University. Stanford, California, www.stanford.edu/~coppock/promise.pdf; (2005); p. 1.

CSCS, (2004). *Semiotics,* Notebooks, 2004; Center for the Study of Complex Systems, College of Literature, Science and the Arts (LSA) at the University of Michigan in Ann Arbor, Michigan, cscs.umich.edu/~crshalizi/notebooks/semiotics.html

CSCS, (2005). *Information Theory Center for the Study of Complex Systems,* Uni. of Michigan, http://cscs.umich.edu, p.1.

CSMINTL, (2002). *Centre for strategic management,* Business leadership, strategy, systems thinking, learning, & facilitating strategic change, Centre for Strategic management International (CSMINTL), CSM Alliances, Haines Centre International http:www.csmintl.com, 1–3.

Daniel, D.; (2009). *A Futurist Weighs in on Techies' Tomorrows;* Dr. James Canton of the Institute of Global Futures tells what IT managers should be doing to lead future projects; CIO magazine; 31 March, 2009; http://www.cio.com.au/article/297362/futurist_weighs_techies_tomorrows; (2009) p. 1.

Dictionary; (2008). *Dictionary.reference.com;* http://dictionary.reference.com; (2008); p. 1.

Eiter, T.; Subrahmanian V.S.; and Pick G., (1999). *Heterogeneous Active Agents, I: Semantics, Artificial Intelligence Journal,* Vol. 108, Nr. 1-2, pp. 179-255, 1999, http://www.cs.mu.oz.au/481/biblio/Year/1999.complete.html#Eiter1999b, (1999), p. 179.

Engelbart, D.D., (1968). *Study for the development of Human Augmentation Techniques.* Final Report under Contract NAS1-5904, SRI Project 5890 for NASA Langley Research Center, Stanford Research Institute, Menlo Park, Ca., July 1968.

FEDEE, (2002). *Relocating and integrating business operations,* Federation of European Employers (EDEE), The Strand, London, Available: www.fedee.com/natlaw.html, p. 1.

Fu-Berlin, (2010). *Introduction to Dahlem Research School (DRS),* Freie Universität Berlin; Available: http://www.fu-berlin.de/sites/en/promovieren/drs/index.html, p. 1.

Goldsworthy A., (2002). *The Heart and Soul of Leadership,* Leadership in the Networked World, Australian Institute of Management; Executive Summary, Available http://www.aim.com.au; (2002); p. 1.

Golec, P.; (2004). *Feedback Economics Web Institute* http://www.economicswebinstitute.org/glossary/feedback.htm; (2004); p. 1.

Goold, M. & Campbell, A., (2002). *Parenting in complex structures,* Long Range Planning, vol. 35, no. 3, pp. 219–243.

Gregersen, H., Mark, L., & Jensen, C.S., (1998). *Mapping Temporal ER Diagrams to Relational Schemas,* December 4, 1998, A TIMECENTER Technical Report, citeseerx.ist.psu.edu/viewdoc/download?doi=10.1.1.43.9078&rep=rep1&

Hatten, R.; Knapp, D.; Ruth Salonga, R.; (2000). Action *Research: Comparison with the Concepts of 'The Reflective Practitioner' and 'Quality Assurance;* September 2000; http://www2.fhs.usyd.edu.au/arow/arer/008.htm; (1997); p. 1.

Hawkins, J., (1993). *Strategic Management - Study Guide,* Australian Maritime College, Launceston, 19, 24–224.

He, B.; Zhang, Z.; Chen-Chuan, K., (2005). *MetraQuerier: Querying Structured Web Sources On-the-fly;* Department of Computer Science, Thomas M. Siebel Center for Computer Science, University of Illinois at Urbana-Champaign. http://eagle.cs.uiuc.edu/pubs/2005/querytranslationdemo-sigmod05-hzc-mar05.pdf; (2005); p. 1.

Hobbs, M.L, (2005). *The Value of Urban Design,* Environ. Ministry, www.mfe.govt.nz, p.1.

Ikehara, S; Tokuhisa, M., Murakami, J.; (2007). *Analogical Mapping Method and Semantic Categorization of Japanese Compound and Complex Sentence Patterns;* Proceedings of the 10th Conference of the Pacific Association for Computational Linguistic, http://linguistlist.org/pubs/papers/browse-papers-title.html (2007); pp. 181-190.

Jones, M. G., & Okey, J. R. (1995). *Interface Design for Computer-based Learning Environment* [Online] Available http://www.hbg.psu.edu/bsed/intro/docs/idguide/, February 21, 1995; cited on Georgia State University web site (http://www2.gsu.edu/~wwwitr/docs/idguide/index.html)

Joslyn, C., (2001). *The semiotics of control and modeling relations in complex systems, .Biosystems. Vol 60*, pp. 131-148, Available: www.informatics.indiana.edu/rocha/pattee/joslyn.html, p. 1.

Kiss, T., (2004). *On the Empirical Viability of the Movement Theory of Control*, www.linguistics.ruhr-uni-bochum.de, pp.1-30.

Kiss, T., (2005). *On the Empirical Viability of the Movement Theory of Control*; SprahwissenschaftlichesInstitut; Rur-Universität Bochurn; Germany; www.linguistics.ruhr-uni-bochum.de/~kiss/publications/stc.pdf; (2005); p.1.

Kondratyev, A., Cortadella, J, Kishinevsky, M., Lavagno L. & Yakovlev; A. (1999). *Logic Decomposition of Speed-Independent Circuits*, IEEE, Vol.87, No 2, www.lsi.upc.es, pp. 1-16).

Kremer, R., (1998). *Concept Mapping*, Uni. of Calgary, www.cpsc.ucalgary.ca, pp.1–5.

LeBrasseur, R.; Whissell, R.; Ojha, A.; (2002). *Organisational Learning, Transformational Leadership and Implementation of Continuous Quality Improvement in Canadian Hospitals*; Australian Journal of Management, Vol. 27, No. 2 December 2002; Australian School of Business at The University of New South; http://www.agsm.edu.au/eajm/0212/pdf/lebrasseur.pdf; (2002); pp. 141-162.

Lemke, J.L. (2001). Theories, Brooklyn College, academic.brooklyn.cuny.edu/education/jlemke/theories.htm

Lin, C., (2003). *CMSC 311 - Computer Organization*, Uni. of Maryland, www.cs.umd.edu, 1, (2003).

Lin, C., (2003). *CMSC 311 - Computer Organization*, Uni. of Maryland, www.cs.umd.edu, 1, (2003).

McNeilly, M., (2002). *Gathering information for strategic decisions, routinely*, Strategy & Leadership Journal, May 2002, pp. 29–34.

Mei, Y., (2008). *Asymptotic Optimality Theory for Decentralized Sequential Hypothesis Testing in Sensor Networks*, Information Theory, IEEE, Vol. 54, Issue 5, www.ieee.org, pp. 208.

Merram-Webster, (2010). *MerramWebster Dictionary*, http//www.MerramWebster.com/Dictionary [2010]

Miller, A. & Dess, G. G., (1996). *Strategic Management (Int. ed, 2nd ed)*, McGraw–Hill, New York, 25, 28, 32, 33, 39, 50, 61, 74, 90, 112, 346, 359, 375, 385, 438.

NAVEDTRA, (1998). *Module 13 – Introduction to Number Systems and Logic*, NAVEDTRA 14185, NE&E, United States Navy, http://d.scribd.com, pp. 1-218.

NCHRP, (2006). *Guidelines for Transportation Emergency Training Exercises*; Mccormick Taylor, Inc., TCRP86/NCHRP525 – Transportation Security, Volume 9: Guidelines for Transportation Emergency Training Exercises, Transit Cooperative Research Program and National Cooperative Highway Research Program, Transportation Research Board; Washington, D.C.; 2006; www.TRB.org, pp. 1-7.

Neiroukh, O. (2006). *An Efficient Algorithm for the Analysis of Cyclic Circuits*, In ISVLSI '06: IEEE Computer Society Annual, VLSI T&A, http://www.cs.columbia.edu, p.1.

Nepa, K., Bahar, R.I., Mundy, J., Patterson, W.R., & Zaslavsky, A. (2006). *Designing nanoscale logic circuits based on Markov random fields*, Brown Uni, Division of Engineering, pp.1-14.

NSF (2004) *Nanoscience Classroom Resources*, NSF, USA, www.nsf.gov, p.1.

Nüchter, A.; Hertzberg, J.; (2008). *Towards semantic maps for mobile robots*; Robotics and Autonomous Systems 56 (2008) pp. 915-926; http://kos.informatik.uni-osnabrueck.de/download/ras2008.pdf; (2008); p. 1.

Phan Luong, V., (1999). *Between Well-Founded Semantics and Stable Model Semantics*; ideas, pp. 270-278, 1999 International Database Engineering and Applications Symposium, 1999, http://www2.computer.org/portal/web/csdl/doi/10.1109/IDEAS.1999.787277, (1999), p. 270.

QSA (2004). *Philosophy & Reason, Senior Syllabus*, Queensland Studies, pp. 1-54.

Raimond, P. & Eden, C., (1990). *Making strategy work,* Long Range Planning, vol. 23, no. 5, Reading 9.5, Strategic Management-Readings, Australian Maritime College, Launceston, pp. 98–104.

Riedel, M.D., & Bruck, J. (2003). *The synthesis of cyclic combinational circuits*, In Design Automation Conference (DAC), http://www.paradise.caltech.edu/papers/etr052.pdf, p.1.

Riepe, M.A., Marques Silva, J.P., Sakallah, K.A., & Brown, R.B. (1994). *Ravel-XL:A Hardware Accelerator for Assigned-Delay Compiled-Code Logic Gate Simulation* Uni. of Michigan, pp.1-39.

Roh, F.R.; (2006). *Return on Investment (ROI): Cost Benefit Evaluation of a Management Development Program*; 2006 International Conference; Holiday Inn Esplanade, Darwin, Australia; 4 - 7 September 2006; Australasian Evaluation Society; www.aes.asn.au/conferences/2006/papers/006 Frederick Rohs.pdf; (2006); pp. 1-11.

Ronczka, J. (2009). *Wisdom Open-system Semantic Identification (WOSSI) Mapping of Causality Logic Gates*, The First International Workshop on Web & Semantic Technology (WeST-2009) and Third International Conference on Internet Technologies and Applications (ITA 09), http://www.ita09.org, Glyndŵr University North East Wales, UK, p. 1–10

Ronczka, J.P. (2006). *Coalescence Theory–Strategic Management Planning in Australian ports, Australian Maritime College, Launceston, Tasmania*, pp. 11.3–1.11; 2.24–2.39; 3.35–3.48.

Ronczka, J.P. (2009). *C3 semantics modeling – dynamics*, CICSyN2009 1st Int Conference on Computational Intelligence, Communication Systems and Networks, 23 - 25 July 2009, Indore, India, www.cicsyn2009.org.uk, pp. 1-6.

Ronczka, J.P. (2010). *Coalescence Theory application to rheology of entangled, single and multiple chains to suggest biorheology logic gates,* 5th Pacific Rim Conference on Rheology (PRCR-5) in Sapporo Japan, http://prcr2010.com. pp. 1-2.

Ryder, M., (2004). *Semiotics: Language and Culture*, University of Denver, carbon.ucdenver.edu/~mryder/semiotics_este.html

Sambasivan, N. & Moore-Jackson, M. (2007). *Designing Pervasive Brain-Computer Interfaces*, A. Holzinger (Ed.): USAB 2007, LNCS 4799, pp. 267–272, 2007, © Springer-Verlag Berlin Heidelberg 2007; www.ics.uci.edu/~nsambasi/USAB07_DesigningPervasiveBCIs.pdf

Schneider, K., Br, J., Schuele, T., & Tuerk, T. (2005). *Maximal causality analysis*, In Conference on ACSD, http://rsg.informatik.uni-kl.de, p.1.

Schneider, K., Brandt, J., Schucle, T., & Tuerk, T. (2005). *improving Constructiveness in Code Generators*, Uni. of Kaiserslautern; www.es.cs.uni-kl.de; pp. 1-19.

Senese, F., (2005). *General Chemistry Online*, Frostburg State University; http://antoine.frostburg.edu/chem/senese/101/liquids/faq/non-newtonian.shtml; 1; (2005).

Sowa, J.F., (2006). *Concept Mapping*, www.jfsowa.com/talks/cmapping.pdf, (2006), p. 1.

Spector, L., (2001). *CS 263: Artificial Intelligence*, Hampshire College, Amherst MA http://hampshire.edu/lspector/courses/cs263s01-syllabus.html

Sturm, L. (1994). *The interaction between micro-, meso- and macro-levels*, Uni. Tübingen; www.tiss.zdv.uni-tuebingen.de, p.1

Tancredi, C. A., (2007). *Multi-Modal Theory of I-Semantics*, Keio University, http://semanticsarchive.net/Archive/jkxMDI2O/Multi-Model%20Modal%20Theory%20II.pdf, (2007), p. 22.

Terzopoulos, D., (2009). *Artificial Life and Biomechanical Simulation of Humans*; Digital Human Symposium 2009; March 12th, 2009) www.cs.ucla.edu/~dt/papers/dhs09/dhs09.pdf; p. 1.

Uschold, M.; (2001). *Where are the Semantic in the Semantic Web;* Ontologies in Agent Systems workshop, Montreal, June 2001, http://lsdis.cs.uga.edu/SemWebCourse_files/WhereAreSemantics-AI-Mag-FinalSubmittedVersion2.pdf; (2001); p. 1.

Wagner, M.; Noppens, O.; Liebig, T.; Luther, M.; Paolucci, M.; (2005). *Semantic-based Service Discovery on Mobile Devices;* University of Ulm; Germany, Available: http://www.informatik.uni-ulm.de/ki/Noppens/publications/wagner-et-al-demo-iswc05.pdf; p.1

Wander, A.E.; Magalhães, M.C.; Vedovoto, G.L.; Martins, E.C.; (2004). *Using the economic surplus method to assess economic impacts of new technologies: case studies of Embrapa;* Conference on International Agricultural Research for Development; Deutscher Tropentag 2004; Berlin, October 5-7, 2004; http://www.tropentag.de/2004/abstracts/full/48.pdf; (2004); pp. 1-10.

Watkins, T.; (2000). *An introduction to cost benefit analysis;* San Jose State University Department of Economics; San Jose, CA; http://www.sjsu.edu/faculty/watkins/cba.htm; (2000?), p. 1.

Werner, L., (2001). *Scientific method: Observation; Question; Hypothesis; Prediction; Test and Causality loop of test outcome* (support/ does not support Hypothesis) (http://wc.pima.edu/~lwerner/181.htm/StudyGuides/1.Science/SGProcSci.htm).

Wikipedia, (2008). Wikipedia, encyclopedia, www.wikipedia.org, p.1.

Wikipedia, (2009). Wikipedia, encyclopedia, http://en.wikipedia.org, p.1.

WSU; (2003). *e-Extension, Pre-Select Business Case;* Draft November 7, 2003; Washington State University, Pullman WA.; http://ext.wsu.edu/links/BusinessPlan.pdf; (2008); pp. 1-58.

Zizzi, P.A. (2003). *Quantum Computing Spacetime* Uni di Padova, www.mindspring.com, pp.1-12.